J. G. Graham Crawfurd
of Balward
Crieff Perthshire
Nov 1966

WESLEY'S ENGLAND

WESLEY'S ENGLAND

A SURVEY OF XVIIIth CENTURY SOCIAL AND CULTURAL CONDITIONS

BY

J. H. WHITELEY, D.Litt.

LONDON: THE EPWORTH PRESS

THE EPWORTH PRESS
(FRANK H. CUMBERS)
25-35 City Road, London, E.C.1

MELBOURNE   CAPE TOWN
NEW YORK   TORONTO

Printed in Great Britain by
The Camelot Press Ltd., London and Southampton

TO MY WIFE

TO MY WIFE

CONTENTS

Chapter　　　　　　　　　　　　　　　　　　　　　　　　　*page*

FOREWORD

THE forthcoming celebration of the two-hundredth anniversary of John Wesley's conversion, provides an obvious occasion for mental and moral stocktaking among Methodists. All but those incapable of serious thought must feel an impulse, if not more than transient, to look back not merely at this epoch-making event, but at the England in which he lived.

He is no longer enveloped in thick clouds of conventional piety and sectarian adulation. In 1938 he can assume the dignity of an ancient and claim the privilege of established fame and prescriptive veneration. A man so amazingly vivid, and whose fiery spirit persisted in his shining old age, has a glory that will throw a lustre over the name of England when time has paled the light reflected from her warriors. But if this glory is to be appreciated by Methodists living in the spacious days of the twentieth century, a brief rehearsal of some chapters of English eighteenth-century history is imperatively needed. Men and women are now enfranchised; education is universal; Dissenters are no longer despised; laws, prisons, schools, army, navy, and work have been humanized; railways and motor-cars make life circulate freely. It was far other in Wesley's days. Eighteenth-century customs and habits, its modes of life and thought, its quaint sayings, captivating phrasings and weird superstitions have disappeared or are fast fading away. Wesley's very personality is receding into the distance, and the astonishing brilliance of his career will appear luminous only when his historical background is realized.

Wesley's span of years practically covered the whole eighteenth century, and as the aim of the book is merely to depict English life as Wesley would know it, the writer has had no hesitation in dealing with pertinent detail which happened just outside Wesley's lifetime. The history that has been selected to reconstruct this background is of the scrap-book order, but it is hoped that the items chosen are significant and fundamental. No attempt has been made to deal with the century's sailors, soldiers, statesmen or empire-builders; even the Evangelical Revival is substantially ignored, although it is implicitly present. Emphasis has been laid on such tracts of history as interested Wesley, such as the conditions of life then existing for ordinary folk, the virtues and vices of the different classes, their work, speech, education, literature, social and religious life. On a few of these aspects, some light has been thrown by an examination of one or two disinterred account-books of early Methodist chapels; these, like contemporary letters, diaries, newspapers, lampoons, &c., cast interesting asides on the social and commercial life of the eighteenth century.

For the learned world there is an enormous literature of critical studies, commentaries and monographs on almost every conceivable aspect of Wesley and of the eighteenth century. In addition to the information gathered from the monumental studies on the eighteenth century, the following pages owe much to Phillips and Tomkinson's book *English Women and Life and Letters*, to Turberville's *Johnson's England* and *English Men and Manners in the Eighteenth Century*, whilst the illustrations to be found in these publications of the Oxford University Press, place all readers under a perpetual debt. The writer has tried to perform a service by gathering the fruits of such scholarship in a form more attractive to the ordinary reader than to the student. So he has refrained from drawing up a list of authors to whom his acknowledgements are due, and is content to admit that no claim is made for originality on behalf of anything that may command assent. With Montaigne, he could say, 'I have gathered a posie of other men's flowers and nothing but the thread that binds them is mine own'. This admission will, it is hoped, justify the omission of a long list of works that have been studied, as well as the innumerable footnote-references which would have given point to the quotations. The best hopes of the writer will be realized if he prove to have succeeded in interesting the ordinary reader in the England Wesley knew, and in placing in an accessible form some important pictures, statements and conclusions which are buried in eighteenth-century novels, pamphlets, parish and church records, philosophical and historical treatises.

The difficulties of the project are manifold, for this is a century of England's story whose details are surprisingly contradictory and elusive, and in whose latter end, complications increase so fast, that a narrative becomes difficult to organize without tedium or confusion. During Wesley's long life much of England's thought, ideals, life, language and so on were frequently re-shaped by the inevitable external pressures to which they were subjected, as well as by the internal stresses arising from the new national consciousness caused by the spread of Methodism. The inexorable limitations of space preclude adequacy of treatment for many themes, and it has led to generalizations which of course require much modification in detail; but like all generalizations, they may serve as a useful starting point, provided that this need for modification is borne in mind. The unity of purpose which pervades the following chapters is pleaded as a justification for publishing those selected. Omission of any of those chosen could not have been made, if clearness and comparative completeness of the background of Wesley's life were to be secured.

For valuable advice, generous help, careful and critical reading of the typescript my thanks are due to several friends, notably the Rev. Luke Beaumont, Mr. Coomer, the Rev. J. R. Course, Dr. Pascoe, Mr. Priestley, and the Rev. Dr. Wright.

CHAPTER I

JOHN WESLEY

I

IT is almost ironical that a Churchman of the calibre and conviction of Wesley should leave behind him, as his permanent contribution to religion, a denomination quite separate from and claiming more adherents than the Church to which he always professed loyalty.

Such a situation would be an amazing and incredible paradox, if one revolutionary cause were forgotten. Wesley himself probably would have assigned his present standing in history to adherence to high-Church rules of living; some of his contemporaries might have attributed it to his ancestry and scholastic training; others would have thought his organizing genius and untiring energy were the main factors. But most Methodists would see that Wesley's astounding achievements were, in the final issue, due to his epoch-making experience in Aldersgate Street on the evening of May 24, 1738, when 'I felt my heart strangely warmed'. From that moment he was a changed man as his *Journal*, hymns, sermons and passionate evangelism abundantly show. Henceforth he had but one purpose and he never wearied of telling his helpers, 'You have nothing to do but save souls'; . . . 'Spend and be spent in this work'; . . . 'Go always not to those who want you but to those who want you most'. The modern layman can but look back with wistful wonder, that most religious leaders of England did not gladly claim such a mighty and successful evangelist as an ally, instead of considering him a despised renegade.

By birth and culture he had right of place among the privileged classes. Heredity, Charterhouse and Oxford naturally put him into contact with those who led eighteenth-century society, politics and State Church, whilst he, and his elder brother Samuel and the younger Charles, often met Pope, Swift, Burke, Johnson and the more musical aristocrats on terms of mental equality. John Wesley was esteemed by such bishops as Potter, Gibson and Lowth, and contemporary theologians like Butler, Paley, Lavington, Warburton, respected or feared him. Throughout his long life he never regarded himself as the founder of a new denomination, but simply as one who advocated a mere society, standing for certain things that were then neglected by his mother Church. To the end of his life he proclaimed his adherence to the Church of England. In 1787 he delivered the falsified prediction 'when Methodists leave the Church of England, God will leave them'. Four years earlier he wrote: 'If ever the Methodists in general were to leave the Church, I must leave them', and later he affirmed, 'I live and die a member of the Church of England and none who regard my judgement and advice will ever separate from it'. Throughout his lengthy preaching career, he always showed a deep sense of the spiritual value of liturgical worship, of symbol, of sacrament, and always spoke of these with the understanding born of experience. He never formulated a new doctrine that his mother Church could not have accepted, and he was never at variance with the bishops on theological grounds. Like most of them he had not much patience with abstract thought, mystical analysis or speculative theology; like them he prided himself on possessing common sense and on sincerity in facing facts. Further, he appreciated the Church's idea of a parish with all its sanctified and benign possibilities, and he never showed any disposition to displace worthy vicars and curates from their manses where they dispensed their modest bounties, temporal, spiritual and mental, for the clamant hedge-preacher, with his gospel of zeal rather than of peace, of dogma rather than of charity.

But perhaps Wesley remained attached to the Church of his ordination rather by ties of affection than by bonds of reason, for his fastidious, critical eye saw the State Church's defects. He realized that the Anglicans who held solid preferments were in the main the relatives, henchmen or sycophants of the aristocracy; that their vaunted broad-mindedness was sometimes a mere disguise for empty-mindedness, shallow indifference or even flippant scepticism; that the sacredness of their office was in many cases but little recognized, and that the services in thousands of churches were negligent and infrequent. Where the clergy were good men they were often poles apart from their illiterate parishioners and so many of them failed to see that the Church should stand for service to others, for fraternity and benevolence, and that it should be a group of people associated for mutual helpfulness and fellowship. Wesley gradually grew to realize that such fellowship should be central to the Church's life and that the Church should meet special needs and serve particular types of people. When charged with destroying the fellowship of the State Church, he replied with the famous passage:

'Which of those true Christians had any such fellowship with these? Who watched over them in love? Who marked their growth in grace? Who advised and exhorted them from time to time? Who prayed with them and for them as they had need? This, and this alone, is Christian fellowship; but, alas, where is it to be found? Look east and west, north and south; name what parish you please; is this Christian fellowship there? Rather, are not the bulk of the parishioners a mere rope of sand? . . . What a mere jest it is, then, to talk so gravely of destroying what never was! The real truth is just the reverse of this; *we* introduce Christian fellowship where it was utterly destroyed. And the fruits of it have been peace, joy, love, and zeal for every good word and work.'

His letters to the different Churches that he had founded, also indicate that he always stressed this fellowship, and considered it central to the life of the Church of Christ. He knew too that religion and morals were quite out of fashion in society; that the majority of the politicians were avowedly indifferent or professedly unbelieving, and that there was blatant atheism at both universities where scores of dons delighted to proclaim their infidelity. After preaching in St. Mary's, Oxford, he notes in his *Journal* in 1744: 'I preached this day for the last time, I suppose, at St. Mary's. Be it so. I am now clear of the blood of these men. I have fully delivered my own soul. The beadle came to me afterwards and told me that the Vice-Chancellor had sent him for my notes. I sent them him without delay.' A mind like his, viewing such conditions, would realize that if the State Church were to live and do its duty, it must alter its ways, must advance, be reformed from within, be developed, and that its stalwarts must abandon their sheer prejudices and fixed traditions, and must no longer idle away their time in disgraceful or dilettante fashion. All that this religious revolutionary wanted was for his mother Church to realize her duty to individuals, and so to make religious life more vivid by the spread of the Gospel, to be a vigilant guardian of order and morals and one that was prepared to do her duty to all individuals however poor and lowly. The improvement of the quality of the race was his vital object. To stem the torrent of vice and irreligion and to 'spread scriptural holiness throughout the land' were his motives. To him, individual character and intellect were the prime movers in human progress; not the thoughts and deliberations of a few learned critics, however distinguished they might be.

He therefore set in motion an organization well designed to get at the separate individuals; an organization which he hoped would supplement and not supplant the work of the National Church. This organization, called the class meeting, emphasized personal experience; it demanded from its units the very secrets of their hearts and made each and all accountable to and for their fellows. The pulpit might supply the preaching power, but the class-room was the scene of private and personal influence. These small gatherings guided the converts, made them perceive the inner light, grasp the fact that religion often implied reformation and revelation, and led them to surrender any personal prejudices in a sincere desire to know what was the will of God. This new organization was admirably calculated to achieve these worthy ends, and eventually it proved to be the agency which liberated forces that changed the religious and political history of England. As religious agencies the class meetings had distinct advantages; they could, where necessary in a dialect-speaking England, be conducted in the prevailing vernacular and thereby generate genuine lay-piety, and so lead the separate individuals to become honest, industrious, thinking Christians.

Some Churchmen saw the sense of Wesley's objectives and machinery. Like him, Hervey, Walker, Grimshaw, Berridge, Fletcher realized that the measure of a nation or of a Church depends ultimately on the standard of its units. These few clergymen of his school of thought, said to number six or seven in 1748, offered him the hospitality of their pulpits; they at least saw nothing against their vows in supporting his methods and principles, and they believed his oft-proclaimed adherence to the State Church; they were the pioneers of the evangelical party of clergymen which in 1788 numbered upwards of 500. The earlier half-dozen or the later 500 would agree with Southey's declaration that 'Wesley simply hoped to give new impulse to the Church of England, to awaken its dormant zeal, infuse life into a body where nothing but life was wanting, and lead the way to the performance of duties which the State had blindly overlooked and the Church had scandalously neglected'. Nowadays such an ideal does not seem flagrant, but in the eighteenth century it raised for Wesley a host of clerical enemies who left him, for many years, little rest either day or night, and who were continually galling him with the shafts of poisoned malice.

Actually the times were very difficult for the State Church;

political morality was at a low ebb; 'great public men were living in open defiance of the laws of morality, the Court was profligate, institutions teemed with the grossest abuses', and literature was markedly impure. And though very many of the incumbents were leading exemplary lives according to eighteenth-century standards 'the Church administration was corrupt and apparently unable to awake from its lethargy or become infused with new life'. Archbishop Secker mournfully declared in 1753 that 'immorality and irreligion were grown beyond ecclesiastical power'. Such evidence proves that she was totally unequal to the work that then faced her, and so in the words of Goldwin Smith, 'the new wine of the Gospel burst the old bottle of State religion, and the evangelist in his own despite was driven forth to found outside the Church of England the free Church of the poor'.

This inability to cope with the nation's religious needs was also shared by the existing eighteenth-century Nonconformist bodies. 'The tranquil tarrying and spiritual quiet of the Quakers was already losing its influence.' A Nonconformist in 1730 lamented that 'a real decay of serious religion, both in the Church of England and out of it, was very visible'. Another Free Churchman then saw 'breadth of thought and charity of sentiment increasing, but religious activity was not'. Even Defoe had sensed a decline in dissenting power 'not so much as regards wealth and numbers as in the qualifications of its ministers and in the decay of piety'.

The 'new wine of the Gospel' of which Goldwin Smith spoke, not only founded a new free Church for the poor, it also infused new life into the State Church in due course, and regenerated the old Nonconformity. Best of all, it gradually pervaded the mass of the population and made them alive to a better world. It also proved to be a sobering influence on the people's thoughts and actions at a time when the political institutions of England were unstable, and when there were most of the elements of revolution in the country.

Wesley had to start his evangelizing movement without any administrative advantages. He had to make himself the shifting centre of an organization without a material focal point, to develop a heterogeneous population into a Methodist fellowship, to create the whole Methodist organization without a conference, without funds, without machinery. And he had to do all this not only without previous experience, but frequently against all his conservative pre-suppositions. Almost from the outset he had to allay internal religious jealousies, to dissipate what his opponents called 'the vapouring heresies of Methodism', and to correct his assistants' eccentric style of preaching and doctrinal extravagancies. Other obstacles blocked his path. The classes were poles apart in civil ideas, interests and even speech, and millions of the people could not read. He had to face the disapproval of good men like Whitefield, Law and the leading Quakers and Independents as well as of 'Orator Henley', the famous preaching-quack of those days. He had to defend himself from the bishops; writing to the Bishop of Lincoln he says:

'I write without ceremony as neither hoping nor fearing anything from your Lordship, or from any living man, and I ask in the name and in the presence of Him, to whom both you and I are shortly to give an account, why do you trouble those that are quiet in the land; those that fear God and work righteousness?'

He was called upon to face the baptism of fire. Gipsies, privateers, tramps, highwaymen, smugglers haunted the countryside and they together with mob-ruled towns provided him with physical handicaps. His splendid courage rebuked the violence of many bent on disturbance, whilst his voice and message could sway turbulent assemblies. His words and thoughts went home to every listening heart that he addressed, not so much from the ideas or oratory as from the living man himself, whose anvil strokes prevailed less by their massive strength and iteration, than by the burning-glow of the heart fire. The Mercy of God, the Grace of God, the Forgiving Love of God to all mankind, and Duty were his ever unexhausted themes, which his reality left impressed on every audience with breadth and simplicity more striking every year. His message was accepted in regions hoary with antiquity as well as in the mushroom-like new towns; and appealed to those speaking the hundred and one dialects within England's shores.

Perhaps there was an even bigger victory. For the refined don must often have flinched instinctively from the bluff, inartistic, enthusiastic, broad-spoken, coarse-thoughted converts who 'battered the gates of Heaven with storms of prayer'. Few things could have been more galling to eighteenth-century reserved, academic, high-Churchmanship than to be brought into contact with noisy, demonstrative, religious ardour or with a luscious manner, and with addresses compounded of mysticism and water, heavily sugared in sentimentality. Wesley had to encounter all these varieties as well as the stolidity of the commonplace mind with its

inability to understand. All must have been intolerable to him
again and again. But thanks to his spirit of interior humility
and constant prayer, he overcame the handicaps provided by
temperament, foe and friend.

Thus the personality of this don's long life grew and grew; it was
always the consistent growth of a genuine character from its bud-
ding promise to its supreme dominance. To-day we see the vast-
ness of its fruits, the beneficence of its influence beyond its visible
operations, its conquest over popular follies and faults, its acceptance by peoples infinitely varied in thought, feelings and customs.
To fight a way through all the obstacles to such a blinding triumph
called for courage, endurance, self-devotion and statesmanship.

Few men ever deserve the monumental panegyrics raised to
their memory, but nobody would question the sobriety of the
inscription to Wesley in City Road Chapel. The serene purity of
his life, his lofty purposes, his nobility of nature certainly cause
him to stand out most conspicuously in the strange, cynical, cruel
world of life and thought in the eighteenth century; for naturally
his influence on that century was equally conspicuous. Sir Leslie
Stephen, who does not pose as a favourable critic of Wesley,
declares however: 'Wesleyanism is the most important phen-
omenon of the eighteenth century . . . no such leader of men
appeared anywhere as Wesley'. Properly to evaluate this judgement, it must be borne in mind that this was the century of
leaders of men like Marlborough at the one end and of Nelson and
Wellington at the other, with Clive and Hastings in between; of
the two Pitts, Burke, Fox and Sheridan; of Rousseau and Voltaire;
of Hume and Gibbon; of Law and Whitefield. It was the century
of Washington in the United States, of the Fredericks in Prussia
and of Catherine of Russia. The century also saw Swedenborg
display an insatiable curiosity of knowledge and propound a new
theosophic system which has won a following in every centre of
thought on the globe.

II

When dealing with personalities of such penetrating charm the
temptation to pursue the thread of fancy is great. Had John
Wesley followed his father's wish, and succeeded him at Epworth,
how different things might have been. For, with the family influence and all his natural abilities, he must surely have risen to the

episcopal bench. From there he would have thundered moral doctrines into the ears of thousands who had never heeded or heard them before; he would have pierced the vulgar, dull, contaminated hideousness of the vicious social life that surrounded the throne, and sent streaming in on it the light of a higher world and better law, just as he inspired the souls of the poor with all the zealot's fire and all the martyr's endurance. Had his mother been a Papist, 'It is quite probable that the Roman Catholic Mass would now be celebrated on the altars of Westminster and St. Paul's', declares Oemler. And as every Methodist knows, his course of life was always as severe as the rule of a monastic order. Had he elected to remain at Oxford and sit in a professorial chair, his sagacious, contentious, dogmatic mind would have been most salutary in that then castle of indolence.

He was one of the ablest scholars of his generation as is evidenced by his masterly translations of poems from German, French and Spanish sources. In these versions he reproduced the full flavour of the originals; a task demanding the highest powers of scholarship, insight, skill and taste both in thought and expression. His *Notes on the New Testament* again indicate his excellent scholarship, and show that he had a sounder knowledge of Greek than that displayed by the translators in 1611. They show too that he suggested English phrasings and vocabularies that very largely anticipated the 3,000 findings of the Revisers in 1881. This literary ability also revealed itself in his substitutions of words and phrases in hymns composed by colleagues before admitting them into his anthology. In so doing he added to the richness of the imagery, symmetry of the form or grandeur of the original versions. Had he decided to enter business he would unquestionably have been a very wealthy man. His financial success as a publisher was phenomenal, for he perceived what the masses needed, and brought to them the literary wealth of the past in cheap and attractive form. At the same time he took effective steps from being defrauded of profits by the piracy of knavish printers and booksellers who battened on every famous writer of his century. It is simple fact that he received some thousands of pounds as profits from his writings alone; it is no less true that such was his amazing generosity, that when he died he left eighteen pence and a half a dozen silver teaspoons. It seems within just surmise, too, that if he had been drawn to politics, his resonant eloquence and masterly handling of facts would have given him

Cabinet rank. His private and public actions would have been regulated by reference to a code higher than that of mere prudence or worldly wisdom, since he ever lived in the habitual contemplation of the unseen world.

A second characteristic, less prominent than the first, was his love of power, which would have been a potent factor had he embarked on a political career. Yet this ambition would have had little in common with the eighteenth-century vulgar eagerness for place, pay and social standing. It would rather have been a resolute determination to possess that complete control over the machine of State which would have enabled him to fulfil, without let or hindrance, the mission with which he believed that Providence had charged him. Further, this love of power was supported by splendid fearlessness born of his implicit trust; no dangers were too threatening for him to face, no obstacles too formidable, no tasks too laborious, no heights too steep. His *Journal* contains numberless instances of feats of endurance, escapes from perils and deliverances from death. He had the eloquence, knowledge, financial skill, moral fibre, self-mastery, concentrative power which made him superior to any of the contemporary statesmen, whether judged by the mental powers of Pitt, Fox, Burke and Rockingham, or by the stainless lives of Somers, Cowper, Townshend and Grenville, whilst there can be no doubt that he would never have descended to the bribery and corruption practised by Walpole, Newcastle, Carteret, Bute, &c. His writings, especially his 'rules' and *Journal*, prove that he had the statesmanlike quality of writing excellent 'minutes', which, however severely condensed, are couched in the clearest English.

Macaulay goes still farther when supporting Wesley's political possibilities and attributes, and declares him to be the equal of Richelieu, the cardinal who gave seventeenth-century France unity and glory. Certainly they resemble each other as men of inflexible will, vigorous abilities and patrons of learnings, and both had the clearest ideas of what they desired their countries should be. Lecky, Green and Birrell too, have placed Wesley high in history's niches; they suggest, and modern authorities like Halévy and Piette confirm, that he saved the English poor from glutting their revenge in the blood of their oppressors. Like France, England then laboured under a complication of great evils, which must lead to some great national calamity, unless there is a powerful restraining influence. Reckless corruption and selfish

contempt of the interests of the people, had during many years
aggravated and irritated the populace, whilst a school of so-called
philosophers were industriously disseminating principles which
tended to undermine the existing framework of society. These
foreign critics, who at any rate can view Wesley dispassionately,
and not through the mists which partisanship would fain raise
round him, suggest that his teachings kept the English people from
the volcanic fires of revolution by reconciling them to their situation, making them patient of their burdens through the acceptance of the philosophy of fortitude which their new region of
thought had opened for them, with the doctrine of posthumous
rewards and punishments. There is a further point of view. The
90,000 or so Methodists living at the end of the century had been
impregnated with Wesley's invincible belief in the perfectibility
of the human race. And the class meetings, which these enormous
numbers shared, were gatherings of people who resolutely put
aside social class grievances and who tried to live in glowing peace.
Finally, by such class meetings, the adherents had been trained to
influence others who did not necessarily see eye to eye with them.

III

Although Wesley does not seem to have been caricatured by
Sayer, Gillray and Hogarth as were his great Nonconformist
compeers, Drs. Priestley, Price, Clarke, he like every other great
man, had his detractors.

As for the charges of ominous fanaticism, impudent hypocrisy,
egregious enthusiasm or personal ambition, time has resolved
them as baseless. The distinctive peculiarities of his work undoubtedly ran counter to the instinct of most of the State Church
and Dissenting leaders of the period. To these men of lesser
mould, his versatility and selflessness might well seem unnatural
and therefore be judged insincere. Nor need the contemptuous
opinions of Beau Nash or Horace Walpole or other meretricious
gentry on his deeds and preaching power detain a reader for a
moment. The same attitude might be assumed regarding the
criticisms of some modern writers, who seem to find it easy to
reproach him with sunless creeds and declarations of mental in-
solvency. Wesley, like other great people of the past, now and
then receives scurvy treatment at the hands of modernists who

would 'discount' the great dead. Of such estimates one competent Methodist historiographer says: 'Fear, fanaticism, credulity and philandering are made the dominant facts of his life . . . the mere disproportion of treatment is amazing . . . the nobility of his life and his labours is insufficiently recognized . . . it is not worth while to waste words in refuting this frantic rubbish.' The excessive praise with which Wesleyan historiography surrounded the Founder, may have been the reason for contemporary and modern belittling statements. In their *English Church in the Eighteenth Century*, Abbey and Overton rightly say: 'It is peculiarly cruel to represent him as a faultless being, a sort of deified angel.' But it is equally cruel for critics judging by twentieth-century standards of thought and finesse, to censure him for being what he was,'such a thorough man of the eighteenth century', and to refuse to cover his so-called weaknesses (due to the age in which he lived) with the kindly and oblivious veil of lapsing time. If it were only a legend that Wesley was the founder of a freer and better England, it has been a powerful legend and one believed in by eminent historians, who saw in him a fiery spirit endowed with indomitable courage, and who have found him to be a source of joy and pride for succeeding generations. More ordinary people have found his sermons and tracts manly in spirit, sure in the progress of the argument, inexpugnable in their foundations, and found the man to be tender, sympathetic, wide and rich of vision, and the precursor of philosophical radicals. A recollection of great moves and great men of the past is, moreover, always needed to keep ordinary folks safe on the heights of present and future.

Now and then Wesley's wordy warfare with Law, Toplady, Whitefield, Cennick, Zinzendorf and the bishops reveals literary brutality. But it must be remembered that in this century, religious stride was generally conducted with a zest and acerbity not consonant with present notions of decorum. Eighteenth-century opinions, whether of art, literature, politics or religion, were invariably extreme, and like all extreme opinions, they were only too liable to generate the opposites in fervid minds, who are in no wise apt to base their convictions upon sweet reasonableness or to phrase their replies in a courteous, conciliatory fashion.

Sometimes he is accused of being romantically superstitious, of believing in omens, of seeing visions, and there is little doubt that he credited and repeated stories of apparitions, witchcraft, devil-possession which are incredible in these days; stories curiously opposed to his notoriously sturdy, not to say impatient, common sense. But because of the extremely bad means of communication and the almost total absence of education, these were the days of folk-lore. Nature was then awe-inspiring; temperaments were nervous, control of the judgement was unstable. Millions of people saw wraiths, spooks, wizards, ghosts, hobgoblins, and scores of the eighteenth-century novels read like the riotings of a disordered brain. Newton, Davy, Leibnitz, Price, the distinguished scientists of the times, were firm believers in alchemy and animal magnetism; a great doctor-author like Sir Thomas Browne maintained that disease and death could be caused by malevolent apparition; an enlightened man like Addison was a firm believer in witchcraft, and a robust soldier like Clive was most superstitious. This was the century of the Rosicrucians with their philosopher's stone and their elixir of life; the age of mesmerism and of secret societies with their mysterious rituals and significant symbols. Belief in the supernatural persisted long years after Wesley's death. Coleridge based his *Ancient Mariner, Christabel, Kubla Khan* on prevailing wild tales of fairy-land; he and Wordsworth treated supernatural subjects in *Lyrical Ballads*; Scott assiduously collected tales of demonology and his *Lay of the Last Minstrel*, with the ever-burning lamp, just satisfied the superstitions of the day; the staple materials of Southey's *Thalaba* and *Kehama* are current wizard tricks and demon enchantments.

The truth of the matter as regards Wesley's tepid interest in politics, virulent disputes with other clergymen or his childlike credulity can only be appreciated justly by a knowledge of the sort of place England really was in the eighteenth century. Or as it is expressed by Pattison: 'What is important for us to know of any age is not its peculiar opinions, but the complex elements of that moral feeling and character in which, as in their congenial soil, such opinions grow.' Like every other great preacher, poet, painter, politician he was necessarily the product of his age more or less. Nor should it be forgotten that important eras in human progress and national salvation are generally inaugurated and moulded by a man who has an understanding of his times.

CHAPTER II

BROAD VIEWS AND WIDE CONTRASTS

I

THE eighteenth century saw an almost complete transformation of England for it was crowded with great happenings. Its beginning found England, Scotland and Ireland three separate countries as far as Parliament was concerned; its close left them nominally united. In no century did politics change so much as in this; the establishment of the Hanoverian dynasty opened up great possibilities of limiting the royal prerogative; it saw the steady growth of parliamentary government, and the slow emergence of the Cabinet as the central feature of the Constitution; it witnessed the establishment of the two-party House of Commons and the foundation of the Leadership of the Opposition. Under Walpole the sceptre of government passed to the Commons and in Onslow it saw one of its best Speakers. The century opened in an age 'pregnant with dynastic changes and political revolutions; it went out amid the throes of social revolutions. America had gained her independence; France after regenerating herself was employed upon the singular mission of regenerating Europe. Everywhere the rights of man were receiving a practical illustration whether from the pen of the theorist, the sword of the warrior or the axe of the executioner. All human institutions were shaken to their foundations, all past authority was ignored or repudiated; the old system of society was crumbling into ruin', says one historian.

In England, the century saw the three great silent revolutions in agriculture, industry and religion. It resounded with tumult; it saw rebellions in 1715, 1745 and 1800; it lost us the American colonies, but it gave us Canada, India, New Zealand and Australia. The century's first years saw the land battles of Blenheim, Ramillies, Oudenarde and Malplaquet; its middle years saw those of Culloden, Plassey and Quebec, and its closing ones the naval battles of Camperdown, St. Vincent and the Nile. In other words, the century saw England engaged in four great wars: the Austrian Succession, the Seven Years War, the War of American Independence and the first half of the great French war, and it only just missed the new projectile invented by Shrapnel.

Its earlier half witnessed the close of the long period of stagnation which, for centuries, had kept the English almost unprogressively to their insular selves; its last fifty years saw the birth of a new expansion which has since reached such dimensions as are unparalleled in history. In those years:

The foundation of the British Empire was laid in five continents. The supremacy of the British Navy was established by the seamanship of Vernon, Duncan, Rodney and Nelson.

The industrial dominance of Britain was secured by the inventions of the art of smelting iron by means of coal; the steam engine of Watt; the spinning jennies and mules of Hargreaves, Arkwright and Crompton; the foundation of the woollen industry in the West Riding through the genius of the Doncastrian parson Cartwright; Wedgwood's discovery of porcelain manufacture; and the improvement of transit by the canals of Brindley and the roads of Telford and Blind Jack of Knaresborough.

The century too has a peculiar charm for lovers of other forms of the English past. All the foregoing outburst of exuberant vitality was accompanied by equal splendour in other realms. Addison, Steele, Pope and Swift are some of its early literary lights; middle-century writers like Richardson and Fielding gave birth to the novel as we understand it to-day; Sheridan, Campbell, Coleridge, Scott, Southey are only some of the great writers at its close. On the Stage eighteenth-century Garrick and Mrs. Siddons still remain unmatched. In Art, Kneller, Reynolds, Wilson, Romney, Gainsborough, Raeburn and George Morland have few superiors. In Hogarth, Sayer, Rowlandson, Sandby and Collet it saw some of the greatest of English cartoonists, and by the end of the century, Britannia and her lion were not the only representatives in the caricatures; for in Gillray's hands, John Bull took pictorial form and became the plump, sleek, good-humoured individual we are in the habit of beholding. In Music, Purcell had been succeeded by Arne, Boyce and Attwood and by such foreign giants as Handel, Bach, Haydn, Mozart and Beethoven, many of whom owed much to eighteenth-century England. In Architecture, it saw the completion of St. Paul's and the erection of Radcliffe Camera at Oxford and the Senate House at Cambridge. In Science, great names stand round those of Davy, Newton and Priestley; there was Cavendish, the great chemist of the eighteenth century and Dollond, who then invented the achromatic telescope; in 1731 Hadley's quadrant superseded the old astrolabe and cross-staff, and together with the sextant, this quadrant solved for sailors the problem of latitude, whilst thirty years later Harrison's chronometer solved that of longitude, the other outstanding problem for mariners. In Medicine, the century's last decade saw the work of the two Hunters, Cruikshank and Haller lead to enormous strides being made in anatomical studies. Eighteenth-century parliaments boasted such figures as Chatham, Burke, Pitt, Fox and Sheridan who still hold the highest place among orators. In Religion, it saw Wesley awake the national Church from her long, devitalizing slumber, rouse the Dissenters out of their droning condition and found a fellowship destined to fling society on better paths. In every department of life, English thinkers and workers of this century opened the ways and initiated the processes for the astounding developments which will ever mark the nineteenth in the story of England's progress.

II

The Englishmen who accomplished all these great tasks must have been mighty ones, and eighteenth-century England is one that we are rightly called upon to admire respectfully, if a little dizzily, in our scholastic youth.

But there is a reverse side of that stately façade of British cultural and religious expansion, and the price for Britain's commercial and imperial supremacy and all our comfortable wealth and pensioned philosophy, had to be paid for one way or another. Orthodox historians dealing with weighty things like political, constitutional, military and naval history do not throw very illuminating glimpses into the more intimate life of the times. Such intimacy can, however, be found in the records of eighteenth-century travellers like Defoe, Young, Johnson, Macky, Le Blanc, Grosely, Pennant, Howard and Wesley; in the novels, diaries and letters of the period; in the ballads and newspapers of the day; in the eighteenth-century story of the cotton, woollen, linen and hosiery developments, and especially in the MS. records of different eighteenth-century commercial communities, religious societies or parish records; in the contemporary caricatures and such illustrations as Schopper's 'Panoplia', 'Cryes of London', and in racy accounts like *Ramblin Jack* (the journal of Captain John Cremer 1700–84), *Life and Adventures of John Nicol Mariner*, *Log of the Bounty*, *Mr. Bulkeley and the Pirate*, &c. The history in them is perhaps little more than the essence of gossip, and perhaps many of the writers had no respect whatever for the idols of society, parliament and the market-place. But they were written from the inside by those who were born and who grew up within the material to which they had the master-key. They are freely referred to in these pages because they deal with people and things in which John Wesley was primarily interested.

From them one gathers other broad views of a century cara-coling in stately fashion to its close. Behind the splendid names of Rodney and Nelson were cruel captains and mates; mutiny in the Royal Navy was quite a common thing throughout the century and insubordination in the Army was not infrequent. These were the days of the cat-o'-nine-tails and the press-gang; the gang that sandbagged strapping young men from the fishing villages and coastal towns and pressed them willy-nilly into the King's Navy, and that stole the villagers' cattle and corn for His Majesty's Service, and when the defence forces were recruited from gaols and workhouses. The lives of the workers, the poor and the felons were considered negligible, and so the high mortality and serious invalidism of convict ships, debt prisons, workhouses and factories occasioned neither surprise nor distress; indeed, they scarcely evoked comment. The slave-complex governed the English rulers. During this century Parliament passed twenty-three Acts genially regulating the slave trade. By the Treaty of Utrecht of 1713, England undertook to supply annually some 5,000 slaves to South America for thirty years and in 1748 it actually renewed the contract. Even the State Church was indifferent to what Wesley called 'that execrable villainy', and a bishop breathing the rarefied atmosphere of the episcopal bench, declared that 'Christianity and the embracing of the Gospel does not make the least alteration in civil property, even when that property consists of human flesh and blood'.

It was the poor living under abominable conditions and developing regrettable moral obliquity. Fielding, who was a Westminster magistrate and as such had close acquaintance with them, said:

'The poor are a very great burden and even a nuisance in the kingdom . . . there are whole families in want of every necessity of life, oppressed with hunger, cold, nakedness and filth and disease. The sufferings indeed of the poor are less known than their misdeeds; and therefore we are less apt to pity them. They starve and freeze and rot among themselves; but they steal and beg and rob among their betters. There is not a parish in the kingdom which doth not swarm all day with beggars and all night with thieves.'

The high roads were infested with robbers, the streets were mob-ruled and hordes of smugglers and ship-wreckers lured thousands of vessels to their doom on wild and rocky shores. Nevertheless, it was a century of savage justice designed to crush misdeeds by its death-sentence for hundreds of felonies. But this 'justice' was often farcical, as it was administered by men who had bought their judicial privileges. Moreover, the laws themselves were often the product of members of Parliament whose brains and morals were devitalized by the fumes of brandy and port, who pretended to legislate after whole nights spent in gambling and whose vote could always be bought.

It was an age of gambling and speculation mania, when hundreds of madcap schemes for getting rich quick were floated; it saw a time when the great majority of the banks had to stop payment, and when the coinage was debased almost beyond control. It was the century of stories of superstition and when a belief in witchcraft prevailed. During its first part poor old women, held to be in communication with the powers of darkness, were officially hurried to the stake or left to be drowned in the rising tide, whilst its late years saw the mob wreak their ignorant vengeance on these unfortunates.

It was the century when people seemed to live to eat rather than eat to live, and when England qualified herself for her sad pre-eminence as the most drunken nation in the world. It was a time when many aristocrats were sodden lumps of flesh preserved in alcohol, and when crudeness, unchecked passions, bitter feuds and love of cruel sports characterized the majority of mankind. The century's sports, fairs and public entertainments were coarse beyond words. Its most popular books, poems and songs were mere licentious pictures; a kind of literary photography of all that we avert our eyes from in Nature. Adherents of parties and sects, representatives of different classes hated, loathed, despised, decried and calumniated one another. Religious strife and political differences were remarkable for the unredeemed, gratuitous vulgarities, clashing factions produced. In vain the really cultured protested against the prevailing practice of cursing and swearing; verbal refinement was not even thought of by the educated till the century was half spent. Its earlier journalists and pamphleteers freely indulged the blast and counterblast style of expressing their clashing opinions, whilst its later practitioners indulged in vulgar familiarity, nauseating innuendo, and were simply pert and fatuous, when they thought they were arch and facetious. These and other broad views of the century show that behind the customary glowing and inspiring picture of a dominating England, were many deep shadows and harsh lines.

The century saw its population increase from five and a half millions to over nine; a stupendous progression when the very high rates of mortality then prevailing, are remembered. Such growth meant big changes in the very appearances of towns. In Wesley's boyhood London boasted some fairly wide streets and brick houses, and some open spaces. But all around the old Houses of Parliament were streets and gateways covering the present broad thoroughfares, and where there are now wide spaces then there were narrow alleys and densely crowded houses. Trafalgar Square was then occupied with tenements and the royal mews; Westminster Hall had rows of little shops or booths ranged all along each inside wall. London Bridge was the principal means of crossing the river; it was a wooden construction with three-storied houses on either side which remained till 1757 when they were demolished to make room for the increasing traffic, and incidentally add to the toll revenue derived from it. The bridges at Westminster, Putney and Blackfriars were not built till Wesley's prime or old age.

Quite out in the country were Marylebone and St. Pancras. Tottenham Court Road ran through fields and was lined with farms and cowsheds, and there was open country to the north beyond Bloomsbury Square. As late as 1800 the country all about Paddington was covered with farms, a lovely rural part where footpads lurked, and from whose activities the district took its name. Covent Garden was then an open space with a sun-dial; Soho and Seven Dials were fashionable neighbourhoods; Mayfair was the scene of a real country fair that lasted six weeks. Wesley was thirty-two when 10 Downing Street got the seal of respectability by becoming the residence of Walpole and succeeding prime ministers; he was fifty when the British Museum was opened and nearly sixty before Buckingham Palace became a royal residence. He would know Vauxhall and Ranelagh as pleasure gardens and St. James's Park, Kensington Gardens, &c., as semi-royal privileged preserves; he would know that London was ringed round with thousands of acres of public commons, and he would find that these commons and parks were mere wastes, unkempt and rugged. When Wesley was young, Glasgow was a pleasant little town of four streets only, but even then possessing a cathedral and university. Across the High Street were the college gardens and green pleasant orchards where the undergraduates played, and through its centre ran the clear Molendinar burn, whilst the Clyde was a silver stream teeming with salmon and blocked with sandbanks.

In Wesley's youth most of our present big towns were then but little more than thriving market-towns with only one main street; only the biggest of them like Bristol, Norwich, York, Nottingham, &c., had more than one State Church. When he was an old man, Manchester was only beginning to grow, and when he opened his new chapel in Oldham Street in 1781, the only objection that he could raise, was 'that it was so far out of the town'. Even when it began to grow, this city failed to arouse favourable comment from visitors. In 1806 Southey asserts, 'a place more destitute of all interesting objects than Manchester, is not easy to conceive', and he then proceeds to condemn the new dwellings for the poor and the new factories and factory-system. When Wesley was in his sixties, Wigan had sulphur springs, and according to *England Illustrated* 'it enjoyed all the eighteenth-century appurtenances of a fashionable spaw'. In Wesley's youth Liverpool had a flat boggy plain about Abercromby Square which was generally covered with water, and in London Road there was a supply reservoir which remained till 1800; when he was over seventy years old, Byrom Street was a country lane and Church Street mainly an orchard. At his death, Liverpool's Scotland Road district was a kind of seaside resort, and was regarded as 'a very desirable spot for any person who wishes the advantage of a pleasant retirement'. For among other amenities this neighbourhood then boasted that its houses had gardens twenty yards long in front and more spacious ones in the rear. Other towns, too, would offer equally bewildering contrasts with modern conditions. Perhaps some small towns like Sudbury (Suffolk), Chipping Norton and Appleby have preserved much of the outward appearance they would present in the eighteenth-century days.

III

In the course of a hundred years it is only natural that England would furnish wide contrasts of appearance, labour and public opinion. The century saw the great farming advances made by Coke, Tull and Bakewell; 10,000 square miles of untilled land was reclaimed and added to general cultivation. Up to 1760 England was a corn-exporting country, but by 1800 she could no longer satisfy her own needs. In 1700 tin was the most valuable mineral got from English mines; the yield of salt and iron was then very inconsiderable, whilst coal-hewing was in its infancy. By 1800 the picture was far other; by then coal had sounded the death-knell of the iron, spinning and weaving industries of the south and west and was determining the trade destiny of many another division.

The century had its problem of social relationships which offered the most amazing contrasts, and one has difficulty in tracing the decency and kindliness of ordinary humanity, essential in such relationships, through all the sordidness of this century's course. The *Tale of Two Cities* reveals the period as one of violent class contrasts, and not only in England but on the Continent. Not merely London, but Paris and especially Venice, were then sinking into shameless eclipse; their wealthy ones were dancing through riotous nights and carrying ribaldry into the cloisters and convents; everywhere aristocracy were plunging headlong down its degenerate course; everywhere it was a time of spendthrift immorality, laughing intrigue and gorgeous pageantry of costume for the nobility. Cheek by jowl were the ridiculous side of rich pomposities, the high traditions of antique aristocracy and un-believable poverty; the differences between the very few rich and educated and the millions of common people living in a manner almost bestial, were appalling and dangerous. England and France had some objectors to the grossly unfair division of wealth and comfort; in France Voltaire and Rousseau raised the flag of revolt against the flaunting pretensions of royalty and nobility, and ridiculed effectively the flamboyant insolence of priests.

Half-way through the century England, too, heard rude protests in the *Address to that Honest Part of the Nation called the Lower Sort*, and in *Protests on Behalf of the People*, whilst at the end Tom Paine and William Cobbett bawled loudly and long for an age of reason and the rights of man. Both attacked licentious politics, privilege of place and position, nepotism, corruption, ignorance, injustice, flogging in the services and so forth. Both held extreme views for the times in which they lived on these and kindred subjects, and were vigorous in debate and print; both had firm wills, strong brains and an intense love of fighting for its own sake; both poured coarse and unceremonious ridicule on what they considered super-stition, and both were ribald scoffers against religion as then practised. Distress and poverty did not make all the eighteenth-century English servile; rather it made a Johnson reckless and ungovernable; affronts to a Cobbett made him rude to ferocity, whilst an insulted Paine replied with the *Commonsense Pamphlet* which sealed the fate of British rule in the revolted colonies, and his *Rights of Man* was so uncompromising in its enforcement of democratic principles, that he was outlawed by an alarmed government. Now and then units of the ruling class protested against the sinister interests and mischievous prejudices of power; both Bentham and Blackstone, the eminent jurists of the eighteenth century, felt the need for a solid foundation for morality, and although the great bulk of the members of parliament throughout the era upheld and multiplied the barriers of race and caste and ancient prejudice, yet in 1780 the Duke of Richmond was so modern as to propose manhood suffrage. It was a similar story regarding eighteenth-century taxation. Then parliamentarians hated the idea of direct taxation on land and property, and preferred the elastic and fertile revenues derivable from taxes on the commonest things like salt, soap, windows, bricks, candles, newspapers and even on articles of clothing; yet in 1798 Pitt imposed a graduated income-tax. Although this much hated tax had to be withdrawn in 1801, the political financiers had realized its efficacy and fairness, and so, despite subsequent withdrawals and reimpositions, this eighteenth-century taxation device was destined to become a permanent feature of English legislation.

The eighteenth-century story of the land question is also illuminating and contradictory. In England the beginning of the era showed some 180,000 small farmers or yeomen who had almost disappeared by 1800. In Scotland the inveterate arrogance of some lairds depopulated entire countrysides to make deer forests or sheep runs. In Ireland it saw the wealthy ruthlessly waste the land for their own immediate enrichment, forests of oak were hastily destroyed for quick profits, woods were cut down for charcoal to smelt iron, and thousands of Irish were outlawed on religious grounds. In that country the first decades saw some 20,000 Irish men, women and children sold into the service of the planters of Virginia and the Carolinas, whilst uncounted thousands sailed to America during those hundred years, and some half million Irish left their homes to fight for France against England. Irish property, Irish positions, whether clerical or legal, were then all sold or given to English Church folk. Yet at least one man

C

questioned the rightness of such treatment, and in the *Querist* Bishop Berkeley wrote the most searching study of the Irish people's grief and its remedies.

These arresting contrasts can be continued. This was a century of quacks among doctors, yet it saw the work of Harvey, Jenner and the Hunters, the use of vaccination and the spread of infirmaries. It was a time when the standard of cleanliness, both personal, domestic and civic, was deplorably low; yet in 1704 it saw the establishment of public baths in Liverpool, the first ever known in England. It had chemists of the eminence of Stahl, Black, Cavendish, Priestley, Lavoisier, but the prevailing knowledge of drugs was very meagre, and mainly acquired by drastic and empirical methods tried out on animals and prisoners; its chemists had in 1747 discovered the existence of sugar in beet, yet throughout the century, people who could afford sugar were dependent for their supply on the cane; its brewers depended on rule of thumb methods till 1785 when, reluctant, they began to use the thermometer and hydrometer.

The century saw Le Sage and Lomond make electric telegraphy possible, Harrison and Hadley rid seamanship of two of its terrors with the chronometer and sextant, Eüler and Herschel improve the telescope; it even saw the start of photography. It saw come into being the troy pound and a new standard yard as well as secondary measurements, all commanded by Parliament in 1758. Six years earlier, it had seen a new calendar re-arrangement. The inconvenience of having a different time system from the rest of the world could no longer be ignored, and Chesterfield's Bill, in recommending the adoption of the Gregorian Calendar, enacted that the legal year 1752 should begin on January 1 instead of the old March 25, and that in 1751, September 2 should be followed immediately by September 14. This step was vigorously opposed by those parliamentarians who were firmly convinced that the reform had robbed them of eleven days, and has led to the insertion of o.s. and n.s. for eighteenth-century dates before and after 1752, and has affected such details as Wesley's birth and death, and the momentous Wednesday, May 24, 1738. Yet the same century's statesmen and inventors were to allow the national coinage to become greatly debased and to be largely replaced by a form of barter. It saw the national Church start off very well indeed, especially in regard to its S.P.G. and S.P.C.K. and in its advocacy of charity schools; later, however, it was to become 'riddled with nepotism and corruption, and cursed with a race of clerics the worst the world has ever known'. Yet in striking contrast it was to see the work of such religious leaders as Law, Whitefield, Toplady, Priestley, Gibson, Horsley, Paley, Lowth, Berkeley, Fletcher, Venn, Stackhouse, Seed, Price and John Wesley. About its last year it taught the people to sing 'Home, Sweet Home'; but a quarter of a century or so before, it had heard Johnson declaring in striking contrast: 'There is no private house in which people can enjoy themselves so well as at a capital tavern. You are sure of a welcome there, and the more good things you call for, the welcomer you are. There is nothing which has yet been contrived by man by which so much happiness is produced as by a good inn'. And considering the sort of homes in which the great bulk of the people lived, Johnson's declaration is not so very surprising.

But the biggest contrast that this century saw was the revolution effected by the whirr of machinery, when industry was dragged from the cottage to the factory. This development was the logical outcome of decades of efforts, whose sum-total at a given moment was suddenly vivified and increased by a remarkable spate of inventions. The new machines, together with the new power, trained the human beings who tended them to renounce their old desultory habits of work, and made them identify themselves with the unvarying and unwearying regularity of an automaton. They made hundreds of thousands of men, women and children lead an existence far worse than that of slaves at a time when they had learned to sing, 'Britons, never, never shall be slaves'. Not only were the machines fraught with peril to the bodies of the workers, but daily attendance for stretches of twelve to fourteen hours called for that 'monotony of attention which sears the soul'. Pitt, through inertia, spiritual opacity, contempt or possibly through design, simply ignored the ugly ways into which industry was falling, and in 1794 could only comment that the new class of workers were 'most ignorant and profligate', accept the declaration of another public man that 'the new employers are quite uneducated, of coarse habits, sensual in their enjoyments, partaking of the rude revelry of their dependants, and totally overwhelmed with their success', and when trade slumps came, he could only suggest the still greater use of child-employment as a cure. This fresh phase of industry was a new problem for eighteenth-century statesmen and completely baffled them. It also baffled or was ignored by the leading Churchmen and philanthropists, whilst the new class of employers never seem to have had the slightest conception of the human needs of labour.

To devise and administer a successful code of factory discipline was a mighty enterprise in that century, and called from an Arkwright the nerve and ambition of a Napoleon, for it was indeed a gigantic task to subdue the refractory tempers of men and women accustomed to centuries of irregular spasms of diligence. In 1700 one chronicler referring to the life led by a countryman says: 'He had fish in his stew, the hives in his garden provided him with honey, the home-brew'd beer he drank was the product of the hops he grew and the barley he malted . . . practically all his wants were met by his labour . . . the simple life of his self-supporting household meant a comfortable existence . . . he was his own master and could smoke or eat, drink or dig or sleep as he pleased.' And Defoe concludes his survey of industries in the first decades of the eighteenth century with: 'Under such circumstances hard labour is naturally attended with the blessing of health and happiness if not riches . . . not a beggar to be seen anywhere or any idle person.' By contrast, Dean Farrar has another picture of England soon after the eighteenth century had passed away. 'Greedy sweaters, uncontrolled by any legal enactment, ground down the faces of the poor; women, half-naked, yoked to trucks like horses, crawling on all fours like dogs, began their labours often at the age of six; grew double with hideous deformity and depraved morals in the black galleries of the mines . . . poor little climbing boys, grimed with soot were maimed, suffocated in crooked and choked chimneys; children were worked in cotton mills for unbroken hours which would have been crushing to grown men; they were brutally treated in brick fields, in canal boats, in agricultural gangs. Waifs and strays, criminals and semi-criminals, unwashed, unfed, untaught weltered in an atmosphere of blasphemy, in lairs and dens of human wild beasts.'

With the century's characteristic cynicism, these inventions which did so much to secure for England the manufacturing supremacy of the world, did little or nothing for most of their creators. Kay died neglected and poor; Hargreaves was driven from his home; Crompton was reduced to absolute penury and Cort died a bankrupt. Such contrasting aspects of this century could be continued; but it may be well to descend from panoramic outlooks and consider significant detail.

IV

From the Pay-book of the Tower Garrison in the days of Queen Anne one gathers the following particulars of their daily pay.

'Governour £1–18–4¼; deputy-governour 16/5¼; chaplain 6/8; town major and sergeants got 4/– each; corporals 3/– each; gateman 1/4; hautboys, privates, &c., 2/6 each; master-gunner 2/– and other gunners 1/– each; warders 1/2 each, gaoler 1/1⅛, water-pumper –/7⅞, scavenger –/4; clock-keeper –/2⅝; chimney-sweeper 1/3¼ and that the "fewil" for warders was –/4¾ a day. The rat-killer and mole-killer got salaries of £48–3–4 and £8–1–8 respectively per annum. The "chirugeon", "physitian" and apothecary got per day respectively 2/6, 1/1⅛ and –/6½.'

One can understand the diversity of wages for governor, deputy and chaplain; they would, of course, belong to the privileged classes and would have bought or inherited their jobs. At first sight it causes a shock to see the surgeon financially assessed alongside a private, and that the doctor and chemist are not valued as highly as the chimney-sweep and much less than the rat-catcher. Maid-servants about this time got 1/6 a week according to Pepys. Round about 1770 Young suggests that skilled workers in and about Manchester were getting 7/6 a week, unskilled about 5/–, that women's wages were nearly as great as those paid to men and that children received about 1/6 weekly. Eden states that round about 1800, skilled men got 18/– a week, women from 6/– to 12/– and unskilled workers something like 12/–. These wage estimates have to be treated with caution, for in some areas the workers had to provide such things as light and firing if not actual manufacturing things; then there was a formidable list of 'fines', whilst 'tommy-shop' tokens, factory-owned houses, &c., helped to invalidate wage calculations. Other authorities suggest that sailors in the Royal Navy got 19/– a month, and that their widows were entitled to one year's pay in the event of the seaman's death. The men who came through a successful fight were entitled to 'prize' money, which was sometimes a thousandth part of the value of the prize taken. There is evidence too, that miners in Somerset went on strike for 12/– a week towards the close of the century, and they were unsuccessful in their efforts.

The Methodist Chapel Book suggests that this company too paid their servants low wages.

'Pd robᵗ Young, caretaker of chappell, one quarters wages'   vis–vid.
'pd Sarᵃ Joness washing preechers linnen for a querter'   is–ood.

As for the preachers themselves, it appears that Wesley's first helpers were sent forth without much money or income; the men got something like £20 a year whilst their wives were allowed 4/– a week and each child 1/6. During the same period probably there were thousands of curates receiving less than a pound a week and hundreds of them getting under 10/–, whilst parish school-masters were equally badly paid for their services. Stipends prob-ably increased but little during the second half of the century, and certainly the pasturage for the first Primitive Methodist minister in the dawn of the nineteenth century was quite as scanty. The Rev. William Clowes got 10/– a week for himself and his family; no wonder he and they had 'to use coarse food, dine on a little suet and potatoes, or a piece of bread and a drink of water'.

Sometimes the ministers' stipends were supplemented with food. The Methodist pay-book has a regular series of weekly entries from 1774 such as:

'Preachers dyatt' (diet, dyett, diatt, eatage)   viis–ood.

Sometimes the entries suggest that the daily shilling sufficed for the preachers' wives as well:

'forr tow preachers dyet for eight nights'   viiis–ood.
'Pd 3 preachers and 2 wifes forr 3 nights'   iiis–ood.

Alongside the visits of some itinerants, those paid by Wesley seem to have been expensive luxuries:

1775	'Butter, suger and bred for Mr. Wesley'	5–4
	'Hay and corn for Mr. Wesley's horse'	1–12–3
	'To Hossler'	2–0
1777	'Painting Mr. Wesley's chaise'	4–17–1
	'By cash omitted for Mr. Wesley'	18–0
	'By cash expences for Mr. Wesley'	13–1
	'Mr. Wesley's expences to Wiggan'	1– 0–1
1778	'Wine &c. for Mr. Wessley'	7–0
	'Mr. Wesslyes chaise bill for Warington'	1– 0–2
	'Mr. Wessleys horses bill at hottle'	0–18–7
	'Mr. Wessleys gratuity'	3– 3–0
1790	'Mr. Westlays chaise bill hire'	3–18–9

Horses are rarely mentioned in connexion with the visits of the other Methodist preachers, and one of these itinerants records that he walked over 2,000 miles a year for twenty-two years on his preaching tours.

Advocates of temperance will have experienced a shock at one

of the previous sample items: the following from the same Methodist register of accounts are equally indicative of the times:

'One gallun of rum for yᵉ preachers'	ixs–ood.
'pd Haynes for wines for yᵉ „	xs–oid.
'Thos. Haines bill for liquour'	iii£–xiis–oid.

They suggest that total abstinence was not expected even amongst
Methodist preachers nor yet from the choir on special occasions;
certainly the stewards provided quantities of rum, wine and ale
for such helpers. Churchmen did not expect total abstinence from
their clergy; indeed there is every evidence that drunkenness was
not uncommon amongst them. Parson Woodforde, who was
educated and refined and who, according to eighteenth-century
standards, lived a life of simple piety and plain duty, seems to
have encouraged hearty eating and drinking at his 'tithe frolics'.
His tithe payers were then rewarded with 'six bottles of wine, one
and a half gallons of rum and as much ale and punch as they
pleased'. Current diaries show that the ordinary men and women
were hard drinkers and that daily drunkenness, coarse feeding and
violent temper did not appear to women folks as faults, but
merely the necessary eighteenth-century masculine attributes.
Diaries often give precise details of such eating and drinking, and
it is significant that according to the pay-book of the Tower
Garrison, it was necessary to allow daily $75\frac{1}{2}$ gallons of beer
together with '$51\frac{1}{2}$ more bottels of other Liquour, comprising Ale
4, Claret 32, White Wine 3, Rhenish 2, Sherry $10\frac{1}{2}$' for the 77 men
and women who had their dinner and supper at the queen's table.
Further, catering for the 52 who had their dinner and the 25
who took supper was an expensive affair and amounted to £26,000
per annum or well over a sovereign a day per person. And yet
within a stone's-throw of St. James's Palace, there were thousands
of people living in a chronic state of semi-starvation.

Statements of the cost of household articles in the eighteenth
century crop up in this Methodist account book.

'A new beasom'	oos–iid.
'iii best pewter spunes'	oos–ixd.
'tea ketel'	oos–vd.
'bason, playtes, glassen'	ois–iiid.
'tin fender'	oos–xid.

By this time brushes of all sorts were known: hair, shaving, clothes
and even for chimney-sweeping; but the poor possessed few of
them. Till well towards the end of the century plates, mugs and

dishes for the poor were made of pewter or wood rather than of glass or china, both of which were still comparatively expensive. They possessed a somewhat coarse delft for kitchen purposes and grey-mottled stoneware was used for sack-jugs, &c., in many a home. Reversible wooden plates which enabled the same utensil to serve for two courses, were still used even in comfortable farm-steads, whilst cruet-stands, handles of knives and forks were gener-ally made of cherry wood and spoons were of wood or horn. But there would be no superfluity of such table-ware and people in this station of life were expected to produce their own knife, rude two-pronged fork, spoon, wooden plate, leather bottle or pewter mug when invited out to dine at another yeoman's home. Pro-bably by then, men like Methodist ministers had learned to employ forks for eating as well as serving even though their hosts did not. Their knives were probably of the 'jack-type' and made to shut in a groove in the handle, but fitted without a spring; and it is very doubtful if any men in this century ever owned pocket-knives fitted with a spring.

A reference to the purchase of a 'Dutch ooven' for 3/9 brings to the mind the eighteenth-century cooking utensils. The wide hearth in the manse-kitchen would be equipped with a 'spit' and roasting-jack. Some manses would also have an oven made of stone or brick. These were shaped like a beehive and about three feet tall; a charcoal fire was made inside the construction and when it was very hot, the fire was raked out and the bread &c., put in. None of the manses would possess all the cooking utensils and appliances described in Mrs. Powys' diary or listed in late eighteenth-century auctioneer catalogues, and it is unlikely, for example, that the minister would have a 'spit' worked by a dog inside a wheel. This wheel when once set in motion, forced the animal to continue running and thereby turn the spit, and few of them would own an 'ice-house' as keeping places. These were small caverns dug in the sloping ground and built of bricks; the chambers were then packed with snow and for months provided cold storage for food and game for the well-to-do.

About 1780 one finds that a quilt for 'ye preachers bed' cost 11/6 and that the stewards paid 'forr chaf bed' 5/- and 'forr coverlid and blankitt' 3/1. There is no definite mention of an eiderdown in these recitals, although eiderdowns were known in the eighteenth century. Some who could afford them considered them quite unnecessary, and a royal princess hearing of this late

eighteenth-century invention for keeping people warm in bed,
declared the device to be superfluous for: 'what keeps me warm in
bed at nights, are six little doggies that lie around me.' As for
very poor people, the great majority of them would have no beds
at all as the term is now understood; probably few of them ever
undressed and so, though blankets were produced quite early in
the century, the Witney output was small.

Now and then there are references to the purchase of garments;
probably for the poor rather than for the preachers.

1773   'Pd forr a pare of lether britches'   00£–03s–00d.
       'Pd for half yeard of linnen cloath'   00s–0vd.

Shoes are mentioned as costing 3/6, clogs ranged from 3d. to 11d.
and stockings from 6d. to 9d. a pair. Later there is mention of a
'shuite of cloathes' without details as to destination. The price
(10/4) suggests that we were still a long way off the nineteenth-
century familiar type of self-made Methodist, who having done
well in business, affected the grand seigneur to a degree with his
ample waist, gold-fob, stately tread; with abundance, prosperity,
self-assurance, self-importance exuding from every joint.

If the local society did not act as provider of clothing for its
preachers, it certainly made itself responsible for their facial
appearance.

'Hary Gregsons bil for quarter shaving of mr. Olivers'   xs–00d.
'To geo. walsh forr fower months shaving of ye preachers'   viis–0iid.

And such items bring to the mind's eye the old Methodist fashion
of shaving lips and chin and of leaving whiskers round the face and
throat.

One item in 1788 has reference to a 'hanway ombrelle'. Then
umbrellas were far from popular and very probably the one
bought for the preacher would, like other northern ones, be rudely
described as a 'walking-stick with petticoats', and become a target
for stones and mud. A little later umbrellas were followed by
sunshades and both, like eighteenth-century candlesticks, were
then furnished with an elbow joint just below the head. Although
Hanway has many other claims to remembrance, he is likely to
go down to history for the two minor ventures of his busy life: as
being the first to use umbrellas in the streets of London, and for his
attack on tea-drinking, which drew a ferocious reply from Johnson.
Nevertheless he was a great writer and traveller and added considerably to the later eighteenth-century knowledge of Russia and

Persia. Moreover, in the course of some seventy books and pamphlets, he sought and not altogether in vain, to win sympathy for chimney-sweeps, pauper children and other social outcasts, as well as to improve conditions in prisons and to modify the terrible code of punishment then in force.

Sometimes in the records are references to the purchase of coal. The fuel was classified under cart-load, horse-load or basket with prices ranging for the first from 4/9 to 7/9, for the second from 1/– to 1/6 and for the third from 5d. to 8d. The classification suggests the eighteenth-century method of goods conveyance, concerning which more will be stated elsewhere. Lighting is often mentioned.

'iii punds of mold candels'	iiis–ood.
'ix pounds of cannels'	vs–iid.
'iii duzzens of mowld kandells'	xs–oid.

In those days there was a tax on bought candles ranging from a halfpenny a pound on tallow ones to $3\frac{1}{2}d$. on mould ones. Thus many candles were made at the manses and at homes of officials during the long winter evenings and in diaries, &c., one reads of 'the wife made 231 candels in fore sizes: greatest, lesse, lesser, and least', and 'that they were made of mutton or ox tallow'. The infrequent references to the purchase of 'flints' or 'tinder-boxes' or 'spunks' (sulphur-tipped splints of wood) remind the reader that matches had not yet been invented; it was not till 1827 that really practical friction-matches were made by a Stockton chemist.

From the eighteenth-century records of a country State church come the following items:

'Pd barnes forr rushing place at rushberrin'	iis–ood.
'Rushingg church'	iiis–oid.
'Forr rushh carrt'	is–vid.
'Forr bear at rush carrt'	iis–ixd.

Slightly later ones run on similar lines:

'Pd forr one trusse of strawe'	oos–viid.
'Ate yerds ov fustyan for daunsers cotes'	is–xid.
'Bellys for horses for drawing rushcarrt'	xs–xid.
'Tow duzzen of morris bellys'	iis–xd.

These items suggest that rushes and straw were used in many country churches as floor coverings, whilst later entries indicate that sand was often placed on the floors. They would occasion no surprise to the worshippers, for the vast majority of them would be familiar with such 'carpets' in their homes.

Here are two contiguous items that need to be taken together to be intellgible.

1784 'Pd Ge. reobotom for brimston'   iiis–ivd.
         'To mr. Robinson for cureing buggs'   vis–oid.

These vermin are mentioned again and again in these records; on one occasion the price of their destruction had risen to 15/–; perhaps that included the brimstone. The entries indicate the prevailing standard of cleanliness and of domestic comfort, when such expenditures are solemnly recorded in circuit accounts with reference to the requirements of the manse and chapel. But the national churches were probably quite as bad. Archbishop Secker had often to comment on the 'damp, dirty, unwholesome, offensive churches' in his episcopate; Bishop Butler suggests that they are verminous in his see, and Bishop Horne said: 'judging from the conditions of the churches, cleanliness was no essential to devotion.'

In this moving picture of the eighteenth century as unfolded by these chapel records, the coinage comes into view.

'By light gold and counterfeits that came back from
      two years collection 1772 and 1773'   ov£.–xviis–xd.
'bad money'   ixs–ivd.

'return'd to thos. lether a bad shilling'
'tokens that were not took'   vs–iiid.

These entries remind one of the debased coinage under George III, by which time it had become intolerably wretched. They do not, however, suggest the percentage of loss incurred to the Society. Preserved accounts of municipal bodies and of toll-keepers operating much about the same time, indicate that their losses through 'false' or 'light' money averaged roughly about 8 per cent. of the total. 'Bad' shillings were still being sold at the close of the century to shop-keepers, turnpike men, waiters at coffee-houses and taverns at the rate of twenty such shillings for 5/6 according to an article in *The Times* in 1794. For it was not till the century's close that Matthew Boulton, who developed Watt's steam-engine, the hydraulic ram, the artistic manufacture of Sheffield plate, ormolu, silver plate and mechanical paintings, revolutionized the coining of money. Up to then it had been possible to clip or sweat coins and so to decrease their value; for banks reckoned by weight and not by tale, and as in the case of this Methodist chapel, the possessor might suffer considerable loss.

No wonder that in those days it was customary for prudent trades-men to carry with them small pocket balances in order to weigh the coins they received. Foreign money, especially Spanish and Portuguese, was legal tender and moidores, double pistoles and bulky 'Maria Theresa' dollars were freely used. Coiners did a thriving trade round about 1770 by buying brand-new guineas for 22/–, then shaving off the edges, filing new ones and returning them into circulation at 21/–. The gold clippings were preserved, melted down and struck into imitation moidores at 27/–. So blatant were some of these coiners, that it is asserted that counter-feiting was actually carried on in Newgate prison as late as 1796.

In addition to the foreign coins already mentioned, Wesley would be familiar with the silver penny; a square-shaped coin in-dented with a deep cross dividing it into four equal parts, which could easily be broken off for the payment of small amounts. He would also know the golden guinea piece, the double guinea, the five-guinea piece, the half and the third guinea, the mark (repre-senting two-thirds of a guinea), most silver coins, the groat and the farthing. He would not know, however, the silver florin nor the weighty copper penny and twopenny pieces, for these were minted after his death. He would also be familiar with some of the thousand 'tokens' issued by banks, corporations and firms for all sorts of amounts such as pence, 1/6, 3/4, &c. &c. These tokens were metal or paper pieces and were very freely used throughout the century. The radius within which each was accepted was very limited, and a traveller from Manchester to Liverpool who had received tokens in the one town would find them quite valueless in the other. He would know that many of his humble followers were paid wages in the form of 'tommy-shop' tokens and that these tokens were only accepted at the shops owned by their employers. He would also find that 'barter' was freely adopted in business transactions among the poor, and typical items from Tim Bobbin's diary like the following, would occasion him no surprise.

1770   'Pd John Kenyon a book for a wig.'
      'Exchanged a book for 3 lbs of thread, blue tape and gross of laces.'

He would be familiar with such receipts as wooden tallies. Notches on sticks were still used as a primitive method of account-ancy, and a phrase like 'he notched me half a day' was employed for 'he deducted so much from my wages'. But wooden tallies were used not solely by poor workers in the eighteenth century; even the Court of Exchequer employed them as acknowledgements for quite large sums.

The account-book makes no mention of any dealing with banks. And yet the banking system was then well spread. The Bank of England was started in the closing years of the seventeenth century, whilst the eighteenth saw the establishment of many private banking houses in provincial towns. Many of these private banks seem to have started as side-lines to a merchant's business; Coutts was primarily an Edinburgh corn-dealer, Lloyd was a Birmingham ironmaster, Smith was a mercer. By the end of the century, every market town seems to have had its own bank, and in the year Wesley died, probably there were at least 400 country banking systems. All of them seem to have issued a lot of paper money or tokens quite regardless of their genuine stability to redeem them in cash. Thus in 1797 when the country was apprehensive of a French invasion, there was a rush to convert tokens and paper money into cash, and the great bulk of the 400 banks were forced to stop payment, and by their fall, produced an extent of bankruptcy and misery till then unknown in the country.

The postal service is mentioned in these accounts:

'Postage of a lettre'	oos–ixd.
'Forr postage of letter from Bristole'	iiis–viid.
'Sundrey letters for mr. Westley'	ixs–vd.

The accession of James I to the English throne necessitated a more frequent and reliable means of communication between London and Edinburgh, and so led to some rudimentary form of postal service. It demanded that 'those riding in post' should enjoy the privilege of having without question 'post-horses' at the rate of $2\frac{1}{2}d$. a mile and that the 'postmasters' should keep at least two horses in readiness for their use. Round about 1650 a York attorney arranged for relays of horses between York and London to convey letters and parcels for the public. A few decades later, London is said to have had many receiving houses at which letters could be left by the coaches and collected by 'runners'. Other towns, too, had privately owned similar concerns for the collection and transport of letters and parcels, and about 1710 these enterprises were consolidated, and so the germ of the Post Office was founded. Its latent powers as a public agency and as a source of revenue were quickly grasped. It suffered greatly from the eighteenth-century system of 'farming out' national institutions, and of saddling them with pensions for political or royal favourites, as well as from high-waymen. To overcome the perils of the road, Palmer of Bath sug-gested, in 1783, the desirability of having special coaches calcu-lated to minimize the attention of robbers, and to ensure greater speed and regularity of service, and his suggestion is said to have raised the net revenue during the next twenty years from under £200,000 to about £1,000,000, even though quite a twelfth of the matter conveyed was 'franked free' by Parliament or the Royal Household. No envelopes were then used; the sheet was merely folded down and sealed, whilst adhesive stamps were not employed till Queen Victoria's day.

Strype, vaunting London's postage system in 1715, says that the 'runners' called at the post houses every hour or so, and that letters and parcels delivered within the city cost a penny each and two-pence for those outside the boundary. Elsewhere too, the scale of postage seems to have been based on mileage, ranging from 4d. for fifteen miles to a shilling for 300 miles with an additional penny for each 100 miles thereafter. To have the benefit of this minimum rate, one's missive had to be limited to a single sheet; those who burdened the post with more than one ounce, paid an additional rate for each quarter ounce; so a two-ounce letter from Manches-ter to London cost 7/4. It was not till 1837 that Rowland Hill exposed the fallacy that costs of conveyance were closely related to distance covered, and advocated a uniform rate of postage based solely on weight.

An item in the Methodist pay-book in 1783 suggests that the local chapel made itself responsible for some interment expenses.

'To Mr. Myles coffin and berial expences'   £6-1- 9.
'Miss Roberts bill for scarfs, crap gloves at Mr. Myles
    funerall'   £2-5-11.

The cost of the coffin suggests that it must have been the funeral of some principal person, perhaps the preacher; whilst the crape scarves and gloves recall eighteenth-century mourning customs. In those days people freely indulged in the luxury of woe and gave grounds for Le Blanc's comment that 'these English seem to find more pleasure in dying than in living'. Funereal decorations were hung in the front of the deceased's home; cards of invitation were adorned with pictures of grief and loss: skulls, skeletons, coffins and gravestones. Usually horses, coaches, churches, drivers as well as mourners were heavily swathed in black, and relatives were expected to wear long black cloaks, black gloves; flowing black scarves festooned their necks whilst their beavers were wreathed with more black crape. Garlands were carried before the corpse and later suspended in a conspicuous place within the church. If the deceased were a maid or bachelor, then this mourning was a study in black and white; even the coffin might be in black and white, whilst white and black plumes would alternate on the horses, and the coachman would sport both colours. To add to the gloom, not infrequently funerals took place at night and the procession, headed by beadles and a dozen or so pall-bearers, would set forth escorted by torch-bearers.

This account does not list another item of expenditure usually connected with eighteenth-century funerals and there is no direct reference to cake, wine or ale served out to each person before starting, and to the bearers of the corpse being liberally supplied with rum, gin or brandy. Instances are on record of a barrel of beer, two gallons of sack and four gallons of claret being consumed, and where the cost of wine has been five times that of the coffin. In those days mourners were in the habit of assembling in the inn-kitchen, there to talk about the deceased and wash him down with reverent quarts. Perhaps by 1783 the fashion was not considered seemly among Methodists; yet the old custom was not dead if one judges from the comments of a writer to *Gentleman's Magazine* about the same year. 'Our Antient Funeralls as well as some Modern Ones, were always closed with Merry-Makings, at least equal to the Preceding Sorrow; most of the Testators directing Victuals and Drink to be Distributed at their Exequies.' The pay-book is also silent as to whether any subsequent memorial was erected to the memory of Mr. Myles. This omission is astonishing, for eighteenth-century mourners had a habit of lavishly setting forth the virtues, talents and deeds of those described as not lost but gone before. It was an age of flowery epitaphs and one still reads with silent awe the interminable list of the virtues and capacities of the eighteenth-century dead. Nothing that rude rhyme and shapeless sculpture could do to preserve the memory of the departed was then omitted, and hundreds of these uncouth rhymes fashioned by verbose, appreciative relatives are still to be seen, defiling rather than edifying church walls and graveyards. Virtues, qualities, accomplishments were muddled together in whimsical fashion. The following are of the period and taken from widely separated districts:

'Here lies the body of Lady O'Looney, great niece of Burke, commonly called the Sublime. She was bland, passionate and deeply religious; also she painted in water-colours and sent several pictures to the Exhibition. She was first cousin to Lady Jones, and of such is the Kingdom of Heaven.'

The gravestone of a mid-century Rector said of his wife:

> She was truely Religious,
> Meek in Apprehension,
> Expert in Geographie,
> Compassionate and Charitable.

To the Memory of Wm. Scrivenor, Cook to this Corporation.

> Alas, Alas, Wil Scrivenor's dead, who by His Arte
> Coude make Deth's Skelington edible in each part,
> Mourn squeamish Stummicks and ye curious Palates,
> You've lost your dainty Dishes and your Salates;
> Mourn for Yourselves, but not for him i-th-least,
> He's gone to taste of a More Heavenly Feast.

Here lies Wm. Smith, and what is somewhat rarish,
He was born, bred and hang'd in this here parish.

> Beneath this Stone, in Hopes of Zion,
> Doth Lie the Landlord of the Lion;
> Resign'd unto the Heavenly Will,
> His Son keeps on the Business still.

Some epitaphs were designedly more candid than complimentary:

> Here lies the Body of P. M. Haskell
> He liv'd a Knave and Died a Rascal.

> Here lies my poore wife, without bed or blankit,
> But dead as a door nail—God be thankit.

> Here lyeth the body of Martha Dias,
> Always noisy and not very pious;
> Who liv'd to the age of three score and ten,
> And gave to Worms what she refus'd to men.

Some of the memorials attempted to pun:

> Here lies a certaine Elizabeth Mann,—
> Who liv'd an old Maid and died an old Mann.

And the epitaph of the celebrated comedian Foote, runs:

> Foote from his early stage, alas, is hurled;
> Death took him off, who took off the World.

A notorious smuggler of the century was remembered by the method of his dying:

> Here I lies,
> Kill'd by th' Excise.

Others also deal with the cause of death:

> Here I lie with my three daughters,
> All along o' drinking Cheltenham waters;
> Had we stay'd at home and kept to Epsom salts,
> We should not have been lying in these here vaults.

> Here lies entomb'd one Roger Morton,
> Whose sudden death was early brought on;
> Trying one day his corn to mow off,
> The Rayzer slipp'd and cut his toe off.

Some are simply doleful:

> At threescore winters' end I dyed,
>   A cheerless being, sole and sad;
> The nuptial knot I never tyed,
>   And wish my father never had.

> Underneath this ancient mill
> Lies the Body of poor Will;
> Odd he liv'd and odd he di'd,
> And at his funerall nobody cri'd;
> Where he's gone and how he fares,
> Nobody knows and nobody cares.

And there is distinct reference to the ghoulish coffin and body-stealers in:

> Here lies my guid and gracious Auntie,
> Wham Death has pack'd in his portmanty;
> Threescore and ten years God did gift her,
> And here she lies wha deil daurs lift her.

Such memorials are perhaps more indicative of eighteenth-century general characteristics like pride of birth, love of eating, grim humour, grim trades, punning, verbal ferocity, blatant advertisement, &c., rather than of real bereavement. But as is usual, they had their striking contrasts, and some tombstone-inscriptions were exquisite, and touched the very root of the deceased's work or life, as for example, those of Wren, Wesley and Hood in St. Paul's, City Road Chapel and Kensal Green Cemetery, whilst from many unknown and neglected graves shone forth such phrases as: 'This poor Woman did what She could', 'He made the Widow's Heart to sing for Joy', 'They gave of their Abundance, but She all that she had'.

D

As it was not till well into the nineteenth century that marriages
were solemnized in Methodist chapels, the account-books under
review make no mention of eighteenth-century weddings. Copious
details of them are however to be found elsewhere, and weddings
of the compulsory order, and called 'hop-pole', 'knob-stick', or
'broomstick', &c. marriages, are freely mentioned. As with
funerals, weddings seem to have been an occasion for all the display and hospitality that the family could afford. When the contracting parties were poor, it was customary to have 'penny' weddings at which guests gave a penny or penny-multiples, so as to
help on the festivities. At them girls wore blue and green streamers,
whilst the men sported cockades and topknots of the same colours.
All carried rosemary which had to be dipped into the circulating
bowls of 'bridal ale' before they pledged the couple. The poor
rarely indulged in honeymoons; but they were expected to put
in an appearance at church the Sunday following, when they were
the centre of much attention.

Plays and diaries suggest that fashionable weddings were con-
tracts arranged by interested people, and *Headlong Hall* especially,
implies that the arrangements were most casual and that 'marriage
broking' was not uncommon even at the end of the century. Such
sources would suggest also that many men showed little hesitation
over marriage, and that even the little hesitation was of the laughing sort, and not much more serious one way or the other, than
that of Panurge. Certainly as husbands many of them did not
amount to much, and Dryden probably expressed the thoughts
of many when he decided that 'wives, like almanachs, should
always be changed every year'. A very large number of couples
were married at 'wedding-shops'. Outside these dreadful holes
were signs announcing 'Marriages performed Within', for until
1754 no banns were necessary. Pennant is speaking of one of
these shops when he says: 'A dirty fellow invited you inside the
booth; nearby the parson was seen walking before his Shop; a
squalid, profligate figure clad in a tattered, plaid nightgown with
a fiery face and ready to couple you for a dram of gin or a roll of
tobacco.' One of these parsons is said to have married 40,000
couples in twenty-seven years. Keith's Chapel in Mayfair was
said to be the scene of 6,000 marriages per annum, and on the day
before Hardwicke's Bill illegalized such couplings, more than a
thousand ceremonies were performed in these booths. When they
were forbidden in England, the Gretna and Sark toll marriages

became popular, and it is estimated that they numbered well over a thousand a year. Less known than the Border places for run-away weddings, was the Charles Church in the Peak Forest. For some unknown reason this particular church was outside the control of the bishop of the diocese, and thus became a rival to Gretna.

Despite the ease with which eighteenth-century men could marry, many of its celebrated men remained bachelors. Among these were Pope, Cowper, Goldsmith, Berridge, Watts, Thomson, Rogers, Hume, Gibbon, Pitt, Horace Walpole and Beau Brummell. An equal number of that century's *élite* also managed to make a poor job at choosing their life-partners, amongst them being Addison, Sterne, Arkwright, Whitefield and Wesley. Although marriage was such an easy matter to arrange in that century, divorce was a very difficult affair. There was no Divorce Court and before a petition could be considered, it had to be preceded by a special Bill presented to Parliament which authorized the particular case to be tried.

Now and then this Methodist pay-book suggests another eighteenth-century custom; that of misdemeanour within a place of worship.

1779 'Got from wm. yung iis–ood; but he should have payed iis–vid; so must bring vid next quarter'
1782 'Pd Mr. Clemens for His Advise concerning rostherne' xs–vid.
'Pd Constable for takeing rostherne to yᵉ cole hole' iis–ood.

Perhaps the aforesaid Rostherne had been guilty of misbehaviour in chapel. If so, he would simply have been emulating his social superiors in the national Church; for, as is stated elsewhere, frequently they showed little reverence when at divine worship. Perhaps he was a stalwart of the State Church and had come along to insult or offer assault and battery to these Methodist enthusiasts; for an almost contemporary entry in a Poole account-book shows that these brawlers were sometimes paid for their sacrilege.

'Subsequent expences at Ann Garball's on Driving the
  Methodists' ixs–ood.

Perhaps he was simply a very noisy, ungodly worshipper, the type of which Wesley was thinking, when he declared in 1782, 'ungodliness is our universal, our constant, our peculiar character'. We shall never know. Rostherne's items, like many another in such records, are of an England that has utterly passed away.

CHAPTER III

POPULATION AND COMMUNICATION

I

STATISTICS regarding population before 1801 are unreliable, for that year saw taken the first official census. Parliament had considered the desirability of learning such figures earlier, but all efforts to that end had been defeated. Actually it was not till 1837 that the first national registration system came into force, and then against strong opposition on religious and political grounds. By some, such registration was regarded as 'impious', by others as 'subversive of the last remnants of English liberty'.

Estimates of the population for 1700 indicate that it numbered between five and six millions. In the closing years of the seventeenth century, England's population had been enriched both in number and quality by the 50,000 or so Huguenots who fled to our shores after the revocation of the Edict of Nantes in 1685. In October of that year Louis XIV suddenly attacked the 400,000 Huguenots who were the best of his people; intelligent, industrious, careful, and who, moreover, practically controlled the industries of France. About half the number managed to escape his galleys and jails, and it is estimated that a quarter of the survivors fled to England and reinforced our country by this transference of skilled industrialists, just at the moment when France was at the outset of potential industrial dominance. These refugees spread throughout England and established themselves as calico makers at Bromley, cotton spinners at Bideford, weavers at Canterbury, cambric makers at Edinburgh, tapestry weavers at Exeter, sailcloth makers at Ipswich, paper makers at Laverstock, kersey makers at Norwich, glass workers in Sussex, silk weavers in Spitalfields, hat makers at Wandsworth and carpet weavers at Kidderminster. Those who settled in Manchester were engaged in making textile materials consisting of linen one way and wool the other; those who settled in Clerkenwell started the trinket, jewellery and watch trades, and Huguenots originated the pottery trade in Burslem and the glass trade in St. Helens. Our late seventeenth-century forebears collected the then very heavy amount of £40,000 for the relief of the more indigent persons amongst their Huguenot guests. Perhaps the collection was not voluntary if one judges from Defoe's *True-born Englishman*. Such lines as:

> Hither for God's sake and their own they fled;
> Some for religion came, and some for bread.
> Four hundred thousand wooden pair of shoes,
> Who God be thank'd, had nothing left to lose,
> To heaven's great praise, did for religion fly,
> To make us starve our poor in charity;

suggest not only humorous dismay at the sight of the crowd of the immigrants, but imply that the self-denying benevolence had been strained.

In 1801 the population for England and Scotland numbered 9,187,000 or for England alone 8,331,434, that is, the total for England alone was a little more than the present size of London. The population probably increased by a million and a quarter between 1700 and 1760 and by over two millions between 1760 and 1800; in other words, it might be asserted that the population increased by 50 per cent during Wesley's lifetime. Such increase was probably less due to bigger families than to a drop in the death-rate, arising from a slightly better dietary and improving medical services. It is just as necessary to speak with caution about the sizes of towns in the eighteenth century, for travellers then gave very different estimates of their populations. Young, Harwood and Parker vary enormously in their estimates, and often differ from Price's figures in his *Essay on the Population of England*. Young suggested that Liverpool in 1769 had 40,000 people, but Price only gives it 34,500 in 1773. The following are some of the suggested populations round about 1770: Birmingham 30,000, Manchester and Salford together 27,000, Leeds and Nottingham 17,000, Hull and Sheffield 20,000, Northampton and Bolton 5,000, Bradford 4,000 and Oldham a nice little village with about 500. On the other hand, London was said to have 800,000 people and its immense size was supposed to constitute a national menace; Bristol with 75,000 was the second city in size and Norwich had 60,000. Gloucester, Somerset, Sussex, Wiltshire and Norfolk were still the centres of industrial activity. But the impending industrial revolution changed the population statistics greatly, and during the century, towns like Birmingham and Sheffield probably increased their population sevenfold and Liverpool tenfold.

The net statistics might suggest that eighteenth-century parents went in for small families. Actually the opposite was the rule; wives were expected to produce a swift and steady succession of offspring; boys and girls were married at youthful ages, and judging from eighteenth-century diaries and letters, social strategy took but little account of the contracting parties' likes and dislikes. The famous Mrs. Delany's first wedding was in her early teens to a disreputable Cornish squire of sixty, whilst there is at least one instance, where the Archbishop of Canterbury did not scruple to perform the marriage service over a bride aged eight. With such early marriages one would expect most parents to have many children and probably they had. Soricold, a brilliant water-engineer, a man of widespread activities, of excellent family, who flourished in the early eighteenth century and who designed the first Liverpool docks, was married at the age of sixteen and had thirteen children before he was twenty-eight. But the appalling death-rates mowed down the number of infants born of all marriages. Queen Anne had seventeen or nineteen children—historical records are dubious about the exact number. But whether seventeen or nineteen was the total, it is certain that only one of the royal family reached double figures, and then that died at the age of eleven. So if a queen was unsuccessful in the task of raising a family, it is no wonder that in the records of this century, one finds after whole rows of children, the phrase 'died in infancy'. When an infant started at birth with a good physique, his first nurses were so ignorant and stupid that they not infrequently cut short his life. Steele has a very lively account of what an eighteenth-century baby might expect from his first nurses, in which essay, after describing some of the activities of the forerunners of Betsy Prig and Sairey Gamp, he concludes with the significant phrase, 'where I had the good fortune to be drowned'. Summer diarrhoea accounted for thousands of infants in one month in London alone, and London was then the only town boasting of any sort of sanitary system, so its suggested mortality of eighty per thousand would most probably be lighter than that of other towns. As for adults, they had to face almost annual scourges of smallpox, jail fever, scarlet fever and plague which often wiped out entire families. In those days ships could scarcely keep the seas because of scurvy, whilst even the newly established hospitals were hotbeds of fatal diseases.

Maternity was no monopoly of the marriage state in that century; probably more than half the children were born 'out of wedlock', for even as late as 1834 it was estimated that illegitimate children were quite as numerous as legitimate ones. The law allowed these 'bastards', as they were termed, to be taken from their mothers and put to the care of the parishes, and records indicate that parish officers were controlling 70,000 of these unfortunates, over whom they had complete power. In 1767 the child-population in workhouses had increased to such enormous dimensions, that the authorities were obliged to board them out; 'whereupon', says Hanway, 'the annual death-rate rose to 70%'. To lower such mortality, this philanthropist succeeded in getting through Parliament an Act by which foster-parents were paid half a crown a week per infant and 'an additional bonus of 10/– per child per annum for every successful nurse'.

Another factor affecting the quality of the eighteenth-century population, was the isolation of place consequent on very bad communications. In-breeding was necessarily very frequent and the physique of a district became markedly distinctive, as was shown in the grey eyes, brown hair, good complexions in Northumberland. The segregation showed itself, too, in the preservation of dialects and manners, which led Wesley frequently to note: 'how the country people stared at me', and to marvel at the frequency with which he 'became a subject of excited amazement and a thrilling topic of conversation in the ale house and at the hearthside.'

II

These bad roads were a real barrier to any intermingling of the people and precluded changes. Thorold Rogers says: 'No changes had taken place in English village life for five centuries.' Almost up to the end of the century, Lancashire consisted partly of swampy plains that were wellnigh impassable, whilst stilts were needed to cross the Fens. So-called roads connecting towns and villages were proverbial 'for their abysmal depths of mire'.

From the Stuarts onwards, the care of highways was a parochial concern, so no wonder that they got into deplorable conditions. Eighteenth-century parliaments, broadly speaking, never worried about commercial transport and means of communication. But because of the threat of a Stuart rebellion, military roads were constructed here and there, and in 1730 General Wade opened up the civilization of Scotland by means of his roads. More than

250 miles of track were then constructed by this great soldier-engineer, as well as many fine bridges, such as that still spanning the Tay at Aberfeldy.

In the later half of the century, new roads were built by 'turnpike trusts', private enterprises which depended for their financial success on the payment of tolls. With the majority of the people, these tolls were most unpopular and there were many serious turnpike riots. Despite riots, new roads were constantly opened up and the old major ones neglected. Between 1760 and 1800, no fewer than 2,000 enabling Acts were granted by Parliament for the making of such new roads. It was in this period that Telford built the famous London to Holyhead highroad and that Blind Jack Metcalf of Knaresborough—without even the aid of a spirit-level—built the Bury–Blackburn, Bury–Haslingden, Haslingden–Accrington, &c., roads and constructed some 180 miles of turnpike roads in Lancashire alone; engineering triumphs over geographical obstacles and incredible personal handicaps that will ever make this man an eighteenth-century worthy. These two men, together with the later Macadam, brought scientific principles and regular system to road-making and repairing. All three insisted on thorough drainage, on the use of carefully selected materials and adopted a uniform cross-section of moderate curvature. But most of the other turnpike roads were constructed by ignorant and incompetent engineers and the majority of their roads were as unsatisfactory and dangerous as were the old parochial ones. A writer to the *Gentleman's Magazine* in the late part of the century, described such turnpike roads as 'a cursed string of hills and holes'. And he was probably very near the truth.

In 1770 Arthur Young asserted that in the whole of England 'there are but four good roads; the rest it would be a Prostitution of Language to call Turnpikes'. He said 'the infernal road between Preston and Wigan was Most Execrably Vile with Ruts four Feet Deep'. He warned 'that all travelling should Avoid this Terrible County as they would the Divell, for a Thousand to One they break their Necks or their Limbs by Overthrowings or Breakings-down'. Wesley, too, found these Lancashire roads very bad; in 1788 he described those about Bury and Rossendale as the worst he had ever travelled. Ogilby and Morgan in their *Book of Roads*, Defoe, Smollett, Pococke, Tucker, Pennant and Cobbett add their testimony to such descriptions of the country's whole road system and for the century as a whole. Foreign visitors like

Moritz, Le Blanc, Grosely, Archenholtz and Wendeborn confirm them. Howard, who travelled more than 50,000 miles on his prison reform, and Wesley who journeyed more than 250,000 miles on his preaching tours, are equally emphatic. All refer to the steep gradients, deep runnels, projecting rocks, morasses, quagmires, by courtesy called roads.

The turnpikes did, however, speed up travel. In 1741 stage coaches promised to do the journey between Norwich and London in two days in summer and in three in winter 'if God permit'. In 1753 the journey from Liverpool to London occupied four days; but that speed was considered express travelling, for the Lancashire and Cheshire mail-coach then took ten days in summer, and twelve or more in winter on the same journey. In 1754 a 'Flying Coach' was advertised between Manchester and London and affirmed 'that however incredible it might appear, this coach will certainly do the journey in four days and one half'. About 1770 Young is often noting that 'two miles an hour is the utmost you can count upon about here'. But in 1780 a Liverpool citizen is boasting that his coach has done the 200 miles between his home and the metropolis in two days and three hours, whilst in 1788, Manchester's 'Flying Coach' was proclaiming that it only took twenty-eight hours to reach London. Palmer's mail-coach design and the improved turnpike roads had evidently worked wonders. By then, along the famous Great North Road, it was affirmed that the post could go from York to London and back in thirty-four hours. Perhaps by this era coaches had attained their maximum speed, for in 1798 a traveller proudly asserts that 'he has done ninety miles in seventeen hours'. And when Peel was first appointed Prime Minister in 1834, it took him twelve days to come from Rome to Dover travelling day and night.

Besides the deterrents to comfort and speed arising from the nature of the roads themselves, there were other obstacles. For the most part, pack-horses were employed for the transport of all kinds of commodities, and on such roads the beasts could carry little more than one hundred pounds. They moved in Indian file, laden with sacks or baskets containing coal, wool, yarn, flour, &c. Wagons were not well known, and as late as 1763 a cart was such a wonder in some parts that people flocked to see it pass by. These first vehicles were springless contraptions and fitted with inferior locks, so they were very difficult to turn and were often bogged, blocking completely the narrow execrable roads. Defoe describes how he saw a team of twenty-two oxen tugging at a single oak along such roads, whilst another account says that towards the end of the century, it took a wagon with a load of four tons, drawn by eight horses, three weeks to go from London to Edinburgh by the vaunted turnpike roads. But movement on parochial roads and transport highways was not only impeded by cumbrous commercial transport, but also by the conservatism of the older aristocracy; far into the century family coaches were drawn by leisurely moving teams of a dozen oxen, for not all the rich used horses drawing stylish perch-phaetons, curricles and gigs. And some of the other users relied on mules, donkeys, ponies and many a poor man possessed and drove his own 'dog-cart'; for dogs were freely employed for draught and carriage purposes in that century. Such means of conveyance gave peculiar significance to words like 'slowcoach', 'post-haste', &c. There was also a further deterrent to speed. Many of the highways ran mostly through open common and moorlands which were frequented by highwaymen, who took their toll of the travellers' time, money, limb and even life.

'John Wesley paid more turnpike tolls than any man who ever bestrode a beast', says Birrell; a statement that leads one to consider these eighteenth-century exactments. They seem to have varied greatly and to have been quite arbitrary; there was no uniformity for example at the hundred and more toll-gates in and about London. An analysis of the preserved lists suggests that charges averaged 1/- for a coach, 6d. for a cart and a ½d. for each foot-passenger and each animal in a drove, and that tolls were doubled on the Sabbath Day. Cary's *New Itinerary* gives many details of the tolls and of their contradictory charges; it implies that a stage-coach or private coach with outriders might have to pay as much as 7/- to get through one toll-gate, that on the London to Birmingham turnpike road there were upwards of thirty tolls and that a conveyance might have had to pay nearly £4 in tolls before completing the journey. As the freeing of the highways was a protracted undertaking—even London Bridge was not freed from tolls till 1782—and as the number of coaches was greatly multiplied after Palmer's postal invention, these toll-rights for different bridges and roads were a great source of income. Not infrequently they were auctioned annually, and sold for sums ranging from £100 to £20,000, nor did the town councils or private bodies disposing of such rights, trouble much about

insisting that the buyers kept the roads and bridges in repair.
Turnpike Gate, a comic opera of 1799, gives one an idea of the
difficulties, humour, &c., of coach journeys and of the light-
hearted attitude assumed by the majority regarding the mainten-
ance of such highways.

Naturally the tolls affected the cost of the conveyance of the
travellers, but fares varied not only according to the number of
tolls, but whether one rode inside or outside, the season and the
year. A preserved ticket issued in 1779 shows that it cost £4 10s.
to go from London to Edinburgh, but in 1800 the fare had been
practically doubled. A journey from York to London apparently
cost £3 6s. 3d., whilst the schedule of fares from Manchester to
London runs as follows in 1801:

		Inside			Outside		
		£	s.	d.	£	s.	d.
Manchester to	Buxton		10	6		6	0
„	Ashburn	1	1	0		12	0
„	Derby	1	6	0		15	0
„	Loughborough	1	15	0	1	0	0
„	Leicester	1	18	0	1	1	0
„	Northampton	2	10	0	1	6	0
„	Newport	2	15	0	1	8	0
„	Woburn	2	18	0	1	9	0
„	Dunstable	3	0	0	1	10	0
„	London	3	3	0	1	11	6

The traveller who in 1798 is heard congratulating himself on
having done ninety miles in seventeen hours, is also very proud of
the fact that he did it 'on the very small sum of £4–9–6 which
included conveyance, breakfast, dinner and tea'. This reference
to breakfast may occasion surprise; but in those days it was
customary to start off on coach-journeys at 4.0 a.m. or earlier.

Except for those bent on express travel, it was usual to make a
halt on Sunday in some town where long-distance travellers might
attend divine service.

'A counterpart of this divine practice and remnant of old English
hospitality, was that the landlord of a principal inn, laid aside his character of publican on the seventh day, and invited the guests who
chanced to be within his walls, to take a part of his family beef and pudding. This invitation was usually complied with by all whose distinguished rank did not induce them to think compliance a derogation.
And the proposal of a bottle of wine after dinner, to drink the landlord's health, was the only recompense ever offered or accepted,' says
Scott in *Rob Roy*.

Besides building turnpike roads, the century also developed its canals. Brindley constructed the Bridgewater one round about 1770, and from the outset it quickly showed immense possibilities, and particularly so after 1788 when Symington's steam-boats moved along it and others, at about five miles per hour. Although these first canals showed great potencies, it is difficult to say by how much canal transport cheapened conveyance. Some statements assert that goods could be sent from Manchester to Liverpool for round about 12/- a ton by canal as compared with 50/- or more by road. And a preserved bill of about 1800 indicates that it was then costing over thirteen guineas a ton to move goods from Leeds to London by road. As England was at the dawn of an enormous trade expansion, it was imperative that the means of trade communication should be both improved and cheapened if not quickened. So the canals had their chance and were greatly boomed, and by 1800 there were nearly 3,000 miles of navigable waterways. Sometimes they were used for passenger transport, and Wesley refers to a journey from Wigan to Liverpool by boat; a journey that took him upwards of ten hours.

Canal construction changed the very appearance of the countryside, and according to Wesley, particularly so around the Potteries. Late in the century he notes: 'How is the whole face of this country changed in about twenty years; and the country is not more improved than the people.' Such construction led to the erection of thousands of bridges and to fundamental alterations in their building design and building materials. Telford alone is credited with the construction of at least 1,200 such bridges including those at Conway and Menai (in 1821). In the latter part of the century, iron was more freely used in their erection, and 1779 saw the first completely iron one span the Severn at Broseley. All were in marked contrast with the London Bridge of 1700, a construction of wood and carrying three-storied houses on either side.

III

As for the streets in the towns themselves, they seem to have been little better than the arterial roads, and many a writer recalls the applicability of the passage in *Pilgrim's Progress* to them: 'the way also here was very wearisome, through dirt and slabbiness.' Even in London itself the means of communication were so bad, that its various districts knew nothing of each other. Many of the streets were little more than six feet wide and some were narrower; there were no footpaths and the street itself was often only trampled mud into which household filth was flung. Street widening for London was urged round about 1757, the problem was discussed in Parliament, but it was not till ten years later that much was done, and that raised footpaths and the use of square granite blocks were introduced into the city's principal streets. Perhaps the first attempts at paving were unsuccessful; at any rate, Grosely in his *Tour from France to London* says, in 1770: 'the streets of London are paved in such a manner that it is scarce possible to find a place to set one's foot, and one is eternally covered with dirt . . . in the most beautiful part of the Strand, the middle of the street is constantly foul with a dirty puddle; these splashings cover those who walk on foot, fill coaches and chairs when their windows happen not to be up, and bedaub all the lower parts of such houses as are exposed to it.' With such streets it is no wonder that rivers were used wherever possible as means of communication, and the 'watermen' who transported customers in boats not unlike gondolas, were a particularly numerous company in London.

London's street lighting was also defective. Before Wesley's birth some attempt had been made to illuminate the streets with oil lamps not unlike frying-pans, stuck outside every tenth house or so. They seem to have been of little service as the oil was inferior illuminant and made from the intestines of slaughtered animals. By 1736 London had improved its lighting system and used oil glass lamps placed at every sixth house or so. For many years much delight was expressed with that lighting system, and in 1780, Hutton, describing his journey from London to Birmingham speaks of the 'brilliant' illumination of city streets where 'not only were there oil lamps at stated intervals, but the shop-windows were full of light'. In one such window that excited his special admiration, he 'counted no fewer than twenty-two candles'.

Actually of course such street lighting was of little service for guidance even in the main roads, and the vast majority of people depended on the host of ragged, quarrelling 'link-boys' to light them home, and iron stands for these guides' torches were fixed to all public buildings and wealthy houses. It was not till 1794 that Murdoch, the friend of James Watt, invented coal gas as an illuminant and lighted his cottage with gas. A few years later,

Watt and Boulton adopted the device so as to light their Soho works; but it was not till the nineteenth century that a Frenchman first lighted a stretch of London streets with gas.

Even in London very few streets had names and the houses were unnumbered; up to 1766, residences in cities were known only by their own particular sign or their vicinity to some sign. Of these signs Addison said: 'Our streets are filled with Blue Boars, Black Swans, Red Lions, not to mention Flying Pigs and Hogs in Armour, with many other Creatures more extraordinary that any in the Deserts of Africa'; usually they were elaborate creations of carved wood, painted and gilded and stretching half across the thoroughfare. There were 'Green Dragons', 'Black Knights' and 'Mitres and Crowns', &c. in every fashionable street and a man lived at 'the Red Bodice' or 'over against the Pestle'. Gore, of directory fame, badgered various councils to regularize the situation, and so early in the nineteenth century streets were named and houses numbered, not so much for the householder's convenience, but rather to conduce to the more regular collection of taxes.

In the countryside the favourite way of visiting was on horse-back and stone mounting-blocks were found before most houses and all inns. Older and wealthier people throughout the century used hackney coaches, and sumptuous examples of these can still be seen in the King's official coaches and that of the Lord Mayor of London; all are typical of the then very weighty, wonderful and most richly ornamented vehicles, supported by straps and not by springs. The wealthy emulated one another in the number of their outriders, the richness of their lackeys' dress and the beauty of the paintings on the coaches. Beau Nash made himself distin-guishable if not disinguished by an immense white hat, clothes richly embroidered, and especially with his chariot and six greys, laced flunkeys and outriders with French horns, whilst the older Pitt's coach and six with blue and silver liveries equalled the equipage of the King. Wealthy old people still preferred their family coach to be drawn by a dozen oxen, but by the end of the century their grandsons had set up perch-phaetons, smart sport-ing conveyances with double perches of swan-neck pattern, with very small bodies, hung high on very high wheels and raised as much as eight feet from the ground. Coaches of a less ornate nature were being used for public hire towards the middle of the century, and Manchester had a stand for them in St. Ann's Square in 1750. Gradually these were ousted by the sedan chair, and by 1770 we are told that 'few country towns were better supplied with sedans than was Manchester', and that 'by then people still actually engaged in business had set up their own coach or sedan'. Such eighteenth-century changes in roads, conveyance as well as in dress, toilettes, &c., are caricatured in Sheridan's prologue to *Trip to Scarborough*.

IV

This isolation of place arising from wretched communications and inferior conveyance told heavily on the physique, habits and thoughts of the ordinary people. Because of these conditions, there was not only a clutter of dialects but also a lumber of folk-lore, whilst even moral life was to a considerable extent determined by the primitive emotions of terror and awe. Thus the people as a body were steeped in fancies and superstitions. Every woman knew of the kindly spirits whose unseen hands helped on the household work, and for whom she left cups of cream and dainty bits; every mid-century miner knew of the 'knocker', a goblin dwelling in mines and who indicated the presence of ore by knocking; every farm-labourer believed in the fairies and lobs who turned his garden from a nursery of slugs and snails into a glowing patch of luxuriant blossoming. Peculiar customs and rites were then bound up with every stage of human life, and especially with birth, marriage and death. It was unlucky to weigh new-born babies or to cut their nails for at least a year.

> If you marry in Lent,
> You'll live to Repent;

and

> From the marriages in May
> All the bairns die and decay.

They had hundreds of beliefs concerning 'gifts on finger nails', on the cutting of nails, yew in houses, starting work on Friday, seeing the moon, the use of salt and about howling dogs. They watched in the church porch on St. Mark's night to see their future life-partners. Christening was not simply a religious rite but a cure for sickness, whilst confirmation to many was a specific against rheumatism. Their 'Good-Friday Bread' was preserved for months to be used as a medicine; 'dumb-cake' was an antidote to certain ailments, whilst many a practice was linked on to 'brides-cake' and 'groaning cake'. Every district had its wishing wells, &c., whilst local customs, feasts and pageants were redolent with ancient superstitions. Even the foolhardy tried to escape the attentions of Tom Poker, Old Shock, Jack o' Lanthorn, Will o' the Wisp, the Mawth Dog, Roger's Blast, &c.; otherwise they suffered dire distress. But there were more dreadful supernatural beings than these. As Blackwood puts it: 'Lycanthropy or the power of war-locks to change themselves into wolves was everywhere believed in, and the ability of witches to transform themselves into cats, by rubbing their bodies with a special salve or ointment provided by Satan, found equal credence. . . . A ghoulish spirit could always take up its abode in a living man or woman, conferring super-natural powers of bat-like flight on its owner, and glutting itself with nocturnal bloodfeasts. When its host died it continued to dwell in the corpse, which remained undecayed. By day it rested, by night it left the grave and went on its awful errands.'

Everything conspired together to render the people of this century superstitious. Astrology permeated its early science, religion and even politics. Eighteenth-century words like 'con-template, consider, jovial, mercurial, saturnine, martial, ascend-ing, disastrous' would be somewhat unintelligible without refer-ence to these ancient beliefs, whilst 'ill-starred' no longer yields its old dreadful thrill to the hearer. Swift's squib *Prediction for the Year 1708* had given astrology a shrewd blow, but it by no means destroyed general belief in the power of the stars on mundane events and human actions.

The peculiar atmosphere evoked by the eighteenth-century wild environment of trackless wastes and pestilential swamps must also be taken into consideration. There was the rugged grandeur of inaccessible mountains, the solemn influence of widespreading moors, the dark face of mountain lochs, the wild and rocky coast lines, the mysterious babbling of brooks. These, seen and heard in the chilly and spectral air, by the flying gleams of moonlight, would have a great effect on ignorant minds. In such surround-ings, shadows would have terrible forms and the voice of the wind that moaned, wailed, screamed, howled was naturally mistaken for the shriek of a tortured soul. When men wandered about on a stormy night, along narrow roads littered with rough boulders, punctuated with deep holes, when they tripped and stumbled and were slashed by the brambles, thorns and gorse, it is little wonder that ordinary things were invested with malignant animation and that the night was full of mad terror. They then recalled all the things that went by night: hellhounds, headless horsemen, warlocks; quickly the air to them was full of witches on broomsticks and demons on black stallions stampeding up the valleys on dreadful hunts, and they could hear the blood-freezing halloes, the blare of horns and the baying of unspeakable hounds.

Not merely places but particular houses could then strike terror into the hearts of people. Something intangible seemed to brood under certain roofs; scores of houses were left in possession of ancestral phantoms and illusive ghosts, whose weird shapes and fearsome activities tried beyond human endurance the nerves of the people who lived in them. Tormented souls were thought to be earth-bound; fast anchored to some room or spot. Rat-infested houses were bound to be full of mysterious squeals. Wesley's boyhood home at Epworth had supernatural disturbances by a lively poltergeist which gave data out of which were created fascinating stories. Many of the Wesleys half believed in the ghost's existence; full records of its activities were made, and an enlightened man like Priestley investigated the records, and came to the conclusion that the things were supernatural.

The eighteenth century saw official belief in witchcraft, &c., die, for in 1736 laws against witchcraft were repealed. In this case Parliament was well ahead of public opinion. In the very same year, the Associated Presbytery of Scotland passed a resolution affirming their belief in witchcraft and deploring the parliamentary scepticism. As for the vast majority of the people they remained firm in their faith in the power of lobs, brownies, witches, and could readily conjure up pictures of their familiars, their cats, broomsticks and cauldrons. They were positive that these sibyls made waxen images of their victims, stabbed them with pins, or melted them before a slow fire, and so induced a painful or a lingering death. They were equally certain that the beldams could bewitch their cattle, and that the only remedy was to suspend the affected beast by its four legs, and slowly roast it alive over an open fire. By so doing, they held by the theory of spontaneous combustion, that the malefic spirit would be attacked by the same fire, and thereby compelled to acknowledge the bewitching, or else be burned to death. As late as 1799, the *Ipswich Magazine* gave an account of such a happening in East Anglia. They were very familiar, too, with the seventeenth-century wood-cut pictures of

E

Matthew Hopkins 'Witchfinder-General to the British Government', wearing his large hat and standing among a coven of witches bound cross-legged upon their stools, whilst their confessions are coming out of their mouths upon scrolls. And long after Hopkins's day and after the Acts against witchcraft were repealed, the brutalities of witchfinders continued to flourish. In 1759 the *Gentleman's Magazine* has an account of a woman charged at Aylesbury with bewitching her neighbour's spinning wheel. In 1775 the same paper reports the burning of nine old men and women for a parallel offence in Poland, and Switzerland had a victim as late as 1782. In 1751 a publican at Tring accused an old man and his wife, who were both over seventy, of bewitching him, and demanded that they should be tested to see if they could shed tears and were capable of being submerged in water. The newspaper then goes on:

'The parish officers having remov'd the old couple from the Workhouse into the Church for security, so the mob missing them, broke the workhouse windows, pull'd down the pales, demolish'd part of the town. So the poor wretches were at length for public safety, deliver'd up, stript naked by the mob, their right thumbs tied to their left toes and their left thumbs to their right toes, dragg'd along the road for two miles and flung into a muddy stream. After much ducking and ill-usages, the old woman was thrown quite naked on the bank almost choak'd with mud and expir'd in a few moments, being kick'd and beat with sticks even after she was dead.'

In 1775 the *Daily Journal* has an almost similar recital of incidents at Frome. In 1825, *The Times* refers to the 'testing' of a wizard by dipping as then occurring in Suffolk. And probably research would furnish similar stories for many other parts of England. Even late in the century, one of the most popular cries in Lancashire was 'Thou shalt not suffer a witch to live'; here, they would heartily have agreed with King James, who in his treatise on 'Demonology', said: 'that sparing of witches is no less a sin in the magistrates nor it was in Saul sparing Agag.'

Not only witchfinders, but the widely advertising fortune-tellers and dispensers of love-philtres and antidotes to witchcraft made a lucrative business of all mysteries. For a small consideration they would repeat incantations or conjure up spells and so cure horses of colic, prevent dogs from biting, reveal the location of lost articles, foretell the future and energize laggard lovers. Reared on superstition, in districts that placed balls on the roofs of houses and hung rags about wells to keep off witches, the people seemed to smell magic everywhere. The element of magic played a part in their very moral consciousness; they were haunted by the magic of curses and condemnations; they saw in the imagined antics of witches a form of operative magic, and to them there was moral magic in certain phrases, words and things. A piece of camphor was regarded as a protector of female health, chastity and charm, whilst the protection of male bodies from supernatural enemies, was ensured by belts of garlic, a bit of monkey skin or that of a murderer, charmed dog teeth, a pocket cross of special wood, or by immersion in baths of brimstone when the case was extreme. To protect their homes, the credulous sealed windows and doors with lengths of human hair, or called in the local witch to recite special incantations within the circle or pentacle, and on the side of many a chimney stack was a stone projection, whereon witches could rest when wearied whilst flying to their weekly revels. They believed their churches were protected from satanism by means of the gargoyles or gurgoyles carved in prominent places. Usually these were the termination to a spout which conveyed the water away from the gutters, and these spout endings were made of grotesque figures such as hideous faces, some animal monstrosity, a devil eating a child, and all calculated to catch the wandering, inquisitive eye of the malefic spirit hovering over the sacred precincts.

Satanism and malign incarnation were taken so seriously in some parts of eighteenth-century England, that many people regarded Wednesday or Thursday as the 'Witches' Sabbath', and when these days happened to fall on the night of the full moon, the most ignorant and credulous parsons and parishioners might hold Black Mass in church on such occasions. Then the church would be entered by a side door, the devotees would come hooded and masked, and service to Satan would be conducted. Cases are hinted where young children were decoyed there and killed on the altar as a sacrifice to Satan. What is certain is that the north side of many an eighteenth-century church was called the 'Devils' Side' and the churchyard adjacent was called the 'Devil's Acre'. Many a church then had its 'Devil's Bell', and the 'Devil's Knell' or the 'Devil's Round' was rung from many a belfry. This diabolic influence also showed itself in topography and hardly a corner of the country escaped; much English scenery then got christened 'Devil's Dyke, Devil's Kitchen, Devil's Dressing Room, Devil's

Elbow, Devil's Punch Bowl, Devil's Den, Devil's Cavern, Devil's Jump, Devil's Bridge', &c.

This grisly crew of devils, vampires, sorcerers, monsters of the void, witches, warlocks, banshees, &c., infested the countryside during the whole of the century. Nor was faith in airy visions and muffled sounds limited to the ignorant only. The educated and refined believed in witchcraft, &c., though as the century declined to its close, their imaginations were more patently seized by other forms of supernatural and mysterious power. The earlier Luther, Erasmus, Bacon and Sir Thomas Browne had all declared their faith in witchcraft; a seventeenth-century king of England had affirmed that 'witches can raise Stormes and Tempests in the Aire, either uppon Sea or Lond'. Defoe wrote essays on apparitions and magic, and throughout his life Johnson dallied with the theory of reincarnation, and was well over fifty when he tried to commune with the perturbed spirit said to haunt Cock Lane. Blake believed the Welsh mountains were haunted by supernatural beings with whom the human race could enjoy celestial intercourse. In 1768 Blackstone, the eminent jurist, wrote: 'To deny the possibility, nay actual existence of witchcraft, is flatly to contradict the revealed Word of God.' Wesley declared his undying belief in demonology, &c.: 'With my latest breath will I bear testimony against giving up to the infidels one great proof of the unseen World; I mean that of witchcraft and apparitions, confirmed by the testimony of all ages . . . the giving up of belief in witchcraft is, in effect, giving up the Bible . . . .'

The idea of demoniacal possession was also fairly widespread among the educated. About 1750 Gassner, a Roman Catholic priest in Swabia, declared that most diseases arose from malefic possession and could therefore be cured only by exorcism. Belief in this theory spread with all the intensity of an epidemic. Gassner's most famous pupil, Mesmer the Viennese surgeon and mystic, had much the same faith, so by 1780 many a European capital was thrown into a state of great excitement by the marvellous effects of mesmerism, which the inventor practised in a highly theatrical manner. In view of such beliefs prevailing among the educated, it can occasion no surprise that 'the awful anguish, ecstasy of sorrow, agony of fear, frantic joy and the indescribable tumult of emotion caused by unsparing eloquence at revival meetings, would lead to many forms of physical hysteria, and to physical phenomena not unlike the casting-out of devils'.

Unquestionably Haydon, Maxfield, Pawson, Haime—some of Wesley's great laymen said to have been reclaimed under such violent forms of conversion—would all attribute their salvation to exorcism.

Similarly it is not surprising that this prevailing theme of superstition should permeate the productions of the late eighteenth-century popular writers like Barham and Beckford, Anne Radcliffe and Matthew Lewis. All based their plots on the supernatural, on runes, sprites, ghosts, on witchcraft trials and on the scenes and practices of witchcraft and thereby gave birth to the novel of terror. And in addition to stories about 'the horror that walked by night', these writers dealt with occult, psychical, weird, mental forces and evil powers from a world unknown and unknowable. Later and better writers like Goethe, Schlegel, Andersen, Coleridge, Southey, Shelley, &c., evoked the more famous demons and phantoms that also troubled the eighteenth century. They expressed the century's belief in undying Cains, Esaus, Ishmaels and the other evil wanderers who had offered insult to Jesus. The Wandering Jew was once again made to preside at orgies, diffuse diseases, instigate revolutions and burn cities. He was again endowed with the old miraculous gifts of speech and again never allowed to die. Again and again he was identified with many a tall, ragged, gaunt, bare-footed, long-haired eighteenth-century tramp; in 1769 he was not only seen but interviewed at Hull, where 'four Ministers testified to his miraculous gifts, his incredibly old age, his supernatural doom'.

v

All regions of space then had their own particular demons and phantoms. Better known to sailors than the Wandering Jew or the Wild Huntsman of the Air were the ghost ships, the fabled albatross who bore the souls of dead mariners on his white breast, and the Flying Dutchman whose special mission was that of evoking dreadful storms on sea. Whenever seamen saw his black spectral ship on the horizon, they changed their course and hastened to flee away from the fatal influence of a demon whose boat could never reach a haven. This phantom added considerably to eighteenth-century seamen's worries if not to their dangers.

As for dangers, they had their full quota both from material and human agencies. Just as the highroads had their hordes of high-waymen and innumerable tramps as sources of terror and danger for land travellers, so seamen found their counterparts in the tens of thousands of smugglers and shipwreckers, and in the many buccaneers and pirates; for although piracy then flourished mainly off the African coast, it was to be found on all the seas of the world. Moreover, their dangers were sufficiently great by nature of the ships themselves and by the general state of navigation.

English naval architecture was comparatively well advanced in the seventeenth century thanks to the two Petts and Deane; but such ascendancy as they gave was lost in the eighteenth century, which was a period of stagnation as regards the application of science to shipbuilding. Then France, Spain, Sweden and Denmark were all producing ships that surpassed those of England for size, speed and sea-behaviour. In 1730 an English ship of 750 tons was a leviathan, and Cook's *Endeavour*, the ex-Whitby collier boat that made history in 1769, was only ninety-seven feet between perpendiculars; or in other words only about half as long again as the *Santa Maria* of Columbus in 1492. The last quarter of the century saw merchant ships increase greatly in number and size to cope with the trade expansion, and by 1800 merchantmen of a thousand tons were not a rarity. Ships for the Royal Navy were always bigger than the merchantmen; the *Royal George*, launched in 1756, was 178 feet by 58 feet, of 2,000 tons, carried 100 guns and 800 men and Nelson's *Victory* was a little longer, slightly narrower, had a shade more tonnage and carried about as many guns.

Practically all the ships were built of timber, though in 1780 iron-plated boats were being used for river and coastal trade, and practically all shipping was done by sails, even though paddle-wheels worked by manual power were designed by Hulls in 1737. Slightly earlier, an English clockmaker is credited with having constructed a ship with engines, but they proved to be unreliable and it was about the last decade before Miller, the Edinburgh banker, designed a steam-propelled paddle steamer capable of doing seven miles an hour on the Forth and Clyde canal. Miller's invention almost synchronized with that of Symington and that of John Fitch, who also claimed to have invented 'a small skiff that made seven miles an hour with machinery'. Naval signalling was very elementary during these hundred years, and orders were usually communicated by hailing or by means of small rowing-boats. Kempenfelt in 1780 devised a plan of flag-signalling, but it was not till the nineteenth century that the method of conveying messages by flags was really developed.

Throughout the century ships were grossly overcrowded and overloaded; even the tiny *Endeavour* of 370 tons going to New Zealand had ninety-four men aboard and the *Victory* had just under a thousand. Mortality was high because of the insanitary conditions, scurvy was rife because of the bad feeding system, whilst the ships themselves were often foul, unseaworthy and water-logged. Smollett, who was for some time a ship's surgeon, describes mid-century shipping conditions, and no reader could forget the description of the 'Thunder' in *Roderick Random*, the disorderly tyranny, the cruelty and dirt of officers and men. Deck after deck is seen, each with some new object of offence; likewise the hospital where the hammocks were huddled together with but fourteen-inch space for each man, and the cockpit, far under water, where 'there was an intolerable stench'. Johnson declared in 1773: 'No man will be a sailor who has contrivance enough to get himself into a jail; for being in a ship is being in a jail, with the chance of being drowned ... The man in jail has more room, better food and commonly better company.' The sailor was supposed to get 19/– a month for his services and he hoped to get a pound of biscuit, a pound of salt pork or beef, occasional oatmeal, butter, cheese and a gallon of beer daily. A battle must have been a capital relief, and prize money, bloodily earned and grossly squandered, must have been welcome after such cruel daily life. Even this prize money was unfairly shared out. The flag-officer, who might not even be present at the fight, got an eighth of the total prize, whilst the surviving seamen might get less than a thousandth. Often the seamen were not paid when discharged from the ship, receiving instead 'pay-tickets' which they were forced to sell at a discount for ready cash. Guy, of hospital fame, bought them in large numbers, and thereby accumulated a great fortune which he invested in Government securities.

Conditions for sailors do not seem to have improved as the century wore on. John Newton describes the slightly later revolting barbarities of a sailor's life in the commercial service, aboard one of the 200 vessels engaged in the slave trade. Nicol dealt with life on whalers, warships, and convict-transports in the last quarter. Marryat tells of sailor life in the early nineteenth century and paints in even greater detail the indescribable filth, bad food, long arrears of pay and cruel ill-treatment. The great Vernon declared that 'our fleets, which are defrauded by injustice, are first manned by violence and maintained by cruelty'. It can cause no wonder that insubordination and mutiny by men in the merchant services were regular occurrences, and not infrequent in the Royal Navy in the days of the Spanish Wars, Texel and Camperdown. Nor need one marvel that with such sailors and ships, journeys by sea lasted a very long time, and that as late as 1765 it took anything from six weeks to cross the Atlantic. For as Wesley points out 'such a journey was a serious adventure, calling for great fortitude'. What is a source of wonder is that the century saw admirals like Vernon, Hawke, Rodney, Howe, Hood, Kempenfelt and Nelson and discoverers like Funnell, Bering, Anson, Wallis and Carteret. Such sailors were not deterred by the nature of their ships or by pirates, smugglers and buccaneers, and they did wonderful things. Perhaps they were even out-classed by Dampier, Rogers and Cook in their exploits in Africa, North America and New Zealand, where the three proved themselves to be pioneers with an astonishing genius, boundlessly resourceful and of inexhaustible energy. It is equally surprising that this century saw the inventions of the sextant and chronometer which helped to rid seamanship of two of its most serious problems.

The prevailing public apathy of the eighteenth century towards the sanctity of human life showed itself in the shipping world as in other spheres. Perhaps public feeling was roused a little, when in 1782, the *Royal George*, having been careened to stop a leak, went down in Portsmouth Harbour with 800 men aboard as well as 400 women who had no business there, and that there were practically no survivors. The papers mention the incident but with characteristic fatalism, and even Cowper is more struck with the sentiment than with the shock of the business. The shocking wreck of the *Adventure* off Newcastle in 1789, when the entire crew was drowned in sight of land, also served to stir slightly this general apathy. But public concern in such tragedies was so tepid, that it took nine more years before the first lifeboat was built. Despite the ever enlarging record of wrecks and loss of life on our shores, public interest was not thoroughly aroused till 1823 when Sir William Hillary championed the cause of lifeboats.

Even institutions specially concerned with ships and shipping were dilatory. 'Trinity House' dates back to the days of Henry

VII when it was a religious house with certain monopolies connected with pilotage. Like most degraded religious houses, it lost both usefulness and influence, and in the eighteenth century it did little more than interest itself in the very few privately-owned lighthouses. But it had no powers over these stations and floating lights, which even in 1800 only totalled forty for the whole of Great Britain. Practically all of them were deficient, and it was not till 1836 that the 'House' got mandatory powers over all lights, beacons, buoys, &c. Of these forty, perhaps Eddystone was the most notable of the eighteenth-century lighthouses. Yet it was rarely mentioned in the newspapers of the times; neither writers nor the general public were interested in its work or welfare. Its lamps seem to have been oil ones, and round about 1770 parabolic reflection was first used there to magnify lighthouse illumination.

CHAPTER IV

THE PATRICIANS

I

THE four reigns in which Wesley lived were not distinguished by excellent monarchs. History reports Queen Anne as one fond of epicurean comforts, petty Court ceremonial, gross flattery. She seems to have been a dull ignorant woman, one with decided ideas concerning the position of a queen. Yet at the same time she had vague conceptions of the duties of a monarch and remained firm in her Protestantism. She also had the peculiar courage of great women in affliction, and her sorrows were deeper than those of Queen Elizabeth or Queen Victoria. Her Hanoverian successors were less praiseworthy; for the first Georges seem to have been a lecherous family, full of tragic misfortunes, and their private history is packed with oddities, vehement scenes of family rows and sexual peculiarities. George I was a profligate, fond of drinking and low conversation. His son is described as 'a poor, weak, irresolute, false, lying, dishonest, contemptible wretch' by Horace Walpole. Yet it was to George II that Carey addressed the National Anthem, with a wording slightly more personal and adulatory than is the modern setting, and at whose death Wesley rhetorically asked, 'When will England have a better prince?' Of the third George, John Wolcot, writing as 'Peter Pindar', described and perhaps distorted, royal peculiarities in his *Lousiad* and *Peeps at St. James*. Of him Byron says:

> A better farmer ne'er brushed dew from lawn,
> A worse king never left a realm undone;

whilst Shelley was to be more bitter still in his sonnet on 'an old, mad, blind, despised and dying king'. Later critics, whilst continuing to find fault with this George's foibles and his very troublesome interference in State affairs, are now ready to see in him a decent moral character, one who tried to lead a good domestic life and one, who in the course of a very long life, delivered many a cutting sentence revealing sound judgement on men and events. As his son George IV had to deputize as monarch during his father's periods of lunacy occurring during Wesley's lifetime, some reference to him is also called for. This 'First Gentleman of Europe', as he loved to be called—presumably because of the dazzling quality of his waistcoats and his ability to sweep a magnificent leg—was actually a soulless sot and heartless fop, whom Byron dubbed 'the fourth of the fools and oppressors called George'. Historians like Benson have spoken of him as 'the first bounder in Europe; vain as a peacock, false to his friends, remorseless to those who had offended him, selfish, greedy and quite devoid of decent principles'.

Contemporary caricaturists were as trenchant as the contemporary poets or later writers on these early Hanoverians. Hogarth dealt cuttingly with George II and the Duke of Cumberland, whilst Gillray often reproduced the third George's vulgar manners, awkward shuffling gait and the vacant stare on his face.

Whilst these Hanoverians occupied the throne of England, 'the relations between the Sovereign and the Heir-Apparent for 105 years was a curse to the country; warping the policies of public men, tempting every toady and place-hunter, overheating each crisis of party controversy', says one historian of the century. One of these family feuds nearly cut Walpole's career short; a second lowered the character and prestige of the elder Pitt; a third vitiated the spirit of Fox. These bitter quarrels between royal father and son were notorious and conducted publicly. George II found occasion to refer to his heir as 'my dear first-born is the greatest ass, the greatest liar, the greatest *canaille* and the greatest beast in the whole world, and I heartily wish he were out of it'.

To the eighteenth-century general public, these monarchs were mainly amusing objects that had to be endured, and who provided opportunities for ribaldry and loud jeering when they appeared on State occasions. They never seemed to forget the unfortunate remark made on one occasion by a Hanoverian princeling with an imperfect knowledge of English plurals. Meeting the usual hooting and hissing, the prince had tried to placate the mob by assuring them that he and his type had come to England 'for your goods'. Perhaps the most biting comment on these early Hanoverians was the silent one, that England ruled for three generations by German Sovereigns, completely neglected the German language and ignored the glorious dawn of German literature, whilst English youthful aristocracy pointedly omitted Germany from their itineraries when they made the grand tour.

These eighteenth-century monarchs and many of its lords, also serve to exemplify the falsities of the laws of primogeniture. Although they plucked the joys of heritage and left its duties to look after themselves, some of them are to be pitied, for as Constance Holme admirably expresses it: 'there is something terrible in the relentlessness with which inheritance may force a man into a position he is not framed to fill, thrusting power into his hands and judgements into his mouth, whether he desire their fiery splendours or no.'

II

The superior social section naturally took their tone from the Court, where the standard of morals accepted for reigning princes did not accord with the simplest rules of domestic ethics. Broadly speaking these aristocrats were gay, superficially intellectual and mainly godless throughout the entire century, and undoubtedly the majority frivolled away their time in refinements of luxury and vice which they cultivated with excessive assiduity. No woman of fashion was expected to be virtuous; nor did the times expect from a husband the slightest pretence of affection or fidelity towards his wife. Even in the days of Anne it was affirmed: 'If men had gone into mourning for the immorality of their wives, sisters and daughters, half the Court would have been continually in black.' And under the Georges matters were to be worse, for morals sank to zero during their regime. Scores of earls and dukes were conspicuous only by their vices; they were immorality incarnate. The 'Hell Fire Club' was a rendezvous of ruffling rakes who tried desperately hard to justify the club's name; the 'Medmenham Brotherhood' sought to make their profligacy piquant by a parody of the religious ceremonies of the Christian faith; Lord Sandwich, Sir Francis Dashwood, Thomas Potter and the Duke of Queensberry were all subjects of antique scandals. Able men like Walpole, Chesterfield, Bolingbroke, were frankly irreligious or professing atheists, and Montesquieu, who stayed some time in England, attested that not more than five or six of the 558 Members of Parliament ever attended church. This was the century of duels. They were openly advertised and discussed in the *Spectator* and *Tatler* as well as in less respectable papers. And not merely did young hot-heads engage in them, but such people as Hastings, Fox, Pitt, Pulteney, Sheridan, Winchelsea, Wellington, Castlereagh and Canning fought duels in Hyde Park,

Leicester Fields and Wimbledon Common. George II of England challenged Frederick King of Prussia, to mortal combat and the spot was picked, and perhaps it is a pity for the good of mankind that the duel did not eventuate, as the potential duellists were the most brutal and coarse Sovereigns of the civilized world. Still at least one royal duel was fought, when in 1789 the Duke of York had a pistol affair with an army officer. The correspondence of high-born ladies also shows that it was a coarse and brutal age; one abandoned to gross and shameless pleasures. The sons and daughters of such fathers and mothers kept up the family tradition, and the diaries and novels of the period show that the younger folks were an amorphous gang of noodles struggling for distinction in filthy fooleries, as is evidenced by their amusements, their behaviour in streets and church, and in their antics at Vauxhall and Ranelagh. One set of these ruffians, the 'Mohawks', was particularly notorious. These young bloods sallied out in companies, drunk, armed with swords and delighted to flatten people's noses. Flamboyance and the vulgar varieties of eccentricity were the hall-marks of the young nobility. 'With a ferocious industry they laboured for dominance in freak parties, and toiled assiduously to acquire flashy notoriety.' Character and quiet breeding were not the essentials for success in eighteenth-century society.

This lack of moral feeling and general decency among the wealthy brought about a contempt of the poor people only equalled in slave-holding States. Moneyed worldlings were always surrounded with a throng of servants who had a definite order of procedure. First came the valet, and last the negro slave who waited on my lord or lady with the silver collar of servitude about his neck. Even attendance at church was ceremonial; my lord had to be preceded by two or more footmen in livery and with powdered hair, one carrying a foot-warmer, another food and wine, another a Bible. 'Throughout the century and in all Western Europe the few wealthy aristocrats seem to have recognized that there were some unimportant millions of people who had to be controlled and tolerated, rather than reckoned with and respected. They never seem to have had the slightest sense of right proportion, or to have had a glimmering of the complicated forces outside the smooth current on which they floated' (Benson). One of them doubtlessly expressed the aristocratic attitude towards life in general when he excused his guilt of bigamy with,

'I am you know the Son of a Nobleman, and consequently have those high thoughts and ambitions which are inherent to those of Noble Extraction', whilst the Duke of Rutland had similar opinions of the immense value of the peerage when he carolled:

'Let wealth and commerce, laws and learning die,
But leave us still our Old Nobility.'

Horace Walpole, who knew well the mid-century members of the House of Lords and the 'Squire Westerns' of his generation, said of them: 'They were intoxicated with vanity, indulgence and the indolence of their situation.' Speaking of the later eighteenth-century aristocracy, Sydney Smith, Canon of St. Paul's, said: 'nine-tenths of the English people of quality of the eighteenth century were either knaves or fools' and Wesley, who knew the Sir Rogers of his day, remarks of the wealthy: 'they do me no good, and I fear I can do none to them.'

Of these three criticisms that of Sydney Smith is the most weighty, for by his day many of the eighteenth-century aristocrats were more adaptable. Some had married into wealthy commercial classes and some were participating as mine-owners, iron-masters, owners of flocks of sheep, investors in commercial undertakings in the rapid economic developments of the country.

But all three, and the many other critics of the eighteenth-century aristocracy, knew that the high-bred, languid indifference of the wealthy aristocracy, and their pose of effortless superiority were dropped when they scrambled for money and position. Their native knavery and greed were then revealed unabashed. 'It was thought no shame in those days for the aristocracy to wrangle for pensions, sinecures, decorative posts, bribes, preferments in Church or State, and to gorge upon their ill-gotten gains with the fierce rapacity of famishing wolves,' says McCarthy, whilst Macaulay declares that then 'they were licentious, profane and corrupt; too proud to behave with common politeness but not too proud to pocket illicit gains . . . titles, places, commissions were daily sold in market overt by the great dignitaries of the realm'. In the days of the Georges, this omnivorous rapacity led the Whigs and Tories to hate each other with a ferocity hardly ever known before or since; for the feuds did not arise from differences of political principles, but simply from the possibilities due to the control of the national purse. Such greed led members of the House of Lords to accept bribes of £100,000 from the East India

Company, to Lord Chancellors selling outright masterships in
Chancery, to one lord trying to sell his private volunteers lock,
stock and barrel to the East India Company in 1763. It led them
to get offices by offering bribes; one noble President of the Board
of Trade got his post by giving a king's favourite £500 and a pair
of diamond ear-rings, whilst Clive got from an Indian nabob a
'present' of £210,000 and Marlborough a 'present' of £63,000
from the bread-contractor to the Army. Even at the end of the
century the Paymaster's Office was a mere shop where parliamentary votes were bought and sold like groceries. Earlier,
Robert Walpole looking at the serried ranks of the members, had
remarked, 'all these men have their price'. Nor was this just a
prime minister's idle passing thought; for he wrote to a friend:
'there is scarcely a Member whose purse I do not know to a sixpence, and whose very soul I could not purchase at the offer.'
Like Henry Fox, Walpole knew that the Paymaster's Office
turned honesty of conviction among the ordinary members of
Parliament into mere derision. When the ordinary member had
sold his voting conscience, he not infrequently raised more money,
by selling his parliamentary privilege of franking letters to a
tradesman, and in this way netted another £300 per annum. The
Crown Ministers were little better than the ordinary members,
and the close of the century hears Nelson grumbling that 'they are
as great scoundrels as ever lived'.

In that century Army and Navy appointments were always
given to the sons of the wealthy or to their nominees. Children
in their cradles had cornetcies presented to them, and in 1795 the
Duke of York secured a return of the number of ensigns in each
regiment under the age of twelve and of colonels under the age of
eighteen, and was amazed at the totals. Nelson was aboard ship at
the age of twelve; Rodney's son was a ship's captain when he was
sixteen; Lord Cochrane's cousin commanded a ship at seventeen.
Wolfe was an ensign at fourteen and a major before he was
eighteen. Throughout the century, colonels were the proprietors
of their regiments and captains owned their companies. Army
commissions and even chaplaincies were widely advertised in
the newspapers, and were bought and sold like many other
appointments.

Naturally, too, the wealthy and the aristocrats got all the
eighteenth-century feudal appointments, and discharged the
onerous duties of 'Master of the Horse', 'Head Groom', 'Head

Valet', 'Lord of the Bedchamber', 'Captain of the Gentlemen Pensioners', 'Grand Falconer', &c., at salaries ranging from £1,000 to £2,000 per annum. Other offices of picturesque foolery and medieval mummery, with rather more euphonious titles were 'King's Cock-Crower', 'Yeoman of the Mouth', 'Keeper of the Sweet Coffer'. In these posts at any rate they would be able to do but little mischief beyond drawing their pay.

Not infrequently they held pluralities of such posts, and one eighteenth-century duke held fourteen paid posts at the same time. Quite often they secured new posts whilst receiving pensions, and fairly often they managed to secure pensions for their poorer relatives, who however, had done nothing at all for the country. One scion of nobility was a pensioned naval officer with £500 a year; at the same time he got £2,000 more as Clerk of the Privy Council, and still another £3,000 as Secretary of Emoluments for Jamaica. Towards the end of the century, an earl managed to quarter three of his sisters on to the State for a pension of £1,000, and as these ladies lived another sixty years, that family of confirmed tax-eaters did pretty well. An undistinguished prime minister of the century got £2,000 a year for his widow (and she lived thirty years after) as well as the promise of a sinecure appointment for his son worth £2,700 a year. An Archbishop of Canterbury got his grandson promised 'in due course appointment to a sinecure office of at least £8,500 per annum'. What Fox said of one of them might have described many, for they 'ever showed an eagerness to heap up emoluments and to systematize corruption'.

As landowners, most of the eighteenth-century nobility get harsh treatment at the hands of historians like Froude, Macaulay, or from letter-writers like 'Junius', Martineau, Horace Walpole, Cobbett, whilst students like Kay on the land question are quite as censorious. Gibbon declares 'treason, sacrilege, proscription are often the best titles of our ancient nobility'. As landlords they had the nomination of scores of M.P.s, and hundreds of incumbencies, and they used their privileges to the full. Not only did they dip deep into the State-Church's purse one way or another, but by their pocket-boroughs they had a stranglehold on the House of Commons. Even on the mere land question alone, many of them were corrupt; they exploited the enclosure acts and yeomen farmers disappeared, whilst a Duke of Athol sold 'his entire rights in the Isle of Man' to the Crown for £70,000; an agreement that did not preclude a succeeding duke from screwing out of the nation another £400,000 'for his remaining property and privileges in the island'. The Sutherlands and the Breadalbanes depopulated Scottish countrysides to make deer forests or sheep runs and some 15,000 people were ejected. Such and similar actions led Sir Walter Scott to write: 'In too many cases the Highlands have been drained not of their superfluity of population, but of the whole mass of the inhabitants, dispossessed by an unrelenting avarice, which will, one day, be found to have been as short-sighted as it was unjust and selfish.'

It was the same story in eighteenth-century Ireland. English aristocratic rule there was an appalling tale of horror, despair and cruelty. Of such noble landlords the Commander-in-Chief of Ireland said in 1797: 'Every crime, every cruelty that could be committed by Cossacks has been transacted here . . . the abuses of all kinds I found here can scarcely be believed or enumerated'; whilst an indignant judge there said in 1814 'landlords should build their tenants better houses and give them at least what they have not yet got—the comforts of an English sow——'

III

Although as a body the eighteenth-century nobility were failures as statesmen, legislators, churchmen and landowners, many of them had a most picturesque side to their lives, whilst the exceptions displayed many pleasing characteristics.

Isaac Watts was treated with the truest and most delicate kindness by the Abneys, just as was John Locke by the Mashams. George III gave Herschel £250 a year to be his private astronomer, and he took Benjamin West the painter under his special patronage. Lord Kingston treated Buffon with discernment. The Earl of Derby was kind to the eccentric Alexander Cruden whilst he was engaged in his stupendous task of compiling 130,000 words and giving them Biblical references. The Duke of Buccleuch seems to have been a well-behaved pupil to his tutor Adam Smith, and gave him a life pension of £300 a year. Johnson, too, received much consideration from Hervey, a gay officer of noble family, who did himself honour by patronizing the writer, whose repulsive person, unpolished manners and squalid garb moved many of the petty aristocracy to laughter or disgust. All the exquisites

F

of the period were not subject to false standards of taste and of fashion, false refinements, false intellectualities or given over to the silly pursuit of decadent eccentricities, nor devoted to a life of easy love-making, of luxurious enjoyment of the good things of this world. The Duke of Sussex was a promoter of science, art, literature and philanthropy; Bubb Doddington had many faults, but indifference to the claims of genius and learning was not among them; Bennet Langton was distinguished by his skill in Greek literature and by the sanctity of his life; Newcastle had a genius for jobbery and intrigue, yet, though he held the highest ministerial posts for forty years in a venal age, he left public life £300,000 poorer than when he entered it.

Other aristocrats evidently loved pity, kindliness and mercy. Their diaries often show that they were really concerned about the well-being of their dependants, that actual law was less to them than loyalty in their relationships, and that such relationships were often marked with genuine friendships and mutual understandings and resulted in long service and amity between peasant and patrician, and so minimized clashing interests and warring classes. Moreover, as a body they were sensible and adaptable, and though they possessed power as well as privilege, and were almost totally unwitting of democracy with all its just claims, they showed enough wisdom not to exempt themselves wholly from taxation.

IV

Many picturesque architectural Georgian memorials like Adams' ceilings, Brettingham's mantelpieces and Grinling Gibbons' staircases, have disappeared or are disappearing. It is the same story with some London city squares, Nash's Green Street and such stately homes as Devonshire, Chesterfield, Norfolk and Lansdowne Houses. There still remain, however, some royal palaces, a few city churches, Brunswick, Berkeley, Fitzroy Squares, and such buildings as Dover House (Whitehall), Wentworth House, Fort Belvedere, Harewood, Chatsworth, Blenheim Palace, Houghton Hall, Castle Howard, &c., as well as such edifices as the Admiralty Buildings, Regency Club, Carlton Terrace, the 'Crescent' at Bath and the Registry House, Edinburgh, which express exactly the best qualities of refinement and dignity the century offered to the more fortunate. All are notable for exquisite detail, quiet and restrained lines, dignified proportions and for exemplifying the qualities concerning which Temple wrote: 'Among us the beauty of building and planting is placed chiefly in certain proportions, symmetries and uniformities.' Perhaps some of these examples of the best eighteenth-century architecture have lost some of the spaciousness they would present to Wesley's eyes, owing to the encroaching buildings that were later erected near them. The restoration of a complete area in its early eighteenth-century setting has, however, been attempted at Williamsburg on the Virginia peninsula. In this magnificent effort, everything alien and inharmonious has been removed, and every attempt made to preserve or restore the setting, beauty and charm of eighteenth-century buildings and gardens. Even decorations, furniture, and costumes with historic significance have been introduced. Such restoration, designed to preserve and re-create the symbols and memorials of a creative and colourful period of history, was dedicated 'to the hope and purpose that the future may learn from the past'.

Many of these mansions were built of blocks of millstone granite, although Wren had introduced rubbed bricks as building material —bricks that he and his successors laid end on and with very close joints. The bricks used in Queen Anne's days were usually red ones, but from 1720 onwards grey or yellow ones grew to be more popular.

Most of the early eighteenth-century buildings were many-gabled and many have handsome projecting porches. Gradually architects emphasized this feature, and pillared porticoes elaborately embossed were often stuck on to red-brick Queen Anne houses. Fine doorways were gradually introduced; canopies in the form of a big shell with finely moulded and carved patterns were built and fanlights were constructed. Texts or heraldic door-heads proved the builder to be proud of his ancestry or proclaimed his piety. The outside windows were long, often filling the entire width of the room; they were somewhat low in proportion and were divided into six or more lights by stone mullions which were bevelled. Some houses had circular or rose windows, all deeply recessed into the very thick walls, whilst above every window was a stone moulding which stopped the water from running down the house front. Mansard roofs were known from the mid-seventeenth century. For many years, there were no troughings or fall pipes; the water ran down the gutters of the roof and large stone water-spouts threw the streams clear of the building. But as the century advanced, architectural beauty declined. A love for the merely garish supervened and stucco came into fashion; and the end of the century saw Beckford delighted with his fantastic creations at Bath and Fonthill.

Although gardening did not become much of a passion with ordinary folks till about 1775, the gardens around the stately homes of the eighteenth century were remarkable. One result of the grand tour which was made by most of that century's heirs, was the introduction of new trees, fruits, flowers and bulbs brought to the family mansions by the touring sons. The Duke of Argyle introduced such foreign trees as the weeping willow, acacia, &c.; a Duke of Athol brought back the larch in 1728 and he and his successors were so delighted with it, that they planted upwards of a million of them; the Lombardy poplar brought over in 1750 or so by another aristocrat, also became a national favourite. Others of them were responsible for the sweet-pea in 1732, the fuchsia in 1753 and the dahlia in 1789; for the raspberry in 1733 and the strawberry towards the century's close. Kew Gardens by then boasted the largest and most varied fruit plantations in the country; Princess Augusta, the mother of George III, had extended and beautified them, and her royal son sent collectors to South Africa, South America and the Far East to acquire new and rare trees and plants, with results that made Kew pre-eminent among the botanical gardens of eighteenth-century Europe.

Judging from the many accounts of the baronial gardens given by Grosely, Le Blanc, Horace Walpole, &c., the eighteenth-century private gardens presented a study in symmetry; they were most prim and formal with their geometrical boxwood and holly hedges, intersected by marl and shell walks. One lovely feature was the sundial, the fascination of which has been felt all down the ages, but never more so than in that era. Usually gardeners placed them at the centre of converging paths and with characteristic eighteenth-century incongruity, the dials were silent monitors with their Latin, Greek or English messages about the flight of time. A favourite one of such an admonitory nature in that restless age ran:

> Time was, is past; Thou canst not it recall;
> Time is, Thou hast; employ the portion small;
> The future is not; and may never be;
> The present is the only time for Thee.

As for the public and semi-public gardens of the eighteenth century, they too had their sundials and rare trees and flowers. It was in the latter part of the century that 'Capability' Brown laid out Hyde Park, and that others made St. James's Park, and the Ranelagh and Vauxhall Gardens attractive. Hyde Park and that of St. James were semi-public resorts, supposed to be reserved for the wealthy of whom some 6,000 were expected to pay a guinea a year for a key that admitted them at any hour. But of course false keys were easily made and walls were climbable, so actually, Hyde Park was really a rendezvous of the populace. It and St. James's Park were often full of disorderly people, betting and playing unlawful games, running naked races, &c., and both were usually as noisy as the streets. Vauxhall and Ranelagh were mainly mere pleasure resorts, and on gala nights they were the scenes of open-air dancing, of vocal and instrumental entertainments, &c., entrance to which cost a shilling.

Perhaps the house interiors showed rather more variety than did the gardens. In some cases the main hall—a spacious apartment 60 feet by 30 feet—went up to the open timbered roof and was provided with a gallery and small organ; other halls were more modest in their height and thus supported many upstair rooms. Stairs were made of marble or oak, and all were very wide, gently stepped and handsome. The main rooms were lofty and spacious, their walls were panelled in carved oak or hung with tapestries on which were emblazoned the arms of the nobles who had occupied the palace. Wallpapers were known in that century, but as they were of poor quality they were rarely seen on the walls of the wealthy; pictures began to appear on the walls of drawing-rooms, &c., round about the middle decades of the century. Ceilings were timbered or decorated with lovely paintings and allegorical designs or had oval, elliptical ornamental plaster work, all finished in gilt. The doors were thick and panelled and usually exemplified very fine craftsmanship, and were flanked with fluted Doric columns. Handsomely wrought stoves and irons stood in the very wide fireplaces which were surrounded with magnificent stone or oak mantelpieces, covered with elaborate and ornamental designs. The room floors were made of highly polished woods and dainty little carpets were often stretched before each separate person. From the ceilings hung magnificent chandeliers of Murano glass in which burnt scores of candles, shining on tall mirrors richly carved and gilt with console tables standing below them on bric-à-brac, on the marquetry cabinets, on the gilt chairs ornately carved and upholstered in crimson or blue silk damask. Although most of the mirror glass and chandeliers would then be imported from Italy, glass was nevertheless being manufactured in England. Evelyn notes in 1673 that at Lambeth, 'glass was being blown of finer metal than that of Murano' . . . and that he saw . . . 'looking glasses far larger and better than any that came from Venice'. Despite this evidence, it seems doubtful if England was making much sheet glass before 1760 or plate glass before 1772.

In this century, furniture reached high elegance of form and perfection of detail. Boule and Martin had invented or perfected a lovely system of varied veneerings, whilst Chippendale, Sheraton, Hepplewhite and the two Adams were all busy in the second half of the century. Clocks, too, offered avenues for ingenuity among eighteenth-century furniture makers. The seventeenth century heard the rival claims of Hooke, Harris and Huygens for the honour of inventing the pendulum to regulate the motions of clocks. It had seen public ones installed at Westminster, Canterbury, Glastonbury and Dover, and fitted with two hands to tell minutes as well as hours. The eighteenth saw 'grandfather' models become fairly common in most English homes. Those found in wealthy houses often had a case of scarlet lacquer, decorated with lively gold chinoiserie figures and standing on griffin feet. The wealthy favoured instruments capable of sounding bells, telling time, dates, phases of the moon, and some of them had intricate contrivances in the form of wooden figures, and horses could gallop, knights joust, or the eyes and lips of a human form could open or blink to time. Bedroom furniture was almost as rich and costly as that in the reception-rooms; indeed, in this century, bedrooms were often thrown open for the entertainment of guests. It was the day of the great four-poster bed enclosed in heavy curtains and when woodwork was highly ornamented; over the tester and above the carved pillars of many a one, towered the Chinese grotesques shaped by a Hepplewhite.

Their love of the sumptuous and exquisite in art was also satisfied by the imported work of Cellini and his followers, and around many a room were shelves on which to display the Chinese and Japanese porcelain which was so greatly loved by the eighteenth-century nobility. They favoured Chinese porcelain with its wonderful designs, and Satsuma pottery with its brilliant colours of gold, green, rich red, its brass cloisonné enamel and delicately moulded patterns. They specially loved Eastern pottery that took the form of animals, and replicas of tigers, elephants and camels, spiritedly modelled and covered with green, brown and cream glazes were adored. Dresden ware too was known to them. From about the mid-century French pottery was also in high favour, and that of Sèvres with its brilliant colours, microscopic delicacy of painting and elaborate surface decoration was held in esteem. Of course this neglect of home-made porcelain was not deliberate, for it was not till 1773 that Duesbury at Derby, Wall at Worcester and others at Bristol, Lowestoft and Coalport brought English pottery into any sort of elegance. Wedgwood had started the Etruria works in 1769, and soon after that date, his coffee-pots, tea-pots and jugs were to be seen in many parts of England, but mainly on dressers rather than on display shelves. His jugs for beer, &c., called sack-jugs, toby-jugs and black-jacks, were also being produced in various designs and colours, though the majority of them were of common grey or mottled stoneware. In the third quarter of the century, Josiah Wedgwood, aided by Flaxman, the greatest sculptor that England has produced, began to manufacture the famous ware now associated with the name.

Perhaps as far as pottery is concerned, England then distinguished herself in the production of kitchen crockery. Delft was certainly manufactured in the early eighteenth century in Liverpool, and there are various English claimants for the credit of inventing transfer on china and pottery. In the first half of the century, only a thin white coating disguised the crude red or buff-coloured clay of which delft was made; but round about 1740 they discovered how to make a ware that was white throughout.

Although the poor had to be content with badly glazed, yellow earthenware, and were compelled to use leather-bottles and wood platters when at meat, aristocratic elegance called for stoneware jugs mounted in gold and silver. Similarly, their silver and gold plate was famous throughout the century. The great salt-cellars, salvers, ewers, standing cups, tankards, beakers, porringers, punchbowls, candlesticks, sconces, wine cisterns, casters, cruet-stands, coffee-pots, chocolate-pots, tea-urns, cake baskets were weighty and substantial. At the same time, they were elegant in design and shape, and ornamented with engravings, festoons, medallions, knots of riband and repoussé work. Not only were these things elegant, but they were practically priceless, for they

were made of solid silver and gold, and sometimes encrusted with
diamonds, for it was not till 1837 that electro-plating was made
possible by Thomas Spencer the Liverpool inventor. Their
cutlery was equally elaborate; spoons became more shapely as the
century progressed and the 'apostle' form was prized; forks were
well known, and the wealthy possessed in small numbers both the
three-and four-pronged form even if they rarely relied on them
for ordinary usage. Their soft-furnishings were equally exquisite
and personal. Linen drapery was abundant and sumptuous; very
fine linen or silk was used for sheets, and these and their table-
cloths were often patterned with the face of the nobleman, or the
family coat of arms, and generally fringed with black or white silk
lace. This was usually hand-made, for it was not till 1768 that a
lace-making machine was invented. Very heavy curtains richly
ornamented, would be found in all the principal rooms, as well as
large, beautifully painted screens to keep off the many draughts.
Cushions were probably equally sumptuous. Sometimes indeed,
their very animals had to be provided with cushions, &c., and we
are told that George I had 'a luxury kennel in walnut with green
glass windows and an embroidered silk-cushion for his lap-dog'.

v

Another characteristic of the eighteenth-century aristocracy was
their genuine love for art and music. Most of the big houses built
in the first half of the century had a handsome, spacious, rectan-
gular room which could be used not only for balls, but as a concert
hall. Moreover in those days, they prided themselves on being
'artistical'. Painters like Gainsborough were expert players of the
harp, viol-da-gamba, 'cello, hautboy; famous soldiers like
Wellington freely indulged their taste for music; Wesley is credited
with being an artist of no mean ability. It was quite customary
to have solos, quartettes, &c., after dinner or supper, and not infrequently the host or guest would deliver a lecture on etching,
painting, music or literature at the conclusion of a party; particularly so in the earlier part of the century.

At such gatherings in the first decade of the eighteenth century,
the music was chiefly vocal, and the guests not infrequently sang
glees, madrigals, anthems and songs. Many of these aristocrats
were accomplished executants as well as vocalists. From Pepys one

gathers that then they were familiar with the pipe, flageolet, elementary flutes, drums, some reed instruments, oboes, bassoons, dulcimers, spinets, clavichords, harpsichords, viols, virginals; that they were very fond of guitars and harps of all sizes and shapes; that trumpets were known, and that many of them prided themselves on their accomplishments with the coach horn. Other sources indicate, too, that up to 1750 bell-ringing was an aristocratic pastime.

During the eighteenth century great musicians were hired to amuse the Court and nobility, and the frequent visits or long residence here of Handel, the two Bachs, Haydn and Mozart gradually dispelled the then prevailing notion that the only good music in the world was Italian. The improving taste also led to the resuscitation of compositions by English composers of the sixteenth century such as Tallis, Byrd and Farrant, and of seventeenth-century musicians like Gibbons, Blow and Purcell, and brought into prominence the work of the contemporary Croft, Boyce and Nares as well as that of the still greater Germans. This resulting attitude led to the foundation of such musical societies as 'Noblemen's and Gentlemen's Catch Club', and the 'Academy of Antient Music' which maintained a very high musical standard. Famous players and composers advanced technique in playing and called for the elaboration of instruments. Thus the century saw the viol transformed into the violin, viola, 'cello and double-bass. Violins had been made in the seventeenth century by Amati and others at Cremona; but the eighteenth century saw them reach their supreme form of excellence at the hands of Stradivarius, though even his instruments had to wait more than sixty years before Tourte was making bows worthy to be used on them. These bows also helped to make other stringed instruments more pliable and capable of giving expression to great musical ideas. Wind instruments too, shared in this general improvement, and the former coarse tone and uncertain intonation were largely mitigated. The century saw the piano gradually oust the harpsichord. Italy, France and Germany all claim credit for its invention; but they all agree that it was one of the eighteenth century. Apparently the new instrument did not reach England till the mid-century; and an old play-bill of Covent Gardens dated May 16, 1767, has this announcement:

'Miss Brickler will sing a favourite song accompanied by Mr. Dibdin on a New Instrument called PIANO-FORTE.'

Organs too, became more numerous and efficient during these
hundred years. Some English churches and mansions such as St.
Paul's, Hampton Court, Trinity College Cambridge, had rudimentary ones in the seventeenth century. These few representatives were greatly multiplied in the eighteenth as at Windsor,
Salisbury, Shrewsbury, Bristol, Greenwich and Foundling Hospitals, and 'Father' Smith alone is credited with the erection of no
fewer than forty-five up and down the country. These models
seem to have had keys and pipes, stops and bellows, but the English organs did not have pedals, couplers or swell-box until the
eighteenth century had gone or almost gone. Playing any organ
in that century must have required great physical exertion, for
Barker did not invent the pneumatic lever till well in the nineteenth century, and the pressure of putting down a key with the
wind-pressure against the pallets it actuated, was so strenuous that
it was not unknown for the eighteenth-century organist to strip to
the waist before going into action. Orchestras also developed
greatly during this century, especially in the sense of having a
fixed group of musicians playing different instruments in different
proportions. Their brass instruments too were improved, although
it was not till the nineteenth century that many of them took their
modern shapes and compass, and by means of pistons were made
to yield the full chromatic scale. Eighteenth-century bandsmen
would therefore never know modern piccolos, cor anglais, clarinets
and trombones.

Nor did eighteenth-century musicians know the American
organ, harmonium, concertina, accordion or mouth organ. On
the other hand the people enjoyed barrel organs, musical chairs,
musical snuff-boxes, tin whistles and 'recorders', whilst 'har-
monicas', or musical glasses, were very popular with society ladies
from the mid-century onwards. To this instrument Franklin
applied his genius, and of it, the great musician Gluck asserted
'whatever may be done on a violin or a harp, can be performed on
a Harmonica'.

Under this impetus from the wealthy, the practice of concert-
music grew enormously during the century and there was a rage
for concertos, operas, symphonies, sonatas, oratorios. Hundreds
of such eighteenth-century productions are sung and played to
this day, whilst scores of their glees, madrigals and anthems are
still regularly performed. Even the rude inelegancies of the poor
were affected by this impetus, and part-singing, hymn-singing,

&c., spread among the illiterates. They revived the old songs like 'Integer vitae', 'Dulce Domum', 'Drink to Me Only', 'Passing By', 'Here's a Health unto His Majesty', and they gradually learned 'O Dear, What Can the Matter Be', 'God Save the King', 'Rule Britannia', 'Men of Harlech', 'See the Conquering Hero Comes', 'Hearts of Oak', 'A-hunting We Will Go', 'There is a Tavern in the Town', 'Sally in Our Alley', 'Green Grow the Rushes', 'Ye Banks and Braes', 'Auld Lang Syne', 'Where the Bee Sucks', 'Bay of Biscay', 'Polly Olivers', 'Lass of Richmond Hill', and a hundred other songs and hymn tunes. Wesley's influence on his chapels and evangelical churches, together with the pressure on other churches effected by musical squires, also made an enormous difference to the musical side of public worship in the eighteenth century.

VI

Eighteenth-century aristocrats also seem to have prided themselves on their collections of pictures. Kneller, Reynolds, Gainsborough, Raeburn and Romney were paid to preserve in lasting radiation, the features of many an eighteenth-century beauty or dignitary, whilst a fewer number of them showed genuine interest in Wilson's landscape and Opie's historical paintings. Apart from these artists, perhaps contemporary painting was, on the whole, one of exquisite minor work, chiefly devoted to the embellishment of the intense social life of the times. English painters gradually became most distinguished for their miniatures, and the century's close saw the work of Cosway, Smart, Engleheart, Bone, Ozias Humphrey and the two Plimers. In their own way these men excelled all their European contemporaries. Some of them painted on copper, but more on card, vellum or chicken-skin (pecorella), rough bone or ivory. A few of them painted in oils or enamels, but the great majority used water-colour. The preserved collections of thousands of these miniatures still show this lovely eighteenth-century portraiture, the strength of handling, brightness of the eyes, exuberance of colouring, elaborate finish and detail.

Quite a number of these aristocrats were enthusiastic collectors of books and freely patronized promising writers. One writer on the period says of them: 'Many of them were quite as happy in a library as in the saddle or at the card-table, and no recital of their dissipations and corruptness, can veil the fact that they were also scholars, men of taste and refinement.' Thus their libraries were often exquisite; they had their books covered with transparent vellum and decorated with hand-painted landscapes. Silk and velvet were the coverings for the more costly books in the first half of the century, whilst in the second half, thanks to Roger Payne, English book-binding took a leading place in the artistic finishing of books. He advertised that he bound books: 'in Russia Lether Emborder'd with Ermin expressive of the High Rank of the Noble Patron. The Other Parts Finish'd in the Most Elegant Taste with Gold Borders Studded with Gold and Dimonds.' Many of the more ordinary bindings of this period are in polished tree gilt calf, gold tooled back-panels, gold dentelled borders, engraved title pages, woodcut portraits, whilst on the pages themselves many of the books have lovely border-designs on the wide margins, striking initials and decorative titles.

The actual printing is much less satisfactory. Eighteenth-century taste demanded pretty courtly vignettes, more and more engravings, fanciful head and tail pieces, garlands of roses, cupids and symbols and very ornate coverings and decorations; in short, attractive 'picture' books rather than well printed pages. The type was usually poor and small and somewhat irregular whilst the alinement was imperfect. The letter 's' was indicated by a symbol almost like 'f', and 'ct' were often united in a single symbol. Most English printers then used the old Dutch types of fount and saw no reason to discard them for improvements. Ever since the seventeenth-century issue of the Elzevir classics, there had been a steady decline in materials and printing-workmanship in the printed volumes all over Europe. Moreover, printers in England were in a privileged position, for the law required a certificate for the possession of all presses or types. Thus being protected by monopolies, the printers had no incentives to consider the quality of the work they produced. Yet the century saw William Caslon, one of the greatest designers and founders of type who ever lived, and who by 1720 had cast several founts of type; the mid-century saw the printing of John Baskerville which, like those of Caslon, are exquisite and which became deservedly popular in foreign countries.

By the century's last quarter, quiet reading at home had lost its attraction for the aristocracy. At any rate, so-called public libraries and subscription libraries had become widespread in

London, and by Wesley's death the movement had spread into the provinces. Advertisements about such institutions suggest that these 'public' libraries numbered thousands by 1800. At such rendezvous the wealthy could foregather to gossip, drink coffee, &c., gamble and perhaps read; and probably Anthony Absolute is quite correct when he describes them as 'the evergreen tree of diabolical knowledge'.

VII

But it was not in books alone that the eighteenth-century aristo-crats were extravagant. Extravagance of attire was the keynote of the century, and though this extravagance changed its form according to fashion's decree, it persisted throughout the whole century. Even colour-tone was not neutralized much before the French Revolution; so blue and scarlet, green and gold, crimson and purple were the daily wear of the well-to-do. Even the wide-skirted suit of black broadcloth had to be frogged with silver lace.

The men's satin or silk coats were usually very tight in the waist, full in the skirt and reached to the knee. Under it was a long silk waistcoat, above which tumbled forth a cascade of white frills, whilst at the wrists was still more lace. Knee breeches were very tight fitting and usually made of silk or white calf-skin. On their heads were wigs of all sizes and shapes and crowned with tricorne hats or beavers ranging from 'shorters to toppers'. Unfortunately for them, they never knew the silk hat, which was a nineteenth-century invention. Prince Charlie's dress 'had in it somewhat of elegance. His coat was rose-coloured velvet embroidered in silver and lined with silver tissue; his waistcoat was a rich gold brocade with a spangled gold fringe; the cockade in his hat and the buckles of his shoes were diamonds.' In 1780 Selwyn says that he and other dandies were wearing suits costing 500 guineas, and that a single waistcoast might be anything from fifty guineas. A fop who committed suicide about this time at the age of thirty-two, left a wardrobe that fetched over £15,000 when auctioned. At the close of the century, Colonel Hanger is saying that he spent £900 on dress clothes alone for one winter.

When dressed for a rout or ball, the exquisites among the nobles were most elaborately equipped. The dandy would be proclaimed by delicate shoes with high scarlet heels, studded with diamonds and fastened by large jewelled buckles; the shoes themselves would be of every brilliant hue and set off with gold, silver or diamond embroidery. His face would be surmounted by a white Court wig; round his throat would be bound a cravat fastened with an elaborately jewelled brooch, whilst the star of some order would decorate his breast. Neck, fingers, wrists, knees and even ankles would support gems, gold and silver in the form of rings, brooches, bracelets, necklets, &c. Not infrequently they wore patches on their faces to indicate their political party, whilst their white, blue or scarlet stockings, ornamented with gold and silver 'clocks', were supposed to proclaim their high lineage. Perhaps the colour of stockings was partly dependent on occasion and period; white ones seem to have been essential for fashionable gatherings throughout the century, whilst red was the favourite colour for the first decades and yellow displaced it for ordinary occasions later on, and to avoid the extremes of fashion many a man then wore striped or spotted stockings. Even garters had to be elaborate; they were a yard long and embroidered with the wearer's name, motto or design. Swords were carried by these fashionables till the last quarter of the century when they were replaced by tall elegant canes dangling from the wrist or coat-button. Often the cane-knob was of gold, silver or diamonds; sometimes it was carved into the semblance of a head, grinning to show two rows of thirty-two seed pearls for teeth. These 'bucks' and 'fribbles' were very fond of gold and silver, fine laces and ornaments and were intensely alive to the right ribbon, the right powder, the right flower, the right perfume, the right snuff and snuff-box. Some of these anaemic and tailorish persons even usurped all the frivolous airs of the other sex, and were so feminine in their dress and demeanour, that they tried to look like women; not infrequently these 'macaronies', as they were termed, carried muffs. Usually the 'macaronies' were of the highest class and could boast that they had made the grand tour after coming down from the university; they had their copyists in slightly inferior young men whom the times called 'dandies' and 'jessamies'. These, the better-class newspapers were holding up to scorn in 1799 as 'emaciated beaux with their quilted lapelles and stuffed sleeves'.

Sometimes fashionable eighteenth-century dress was determined by the membership of a special club. Diehard Tories then wore a waistcoat of light blue silk with gold buttons, bordered round with yellow silk, and a dark blue frock-coat with a broad orange-velvet cape with still more buttons three inches in diameter, and on which was inscribed 'October Club'. Such a costume might nowadays render its wearer open to being mistaken for a cinema attendant; but then great noblemen of the realm attended parliament in such party uniform, and even Charles Lamb considered such a rig-out 'a wise and manly thing to wear'. Sporting men in that century hankered to be members of the 'Four Horse Club', membership of which allowed the privileged to drive in procession, in yellow-bodied barouches drawn by four bay horses, from London to Windsor and back every second Thursday in the summer months. More important still, it allowed them to wear the club-waistcoat with its inch-wide yellow and blue stripes, and a greatcoat with fifteen capes and a double row of silver buttons.

Perhaps some idea of more ordinary eighteenth-century dress can be gathered from remaining memorials. In the dress of the Lord Mayor's coachman, modern eyes can see a nobleman's dress of the days of George III; in the powdered attendant found in some clubs that of the fop in George II's times; whilst the page-boy, with his three rows of buttons, wears, in less expensive form, much the same fashionable garb as upper-class boys wore in the eighteenth century. Beau Brummell, the great arbiter of fashion at the end of the century, did his best to introduce smart clothes and super-cut, and to kill the vulgarity of the garments worn by the beaux in 1750. He improved design and workmanship, added to details, and reduced considerably the weight of garments; for till well into the century a man's garments frequently weighed nine or ten times what modern ones do. His initiative also conferred the convenience of wearing trousers for city life, instead of tight breeches with long boots. He managed to lower the scarlet high heels that had been on shoes, and to make fashionable taste prefer round-toed shoes to the square form. These had buckles till the eighties when 'the effeminate shoe-string became popular, and fashion, devoid of feeling and deaf to argument'—as ran the old protest—deserted the buckle. Boots towards the end of the century challenged the public's taste, and so was sounded the death-knell of the old binding buckle. Under Brummell too, the handkerchief was still regarded as a decoration and dangled from the men's pocket. They were used almost exclusively as mere ornaments, for the practice of blowing noses with the fingers was still frequent in the highest circles. He also stressed the use of large, long purple cloaks lined with crimson silk to be worn over their satin cloaks, instead of the great-coat with multiple capes.

Although dress for men was less noticeable for finery, &c., under the Brummell regime, and though great mutations had taken place in male attire by the last quarter, as late as 1796 *The Times* still found it necessary to devote columns to the description of dresses worn by men at public functions. The columns contained such entries as

'The Marquis of Lorn was wearing a brown and blue striped silk coat and breeches, a white silk waistcoat richly embroidered with silver, coloured stones, dentelle and bouquets of flowers; the ensemble producing a beautiful and splendid effect'.

The *Morning Post* also gives a glimpse of these ancient splendours:

'The Prince of Wales was decorated in a manner almost beyond the powers of description; he wore a coquelicot satin, wholly covered with Mosaic embroidery of Silver, Pearls, Stones and Sky-Blue Foil; the seams were also embroidered with additional labour in a superb manner. The Cuffs of the Coat were made of Silver Tissue and a Waistcoat of the same, beautifully ornamented; with a Diamond George, Button, Loop and Star. . . . His Royal Highness wore rather small oblong Buckles of Gold set with Diamonds.'

It was only the very wealthy who carried a watch in those days, for watches were still rare and expensive objects—a reason why the majority of the dandies carried two at once. Robert Hooke, an original and experimental philosopher, by the end of the seventeenth century, had succeeded in regulating the movement of watches by the application of the balance-spring. These first watches were wonderful things: big fob-distending packets of machinery, made of solid gold and usually studded with diamonds. Family coats of arms were blazoned upon the case, and also embroidered in blue silk upon the old-fashioned lining between the inner and outer cases. Many of them had repeater-catches, and little and sweet, true in tone and prompt, the bells responded and reproduced the chimes of some ancient belfry. Lever escapement was invented about 1770 and this device, together with the abandonment of the striking parts, allowed watches to become much smaller; so in the last quarter of the century they had become so small that they could be set in the heads of walking-sticks, in bracelets, in finger rings. They were often encased in crystal, enamel, imitation skulls, decorated with pictures and became subject to all the vicissitudes of eighteenth-century fashion. Other portable heirlooms carried by the eighteenth-century exquisites were the musical snuff-box and patch-box. These, like all their other goods, were most elaborate and often cost hundreds of pounds, for they were made of green or other enamel, solid gold and encrusted with diamonds. Every gentleman and lady had snuff-boxes to match the dress. Even the snuff itself had to vary according to occasion, rather than to mere taste, and there seem to have been as many brands of snuff then as there are of tobacco to-day; it ranged from common brown rappee to Spanish bran which was scented with otto of roses or Strasburg violets, and snuff blending was evidently quite a fine art. Among their other necessaries were their mirror-cases and their perspective glasses, through which they quizzed the passers-by. These too, were mainly composed of ivory, gold, enamel and the expensive like. Platinum was known in those days but was never used for trinket purposes. It was brought to the country round about 1740 and generally called 'white gold'; it was regarded as a mere laboratory plaything and considered inferior even to silver; as late as 1800 it was bought in the rough at about 2/- an ounce.

The more ordinary citizens could not compete with the aristocrats in the matter of dress, &c., but even they shunned neutrality of tint in clothes and wore browns and murreys, bottle-greens and clarets, buffs and lavenders. John Baskerville the great eighteenth-century master-printer and japanned-article manufacturer, walked the streets of Birmingham in the third quarter of the century dressed in a green satin coat edged with gold lace, a scarlet waistcoat lavishly trimmed with gold and sported a small round hat similarly decorated. Not content with making his personal apparel so conspicuous for a mere manufacturer, 'He had a gorgeous chariot built, in which he drove behind six cream-coloured horses caparisoned with net-hangings. The coach was a super-product of his japanning establishment, the panels being emblazoned with decorations of flowers and naked cupids.' In 1786 one sees Burns in his farmer's Sunday-best: boots and buckskins, full blue coat, green waistcoat striped with buff, frilled shirt and stock. Up to the American War, foot-soldiers wore a three-cornered hat, a broad-skirted scarlet coat with white facings, a long low-flapped waistcost in scarlet or blue, red breeches and long white spatterdash gaiters reaching to mid-thigh. The war led to a less conspicuous usage of brown in the men's clothing but it was not till 1834 that they were put into trousers. The end of the century

G

saw Nelson going into battle in his bright blue coat with white lapels, with the epaulettes of his exalted grade, frilled shirt, cuffs striped with gold braid, white knee-breeches and a cocked hat set on his powdered hair which was braided into a queue and tied with a black silk ribbon. To be a still more notable target for sharpshooters, he was wearing his four stars outside his admiral's frock. It saw ordinary well-dressed men wearing white feathers inside the brim of their beavers, whilst rosettes, cockades, favours of all kinds, colours and shapes were used for special occasions or to indicate political leanings.

Even the clergy were dissatisfied with a mere cassock or geneva gown which public opinion expected them to wear in the streets, and they too, took to dressing like persons engaged in secular callings. Swift reports that the Church authorities had constantly to reprove clergymen for such practices, and many of the young aristocrats of the Church were a sporty set and so they affected brilliantly coloured garments. Dean Swift declares that he himself once sported a light green velvet frockcoat faced with red camlet, white calf-skin breeches, cream-coloured silk stockings, and shoes with silver buckles, whilst Goldsmith applied for ordination in scarlet from head to foot. But apparently this dress was too ultra-modern for the bishop, and the future poet-novelist-playwright was speedily turned out of the episcopal palace.

VIII

Eighteenth-century men never questioned the equality of the sexes nor did they think it necessary that their women should be as well taught or dressed as they were. Pepys once reckoning up his household accounts, found that for one quarter his wife had spent £12 on dress and that he himself for the corresponding period had gone through £55. And judging from his comments he regretted that £12 much more than the £55. Despite this masculine attitude, an eighteenth-century society lady's dress was superfine and more fitted to figure in a museum than on the stage of real life. Two features characterized every object down to the minutest and most intimate: elaborateness was sought after by the silk weaver, milliner and goldsmith, and next self-assertion. Lace, embroidery, linen worn next to the skin must always be designed with the crown—the symbol of noble birth. Naturally all garments were expensive, and Mrs. Pepys at the end of the seventeenth century is credited with having bought a 'nightrail' costing £40 and certainly she did not belong to the opulent classes. It seems a big price to pay for a nightdress even in the days when the purchasing power of money has fallen to a ninth or so; but in the eighteenth century fine ladies often received visitors of both sexes in their nightgowns, so, as the chronicler pertinently remarks: 'they might be seen with envy by their visitants.'

Women's dress changed considerably during the first half of this century and still more so during the second half. But throughout its entirety extravagance of attire persisted, even though the extravagance changed its form. The gigantic hoops in which they delighted in the first half, declined about 1760 and were succeeded by a hideous head-dress, when vast pyramids of false hair were piled on heads, pasted together with pomatum, smothered in powder and pricked with feathers. Sometimes from the topmost rung of hair to the heels a woman measured eight feet. Yet what she had gained in height she had lost in circumference; for during the vogue of the hoops, one pamphleteer wrote in 1745 against 'that enormous abomination the Hoop Petticoat, as the fashion now is . . . often as large as to fill the space of six men'. Apparently this tirade had little effect on the fashion, for in 1751 the newspaper *Connoisseur* lamented that 'the town was full of hoops capable of contracting or expanding from the size of a butter-churn to the circumference of six hogsheads', and a poetical description of the ladies' dress in the mid-fifties runs:

> Make your petticoats short, that a hoop eight yards wide,
> May decently show how your garters are tied.

197576

Throughout the century these ladies seem to have delighted in gorgeous and numerous petticoats and in very tight bodices. On this fashion, an irreverent lampoonist wrote the following lines in the last decade:

> Shepherds, I have lost my waist,
> Have you seen my body?
> Sacrificed to modern taste,
> I'm quite a hoddy-doddy.
>
> For fashion I that part forsook
> Where sages place the belly;
> 'Tis gone—and I've not a nook
> For cheesecake, tart or jelly.

Other critics then looking upon fashionable dress said, 'these women are like unto immense, open, inverted tulips'.

Other critics were equally censorious about the late eighteenth-century coiffures. Speaking in *Humphry Clinker*, demure Lydia Melford says: 'the rooms, the dresses, the company, the decorations surpass all description. But as I have no great turn for card-playing, I have not thoroughly entered into the spirit of the place (Bath). Indeed, I am such a country hoyden that I was hardly fit to appear. I was not above five hours under the hands of the hair-dresser, who stuffed my head with as much black wool as would have made a quilted petticoat, and after all, it was the smallest head in the assembly.' The diarists of the period say that in the scaffolding, the hair would be crimped, curled, plaited and surcharged with feathers, ribbons, gauze, wreaths, flowers, pearls and diamonds. Sometimes the structure was made to represent rose-covered trellis, musical instruments, dolls, and even ships. Not infrequently it towered a yard above the brow, and the wearer had to kneel in her sedan or coach when transported to the assemblies. An ode written in 1778 described the lover's possible astonishment at his lady-love's hair:

> When he views your tresses thin,
> Tortur'd by some French friseur;
> Horse-hair, hemp and wool within,
>   Garnish'd with a diamond-skewer.
>
> When he scents the mingled steam
> Which your plaster'd heads are rich in,
> Lard and meal and clouted cream,
>   Can he love a walking kitchen?

Much about this time the immodest practice of exposing the bosom then attained the extreme of indelicacy. Newspaper references to balls remark that some of the fashionable ladies 'appeared at the masked ball as Iphigenias, but so naked that they might have been taken for Andromedas'. This nude cult became more noticeable as the century declined to its close; stylish women were not content with mere paucity of covering, but they had it made of materials of such transparent texture that it rivalled the costume of the ancients. Gillray's *Godiva's Rout, Fashionable Modesty, High Changes in Bond Street*, &c., drawn in the century's closing years, as well as scathing satire in newspapers like *The Times*, indicate the extremely *décolletée* and diaphanous dresses of the period.

There are ample examples of later eighteenth-century costumes

to be seen in the dolls that are preserved in museums. These dolls
were the fashion plates of the day and were sent about to exhibit
what was new in dress. Similarly, eighteenth-century aprons and
fans are available for the interested. By the end of the century
aprons, which had once been a gaudy ornament and worn at balls
and receptions, had disappeared entirely from fashionable throngs
owing to the ban imposed upon them by Beau Nash. Fans on the
other hand maintained their popularity throughout the century.
All the luxurious ornamentation of the day was bestowed on them
as far as they could display it. The sticks were made of mother-of-
pearl, gold, silver or ivory; taffeta, silk and fine parchment were
used for the mounts; occasionally they were mounted with the
finest point lace. Little circles of glass were let into the stick to be
looked through, and sometimes small telescopic glasses were contrived at the pivot of the stick. Artists of distinction like Klingstet,
Herbert, Boquet painted landscapes or scenes or personages connected with political events on them. Not infrequently the ladies
took their fans to church, and it is said that certain gentlemen
objected to the secular designs on them 'because they distracted
their minds from the service'. So in 1790 an ingenious fan-maker
designed a 'church' fan decorated with angels' heads and adorned
with four pious hymns for morning and evening service.

Like their men-folk, women wore a multitude of rings, bracelets,
necklaces. Like them too, they painted or placed patches on their
faces to indicate their political bias; sometimes, however, these
patches must have been more decorative than indicative, for
diarists and novelists refer to ladies wearing circles, crescents, stars,
and even a coach and horses transferred to their faces; sometimes
they sported as many as six of these weird ornaments at one and
the same time.

Indeed, adult and juvenile dress for the eighteenth-century
aristocrat seems to have been nothing but a complicated form of
livery. That for women was certainly astounding, and there must
have been some motive behind their self-immolation on the altar
of fashion. A proposed Act of Parliament suggests one motive. In
1700 an Act was seriously propounded 'to protect men from being
beguiled into matrimony by artificial adornment'. It proposed to
enact 'That all women of whatever rank, profession, degree or
age, whether virgins, maids or widows that shall from and after
such Act, impose upon, seduce and betray into matrimony, any
of His Majesty's Subjects, by the scents, paints, cosmetics, washes,

artificial teeth, false hair, spanish wool, iron stays, hoops, high-heeled shoes, bolstered hips, shall incur the penalty of the Law in force against witch-craft and like Misdemeanours and that the Marriage, upon conviction, shall stand null and void'.

Perhaps some of these beauty-aids had found favour among male and female Methodists; at any rate in 1784 Wesley was urging Quaker plainness of dress and calling for 'no rings, ear-rings, necklaces, ruffles; no velvet, silk or fine linen, coloured waistcoats, shining stocking, costly buckles or buttons or gay perukes. . . . Band-tickets must not be issued to those guilty'. Perhaps these beauty-aids had begun to attract even bachelor Methodist ministers. An old Methodist minister in 1788, writing to a young colleague about his projected marriage, specifies the sixteen qualifications indispensable for a preacher's wife. In the main they are such qualities as might be looked for in any pious woman, but he emphasizes that 'she must be exceeding exemplary in her dress, not using gaudy or costly apparel; if she does, her husband need never say a word against dress, as it will be all lost labour'.

Whether Wesley and his colleagues were successful in toning down Methodist dress, we do not know. Certainly it would appear that all previous sumptuary laws and the proposed Act of 1770, did not stem this eighteenth-century urge for personal adornment. An advertisement for perfumery &c., in one London shop in 1800, gives a list of 250 different perfumes, waters, hair-oils, soaps, pomatums, face powders, &c., purchasable there; whilst other advertisements indicate that most of the tooth, hair, nail and clothes brushes and even those for shaving, were said to be in gold, pearl, enamel, &c.

And yet the eighteenth century had been an age of sumptuary laws. Acts were passed restricting the use of hair and face powder, the wearing of certain stylish or distinguishable dresses, or of certain materials like brocade and of such colours as sky-blue, for the gentry alone. As members of Parliament and their sponsors were primarily interested in sheep and therefore in wool, right up to the last quarter of the century, cotton was handicapped by restrictive laws. In 1720 it was decreed that garments of cotton should be dyed in deep blue only, under a fine of £20 for the seller and of £5 for the wearer of other colours. A year later calico was forbidden for entire garments, and this material was restricted to neckcloths, &c.; it was further handicapped by a heavy excise

duty. Entire cotton goods were not permitted till 1774, and when
Byrom died in 1763 his heirs were fined £5 because they had not
buried him 'in a shirt, shift, sheet or shroud made of sheep's wool'.

Such sumptuary laws not only determined materials and colours
but they even decided cut and shapes. Up to the last quarter of
the century, handkerchiefs were superfine and of all shapes:
oblong, round, triangular, square, &c. Marie Antoinette is
credited with the discovery that it would be more convenient and
much neater if the square form only was used, so in 1785 it was
decreed 'that the length of handkerchiefs shall equal their width
throughout the Kingdom of France'. And oddly enough the
decree seems to have standardized their shape ever since and in
every country.

IX

Perhaps the personal habits of these fine people matched their
adornment in some respects, and Frances Burney, who moved in
Court circles, says in 1791 that the perpetual card-playing,
elaborate dressing, meals, gossip and etiquette wearied and disgusted her. About that time three titled ladies enjoyed such a
high reputation for gambling, that even Parliament considered the
possibility of pillorying them. But as the passion for gambling ran
through all ranks of society and demoralized them all, nothing was
done. In his mock *Journal of a Modern Lady*, Swift gives details of
the wealthy's senseless pursuits. Defoe, Smollett, Richardson,
Crabbe, Fielding and Anstey, when they describe highlife, show
that Swift's strictures were not imaginary ones. From them one
gathers that early in the century, fashionable folk carried about
with them their favourite monkey, whilst at the end of the century,
parrots croaked in every boudoir, and many a grandee boasted of
a punchbowl made out of a famous or beloved skull. In this century fops were essentially fine weather creatures and from November to March, the ladies were laid up, so to speak, for the winter.

On the other hand the personal cleanliness and bodily habits,
&c., of such human peacocks were singularly out of harmony with
this fine raiment. 'The Duke of Norfolk was famed for his indolence, late hours, deep drinking, heavy eating, and reckless
gambling. He was negligent to so great a degree, that he rarely
made use of water for purposes of bodily refreshment and comfort;
nor did he change his linen more frequently than he washed

himself'. *The Times* in 1788 mentions that 'His Grace of Bedford has bet Lord Barrymore that the latter will not be able to eat a live cat for fifty guineas'. Congreve in *Way of the World* makes the young lady say of her titled would-be lover, 'Eh, how he smells! I shall be quite overcome if I stay', and Lady Wishfort adds, 'Smells! he would poison a tallow-chandler and his family! Beastly creature, I know not what to do with him'. Apparently too, whenever a grandee of this century wanted to spit, he simply spat, regardless of occasion. Pepys puts on record that one day a lady by mischance spat on his clothes, and how he was consoled when he observed that she was pretty and clearly of the *élite*. Much later Horace Walpole describes at length, how for a guinea bet, Lord Cobham spat into Lord Hervey's hat, whilst the latter, hat in hand, was gossiping with some fashionable ladies. Spittoons figure in most of the drawings of the century and seem to have been placed in all reception-rooms. Even in church, eighteenth-century fops were largely undisturbed by the presence of crawling vermin of the intimate type and simply re-acted in primitive fashion. Other objectionable practices of theirs were displayed when they passed the time of divine service by calmly looking about them 'quizzing' all the pretty women with their perspective glasses. Equally offensive and out of harmony with fine apparel were their use of vile language, reckless gambling, heavy eating and deep drinking. For in every age, there is a species of degenerate who reacts with great violence from all the traditions of good breeding.

x

Probably one of the most abstemious men of the eighteenth century was John Wesley. He says in one place that for four years he lived entirely on potatoes and declares with pride, that his weight remained for years just under nine stone.

It was far other with most eighteenth-century notables. Here is Dryden describing the dramatist Shadwell at the end of the seventeenth century:

> Og, [Shadwell] from a treason-tavern rolling home,
> Round as a globe and liquour'd every chink;
> Goodly and great he sails behind his link.

Horace Walpole half-way through the century, describes a Court beauty as having 'two acres of cheek spread with crimson, an ocean of neck that overflowed and was not distinguishable from the lower part of the body'.

Thackeray observes: 'Swift was fat; Addison was fat; Gay and Thomson were preposterously fat; all the fuddling and punch-drinking, that club and coffee-house boozing, shortened the lives and enlarged the waistcoats of the men of that age.'

The royal Georges were all obese; Fox and Walpole were massively corpulent. Johnson is seen as a huge, ungainly, slovenly figure, clad in a greasy brown coat, wearing a grey wig with scorched foretop, rolling in his wooden armchair, long past midnight and holding in his dirty hand his nineteenth cup of tea. Garrick declares that 'most actors ate and drank themselves into unseemly unshapes'. Handel was in the habit of ordering dinner for three and of promptly consuming the lot. The Duke of Norfolk was the perpetual president of the 'Sublime Society of Beefsteaks' because of his reported ability to eat more beefsteaks than any other man. George IV is said to have been so fond of mutton chops that he ate fourteen at one sitting. The Duke of York at the end of the century always took three hours over dinner and ate ravenously from 8.0 to 11.0. Even Brillat-Savarin, author of *Physiologie du Goût*, and therefore expected to be a gourmet rather than a gourmand, was said to swallow forty to fifty oysters as an appetizer before a meal, and it is affirmed that he and a friend—also presumably given to elegant dissipation—ate sixteen dozen on one occasion before settling down to dinner.

Eighteenth-century people seem to have had a curious reverence for obesity; perhaps it was a sign of power to them. Fashionable people, statesmen and writers of that age, seem to have had to choose between social disabilities on the one side, and on the other indigestion for themselves and gout for their descendants; no wonder that many were cut off in early manhood or lived martyrs to delirium tremens. One of the most popular sights at late eighteenth-century fairs was the Lancashire worthy Daniel Lambert, who was enthusiastically billed as 'owning the advanced weight of 739 pounds'. Even sportsmen were expected to be good trenchermen. John Nyren the great cricketer of the century, almost rhapsodizes over 'barleycorn such as will put the souls of three butchers into one weaver', and refers to 'the quantity of food my fellows would eat . . . two or three of them would strike dismay into a round of beef'. The record of Cavanagh, the famous fives player of that age, is much the same, and long distance runners

like Powell, who in 1793 went from London to York and back in
5½ days, trained on a diet of raw meat and beer. It is no wonder
that according to a character in *Rob Roy*, the deity most wor-
shipped in eighteenth-century England was 'the belly god'.

These were the days when 'fathers trained their sons gradually to
inure their brains to bear the gentleman-like quantity of liquor of
three or more bottles without brawls or breakings of heads'; when
Johnson declared: 'claret is the liquor for boys, port for men, but
he who aspires to be a hero must drink brandy'; when even a
painter like Morland had a reputation for incessant dissipation;
when a great Greek scholar like Porson was disgraced with the
stain of intoxication and when the great judge Lord Braxfield
'shone peculiarly at tavern meetings'. They were the days when
'statesmen sailed on a sea of claret from one comfortable official
haven to another'; when crown ministers like Walpole, Bolingbroke, Carteret were famous for their powers of absorption, and to
which powers they owed no little of their popularity; when the
ministry of 1742–4 has gone down to history as 'the drunken
administration', because of the conviviality of its leaders; when
Pitt's love for port enabled him, as he expressed it, 'always to see
two Speakers when addressing the House'. The mid-century saw
Parliament decide that neat rum should be served out as the
Navy's standard beverage. The beginning of the century shows
that, according to the Queen Anne account-book, fashionable
people dining at her majesty's table were expected to drink two
gallons a day of beer and wine. Towards its close one reads that
even a Boswell provided his guests with no fewer than ten kinds
of liquor when entertaining at Auchinleck House. With typical
painstaking accuracy he recites the wine list, and records exactly
how much each guest drank of each variety; and the figures
indicate that fashionable people were consuming quite as much
as in the days of Anne. The Duke of Norfolk, who was intimate
with Foote the comedian, was much addicted to the bottle; on a
masquerade night he asked Foote what new character he should
go in. 'Go sober,' answered Foote—a terse and significant suggestion. Neither preachers nor clergymen were expected to be tee-
total in those days, and circuit-stewards had to provide wine, rum,
&c., for their ministers. Hard drinking among fathers and
brothers was regarded as a mere masculine attribute by wives and
sisters.

Nor was excessive drinking confined to the one sex; fashionable

women seem to have been very fond of wines, &c., and not infrequently put rum into their tea. Perhaps it was such a practice
that gave occasion for regarding fashionable tea-parties as noisy
assemblies, and led Swift to write:

> Their chattering makes a louder din,
> Than fishwives o'er a cup of gin;
> Far less the rabble, roar and rail,
> When drunk with sour election ale.

The middle classes, too, were far from total abstainers, Derrick,
Master of Ceremonies at Bath, visiting Liverpool in 1760, writes:

'the rum here is excellent of which the merchants consume considerable
quantities . . . but they pique themselves greatly upon their ale of which
almost every house brews a sufficiency for its own use; and such is the
unanimity prevailing among them, that if by accident, one man's stock
runs short, he sends his pitcher to his neighbour to be filled.'

Before the days of cheap gin in 1723, the poor had probably few
occasions on which to indulge their love for strong drink, except
when they consumed the special 'christening', 'bridal', 'burial',
'election' or 'harvest' ales. Still, they must have had occasional
outbursts, and such a surmise is confirmed by an extract from a
sermon preached by a late seventeenth-century divine, who,
waxing hot, rhetorically asked his flock:

'Did they not swill beer till they were as red as cocks and with as
little sense in their heads as they had in their combs? . . . How much did
they spend on the upholstery of the body and how little on the soul?' . . .

Till the introduction of cheap spirits, the poor had depended on
cider and beer, both home-made, for their drink. Probably before
the Gin Act, consumption of the spirit had not exceeded two
million gallons per annum. After the Act, consumption jumped
sixfold, and by 1725 there were thousands upon thousands of
houses in London alone selling it. Ale-houses had to be licensed,
but the sale of gin was to all intents and purposes unchecked. It
could be bought from street stalls and barrows, from chandlers
and tobacconists. By 1750 Fielding was declaring: 'gin is the
principal sustenance of more than 100,000 people in the
metropolis.'

Details of eighteenth-century drinking among the wealthy are
equalled by the menus of their banqueting delights. Such menus
show that they had mountains of confectionery in the shape of
grottoes, castles, strange animals, from which issued forth live

birds or frogs or perhaps the Court dwarf. Their principal pride
lay, however, in more solid dishes. A 'broadside' of 1746, cele-
brating Culloden's victory, ends with:

> French soupes we do dispise;
> It suiteth not our blood;
> Brown bear and good ros-beef
> Is holesome bri'ish food.

Of the hosts of typical menus to celebrate some local or national
event, here is one sample, that commemorating an election victory
in Lincolnshire in 1784:

1st Course: Soups: Turtle or Swans giblets. Fish: Turbot, smelts, red
mullet, whiting, soles, codfish, stewed eels.

2nd Course: Swan, haunches & saddles of mutton, roast beef, breasts
of veal, fillets of veal, hams, tongues; turkeys, guinea fowl, ducks, geese,
pigeons roast or boiled; pigeon pie.

Entrées: Lobster cutlets, dresden patties, oyster patties, chicken
fricassé, cutlets and tomato sauce; sweetbreads, cocks combs.

(Some of these items may sound crude but they are matched by
an item appearing in Queen Anne's dietary: 'For livers, gizzards,
&c., for our dyet £27–7–6,' by such things as pigs' trotters, cows'
udders, cockles, winkles, which all appeared in slightly earlier
coronation banquets, whilst a very popular dish appearing on
wealthy eighteenth-century dining-tables was 'giblet pie' or its
counterpart 'numble pie', when they seem to have enjoyed eating
the heart, liver, &c., of a deer.)

3rd Course: Snipes, wild fowl, pheasants, partridges, leverets.

4th Course: Plum puddings, bakewell puddings or tarts, plum, goose-
berry, apple, damson, apricot puddings or tarts; cheesecakes, blanc-
manges, swiss creams, jellies, coconut doce, custards, syllabubs.

Dessert: Grapes, pears, filberts, oranges, fruits.

The potables fully matched the eatables in diversity and quality.
No details of the cost of this feast are given; but the Guildhall
dinner of November 9, 1761, is said to have cost £6,898 5s. 4d.
In neither case can the cost per head be calculated. An old
scholars' re-union attended by John Wesley in 1727 puts that
figure at £1 2s. 0d., while the paybook of Tower Garrison shows
that at Queen Anne's table it cost just under £400 a year per
head to feed her daily guests. Parson Woodforde's 'tithe frolics'
show that his twenty guests consumed huge quantities of meat,
wine, punch and ale, whilst the diarists of the period tell one that

the guests usually became very drunk, that dinners lasted for hours and that often people were ill at and after them. Such protracted banquets must have been fruitful sources of human ills and sickness; nor had soda-water been yet invented for their relief. Immermann in his *Münchausen* refers indirectly to these eighteenth-century well-spread banqueting tables, when, after describing how with his balloon and the famous sling he had inherited from King David, he lifted the College of Physicians into the air and kept them suspended there for three months, he says:

'You will naturally inquire what they did for food such a length of time? To this I answer. Had I kept them suspended twice that time they would have experienced no inconvenience on that account; so amply or rather extravagantly had they spread their table for that day's feasting.'

The mere everyday eating and drinking of the wealthy seems to have demanded a prodigious spread. Even the breakfast table was 'copiously furnished with all the apparatus of tea, coffee, chocolate, milk, cream, eggs, rolls, toast, muffins, bread, butter, potted beef, cold fowl, partridge, ham, tongue and anchovy' (*Headlong Hall*) and such a breakfast seems to have been needed after 'a very good supper consisting of veal cutlets, pigeons, asparagus, lamb and salad, apple-pie and tarts'. Diaries and journals also refer to the 'night-repasts' consisting of cold meats, pastry and sweetmeats which were placed in bedrooms, in the event of the gourmand waking up hungry. A substantial supply of provisions was also a very necessary ingredient in all eighteenth-century rural amusements, and in a lady's diary one reads: 'we picknicked at the top of the hill on veal, ham, chickens, gozebury pies, bred, chese, butter, hung leg of mutton, wine, porter, rum, brandy and bitters.'

Fashionable people dined at midday in the days of Queen Anne, at about 3.0 under George II, as late as 6.0 under the third George and at 8.0 in the days of the Regency. On the other hand, breakfasts formed a somewhat late morning meal with them, and Fanny Burney says that in 1786 *circa* 'we breakfast at 10.0, dine precisely at 2.0, drink tea about 6.0 and sup exactly at 9.0'.

More ordinary folk seem to have had other hours for meals. Byrom says: 'eminent manufacturers in 1750 were at their warehouses by 6.0 a.m., after the head of the household and his family had had a plain breakfast consisting of one large dish of water-pottage, made of oatmeal, water and a little salt boiled thick and

poured into a dish. . . . By the side of this dish was a pan of milk
and each dipped his wooden spune first into the one and then
into the other until paterfamilias said "Hold enough!".' His
diary has many entries like the following: 'we had supper of turbot,
turkey, sweetmeats, rabbit and a dessert of cherries, raspberries, a
good custard and then upstairs to wine and punch in bottles.'
Parson Woodforde's diary is equally instructive. He often mentions his dinner of two courses consisting of (1) 'a fine pike
roasted for dinner with a Pudding in his Belly; a leg of mutton
with caper sauce, a pig's face, a neck of pork roasted with gooseberries and a plum pudding and (2) eggs, roast fowl, orange pudding, custards and jellies'. His supper often consisted of 'a brace
of partridges, some cold tongue, potatoes in shells, meat pies and
more tarts'. Another middle-class man, Pepys, describes some of
the early eighteenth-century dishes to which he at any rate was
partial:

'Home from my Office to my Lodging where my wife had got ready
a fine dinner namely a dish of marrow bones, a leg of mutton, a loin of
veal, a dish of fowl, three pullets and two dozen of larks all in a great
tart; then a neat's tongue, a dish of anchovies, a dish of prawns and
cheese.'

Another mixed dish that was very popular in the north country in
the mid-century was called 'ambigu'. In this, meat, vegetables,
fruit were all served up together on a big dish. Here and there
they seem to have preferred their beef to be stuffed with chestnuts.
Much about the same time the people of the south-west had a
supper fancy for 'goose-giblet pie', and 'squab' pie made of
mutton, raisins and onions and queer shaped saffron cakes; the
whole washed down with 'egg-hot', an inspiring compound of
eggs, hot beer, sugar and rum. A fashionable cookery book issued
in the latter part of the century and called *King's Art of Cooking*,
suggests that gooseberries were served with mackerel, fresh or
dried currants with veal, and that honey was poured over cooked
beef and mutton, whilst Johnson always soaked his plum pudding
with lobster sauce.

As for other individual dishes to which eighteenth-century
people were partial, diaries suggest that in the early part of the
century they knew something called 'plum-porridge', for which
Sir Roger de Coverley had a great bias. To it he attributed
unusual potencies, for he declared that 'he had some hope even
for a Dissenter, when he saw one enjoying his plum-porridge'.

George I and George III esteemed boiled mutton and turnips as the daintiest dish that could be set before a king. 'Bubble and Squeak' in which meat and vegetables were fried together for supper was popular in the last quarter of the century, whilst Christmas pudding began to dominate English tables towards the nineties, and both Lamb and Byron were to testify to its excellences. Much about the same time green peas grew into favour, but probably they were restricted to the wealthy; at any rate in 1796 *The Times* has this sentence: 'The Bill for green Peas at Mrs. Mills' supper last night was £75.'

Hannah More's statement that 'the strawberries at my Lady Stormont's breakfast last saterday morning cost one hundred and fifty pounds', suggests that this fruit was both rare and expensive at the end of the century. Yet Byrom often makes reference to both them and raspberries, much earlier in the century; perhaps those he ate were wild ones.

Dr. Aiken has a reference to northern afternoon teas in middle-class society.

'About 1765 this respectable old lady could not bring her self to conform to the new fashioned beverage of coffee or tea; whenever therefor, she made her afternoon calls, her friends presented her with a tankard of ale and a pipe of tobacco. The other ladies would enjoy the usual afternoon's entertainment of wet and dry sweetmeats, different sorts of cakes and gingerbreads, apples or other fruits of the season and a variety of home-made wines. The manufacture of these wines was a great point with all good housewives both in the country and the town; they made an essential part of all feasts and were brought forth on all afternoon visits.'

The foregoing details would suggest that dietetics played no part in eighteenth-century dietary; even the wealthiest depended on meats for their energy and stamina, and completely ignored green foods and vegetable minerals. The quantity of food consumed seems to have been inordinate, and gives much colour to Carlyle's description of the century as 'one with soul extinct, but stomach well alive' and to the frequent passages in diaries where girls are described as hastening from girlish to buxom, from buxom to stout. The prospect of these eighteenth-century masses of food are all the stranger, when it is remembered that by the last decade, Brillat-Savarin had made eating and feeding a fine art in France, and that then England was very deeply influenced by French habits and customs. For not only were the quantity and quality of English feeding open to criticism, but their table manners were equally objectionable. Johnson is depicted as eating sixpenny-worth of meat and a pennyworth of bread in his Drury Lane ale-house, tearing the meat off with his teeth and grunting the while like a famished dog. Fielding is seen dining on tripe in an underground cookshop, and like other customers, wiping his greasy hands on the back of a Newfoundland dog kept there for that purpose. Rowlandson has dozens of cartoons showing eaters scrunching bones with their teeth and biting out the marrow. Hogarth's pictures, too, showed that they gnawed and sucked the bones of birds or beasts, and shovelled green peas into their mouths with their knives, as the two-pronged fork was inadequate to the occasion. His *Modern Midnight Conversation* illustrates with painful realism the attitude, behaviour and expression of a gourmand before dinner, at dinner, after dinner.

XI

Other habits of the eighteenth-century superior social section also left their mark on the nation's life.

Throughout the period coffee-houses played an important part in the social, professional and business life of the times. Men of similar tastes, pursuits or political persuasions gradually flocked together in establishments near their haunts, and where the company would be congenial. In this way many a coffee-tavern became the parent of fashionable clubs or insurance offices. One of the outstanding examples is the tavern of a Mr. Lloyd which became the rendezvous of those interested in maritime matters. The proprietor, in order to satisfy such guests, made himself a reliable source of all shipping news, went so far as to produce a weekly paper furnishing such intelligence, and so gradually a coffee-shop developed into the famous Lloyd's.

Not all of them grew into west-end clubs or business institutions. Many of them sold pills, syrups, powders, quack medicines and were visited daily by doctors, who called at them at specified times to interview patients, and a late-century broadsheet says of such coffee-taverns:

> Of all some, and all conditions,
> Even Vintners, Surgeons and Physicians,
> The blind, the Deaf and Aged Cripple,
> Do here resort and coffee tipple.

Perhaps some of them were mere drinking shops. A writer in 1715 'reckons the number of these here nuisances is quite 2,000'. Perhaps this adverse critic displayed more mathematical imagination than sound arithmetic in his calculation, for an 'estimate' taken in London in 1751 gives the number of 'coffee-taverns' as 551, 'together with 447 other taverns, 600 ale-houses and 200 inns'. Probably there was but little difference between coffee-taverns, mug-houses, inns, &c., in 1751. At nearly all these places, the floor space was divided into boxes, which were big, straight-backed, mahogany compartments not unlike family pews in the older churches, with facing seats and long tables running down the middle of the box. Most of them provided their customers with clay churchwarden pipes, and either sold tobacco at a low price or gave it away because of the excessive smuggling, and all of them, like most homes and clubs, had elaborately-decorated lacquer boxes filled with snuff for the use of their guests.

Gradually many of these 'boxes' in the coffee-taverns became the meeting-places of special guests, and in time the small fellowship there became the germ of a club; which, from time immemorial, has, according to Addison, been 'a natural and necessary offshoot of man's gregarious and social nature'. The nexus of these eighteenth-century clubs was a love of good eating, good drinking and good fellowship. One famous one was the 'Antient Society of Cogers', consisting of citizens of London

'who met to watch the course of events and the conduct of their Representatives in Parliament'.

Actually it was mainly a debating society and had the glory of such presidents as Johnson, Goldsmith and Wilkes. Its name was derived from *cogito, ergo sum*; but its members were quickly nicknamed 'old codgers'. The club movement spread to the provinces. Liverpool had its 'Unanimous' club in 1754; a club so-called because its members were 'unanimous in the belief that good fare, good fun, good wine, good talk promoted good fellowship'. Birmingham has its 'Lunar' club from 1766 and boasted such members as Matthew Boulton, Erasmus Darwin, John Baskerville, William Small. They met for heavy dinners and subsequent convivial entertainment, every Monday nearest the full moon, 'in order to have the benefit of its light when returning home'. Despite its roll of eminent members, the general public quickly nicknamed them the 'looneys'. Manchester by 1770 'had assumed the style and

H

manners of one of the commercial capitals on Europe' and it
started a club for its business men. In this venture northern
caution shackled northern audacity, for 'the club only met in the
evenings, and expences were limited to fourpence for ale and a
half-penny for tobacco per person'. Moreover, it was closed
promptly at 8.0. The new habit of cutting the hair close led men
in 1795 to form the 'crop-club', to which membership was
restricted for those 'docked' in hair.

Secret societies also developed greatly during this century
among the wealthy. The 'Rosicrucians' with their ever-burning
lamp, the elixir of life, the philosopher's stone, the enigma of
alchemy formed a numerous company. Although the first Grand
Lodge of Freemasons was probably instituted only in 1717, there
are evidences that the craft flourished much earlier in England,
and some authorities assert that Inigo Jones and Christopher Wren
were masonic brethren, whilst others adduce evidence from the
plays, sonnets and poems of Shakespeare that it was flourishing in
England in still earlier times. Certainly this company of people,
with its claim of respectable ancestry and remote antiquity,
developed considerably during the eighteenth century, and lodges
of that era refer to the initiation of such noblemen as the Earl of
Bedford, Gresham, Wharton, &c., who very certainly could not
have been made masons for any operative purposes. 'Orange'
Societies also flourished towards the end of the century, and these,
too, seem to have been a vast secret organization with signs and
passwords, a mysterious ritual, significant symbols and dress. All
these and many other societies were thought by many later
eighteenth-century parliamentarians to have been engaged in
definite conspiracies against the state religion or the social order.
In 1799 an Act directed against seditious societies was passed and
this Act made an exception in favour of masonic lodges, and so
dispelled a stupid slander.

XII

Gambling appears to have been one of the curses that afflicted
well-to-do England in many centuries, although perhaps never
more so than in the eighteenth. Legislation had been framed
against it as far back as Henry VII and again under Charles II,
whilst in the reign of George II it was enacted 'that if any man be
convicted upon information of winning or losing at play or by

betting at any time £10 or £20 within twenty-four hours, he should be fined five times the sum for the benefit of the poor in the parish'. If the Act had only been enforced, the poor of the parish would have been extraordinarily well off in London.

Eighteenth-century aristocracy accepted a tradition of imperturbable recklessness in all forms of gambling. Parliament was filled with gamblers. Before he was twenty-four years old, Fox owed the Jews £100,000 lost at cards and dice. According to Gibbon 'Fox prepared himself for that Holy War (repeal of the Test Act), by passing the previous twenty-two hours in the pious exercise of hazard; his devotion costing him only about £500 an hour; in all £11,000'. Sherwin, the great engraver of the age, who was reputed to make £12,000 a year, was another reckless gambler and in constant pecuniary difficulties. Goldsmith was rarely out of debt for the same reason. The Duke of York played whist nightly from 11.0 to 4.0 for £5 points and £25 on the rubber. The Duke of Norfolk in one evening lost the sum of £70,000 in a gaming-house on the right side of St. James's Street. At Almack's gaming club, the stakes were limited to £50, but often there were so many players that frequently there was as much as £10,000 on the table at a time; the tables at other clubs like White's and Boodle's told the same story. General Scott, connected with the highest aristocracy and father-in-law of a nineteenth-century prime minister, boasted that 'he had won honestly no less than £200,000 at White's'. But whist, piquet, faro (i.e. poker) and dicing were not restricted to clubs, they were played at the subscription libraries, taverns, &c. 'Society was one vast casino; wherever half a dozen met, whether for music or dancing, for politics or drinking the waters, the box was sure to be rattled, and the cards cut and shuffled', asserts Trevelyan. Contemporary thinkers had grown alarmed at its evils. Blake with imaginative significance had already written:

> The winner's shout, the loser's curse
> Shall go before dead England's hearse.

In 1798 *The Times* is affirming that 'Gaming, that hydra of calamities, has again made its appearance with its black catalogue of horrors'. About the same time Rowlandson's cartoons and Gillray's *Modern Hospitality* are making one see the very faces of these eighteenth-century roués.

As widespread and insensate as the eighteenth-century gambling craze was the speculation mania of that period. Even the magnates with inordinate rent-rolls, indulged freely, whilst at the same time professing an invincible detestation for all forms of trade. Under Lord North, smuggling was capitalized by rank and wealth in London and profitably employed 40,000 adventurous spirits. In 1720 these 'stockbroking sybarites', as they were contemptuously termed, underwent the South Sea speculation mania, went iron mad in 1765, steam-mill mad about 1780 and canal-mad about 1790. Eighteenth-century history of speculation is both fascinating and amazing, although the earlier periods are most marked by the wild-cat schemes. Among floated enterprises were those for trading in hair, for the universal supply of funerals to all parts, for breeding milk-bearing asses, for a wheel for perpetual motion, for the transmutation of lead into silver and gold. Any project sufficiently preposterous could win a hearing, and propositions 'calculated to enrich the investor at a rate of at least 1,153 per centum per annum' were over-subscribed. They took shares in companies formed to extract gold from sea-water, in expeditions to discover the lost kingdom of Prester John and even 'for carrying on an undertaking of great advantage, but nobody to know what it is'. These madcap schemes for getting rich quick were most popular and the hundred pound shares in the South Sea Company often stood at £2,000. At least one speculator put his winnings to good ends. Guy had £45,000 of the original stock of the South Sea Company, which he sold at great profit and with which he founded his famous hospital. This rage for getting rich at a stroke and without trouble infested all countries, and France then had her nefarious Mississippi scheme which was another South Sea Bubble. The popular tavern for this stock-broking business was Garraway's in Change Alley, to which Swift alludes in:

> There is a gulf where thousands fell,
> Here all the adventurers came,
> A narrow sound, though deep as hell,
> Change Alley is the dreadful name.

> Subscribers here by thousands float,
> And jostle one another down,
> Each paddling in his leaky boat,
> And here they fish for gold—and drown.

> Now buried in the depths below,
> Now mounted up to heaven again,
> They reel and stagger to and fro,
> At their wits' end like drunken men.

Meantime, secure on Gar'way's cliffs,
    A savage race, by shipwrecks fed,
Lie waiting for the founder's skiffs,
    And strip the bodies of the dead.

More popular than Swift's poem was the later eighty-lined lampoon 'South Sea Ballad' that was bawled out day and night, and which helped to bring stock-broking into still greater disrepute.

Although this mid-century saw Pelham consolidate the then fourteen national loans into four, henceforward to be known as 'consols', most of its political financiers preferred raising sums by State lotteries, which were started in 1709 and lasted till 1824. The prizes were usually in the form of terminable or perpetual annuities. Tickets issued at the nominal price of £10 were sold at about £14 or £15 to contractors who re-sold in much smaller units. These lotteries were widely advertised by the contractors, and one alone is said to have spent £36,000 a year on them. The lotteries varied in bait almost annually, but perhaps the following is indicative of their nature. Holders of 'blanks' were entitled to annuities of 14/– a year for thirty-two years and holders of 'winners' to annuities varying from £5 to £1,000 for the same period. They were most popular and it is estimated that governments made well over £300,000 annually out of them. Usually these lotteries were designed to raise loans for particular purposes such as the improvement of London, the construction of Westminster Bridge, purchase of art galleries, &c. They had a demoralizing effect on the people, and especially the 'private' lotteries popularly called 'little-goes' held in most assemblies; no wonder that some eighteenth-century financiers likened their action to mere debasement of money.

CHAPTER V

WORK AND WORKERS

I

COWPER's lines written in the century's closing quarter summarize the general condition of the poor:

> The poor inur'd to drudgery and distress,
> Act without aim, think little and feel less;

and he found occasion to describe some as:

> Sworn foes to sense and law.

Some years later Elliott asks the Lord:

> When wilt Thou save the people. . . .
> From vice, oppression and despair.

Their conditions of life were well calculated to produce such regrettable conditions, and to necessitate such prayers.

Their homes defied every law of sanitation. Cottage homes consisted of one living-room and one bedroom, and it was only towards the end of the century, that reformers were content to urge the provision of another bedroom to separate the children from the parents. The living-room ceiling was very low and supported by rough heavy beams, all the walls were of immense thickness and the whole fabric was made of stone, slate or timber filled in with straw-mixed clay. If the house was built of red, grey or yellow brick, it would cost about twenty-five per cent more than if of stone, since bricks were subject to taxation. Usually the roofs were thatched. Windows were set deep in the gables and walls and so deeply embrasured were these small apertures, that interiors were mere caverns of gloom. Where glass served, it was of a deep green colour and of an extraordinary thickness; but glass was rarely used in the homes of the very poor throughout the century. Before Wesley was born the first window tax had been imposed; it was made more stringent in 1748 and increased in cost in 1788 when Pitt had to compensate the revenue for a reduced tea duty. Consequently most cottage windows were made of horn or oiled paper. Many of the floors were of earth or roughly tiled with stone, crude cement, slate, and now and then with brick.

Such floors were always a little lower than the threshold, so that they might be strewn with rushes, &c. Chimneys were very wide; hearths were of stone, slate or brick so that logs rather than coal might be used for firing; the wide chimney also served to smoke bacon. Round the fireplace was often built a chimney-corner—a cosy stone or brick seat whose high back protected the occupants from draughts. When Parliament imposed the chimney tax, many a householder evaded payment by demolishing the outside stack, and covering the aperture with bars of iron or a large perforated stone. The upstair room was approached sometimes from the inside by a ladder or spiral stairway or from the outside by stone steps fixed into the wall and without protecting rail. This room had a sloping roof, was very low and its floor was often made of a curious crude cement, very rough to the feet; scarcely any bed-room was ever underdrawn. The rough inside walls were prim-arily coloured with wash—a nondescript blue-grey or a yellow ochre—and upon this surface the continual runnings of damp wrought strange devices. For artificial lighting they depended on rushes, home-made candles, or very inferior lamps in which they burnt the intestines of animals soaked in pilchard oil, &c. The open hearth was used for cooking meat which either turned on a spit before the fire or hung from a roasting jack above it. Some cottages and most farmhouses would own their own stone or brick oven, and where the owners were energetic, they might even have their 'ice-house' as a keeping place.

Other rural habitations like farmhouses were little more than glorified cottages with dim connecting passages, low rooms raftered with thick beams, inter-communicating sleeping places and windowless lumber-rooms where fruit was stored. Despite the fact that whole, and sometimes very large families lived in two-roomed cottages, and that the lighting and ventilation and sanita-tion were all wretched, such conditions seem to have satisfied the eighteenth-century rural standards and demands. Most people were undisturbed with homes that were redolent of cooking and stale food, buzzing with flies, swarming with vermin and not infrequently invaded by pigs and poultry. Where the occupants were a less shiftless crew, writers like Hannah More or literary wives of local squires, would have occasion to compliment them on 'their walls creamy with whitewash, the tables scrubbed spot-less, the ranked pans gleaming like copper moons, and on their china dogs with gilt collars and ladies and gentlemen on prancing horses, hawks perched a-wrist'. As for other furniture, practically every cottage home had an old oak cupboard in the angle of the chimney-piece, a round oak table standing firm on three shanks, an oak chest, a spinning-wheel, a copper warming-pan, and a grandfather clock. This last was their pride and would have a bright brass face engraved with the signs of the zodiac and bearing such cautionary words as:

> I mark yᵉ houres but cannot stay their race;
> Nor priest, nor king may buy a moment's grace.
> Prepare to meet thy Maker face to face.

Even in towns, the homes for the poor were usually detached constructions; it was not till after Wesley's death and when the industrial revolution was in full swing, that back-to-back house building started. And yet it is of London at the close of the century that Wordsworth is speaking, when he writes about 'Private courts, gloomy as coffins'.

II

Although the conditions under which the peasant population lived now seem barbarous, the people do not seem to have been unhappy for the greater part of the century. They could fill their stomachs, and if they were sufficiently industrious, they could be covered with clothing. The Eden report of 1795 suggests that workers in towns almost always bought their clothes usually at third or fourth hand. Shops dealing in such garments had been in existence for the bigger part of the century; at any rate the term 'slop-shop' for such emporiums was used from 1723 onwards. In the country districts, and particularly in the north of England and in Scotland, the country poor retained their old habit of spinning, &c., till the end of the century. Even if they did not grow their own wool and flax for clothing, they still had the habit of buying raw materials, of spinning them into yarn and of sending it to the dyers and weavers to be made into cloth. This Eden report goes into eighteenth-century clothing details:

'The usual price of a hat that is worn by labourers is 2/6; a coat purchased costs about 10/– at 2/6 a yard; a waistcoat takes another yard and half; a pair of leather breeches costs 3/6, but these men often wear breeches of flannel or coloured cotton. A tailor charges 3/– for making a whole suit. A linen shirt takes 3¼ yards at 17 pence a yard; this is strong and wears well. About 11 ounces of wool at 8d a pound will make a pair of stockings and these are almost invariably knit at home.'

'. . . A pair of shoes could then be bought in a shop for 3/9; but most of the poor wore clogs or pieces of rope wound round their feet as late as 1779', states another authority, who also adds 'though boots were coming into fashion, their use was restricted to the wealthy.' Eden continues with 'A black stuff hat for a woman costs about 1/8; a linen bed-gown about 5/6, two petticoats of flannel are about 11/6, and a linen shift made at home 3/–. Their stays or bodices are of different prices, but a pair that will last six years costs 6/–.' A coloured necker-chief can be got for 1/– and the cheapest kind of cloak, guaranteed to last four years, is 4/6.'

They always appear to have made poor attempts at a little Sunday bravery in inherited garments irrespective of fit. These bore pathetic testimony to the poverty of these folk and to their simple desire to mark the difference between one day of the seven and the other six. At their weddings their clothing was rather more colourful. At 'Wakes Time', the old-fashioned kitchen in the inn would be filled with brides in beribboned bonnets and quaintly designed paisley shawls, sitting next to grooms in flowered singlets and drab knee-breeches made of a coarse sort of drugget. They had gone there after the communal wedding ceremony, to quaff the 'bridal' ale; a custom that was held to bring good luck to the pairs; for in the eighteenth century no good wishes could possible follow a 'dry' wedding.

In the country and on the fringes of the towns, a suitable house for the poor could be rented at about £2 a year; rates were negligible though taxation was somewhat high; small ale could be made at something like 6d. a gallon even when the home-maker bought the ingredients, whilst the smuggled rum, gin, wine, &c., were little dearer. Tea had dropped in price from 30/– a pound in 1700 to 16/– in 1780; bacon then was about 5d. a pound, butter much the same, cheese 3d., and meat ranged from 2d. to 5d. Round about 1780 prices rose quickly and steeply and soon the commodities were costing two or three times as much; in the closing years of the century, Eden and Hannah More assert that country labourers were living almost entirely on rye or barley bread and potatoes, on brewed tea instead of beer, on whey and water instead of milk. 'Tim Bobbin' was a clergyman's son, yet up to the time he was fourteen years old 'he had to be content with water-pottage, buttermilk and jannock'. Eden gives particular instances of the dietary of different persons about Wesley's death, and states that 'some never bought any meat except a small piece of beef against Christmas . . that clap-bread which is made of oatmeal and water rolled into thin cakes and baked on a stone over the fire, was the chief article of their support'. And Hannah More, in *Shepherd of Salisbury Plain*, recounts how this man with wife and eight children lived on his wages of a shilling a day. The principal meal was in the evening when 'there stood on the table a large dish of potatoes, a brown pitcher and a small piece of coarse loaf'. She and other writers happily found occasions when the poor fed really well, such as 'harvest time', when it was the pleasant practice of the farmers to invite the poor, infirm and aged to join at this celebration, and at which they consumed every species of vegetables which the farm produced, as well as beef, mutton, pork and boiled puddings, apple pies, &c., and drank incredible amounts of 'harvest' ale.

III

In Wesley's youth, farming in England was of the rudest kind, for agriculture had developed but little since the days of Henry VIII. Books written in that reign show that the English knew something of salads, carrots and other edible roots, whilst the Commonwealth books indicate that farmers cultivated hops, clover, barley, potatoes and knew a little about ploughing and manuring. But at the beginning of the eighteenth century ploughs were still made of wood like those used a thousand years before, and for the most part potatoes were rarely sold in greater quantities than the pound. Wheeled vehicles of any kind, wheelbarrows and carts were rarities, and a parish possessing two carts was considered well provided for. Vast parts of the country were still waterlogged. Despite the earlier work of Vermuyden, Thomas and Lovell, most of the Fenland was once again a howling wilderness of reeds producing mainly osiers, some down and a little hemp, and these watery and marshy swamps still called for stilts when traversed by pedestrians. Not only had actual farming and land-reclamation deteriorated, but the early seventeenth-century privileges arising from 'open' or 'unenclosed' land had been invaded. Fifty years before Wesley's birth, the live stock of a district grazed together, arable land was occupied as common-field or run-rig, rye and oats furnished the food of the great body of the people who, in addition to their coarse bread, had three regular things to drink: water, milk or home-made beer and cider. In 1700 the field labourer only got some 5/– a week from an employer; but in addition to these wages many a one had a cow or pig wandering on the common pasture, raised a little crop on a strip of the common-field and took his wood, furze or peat for firing from the waste. Sugar was too dear for him to buy; but honey was plentiful and if necessary could be bought at 2/- a gallon. Then he had not acquired a taste for white bread; only the rich could afford such a delicacy, and even employing farmers depended on the flour from their own rye roughly ground by their own windmill. Meat was very cheap for him especially in the winter; at that time the farmers knew nothing of turnips or oil-cake, and as they had not learned how to keep their cattle in winter, they were obliged to kill almost all their live stock in November, and from then till next summer every one had to eat salt meat. From 1715 to 1765 there was a sequence of abundant harvests and the land workers—who numbered almost half the entire population—had a fairly comfortable life. By 1765 potatoes were grown in fields and not in gardens and sold by the ton and not the pound; corn, too, was extensively grown and was still being exported; wool continued to be exported and sheep enriched the landowners. In 1765 it was thought that the average farmer was making twice as much profit as the new class of rising manu-facturer. A preserved market account round about 1760 shows that he was getting £6 for a bullock, 12/- for a sheep, £1 for a pig, 3/6 for a turkey, 9d. for a duck or hen, 7d. for a rabbit and 2d. for a pigeon. And wheat had risen from the earlier 2/9 a bushel to about 5/-. His expenses had not grown in proportion. Seven shillings a week was considered sufficient for a worker with a family of five; women workers got 9d. a day; girls 4d. to 6d.; boys from 2d. to 8d. Despite this apparent prosperity the farmers seem to have been dissatisfied, and Wesley had occasion to comment 'that farmers are seldom satisfied either with God or man'.

The farm labourers were certainly growing restive, especially those who lived in. Their wages were 3/- a week and 'eatage'. This was a relative term, for the men and women did not get all the courses, and they had to leave the table when the pudding came on and go without it. Even the cottagers were becoming increasingly dissatisfied, as their 'common' rights were being steadily invaded by the farmers, and by then some 200 Acts of Parliament had deprived them of 300,000 acres of common-fields and waste land; or in other words, many a farm-labourer had by then lost the possibility of keeping a cow or pig, or growing cereals

for himself and of getting free firing. Even an easy-going man like
Goldsmith saw danger in this penetration into peasant-rights
arising from these multiplying Acts, and much about this time he
wrote:

> Ill fares the land, to hastening ills a prey,
> Where wealth accumulates and men decay;
> Princes and lords may flourish, or may fade:
> A breath can make them, as a breath has made;
> But a bold peasantry, their country's pride,
> When once destroyed, can never be supplied.

Despite this protest, farmers and landlords steadily pursued their
encroachments on waste and common lands; during the next forty
years or so, they presented 2,000 more Acts of enclosures to com-
plaisant parliaments and thereby secured almost three million
additional acres. Nor did the pilfering stop in 1800 but continued
well into the reign of Queen Victoria, by which time it is thought,
that altogether some 4,000 'Enclosure' Acts had secured for the
wealthy between six and seven million acres. Later writers joined
in the protest initiated by Goldsmith. Arthur Young says:

'A man will love his country the better for a pig. . . . For whom shall
he now save? For the Parish? . . . If I am diligent shall I have leave
to build a cottage? If I am sober, shall I have land for a cow? If I am
frugal, shall I have an acre of potatoes? . . . You offer no motives; you
have but a parish-officer and a workhouse. . . . Bring me therefore
another pot.'

More's *Mendip Annals* and Crabbe's *Village* and *Parish Register*,
whilst offering no protest against the Enclosure Acts and system,
recount in detail the abject poverty, dissipation, depravity and
dishonesty among the rural poor at the end of the century, and
they, like Arthur Young, wrote from personal experience of
country life and manners. This degradation of the peasantry and
the marked rural distress which set in about 1780 was invariably
attributed to Enclosure Acts by the poor. From that date onwards
the increased cost of living meant that hundreds of the rural poor
were subsisting on barley bread or potatoes, with brewed tea
instead of beer and water in place of milk. Fuel was then so dear
that many peasants were unable to afford to cook a meal or bake
bread, but had to take them to the village bakery; meat they never
ate except on Sundays and rarely then. Not only had they been
deprived of their old free firing, the possibility of growing their

own corn and feeding their own cattle and poultry by these Enclosure Acts, but the numerous 'Game Acts' now being passed pressed them severely; for henceforward they poached at the peril of their lives. Acts for preserving game increased almost annually in number and severity under George III, and the death-sentence was a possible penalty for stealing a hare. There was in consequence an increasing amount of malnutrition among the rural workers, and towards the century's end, they and other workers were often on the verge of starvation. Pauperism grew enormously and quite 28 per cent of the total population was in receipt of parish relief. By 1795, when the 'bread-strikes' broke out, the cost of the quartern loaf had risen from 3*d*. to over a shilling; many families were living on bran instead of flour, whilst nettles and raw turnips were in great request. Foodstuffs had doubled or trebled in cost; inferior bacon, cheese and meat was costing 10*d*., 6*d*. and 5*d*. a pound. Wages had scarcely moved upwards, whilst all the old 'perquisities' and means of self-help had disappeared. It is no wonder that an historian like Thorold Rogers declared that 'the lot of the agricultural workers in the days of the Plantagenets was one of far more hope and plenty than it was under the Hanoverians and that wages were, relative to purchasing power, far higher'. The peasants' sense of grievance found expression in the popular rhyme:

> The Law doth Punish Man or Woman,
> That steals the goose from off the Common,
> But lets the greater Villain loose,
> That steals the common from off the Goose.

The employing farmers, too, deteriorated in character and had grounds of complaint. In many an instance, the Enclosure Acts had led farmers to ape the squirearchy in their ways of living and so pose as 'gentleman farmers'. The roads affected the condition and price of the cattle driven over them. After the agricultural revolution, when Norfolk farmers sent their fat cattle to London markets, the journey took fourteen days and the animals lost in value to the extent of £3 a piece, to say nothing of the loss arising from fodder, drovers' wages, &c. Then their troubles were increased by a succession of bad harvests, and the farmers maintained that they could not afford to pay the high and increasing rents demanded by landowners and at the same time to raise their labourers' wages.

Parliament met the impasse in characteristic eighteenth-century fashion. It voted two million pounds to meet the agricultural depression, ostensibly to help the farmers to recoup themselves for their dwindling profits; actually, of course, most of it went to the landowners, who because of these grants, would brook no shrinkage in their rents. It stressed the wisdom of employing still more children on the land, and contractors with gangs of small children and juveniles drawn from the workhouses, toured the countryside with the unfortunates, who, of course, were housed anyway, without the slightest regard to ordinary decencies, and who aggravated still further the local unemployment problem. It allowed farming to be subsidized by supplementing inadequate wages with parish-relief, and it is asserted that between 1750 and 1800 'the cost of feeding this ever-increasing multitude of idle or destitute poor, rose fourfold throughout the land'. In some districts in Sussex, rates rose from 5/– in the £ in 1750 to 34/– in 1800, whilst some areas had poor rates as high as 52/– in the £. Rural workers were pauperized on a wholesale scale, and one parish in Hampshire was said to have 104 paupers out of a population of 139 .

This was the common view of the effects of the Enclosure Acts on the eighteenth-century agricultural problem. Another popular contemporary fallacy was that of regarding the enclosure movement as peculiar to the century. Actually it had made headway during the seventeenth century and by Wesley's day all trace of common-field farming had already disappeared in some parts of the country, whilst in others partial progress had been made. And though there was a sad side to the enclosure movement, there was unquestionably a bright side to the picture.

However Utopian had been rural life with its common rights for planting, grazing and fuel gathering, in actual practice it had encouraged idleness and had led to endless quarrels and to other very bad moral results. It had been inimical to any agricultural progress. When and where the enclosures had been effected, the bigger agriculturists introduced very much better farming methods, demanded better ploughs, threshing machines and other farming implements, sought for better manuring systems to make the soil more productive and discovered that more rational methods of cropping increased the yield. Enclosures led men to reclaim land from fens and moors, and it is estimated that during the century 10,000 square miles of untilled land were added to cultivation; the century saw the Duke of Bedford and his company of 'Gentleman-Adventurers' re-drain the Fens and saw the

Knights, father and son, bring into productivity 20,000 acres of the waste which was Exmoor.

'From the reclaimers, the farming story passes on to those who in this century developed agricultural machinery like Tull, to Coke and Bakewell who by better breeding and feeding improved the weight and health of cattle and sheep. . . . In turn these opened the way for the later pioneers of agricultural science like Davy, Liebig and Gilbert and finally to Mendel who reduced plant-breeding to a science.'

All these actual and potential improvements listed by McCarthy would have been impossible so long as herds and flocks ranged together on common pastures. The century saw the weight of cattle and sheep trebled and quadrupled; it saw satisfied the wealthy's demand for better and more stylish racehorses, hunters, harness-horses, cobs and bulls for the ring. Its close saw animals sold not by mere number, but according to quality and breed. By then its farmers were no longer satisfied with mere bigness as the only criterion of excellence, as they were in 1750 when the widely-advertised 'Lincolnshire Ox' was the standard of unapproachable excellence and which was thus vaunted;

'He is ninteen Hands High and Four Yeards long from his Face to his Rump. The like Beast for Bigness was never seen in the World before.'

Likewise the century saw Lord Townshend introduce the swede-turnip, which together with oil-cake preserved the life, improved the quality of most beasts and certainly made milk possible for a much greater number of people in the winter months. In fields and gardens it saw grown lettuces, lentils, spinach, leeks, radishes, onions and even cucumbers. The geographical range of this agricultural revolution was equally impressive. According to Macaulay, 'it seems highly probable that a fourth part of England had been, in the course of a little more than a century, turned from a wild into a garden'.

IV

As for other forms of work in the century, it is evident that even in the first decades, there was some geographical trade-specialization. From the earliest period of history, the manufacture of cutlery had been peculiarly associated with Sheffield. Colchester in 1700 was famous for its needles; Ashburnham then produced nails; guns for the navy were made in Sussex. The great seat of the woollen industry was in Kent and Norfolk, and the articles manufactured included baize, *crêpes*, serges, bombazines, &c. In the West superfine cloth was manufactured in Wiltshire, especially in Bradford; Devizes was known for its serges; Stroud was a centre of dyed-cloth manufacture, and Taunton had thousands of looms, even if these looms were little different from those used hundreds of years before.

Then came the spate of northern mechanical inventions ranging from Kay's flying shuttle of 1733, Hargreaves' spinning jenny of 1767, Crompton's 'mule' of 1779 and Arkwright's many improvements during the same period. Round about 1785 cylinder printing was invented; but the century's remarkable men never discovered that bleaching could be done by chemicals. So it was not till 1810 that Tennant discovered the possibilities of chlorine to that end, and found that in one week he could bleach what had taken sunlight six months.

Although the 'flying shuttle' enabled weavers to work ten times as fast as they had done previously, the new inventions did not at first upset the labour-market unduly. For the first 'jenny' depended on a handle turned by a boy, Arkwright's developments on a water-wheel, Crompton's 'mule' on a horse, and Cartwright's twenty looms were turned by a bull. All had, of course, diminished the need for men in the first place and in the doggerel of the times appeared:

> Come all you Mayster Coomers and hear o' our Big Ben,
> He'll comb more wool in a day than any fifty men.

But synchronously there had been other inventions which, together with the new machines, were to revolutionize industry. Round about 1760 Smeaton at Carron and Darby in Shropshire, discovered how to make iron profitably by using coal instead of charcoal, and when Cort's blast-furnace was still further reinvigorated in 1790, the ascendancy of coal over charcoal was assured. In 1769 Watt made his first steam-engine and by 1785, he and Boulton introduced steam-power into factories. Combined, the new inventions and power revealed the most amazing potencies and possibilities. They increased Yorkshire's woollen trade tenfold, and whereas cotton in 1760 employed about 50,000 people, in 1800 it needed over a million hands. In the same period the northern output of pig-iron was multiplied twentyfold. These new machines and this new power whether for cotton, wool, silk or linen imported astounding energy into every section of the

English textile world with remarkable increases in the volume of trade. They were prodigious in their potentialities, they were relentless and suffered from no human disabilities, and were prepared to work as long as a sufficient head of steam was maintained. From 1788 to 1803 was the golden age of the cotton manufacture which boomed as no industry before. Old barns, ramshackle buildings of every description were fitted up as loom shops and new cottages with a loom-room attached, sprang up in every direction in Lancashire. In 1700 it is estimated that England imported one million lbs. of cotton but in 1800 it was more than fifty-six times that amount.

Eighteenth-century parliaments never hesitated to impede the developments of any industry which was likely to be inimical to the interests of the landed classes. Throughout the century, cotton suffered from many a shackling restriction, and by 1800 the five million spindles that the industry employed, demanded so much raw material that the national revenue was getting £1,000 a day in excise duty from cotton alone. It was not till 1795 that the 'Woolcombers Act' permitted employers to carry on their trade in any town in Great Britain. Yet on the other hand, acting on the eighteenth-century tradition of no interference between employer and employee, Pitt let the industrial revolution go on its ugly way, and create a squalor unparalleled before in England and to be still more dreadful north of the Tweed. The new steam-driven machines gave the workers no leisure, and they could only employ their non-working hours in the sleep of exhaustion or in the oblivion of drunkenness. The conditions of work inside the new factories were deplorable; brutal masters whipped their workmen whilst their wives similarly drove the workwomen with blows. Work was carried on in very hot rooms; the air was full of dust; men, women and children were on their feet fourteen or more hours a day. During the factory hours the doors were locked except for two intervals of half an hour for dinner and tea; a worker was fined 1/– if he was caught washing, whistling or opening a window; nor was he allowed a drink of water until meal-times. Unbridled competition was allowed among the small employers which, in time, meant very low wages, and late records show 'the man was left with 2/6 a week for meat, drink and clothing'. Strikes designed to correct such conditions, were ruthlessly put down by parliaments, and when the workmen returned to their labours, their masters were allowed to deduct

I

ten per cent. a week from their wages until they had recouped themselves for their losses during the men's strike, whilst victimization of the ring-leaders was regarded as sound common sense. Employer-tokens, 'tommy-shop' tickets, living in the factory-owned houses, payment of wages at factory-owned inns and similar devices were not forbidden by parliaments, and yet all these abuses helped to engender bad feeling and invalidate any wage-calculations. Poverty of the most distressing sort, with sometimes the near prospect of jail, embittered the lives of the diligent poor.

Because of the declared inability to pay higher wages to men and women in these factories, still greater reliance was placed on child-labour, and in 1796, Parliament under Pitt's guidance, thought the problem would be solved if still more children aged four or five were employed in industry. Hapless youngsters were carried in wagons or canal-boats to the mills; men made a profitable trade of collecting superfluous children and 'apprenticing' them to employers. These 'apprenticed' children were controlled by the parish, and it was estimated that about 1797 Lancashire alone had some 30,000 of them in the mills. Manufacturers contracted with masters of the workhouses to send them all their young children, and lots of men toured the countryside with gangs of infants 'skilled and unskilled'. Actually a gang of such children was put up for sale among a bankrupt's effects and publicly advertised as part of the property. Robert Owen, in his evidence before a Royal Commission in the early nineteenth century said 'that overlookers were paid according to the work they could extract from the employees', that 'many of these were adepts with a strap or "billyroller"; that their sole duty was to see that the luckless infants were kept awake'. Other evidence shows that even during the period 1804–19, the friendless innocents were starved to the bone, flogged to their work, sometimes driven to suicide. Usually they worked fourteen hours a day and much of the work had to be done by candle- or oil-light; day and night shifts were worked so that the machines should never stop. One witness said: 'In the dim light they seemed a host of hobgoblins; gaunt-faced, hunch-backed, splay-footed with thin arms and bow-legs . . . when their apprenticeship expired they were admirably trained for swelling the mass of vice and misery in the town.' Even in the famous 'model' factory for apprentices near Manchester, in a place famed for its tolerant attitude and benevolent oversight, the children were worked seventy-four hours a week. Nor was it till 1802 that an Act fixed limits to children's labour in textile factories; but this Act brought no relief to the children who were not 'apprenticed', or to those employed in mines, potteries, agriculture, brick and tile works. The same Act called for better working conditions, as the spread of epidemic disease had decimated the youthful labouring population. From 1802 factory walls had to be whitewashed, some opening windows provided, apprentices must have two suits of clothing and working hours must not exceed seventy-two a week. But the Act did not protect the children who were living with their parents; whilst many an employer nullified its beneficence by calling his factory a 'lace-school', and according to evidence given at Royal Commissions, in these 'women and children, often only three years old were pushed into a cottage-room to work fifteen hours or more a day, and where the smell was unbearable'.

Perhaps more spectacular evidence than that given before Royal Commissions or disclosed by the Acts of Parliament, is that afforded in a series of pictures by Robert Cruikshank and called *English Factory Slaves*.

v

More familiar to ordinary readers is the story of the youthful chimney-sweepers in the eighteenth century. No other European country ever allowed the system which England did not begin even to challenge till the nineteenth century. In those days parents got £4 a head when they 'apprenticed' their sons or daughters to chimney-sweeping at the age of four or five. Usually these children went up the chimneys naked, otherwise they could not have crawled through the narrow and occasionally horizontal flues. The master-sweep 'provided the apprentices with a leather cap with a brass number on it, promised not to hire him to another master-sweep, to see that he washed once a week and agreed to send him to the State Church on Sundays'. And some may have carried out their bond. Yet whilst this hand-sweeping was being carried on, inventors had produced satisfactory brushes for the chimney-sweep; but the brushes were unpopular and 'these were cruel days and human flesh was cheap'. More humane or frugal people sometimes used another form of living chimney-sweep. They got a fair-sized duck or goose and with a cord dragged the unlucky bird up and down the chimney-stack.

The mines too had their juvenile and female labour in the eighteenth century. In the pits boys and girls of five, sometimes worked eighteen to twenty hours without coming up to the surface. Before the introduction of steam into the mines, small boys, girls and women carried loads of coal up ladders from the bottom of the shafts to the surface, or dragged the tubs of coal along the workings to the foot of the shaft. It was not till 1842 that the law forbade the employment of women and children in mines. For such work children up to the age of nine got 5*d*. a day, whilst apparently their fathers proportionally fared little better. In 1792 there was a miners' strike in Somerset for wages of 12/- a week instead of the then 10/- and in this strike the men were beaten.

The same chorus is to be found in other eighteenth-century industries. Giving evidence before a commission early in the nineteenth century, a woman from a brick and tile factory said she made 2,000 tiles a day, the clay was brought to her by two little girls who had to climb with it out of a pit thirty feet deep and then carry it one hundred yards. The quantity of clay carried by the small juveniles in a day's work was ten tons; their day began at 5.0 a.m. and lasted till 8.0 p.m. In 1761, a Mr. Hutton describing his travels in England remarks: 'In some of these midland shops I observed many females, stripped of all their upper garments, wielding the hammer with all the grace of the sex.' Female chain-making long continued to be an abominable form of slavery with unending monotony, degrading conditions, continuous discomfort, unlimited hours and lamentable scale of payment. Gradually it and nail-making fell to the lot of children who had to make 1,000 nails a day, work at least twelve hours and got 5*d*. for their toil. And many an unscrupulous master robbed the workers of some of these pitiful fruits of their labour by false weighing and counting, whilst the prevailing practice of paying wages in a public-house—a practice lasting till well into the nineteenth century—reduced considerably the home-takings of weavers, spinners, miners, iron-workers, &c. When they got into debt, they were shut up in prison merely for inability to pay, and so were forced to associate with the worst of criminals.

Although wages did not increase very much till 1790, perhaps domestic service was one of the best occupations for eighteenth-century women and girls. At its beginning one hears from Pepys of 'a very tall maid applied for the post of cook-maid and asked £5; my wife offered her £3-10-0. Whether she will take it or not,

I know not till to-morrow; but I am a-feared she will be over-high for us'. Other diaries suggest that their wages were doubled in the last decade of the century and that by 1800 many were getting £12 a year. These diaries also suggest that servants were always anxious to get tips which they called 'vails'. Up to the end of the century it appears to have been customary for guests, even those in for dinner or tea, to dispense *pourboires* ranging from a shilling to a guinea. Again judging from diaries, maids seem to have been a constant source of worry to their mistresses, and there were the usual complaints about aping ladies' clothes, manners and speech. Letters to newspapers in the last quarter of the century also swell the chorus of complaint about servants and their exactments, their failure to be subservient, their actual rudeness and familiarity and their bad service in inns. Because well-trained servants were hard to get, many households then employed foreigners, especially negroes.

The conditions of service can be dimly imagined in these large houses which possessed no sort of modern sanitation and which were quite without any labour-saving devices. Apparently the maids had to start the household washing every Monday at 2.0 a.m.; they seem to have slept in the attics and to have worn no mark of uniform. The male servants slept in the cellars, and in the wealthier establishments they had elaborate and distinctive uniforms to distinguish chambermen from valets, footmen from stewards, &c. Probably the male servants fared better than the maids, especially if they did not object to being cuffed about the ears, &c., by their noble employers of both sexes.

VI

Throughout this century employers generally never seem to have grasped the fact that their employees had human needs, and never do factory owners seem to have faced the modern problem of making savings in cost of production without reducing the workers' wages. State and Church seem to have had no sad consciences at the thought of large numbers of men, women and children working hard for a remuneration which left them short of necessaries to say nothing of modest comforts. Paley argued 'that the poor deceived themselves in supposing that they were worse off than the rich'. Jeremy Bentham, who applied rigorous common sense to the facts of society and to public institutions, and who judged everything by one standard—'how far does this thing minister to the increase of human happiness for the greatest number?'—did little or nothing to ameliorate the workers' conditions of life. Henry George, the economist of the mid-nineteenth century, chided the Pope for counselling States to restrict the employment of women and children, and preached the gospel of unrestricted competition, urging that both were calculated to solve the problem of poverty. Like Bentham, politicians of the spirit of Fox, Burke, Sheridan and Romilly tried to soften the penal law, but they were largely unperturbed by conditions of employment. Wilberforce toiled for years for the negroes, but he consistently opposed the formation of trade unions intended to improve working conditions, and he appeared to see nothing wrong in children being broken on the wheels of factory discipline. Later, Cobden was to show himself so far ahead of his times as to proclaim himself an advocate for free education and against the employment of young children in cotton-mills; but he disliked organized demands for working hours and wages, and opposed bills regulating the hours of labour in factories. Most preachers of the day stressed the evil of idle hands, which was the devil's opportunity, and the 'busy bee' received quite unnecessary attention. Teachers of religion and political economy united to impress upon the toilers that work, though regarded in some moods as a punishment for sin and as Adam's curse, was a noble duty and worth doing for its own sake. The attitude of eighteenth- and early nineteenth-century politicians, philanthropists, teachers and preachers is only intelligible when Pattison's wise words are recalled: 'What is important for us to know of any age is not its peculiar opinions, but the complex elements of that moral feeling and character in which, as in their congenial soil, such opinions grow.'

Eighteenth-century writers like Goldsmith, Young, Fielding, Crabbe certainly recognized the conditions of the poor and described their sufferings photographically. Hannah More's political tracts, cast in the form of dialogues and jingles, simply urged the poor to be good and contented with their lot. She was quite ready to compliment them when they managed to be neat and clean. She taught in a Sunday school in a Mendip village where wages were a shilling a day, where 200 people lived in nineteen cottages. Yet it never seems to have occurred to her that such conditions were iniquitous; she only deplored the immorality of the inhabitants and 'rejoiced that the children knew tolerably well the first twenty chapters of Genesis'. Early nineteenth-century writers, when contemplating the simple-living people of the early eighteenth century, and contrasting them with the factory workers at the close, seem to have thought the price paid for luxurious benefits with sweated labour caused by the greedy, soul-destroying competition was scarcely justified by results. Thus Peacock says in *Headlong Hall*:

'Complicated machinery; behold its blessings. Twenty years ago, at the door of every cottage sate the good woman with her spinning wheel: the children, if not more profitably employed than in gathering heath and sticks, at least laid in a stock of health and strength to sustain the labours of maturer years. Where is the spinning wheel now, and every simple and insulated occupation of the industrious cottager? Wherever this boasted machinery is established, the children of the poor are death-doomed from their cradles. Look for one moment at midnight into a cotton mill, amidst the smell of oil, the smoke of lamps, the rattling of wheels, the dizzy and complicated motions of diabolical mechanism; contemplate the little human machines that keep play with the revolutions of iron work, robbed at that hour of their natural rest, as of air and exercise by day; observe their pale and ghastly features, more ghastly in that baleful and malignant light, and tell me if you do not fancy yourself on the threshold of Virgil's hell.'

To Peacock, at any rate, this eighteenth-century progress of civilization through the agency of machinery, had little apparent meaning, and provided inadequate compensations for its difficulties and bewilderments. He concludes his attack with:

'You must at least assent to the following positions: that the many are sacrificed to the few; that ninety-nine in a hundred are occupied in a perpetual struggle for the preservation of a perilous and precarious existence, whilst the remaining one wallows in all the redundancies of luxury that can be wrung from their labours and privations; and that every new want you invent for civilized man, is a new instrument of torture for him who cannot indulge it.'

This is forceful language and the message is thoughtful, moving and burningly sincere; it should have shocked Peacock's contemporaries into a realization of prevailing factory conditions, and made them realize that it was society's duty to end such infamy. But to many early readers, *Headlong Hall* was a mere parade of verbal pyrotechnics. So it was left for still later nineteenth-century propaganda-novelists to help to awake the public conscience to a knowledge of inherited eighteenth-century evils, and publicly to demand that they should be removed. Disraeli's *Sybil* with its poigant picture of child-slavery in mines was the forerunner of more humane factory employment. Dickens' trenchant pen, acute sense of character and clear-eyed understanding, came to grips with such remaining eighteenth-century abuses as the poor-law administration, the nursing profession, slum property, debt prisons, inefficient schools in *Oliver Twist, Martin Chuzzlewit, Bleak House, Pickwick Papers* and *Nicholas Nickleby*. In *Hard Cash*, Reade gave an atmosphere of reality to the continued eighteenth-century abuses in asylums, and he attempted to reform lingering abuses in prison discipline in his *It's Never Too Late to Mend*. It was left for Mrs. Gaskell to deal with the strange giant forces at work in the new industrialism. These writers were much more active social forces than had been any of those writing in the eighteenth century, and 'never was literary art more earnest and effective in stirring the heart to wise and urgent public ends . . . their concrete pictures kindled a new feeling for our unfortunate fellows, new knowledge of them and their ways, and new anger against the gross and stupid wrongs, social and legal, from which they suffered'. Most of these cruel mischiefs had been inherited from the eighteenth century, but the writers of that epoch, whilst photographing the conditions fairly accurately, did not attack them with real responsibility, sincerity, independence and power.

VII

Perhaps this eighteenth-century blindness to the sufferings of the poor shown by most of the leaders of politics, Church, literature, as well as by employers, arose from the fact that the leaders and the wealthy had the slave-complex. Right up to the American War, England had 200 ships engaged exclusively in the trade; these ships sailed mainly from London, Liverpool and Bristol and could carry 50,000. It was not till 1788—and after the super-human efforts of Thomas Clarkson—that a Mr. Dolbin got through the Commons some slight relief for these slaves, by a Bill limiting the number carried by a slaver to its tonnage. But so callous were the parliamentarians and people generally, in those days, that even the slight Clarkson relief was only secured by the advocacy of Pitt, who threatened to resign if the Bill were not accepted. And the Bill only dealt with the number of slaves to be carried and did not attempt to deal with the conditions under which they were carried. Thus these slaves continued to be

herded in pens under wooden gratings, shackled and packed so
tight that they could scarcely move till the journey was over;
unless they died. During the lifetime under review, such treatment was meted out by the people of Britain to perhaps a million
of their fellow human creatures. Wilberforce had been urging the
abolition of the trade since 1790, but it was not till 1805 that the
Government issued its first order against the trade; nor was it till
1833 that the West Indies were compelled to give up the horrible
brandings for identification, floggings, and mutilations.

Perhaps this slave-complex was responsible for the long con-
tinuation of the press-gang which was little else than illegitimate
slavery. This system of recruitment for army and navy had been
in vogue ever since the fourteenth century, and though declared
illegal in 1641, it was nevertheless carried on right up to 1835.
Because of its antiquity, an eminent and humane eighteenth-
century judge like Lord Mansfield, defended the practice because
'it was founded upon immemorial usage allowed for ages'. It was
not till 1777 that even London dared to challenge the Admiralty's
right to impress men living within the city. This 'right' continued
to be exercised long after 1800 even in the City, and there are
frequent references to the 'hot', 'vigilant', 'successful', 'unscrupulous' pressers in newspapers like *The Times*. Other towns made
no public or effective protests against the abduction of their
townsfolk. Animated pictures of the activities of these nefarious
gangs are given by Smollett for the mid-century and by Marryat
for its closing years. And at least one admiral was under no
delusion about the wrongness of the system when he declared:
'Our fleets which are defrauded by injustice, are first manned by
violence and maintained by cruelty'. In the twenty years in which
Pitt practically doubled the tonnage of the Royal Fleet, the necessary increase in personnel must have entailed many 'keen' press-
gangs, absorbed thousands of poor, decimated the population in
prisons and reduced to perhaps countable numbers those in workhouses or houses of correction.

Little removed from press-gang methods and slave-recruitment
were the ways by which paupers, vagrants, debtors, 'pardoned'
prisoners, offending Methodists and other 'incorrigible rogues'
were pushed into the fighting forces when England was then at
war. Even in the third quarter of the century, enlistment in Navy
or Army was a form of slavery, for on the one hand the recruit was
the personal soldier of his colonel or captain by whom he was

clothed and fed; the charge being ultimately defrayed by the 'stock-fund'. It can therefore occasion little surprise that a duke once tried to sell his regiment lock, stock and barrel and men to the East India Company; he would regard the men as really being his live property. Perhaps the Army accommodation suggested the slave-complex too. Round about 1700 there was barrack accommodation for 5,000 soldiers; the rest of the men were pushed into camps or billeted in protesting homes; in 1792 barrack accommodation had risen to 20,000 places, but even with this increase of accommodation, a large part of the Forces was still in camps and billets. Most of the barracks were mere hovels, whilst the billets caused endless complaints and quarrels. Another effect of the billets was that the soldiers living in them not infrequently took the side of the rioters in civil disturbances they were called upon to quell. This was particularly noticeable in 1795 during the 'bread riots'.

A semi-form of slavery was invested even in the 'militia' which was formed in 1757. Parliament was trying to break down the existing form of personal service then existing in Army recruitment, and it called upon each township to prepare lists of men between the ages of eighteen and forty-five for 'militia' service. The persons chosen from this source were selected by ballot. So as to evade the result of the ballot, many members paid a guinea and a half every year, and these sums were used to pay for substitutes for the chosen well-to-do. And till well towards the century's close it was impossible for a Nonconformist or a Roman Catholic to enlist voluntarily. No wonder with such systems of manning the land forces, the militia often proved utterly untrustworthy, whilst the Regular Army's history became chequered. In the days of the great wars of Queen Anne the English Army distinguished itself at Blenheim, Ramillies, Oudenarde, Malplaquet; in the middle years it conquered at Minden, Plassey and Quebec. Then its history darkened with Saratoga and Yorktown, so that by the time it entered on the long French war, the Army's character stood very low and its administration was both defective and corrupt.

Even the general disciplinary methods adopted by eighteenth-century officers, officials and employers suggest the slave-complex. The lash was freely used in barracks and on ships, the cat-o'-nine-tails in prisons, the 'billyroller' in factories and mines. Every convict settlement had its official 'scourger', and every workhouse its 'correction' room. The very accommodation in prisons, settlements, barracks and on ships was equally indicative of the slave-complex. And finally, many a one will see but little difference between child-slavery and the eighteenth-century practice of 'apprenticing' children to the cotton trade, chimney-sweeping, &c.

Judged from the stories written in or about this century, it would seem that the eighteenth-century poor possessed the uninquiring mind of the serf; they all drudged; they were totally uneducated in the modern sense of that term; they were expected to respect their 'betters'; even the best of them seem to have been loutish, easily pleased and readily satisfied. 'Days of propaganda were still far away; society was permanent; old institutions looked like lasting for ever; they were not called upon to think nationally or internationally; they were not perplexed with economic theories,' says a modern writer. Though he is speaking of another period, his words are applicable to the eighteenth-century poor. Equally so are his further comments: 'Nor were they maddened with relentless ambition. Fate had willed that their lives should be occupied with a series of small struggles with the odds heavily against them and had decreed that they had no business with vital religious or state questions.' Thus as a body they accepted their 'place'; and their subservient ignorance made them content with the glaring falsities and stagnant mummery of eighteenth-century England. Legitimate slavery could scarcely have induced a more docile temperament.

Wesley never lived to see the factory system at its very worst, but he always deplored the accumulation of mere wealth. Although he and his friends drew the attention of the legislator or the philanthropist to the workers in the mine, field and factory, it is also true that he suggested no solution of the everlasting quarrel between capital and labour, except as Rattenbury puts it 'so far as quick sympathy and instinctive personal happiness serve to smooth all such antagonisms'. But he always preached against all forms of slavery and it formed the subject of his last protest. On his death-bed he wrote to Wilberforce: 'I see not how you can go through your glorious enterprise in opposing that execrable villainy, which is the scandal of religion, of England and of human nature. . . . Unless God has raised you up for this very thing, you will be worn out by the opposition of men and devils.'

CHAPTER VI

CLASS CONTACTS

I

As has been shown, the old pressure of worn-out institutions continued to encumber all England throughout the eighteenth century and with their dead weight pressed men down. Towards the close, as Benson has it, 'the hoarse murmurings, mutterings and occasional seethings of the common people were making the upper and landed classes somewhat apprehensive of their ancient buttresses of property and privileges'. As a body, however, they knew nothing of the working classes, 'of the barbarous beggary, of the poverty & suffering & squalor in which they lived'. They regarded them as suitable material 'to be milled into money and starved and sweated by their callous employers'. And though the ruling class were only very dimly conscious of 'this very large quantity of dim human beings', such institutions as the Church and amusements, roads and streets made the aristocrats aware of their existence, whilst pestilence and fire refused to recognize the eighteenth-century separateness of the classes.

The Great Fire of London in 1666 spared neither rich nor poor and in three days consumed the buildings on 436 acres in 400 streets. By it were destroyed 52 halls, 86 churches and 13,200 houses. A year later, Glasgow was totally burnt out and Edinburgh left a blackened ruin from St. Giles to the Tron. As most of these buildings then consisted of timber framework filled in with lath and plaster, situated in very narrow streets and unsupplied with an internal water-system, the extent of the destruction is not surprising.

Such extensive fires naturally gave architects an opportunity of building better in the affected towns, and London at any rate determined to improve its housing conditions. According to Strype, 'In 1720 there is now not a street in London but water runs through it in pipes underground and from the pipes there is scarce a house whose rent is £20 per annum but hath the convenience of water brought into it' . . . while . . . 'for the smaller tenements there is generally a cock or pump convenient to the inhabitants'. Steele, five years later, declares that London had

well-disposed streets, magnificent public structures and gay,
wealthy shops. The City, too, boasted that its drains and sewers
had stood the test of time, seeing they had been in existence since
the seventeenth century, and round about 1783 an inventor
named Bramah had designed some mechanism for water-
closets.

Despite such patents and attestations, it is however, certain that
even at the end of the eighteenth century London was still taking
some of its drinking-water from the Thames just below the place
where several sewers emptied into the river. A mid-century
grumbler confirms this suggestion of the pollution of rivers, &c.,
when, writing to the newspapers, he says: 'If I would drink
water, I must quaff the mawkish contents of an open aqueduct
expos'd to all manner of defilement or swallow that which comes
from the Thames, impregnated with all the filth of London and
Westminster.' In 1770 a foreign visitor declares that in London,
water was only distributed to the householders three times a week,
and that it was stored in the houses in lead cisterns. The internal
water-supply to the houses, which had roused Strype's admiration,
was proving to be insufficient and the outside drains too dubious
for any widespread adoption of Bramah's w.c. patent. The Fleet
Ditch was often a mere trickling puddle, which the fastidious
passed with an orange stuffed with cloves held to their noses; the
special sewage wells, when full, were still pumped into the
'kennels' of the streets; Rosamond's Pond and the Decoy and its
ditches in Hyde Park were still there in 1770. Steele's pride in
London's 'well-disposed' streets seems to have been somewhat ill-
founded, for a mid-century diarist refers to the fact that 'the
residents of the fashionable St. James's Court had engaged a
private scavenger of their own to remove their refuse, and by such
action had proclaimed themselves to be aloof and squeamish'. A
French visitor found the Strand to be in a regrettable condition in
the last quarter of the century.

In London mansions there was not a single bath, as the term
is now understood, and the standard of personal cleanliness of
rich and poor alike was probably deplorably low till well into the
third quarter. To Samuel Pepys the idea of washing himself
regularly seems to have been strange; at any rate he thinks the
occasion worthy of mention in his diary:

'Up and to the Office where busy till noon, my wife being busy in
going with her woman to an hothouse there to bathe herself after being

so long within doors in the dirt, so that now she pretends to a resolution of being hereafter clean. How long it will hold I cannot say. . . . At night late home and to clean myself my wife will have me, because she do herself.'

Other diarists living in London also make mention of similar washing experience, of 'hothouses' and 'banios', whilst Edinburgh boasts that its Royal Infirmary possessed 'two or three baths' in 1778. It would appear that the public baths which the Romans built wherever they settled, had in many instances fallen into a state of disrepair or into disuse in England. Yet despite this complete absence of baths from private homes, their fewness in hospitals and towns and the unsatisfactory water-supply to the houses, foreign visitors from 1780 onwards, seem to have been struck with the cleanliness of eighteenth-century Britons. Some call these Britons 'slaves to cleanliness . . . not a day passes by without their washing their hands, arms, necks and throats in cold water, and that in winter as well as in summer . . . houses are washed twice in the seven days and that from top to bottom . . . even the large hammers and the locks on the door are rubbed and shine brightly'. Perhaps Wesley's firm belief in and advocacy of cold water had begun to bear fruit.

As for other towns that did not boast of a water-supply, or of any form of drainage, or of well disposed streets, conditions there can only be dimly imagined. Liverpool is credited with having a privately-owned bath for public use in the first decade of the century and Manchester had one in the fifth decade. But it is an historical fact that it was not till 1846 that 'civic authorities should be encouraged to establish public baths for the health, comfort and welfare of the inhabitants of towns'. Even progressive Liverpool well in the nineteenth century had 2,400 close-courts with only one water-tap each; and every one of these courts would be densely peopled. Perhaps conditions were still worse in other places. For the vast majority of England's eighteenth-century population, contemporary novelists and diarists suggest that water for domestic use had to be bought from a hawker or fetched from a well, spring or river, which, as often as not, was also the people's sewer.

Their streets were mainly trampled, bouldered approaches to houses into which was flung all the household filth and refuse, there to putrefy and make the most noisome mud in wet weather. The historian MacCarthy is speaking of Edinburgh when he says:

'At 10.0 p.m. the taverns and clubs disgorged their crowds; every-body rushed for home; up and down the streets rang the most effective curfew of "Gardy-loo" (Gardez l'eau). Down poured trash and gar-bage from hundreds of windows and unfortunate is he who has not reached a shelter.' In the last quarter of the century, Boswell says: 'I could not prevent his (Johnson) being assailed by the evening effluvia of Edinburgh.'

An even more detailed account of this nightly practice is given in graphic terms in *Humphry Clinker*, and other writers dwell upon 'the picture of cats, dogs, rats and mice feeding on the garbage and on themselves; of the swarms of flies and of the evil-smelling, repulsive looking flood washed down the street kennels when the rain came'. Diarists and novelists suggest that this nightly practice in towns had its humorous side; this accepted method of dealing with refuse from home, inn, club or coffee-tavern, occasionally pro-vided a means for the gratification of revenge by some servant on the slights offered by a passing dandy. That this primitive system of sanitation continued well into the nineteenth century is dis-closed by the later numerous outbreaks of 'putrid' fever, &c. As late as 1832 there was a cholera outbreak when out of 82,000 stricken down, 31,000 cases proved fatal—a result largely due to the generally unsatisfactory and insanitary conditions in which the masses of the people lived. For naturally in addition to the vermin seen in the streets, the houses were rat and bug infested. More-over, the main way of keeping down these fever epidemics in those days, was simply to burn brimstone or saltpetre in the houses or at the street corners. Since neither brimstone nor saltpetre pleased the nostrils of the wealthy, they disinfected their reception and bedrooms by fumigating them with eau-de-Cologne dropped on red-hot pokers.

II

In the towns, and particularly in Scotland, fashionable people made their homes in the lower flats while workmen, hawkers, &c., lived in the garrets of the same building. Practically every room in such houses was a sleeping place, and the bulk of the poor had no bedsteads at all and never undressed at night. Sometimes the poor lived in the cellars of such houses and as late as 1837 it is estimated that one-tenth of the people of Manchester lived in such cellars without ventilation or drainage, and much about the same period it is calculated that a seventh of Liverpool's inhabitants were living in 8,000 cellar-dwellings. These dwellings were dark, damp, confined, dirty and miserably over-crowded. When the conditions of one street were investigated, it was found to be 160 yards long and had one water-tap for its 1,285 inhabitants. No wonder it was calculated that one person out of every six of the inhabitants of that city developed fever. Nor was it till Victorian days that the First Public Health Act was passed in this country.

Rents were not high in the early part of the eighteenth century. Riverside houses near London let at £5 per annum and one in Golden Square (Charing Cross) with stables, coach-house, gardens, &c., was rented at £60 a year. The hostelry called 'George Inn' at Southwark and made famous in *Pickwick Papers* was then let at £50 per annum. Like other eighteenth-century inns it had an arched entry, a spacious courtyard big enough for a theatre, contained a stage on which strolling players performed, and surrounded with wooden galleries. It had reception-hall, coffee-room, dining-parlour as well as minor apartments for special guests, and known not by numbers but by intriguing names like Sun, Moon, Star, Crescent, &c. It had forty bedrooms, stabling for fifty horses and a half a dozen coach-houses. Swift complains bitterly that he had to pay 8/- a week for a dining-room and front bedroom when he lodged in Bury Street, London; he was more familiar with rents of about ninepence a week; at that price he could have obtained possession of any country cottage.

None of these inns or houses, whether in town or city, would be lit by gas; all depended on candles or oil lamps. House-bells worked with wires came into fashionable use towards the end of the century; up to then employers and callers had relied on hand-bells, and before them on the horn, whistle, rattle or the big door-knocker. This knocker had always been very popular, and Steele has an account of the amusement they afforded the wealthy young in his day, and how they found great fun in rapping them or wrenching them off; a practice indicating the origin of the eighteenth-century expression 'up to the knocker'. The house doors were very stout, made of oak, possessed no handles and were often without locks, so they were secured by drop-latches or sliding oak bars. But locks were being made in the century and Barron's patent had several tumblers in its mechanism. Winifred Jenkins, the maid appearing in *Humphry Clinker*, seems to think, however, that locks were of little use and says:

'You must know Molly, I missed three quarters of blind lace and a remnant of muslin and my silvern thimble; they were all in my work-basket that I left upon the table when mistresses bell rung; but if they had been under lock and key it would have been all the same for there are double keys to all the locks in Bath, and they say as how the very teeth aint safe in your head if you sleep with your mouth open.'

III

Despite the inflammability of the houses and the inadequacy of the water-supply, fire insurance seems to have been possible throughout the century. The earliest records of this highly specu-lative form of insurance business, indicate that they charged a 12/- rate; perhaps there is no wonder when it is remembered that even at the close of the century, and even in most large towns, fires could only be extinguished by water delivered in carts and vended at a halfpenny a bucket, and that it seems to have been the custom for the vendor to insist on his account being delivered with the water. Still the prudence of insurance was well recognized, and it is estimated that by 1800 these companies were responsible for over £200,000,000 of property. They received very little assistance from the State, which imposed stamp duties on all their activities; in 1782 there was an annual duty of 1/6 for each £100 insured, a duty that was raised to 2/- and more as time rolled on. Other forms of insurance made many starts during this century, and the temptation to offer generous terms, afforded by the fact that the income of life-assurance companies necessarily exceeds the expenditure during the first generation of insurers, brought many of the early eighteenth-century companies to utter ruin. By 1762, the 'Equitable' would insure a man's life for a fixed sum, and by the time of Wesley's death this company at any rate, had fairly well-developed ideas on 'life-contingencies'. In 1771 Dr. Price wrote pamphlets on annuities, &c. Although to most people this great Nonconformist minister is best known by his consideration of philosophical problems and by the ardour and cool courage he threw into revolutionary turmoil, he is equally famous for his aridities of actuarial calculations and for his tentative schemes of old-age pensions. His insurance book *Reversionary Payments* placed the practice of insurance, for the first time in history, on a sound mathematical foundation. In 1788 the practice of insurance received further help from William Morgan's book on the *Possibilities of Survivorship*, and under this man's control the

K

'Equitable's' capital rose from £33,000 to over nine millions. Friendly societies—really burial clubs—existed during the whole century; each one was rather small, and at one time there appear to have been upwards of ten thousand such concerns. Until 1783 they were purely private affairs, but about that time the State was compelled to recognize their existence because of their activities and malpractices. Societies for the mutual benefit of members in sickness probably did not materialize in this century at all. One of the earliest of these started in 1837, and its original rules would suggest that even then press-gangs were active and that the standard of cleanliness and behaviour still savoured of the eighteenth century. 'Members impressed into the Navy forfeited claims during the period of the impressment, but if discharged fit, could be readmitted into the Society on payment of all arrears.' A fine of one shilling was levied on any committee member who failed to attend a meeting 'in a clean and decent manner'. Fighting at meetings was punished more heavily. 'Any member challenging another to a fight was fined 2/6', and 'should a blow be actually given, the member so offending is to be fined 10/-'. It is also very doubtful if the eighteenth century saw issued any accident policies. On the other hand, in Wesley's early manhood, it was possible to take out policies against 'lying' or 'death from gin-drinking', and even 'female chastity' could be insured.

IV

As for shops, Steele declares that in 1725 London had 'wealthy, well-lit shops'. Johnson thought 'London shops were the greatest in the world', and towards his death, some London shops were certainly being transformed into handsomely decorated saloons, brilliant with mirrors and gilding. In the eighth decade, foreigners like Grosely and Archenholtz speak of the city shops as 'having shop-fronts with large glass windows and a glass door' and they refer to 'the symmetrical arrangements of varied goods'. Another traveller enthuses over 'the city's brilliantly lighted shops'.

Perhaps eighteenth-century standards of shop wealth, splendour and lighting were not those of to-day. Defoe in 1726 describes in detail the somewhat meagre shop-fittings to be found in London. Pictorial representations of shop interiors and exteriors in 1804, indicate that many city shops were little different from what can be seen in small village shops to-day. The traveller who enthused over the brilliant shop lights, added numbers to his description; in one that excited his admiration he 'counted no fewer than twenty-two candles'.

Outside London and the biggest towns most shops were small concerns; their windows were of the bow type containing a dozen or sixteen panes of square glass about ten-inch size and fitted with bottle-green glass and many 'bull's-eyes'. Many shopkeepers made the articles they sold, and really used the shop as a work-room, where they might be seen making shoes or weaving cloth, whilst the town apothecary would be seen preparing in his shop window as advertised: 'all sorts of balsams, decoctions, electuaries, elixirs, emplaisters, infusions, liqueurs, magisteries, oils and oint-ments.' But most country shopping was done at the fairs or on the house doorstep. Dressmakers, milliners, tailors, hairdressers, &c., would call on their customers, do most of the work at their residences, and probably remain for dinner with the family or staff.

Sugar was generally bought at a pharmacy for it was used mainly for medicinal purposes or as a sweetmeat. Until smuggling had made the poor familiar with it, sugar was a rarity and even in unpinched households, the fragment of sugar-loaf was carefully wrapped in gauze paper for further use. Still it grew in popularity in this century; in 1700 estimates indicate that the rich were con-suming some 10,000 tons per annum; a century later, consumption had grown to something like 50,000 tons. To-day we consume something like ninety-six lbs. a person per annum, a century ago the figure was seventeen, and in Wesley's day it must have been much less. Chocolate was manufactured in the eighteenth cen-tury, but for the most part it remained unsweetened. Soap also was then manufactured and in increasing quantities principally in and around Bristol; but patent rights and duties localized its production and impeded its development.

Things that could not be bought in the small or unsatisfactory shops or at the house door, and even commodities that could be purchased there, could always be procured at the eighteenth-century fairs and markets. Most of the old charters gave a town the right to hold a market every week as well as to have a fair once or twice a year. The Winchester Fair lasted sixteen days, whilst those at May Fair and Smithfields, like Houndsditch's 'Rag-fair', seem to have been almost continuous. One near Cambridge was of European reputation; to it Lancashire used to send 1,000 pack-horses laden with textiles. Thanks to Hogarth the fair at Southwark can still be well visualized.

At them there were separate alleys for the sale of different commodities. 'Garlic' alley sold vegetables, whilst the trade done in 'cheese' row, 'book' row, 'braziers' row was self-evident. Hucksters went from alley to alley selling gin, aniseed and fruit, whilst large booths offered meat, cider, punch, gingerbread animals at four a farthing. At them, too, there was a vile traffic in quack papers, pictures, peep-shows, human deformity shows and dreadful toys. They were also used for the annual engagement of servants, and decoys connected with immoral houses plied their trade. In the early days, the charters required all the goods to be satisfactory in quality and price; and officials were appointed to go round to see that the rules were obeyed, and dishonesty was punished in characteristic eighteenth-century picturesque and public fashion. A baker whose bread was of light weight, had a loaf tied round his neck, then he was dragged through the rows and streets, sitting on his bake-board, everybody jeering and throwing dirt at the unfortunate; a seller of bad fish was made to swallow lumps of it and then he was pitched into the river or village pond. Strolling players, degraded gladiators, fireproof ladies, acrobats and ballad-singers were there too, and followed the fairs from place to place in very large numbers. Most of the fairs closed with a fireworks display. Till well towards the middle of the century, fairs were big and thriving concerns, and extremely popular with all classes of society; even a prime minister wearing his red coat did not disdain to visit those in Norfolk. Their great popularity began to decline about 1760 when new roads had been constructed; another reason for their decadence was Wesley's attacks, for he saw in them injury to public morals.

V

The decline in the amusement sections of commercial fairs and markets probably increased the popularity of the eighteenth-century 'wakes', &c. As these had a religious origin, they were less open to adverse attacks from religious men. Like all holidays, they began as holy days and have a direct association with the Church. 'Keeping Wakes' was solemnized in the time of Edward

the Confessor, and one ancient chronicler records how 'in the
begynning of holy Church, men and women comyng to church
over nyghte, wit candelus and other lyghte, hadde woken in the
church alle nyghte in their devocynes'. Even in the Middle Ages,
it was still the custom to pass a great part of the night that preceded certain holy days, or the anniversary of the dedication of the
local church, in devotion and religious exercises. Owing to the
general decay in all religious observances, by the middle of the
eighteenth century these vigils or night watches had taken on a
different complexion and had degenerated; in proportion as the
'love-feasts' deviated from the original design of their institution,
they became more popular and convivial, and so a 'religious
wake' was converted into a secular fair and gargantuan feast.
Another eighteenth-century source of amusement that had a
religious origin, was the 'rush-bearing festival'. The name gives
some idea of what the occasion implied, and the following verse
from a late eighteenth-century hymn confirms the theory of
original sanctity of purpose:

> Our fathers to the House of God,
>   As yet a building rude,
> Bore offerings from the flowery sod,
>   And fragrant rushes shrew'd.

For a good part of this century the floors of most country churches
were still of virgin earth or paved with thick flagstones, and
although the exact religious reason for strewing rushes is lost in
the dim past, there is little doubt that the annual bearing of
rushes to be placed on the sacred floors was losing its religious
significance by 1725. Yet well into the next century, in some districts, rushes were still gathered and piled in a wain called the
'rush-cart', and stacked up twelve or more feet high. Packing to
this height needed special skill; the sides of the structure were
ornamented with religious tokens or symbols at first, but these in
time degenerated into dangling pots, &c. As the religious significance died away from the festival, more and more worldly antics
and items were introduced. Perched on the top of the rickety
structure would be some daring fellow of the village; the cart
itself was drawn by twenty or more men dressed in picturesque
garb. The procession generally led off with some banner; then
came 'Adam & Eve', 'St. George & the Dragon', the 'Virtues', the
'Vices', 'Robin Hood & Maid Marian'; men rode hobby-horses,

sweeps were perched precariously on unruly pigs, whilst hordes of goose-dancers, morris-dancers, &c., followed behind. It took a long time to reach the church, even though a carter with a cracking whip would be urging them on, for dozens of boys and girls with 'alms' boxes would be collecting money to be spent later on drink. The evening was usually wound up with a bull- or bear-baiting, wrestling matches and often ended in riots and brawlings. The old parish perambulations, too, had probably a religious significance for they usually took place during Rogation Week. Wither, the accomplished layman of strong Church principles, had suggested in the seventeenth century that these perambulations were of legal origin:

> That every man might keep his own possessions,
> Our fathers used, in reverent processions,
> With zealous prayer, and with praiseful cheere,
> To walk their parish limits once a yeere.

By the middle of the eighteenth century, all 'wakes', 'rush-bearings' and 'parish walkings', had begun to lose their old solemnity and religious significance.

The poor, plutocracy and aristocracy all joined together at fairs and festivals for one and all were delighted with such 'wakes', 'rush bearings', 'parish walkings', and with such sports as cock-throwing, dog-fighting, bull- and bear-baiting. Indeed, those of the poor as were physically favoured, became paid gladiators themselves and boxed with bare fists, wrestled and indulged in clog-kicking contests not merely to satisfy their own inclinations, but also to afford patrons additional opportunities for betting. Wesley found the Cornish tinners engaged in boxing, kicking, wrestling contests at their fairs and 'in all other manner of wickedness ... they also took their pleasure in hurling, at which limbs are often broken'.

At these fairs all the eighteenth-century love of a ruction came to the front, and screaming and exhortations were incessant. Such ribaldry led *The Times* in 1796 to describe them 'as the congregation of odious vapours ... foul and pestilential to society'.

Tugs-of-war were very popular and provided an opportunity for the infringement of all rules, and afforded spectators a chance of howling, blessing and adjuring the individual members of the two sides. Foot races were popular, especially those between women; often the male competitors ran naked, whilst the women were supposed to wear only a smock. Usually the spectators ran with the competitors, yelling curses, blessings and advice upon them; and more popular than races over a specified distance on a prescribed course, were those in which the runners had to chase and grasp the well-greased tail of a pig. 'Tip-cat', 'knur and spell' provided keen contests, and at every fair was a tall and slippery pole, glistening in its grease and crowned with an ample cheese. Men led about dancing bears and trained wolves or carried live rats in their shirt bosoms, killing the vermin with their teeth at a penny a time. Others would back themselves to take hundreds of lashes for half a crown. Women battled in a ring like men; in such contests the combatants were given a half-crown to clutch in their fists and she lost who first dropped a coin.

VI

As the sports and amusements of an age may indicate a period's mentality and morality, some reference to a further few of those prevailing in the eighteenth century is called for. Verbal relics of some such amusements are to be seen in the 'bull-rings', 'bear-pits', 'cockspur streets', 'cockpit lanes' to be found in many an English town.

Stag-hunting had begun to decline by 1700 although George III was ardently attached to it; archery and falconry had begun to wane even in the first decade; the wealthy knew about grouse and pheasant shooting and were fairly fond of angling. Fox-hunting grew in popularity and so did otter-hunting, while coursing became very popular from 1750.

Bull-baiting was one of the most popular forms of eighteenth-century amusement, nor was it declared illegal till 1835. Its popularity varied according to district and decade. It was held in high esteem in Lancashire, Staffordshire, Shropshire, it was well attended in the south and west, but in Yorkshire and Northumberland it was somewhat suspect. At the beginning of the century Pepys and Evelyn speak of bull- and bear-baiting as 'rude and nasty pleasures' . . . 'butcherley sports or cruelties', whilst later, the great essayists in their *Spectator* and *Tatler* articles, steadily discountenanced 'the brutality which could find pleasure in the sufferings of the brutes'. At the century's end however, Canning regarded the sport 'a most excellent one; it inspired courage and

produced a nobleness of sentiment and elevation of mind'. In
many a town the ceremony was attended by the mayor and corporation in state; in some districts the bull or bear was hunted
through the town, chased by a shouting mob, worried by dogs
and beaten by men armed with special clubs. In some, it was
fastened to the 'bull-anchor', a heavy five-armed grapnel about
four feet long and some eighteen inches across the flukes, and then
beaten to death. Often it was covered with fireworks, whilst in
other districts cats, monkeys, dogs were tied to its legs and tail.

Cock-throwing and cock-fighting grew steadily in favour
throughout the century. Edinburgh had no official pit in 1763,
but twenty years later it had a great number. Cock-throwing
needed no pits; the bird was tied by one leg with a length of rope
and for twopence a thrower, standing twenty-two yards away from
the peg, could hurl a broom-stick at the bird. For cock-fighting
either indoor or outdoor pits were needed, and many an outdoor
one was to be found in the churchyard. The cock-pit was an
arena some six or seven yards square, rounds were timed and
there was a multitude of 'rules' connected with the contests. The
birds were armed with steel spurs three to four inches long, spurs
that were pointed, shaped and grooved in a way calculated to
inflict maximum injury; not infrequently a knavish owner would
wet them with vitriol to add to their horror. Birds were trained
for the contests by massage, special feeding, plucking, comb-
cutting and a dozen other devices to make them more ferocious.
Prizes ranged from a thousand guineas to a fat pig. In this sport
not merely did owner challenge owner, but village challenged
village, town was matched against town and county against
county in 'the innocent pastime of cocking'. Victory was celebrated by merry peals from the church bells. Pegge's *Memoir on
Cockfighting* and the century's novels and diaries abound in descriptions of these 'mains'. A London newspaper of 1800 announced
that

'A main of cocks is to be fought this week at Newmarket. . . . The
match is ostensibly made between Mr. Cussand and Mr. Germain, but
Sir Harry Vane and others we might mention are supposed to be the
real principals. It is for a thousand guineas a side and forty guineas
each battle. Great sums are depending and much money will be
sported. . . . One of the promoters is the P . . . . e of W . . . s.'

Two preserved bills advertising eighteenth-century sports—one
for the north and the other for the south; one for the beginning of

the century and the other at its close—are indicative of the little change that had taken place during these hundred years as far as sport is concerned.

(1) At the Bear Garden in Clarkenwell-Green. These are to give Notice to All Gentlemen and Gamesters that this Present Munday, there will be a Match fought by Four Dogs; two of Westminster against two of Eastcheap, at the Bull for a Guinea. Five Let-goes out of Hand, fairest and furthest it wins all.

And a Mad Bull let loose to be Baited, with fireworks all over Him and Dogs after Him.

With other variety of Bull-Baiting and Bear-Baiting Being a general Day of Sport by all the Old Gamesters.

Beginning at Three a'clock.

The Gentlemen are desir'd to come betimes, because the Sport will be Long.

Vivat Regina.

(2) On Monday morning at eleven o'clock, the Sports will commence with that Most Antient, Loyal, National, Constitutional and Lawful Diversion:

Bear-Baiting

in all its primitive Excellence for which this Place has long been re-nowned. At one a'clock there will be a foot-race; at two a bull or bear-baiting for a horse-collar; at four, donkey-races for a pair of paniers; at five a race for a stuffed hat. The days sport will conclude with bait-ing the Bull Fury for a superior dog-chain. This animal is of gigantic strength and wonderful agility and it is requested that the Fancy will bring their choice dogs on this Occasion. The Bull ring will be stumped and railed round with English oak so that

> The Timid, the Weak, the Strong,
> The Bold, the Brave, the Young,
> The Old, Friend and Stranger,
> Will be Secure from Danger.

On Tuesday the Sports will be repeated; also on Wednesday with the additional attraction of a Smock-Race by Ladies and Women. A main of Cocks will be fought on all the three days for twenty Guineas. The Wakes will be concluded with a fiddling Match by the fiddlers that attend for a Piece of Silver.

The smock-race alluded to in the second advertisement was a race run by young women for a prize of a laced chemise, when the com-petitors had to be attired only in 'smocks'.

Other sports not requiring much skill or courage from the human participants were those in which dogs were dressed out with squibs and crackers tied all over them, when cats were tied to dogs by their tails, when dogs fought monkeys and hunted ducks on the 'ducking ponds' that were surrounded by howling mobs. Sometimes an owl was tied fast to the back of a goose, and apparently the fun consisted in watching the struggles of the terrified birds to free themselves from their unwelcome union. A cock sparrow with clipped wings was put into the crown of a hat and competing men and women, whose arms were tied behind their backs, essayed to bite off the bird's head. 'Goose-riding' was equally barbarous. In this contest the live birds were tied to a rope seven or eight feet from the ground, their necks were well greased and the competitors, mounted on ponies, tried to grab a bird by the neck and so decapitate it as they dashed past. Badger baiting was quite as cruel. In this pastime the badgers were fastened to a stake by a chain passed through their tails and then dogs were set on to them.

Towards Regency days some sports became better organized if not more human. Sometimes the wealthy who posed as thorough-paced Corinthians, would fence and box in public; oftener still, they were satisfied to be prize-fight patrons, and encourage eighteenth-century pugilists of the renown of Figg, Sutton, Johnson, Mendoza, Tom Cribb, Jem Belcher, Jack Slack, 'Gentle-man' Jackson and the 'Game Chicken' who fought bare-fisted. Wrestling also was very popular and dangerous at these fairs. There seem to have been at least four distinct styles, but almost every area had its own peculiar rules, although most concurred on the suitability of prizes taking the form of a ram or fighting cock.

The century had also its more orthodox forms of sport. By 1700 horse-racing already boasted a long lineage, for races at Chester, York, Epsom and Newmarket were run before the century dawned. By that year all cathedral towns had race-courses, not because of ecclesiastical support—though that was not lacking —but because many of them ranked as county towns and were surrounded with wide commons. The century saw the establishment of the Derby, Oaks and St. Leger; it witnessed the start of the Jockey Club and Tattersall's. The latter was, in 1776, a Hyde Park coffee-tavern that gradually became the rendezvous of those interested in horse-racing, sale of animals and turf-betting. Horse-racing was carried on in a slip-shod fashion for the greater part of the century; horses were untrained, courses ill-kept, jockeys were mere brutes and played dastardly tricks on one another, whilst the crowd was out of hand. They rushed on to the course, applied fervent applications of whips and sticks to the racers amidst scorching profanity.

Rowing became popular in that century and from 1715 there were frequent contests between the professional London water-men, and regattas were held every August at Vauxhall and Ranelagh. Then it was laborious exercise, for the barges were big and cumbersome and most ornate. Many of the competing boats needed twenty oarsmen, and a sample of them still exists in the royal one of 1732 preserved in the Victoria and Albert Museum. Eighteenth-century ostentation was shown in the large amount of crimson and gold considered necessary for every boat.

The more ordinary athletic sports, as the term is now under-stood, were hardly known before the battle of Waterloo; certainly school games were not really taught at Sandhurst till about that time, whilst other public schools did not undertake such instruc-tion till 1840.

A sort of cricket had, however, been played in England since the fourteenth century and the game was very popular throughout the eighteenth. Then there were two stumps about a foot high with some six inches between the uprights, so bowling was always underhand though the pitch was always twenty-two yards. Modern pitches were unknown, and the game was often played in a rough field or in the so-called streets. The general public pre-ferred freak cricket matches, and newspapers of the closing years report matches between eleven one-armed men and eleven one-legged men, &c. And yet the century saw many improvements in the game; Kent seems to have led the way for all improvement, but by 1774 Hampshire had become the home of the game. By strange coincidence, John Nyren, the first real writer about cricket, was born in the one county and played for the other. It seems that the players wore toppers of beaver and long, gaily-coloured coats. It was followed by all classes, and the consequent commingling of aristocrats and plebeians on the cricket field was viewed with apprehension, and repeatedly discountenanced by the writers of the day. It was also accompanied by the usual eighteenth-century betting, and in 1748 the King's Bench held 'that it was a manly game, not bad in itself, but only in the ill-use made of it by betting more than ten pounds on it'.

Football also goes back some centuries, although this game never took root among the eighteenth-century aristocracy. A contemporary writer, Misson, then says of it: 'Footeball is a Usefull, Charming Exercice. It is a Lether Ball about as Big as Ones Hed, fill'd with Wind. This is Kick'd about from One to t'uther in Streets by Him or Her thet cann gette it. And thett is all the Arte of it.' A previous century writer had not thought the game 'charming'. Indeed, it must have been very rough. 'By its means sometimes necks are broken, sometimes their legs, sometimes their arms, sometimes their noses gush out with blood, sometimes their eyes start out. . . . And hereof groweth envy, rancour, and mallice and sometimes brawling, murther, homicide and great effusion of blood as experience daily teacheth.' Both accounts suggest that football had fallen into bad repute, and other accounts refer to the violent horse-play and eccentric mannerisms of the players. In the eighteenth century both sexes and all ages seem to have taken part in the game, especially in the Shrove Tuesday matches. Nor do the players seem to have troubled about distinct teams or even goal-posts; everybody kicked the ball anyhow and anywhere, and vague intimations of its ancient form and practice, are still to be seen in those few towns where the custom of playing football in the streets every Shrove Tuesday still obtains.

Instead of football, and in addition to cricket, the wealthy knew of and provided for such games as golf, fives, bowls, rackets, tennis, bagatelle, draughts and billiards in their gardens and homes. But marbles, hoop-bowling, hop-scotch, stool-ball, battledore, peg-tops, see-saw, &c., were not infrequently played by well-to-do eighteenth-century adolescents. Dancing was extremely popular among them in this century; the old practice of kissing forming a not unimportant part of the popularity of the pavane, branle, minuet, gavotte, quadrille, waltz and all ballet dancing. This picturesque practice declined a little towards the end of the century, when ladies preferred to accept bouquets, sweetmeats. &c. The rage for dancing spread outside the mansion walls to Vauxhall and Ranelagh gardens, to the Pantheon and to such famous assembly rooms as White's, Boodle's, Almack's. The century saw Beau Nash, 'Monarch of Bath', draw up a code of rules for the regulation of fashionable dances, which called for an atmosphere of ceremony and courtliness of manner; and one of his inflexible rules was that all dancing stopped promptly at 10.0 p.m. The poor, who naturally did not frequent such assemblies, also loved dancing, and they enjoyed open-air dancing, and throughout the century, they preserved Old-English dances, morris-dances, hornpipes, &c. Unhappily it would seem that many of their open-air dances were mere horse-play and crude buffoonery, if the contemporary writers are to be credited with accuracy.

Professional dancing at the Opera, &c., grew in popularity and boldness during the century. Often the performers danced in the nude, and in the last decade some bishops tried 'to stop these most indecent exhibitions at the Opera, the Gardens and in our theatres'. But the extreme licentiousness which appears to have reigned amid these riotous public entertainments, was perhaps no worse than the immorality and indecency to be found in the fashionable masquerades. Of these, one of the newspapers said: 'towards the end of the debauch, I beheld scenes in the rooms upstairs too gross for repetition . . . these fashionable routs are subversive of virtue and of every noble and domestic point of honour.' And this particular paper was far from strait-laced. Then Ranelagh and Vauxhall gardens offered dancing, vocal and instrumental music for 1/-. They and other gardens also offered walks, lawns, clipped hedges, shrubberies, ornamental water, grottoes, fountains, statues, vistas and fireworks for day and evening amusements. There were also the houses offering variety entertainments like conjurers, contortionists, tight-rope walking, fire-eaters, talking dolls, vanishing figures, magic flutes, magic lanterns, card tricks, and by 1775 the variety stage had eclipsed the legitimate drama in public esteem. The people were familiar with the two Grimaldis, father and son, with Delpini and Scaramouche, the best clowns of the times. Their great amusement hero was called Rich, and he provided them with elaborate scenery, real water on the stage, living animals, and he seems to have been the creator of the pantomime. Philip Astley turned the eighteenth-century craze for horsemanship to circus account. Magicians with their 'temple of magic' had fallen low in legal esteem and they were classed with 'ruffians, blasphemers, thieves, vagabonds, Jews, Turks, hereticks, pagans, sorcerers'. But this classification did not diminish their popular appeal. Towards the end of the century 'panoramas' became the rage and from Edinburgh, their first home, they spread throughout the land. In most towns the places of amusement were excessive, and a London grumbler writes in 1780: 'The number of places of dissipation and pleasure are inconceivable. . . . Sundays are days of riot, excursion and dissipation.' Probably he was quite correct in all he said and especially

so about the 'riot'. Then accommodation at amusement places
was primitive; all the seats were backless and none was bookable
in advance; thus entrances and exits seem to have been regular
scenes of struggling, swearing crowds, and such rowdyism was
itself a very popular form of entertainment.

Eighteenth-century theatres were little better as regards amusement, accommodation and administration than were its variety
halls. Up to 1750 the swells used to sit on the platform itself or in
side boxes on the stage, for which privilege they had to pay
extra. Their footmen and lackeys were admitted free to the upper
gallery, and when in 1780 these prerogative positions were
abolished in the new theatres, there was considerable outcry.
Throughout the century hissing was permissible and declared to
be a lawful practice. Great actors like Garrick, Betterton, Barry,
Quick, and Mrs. Clive, Mrs. Pritchard, Mrs. Yates, Mrs. Jordan,
Mrs. Robinson and the ever famous Mrs. Siddons and Peg
Woffington had all to undergo such indignity. In 1798 the
Morning Post often alludes to riotous scenes in Drury Lane Theatre:
'the pit was so turbulent and riotous that the performance was
again interrupted upwards of half an hour . . . something should
be done to crush the race of disgusting puppies that are a constant
nuisance at the Playhouse every night.' About the same period
The Times has to refer to 'the indecent behaviour of the Box-lobby
loungers; every night they become more disorderly and offensive'.
Yet by that time, public entertainments were no longer disgraced
with some of the earlier habits of theatre-goers, such as eating,
drinking, and dicing during the performance. But throughout the
century and at all entertainments, the people noisily took their
snuff and the rich smoked their pipes made of silver, gold, brass,
glass, ivory, horn and stone-ware, while the poor puffed at the
long clay of Elizabethan days.

The very plays presented were often objectionable. In 1802
Sydney Smith wrote: 'Although Garrick and others had worked
hard to eliminate the coarse, obscene and scandalous from the
stage, its state is still very far from satisfactory.' Twenty years
before, Wesley declared: 'the stage is the sink of all profaneness
and debauchery.' The first comment suggests that some attempt
had been made to raise the standard of the plays produced: a suggestion that is reinforced when one reads William Law's *Absolute
Unlawfulness of Stage Entertainments* in 1750 and Jeremy Collier's
invective of 1698 on the *Immorality and Profaneness of the English*

Stage. Although the eighteenth-century stage had so many distinguished actors and actresses, until the close of the century they did not pay much regard to theatrical decorations, customs, arms, dress, &c., in the way of being historically accurate.

In the last quarter of the century another remarkable form of sport and amusement affected both classes and masses. This was the sudden rage of ascending in balloons. Such ascents were particularly popular in 1784 and invariably excited immense interest; and concerning this new fashion a lampoonist thus delivered himself:

> How few the worldly evils now I dread,
> No more confin'd this narrow earth to tread.
> Should fire or water spread destruction drear,
> Or earthquake shake this sublunary sphere,
> In air-balloon to distant realms I fly,
> And leave the creeping world to sink and die.

Among the more delicate customs of this eighteenth century were their partiality for exquisite visiting cards, &c. On these were lovely sketches, whilst the name and address was limited to a tiny space two inches by half an inch. By the end of the century they had developed a liking for 'valentines'. At first these were very expensive and often designed by the leading artists; not infrequently they were of a useful nature or consisted of perfumed satin sachets in lacy envelopes decorated with daisies and jasmines. The eighteenth-century comic vein crept into the fashion, and one distressing form was that of pasting the silhouette of the unwelcome suitor on a pictured donkey or goose and of adding to the rudeness such lines as:

> Ass upon ass, you ill-looking Brute,
> You never will Me for Valentine Suit.

New Year's Eve was perhaps a more popular festival than Christmas Eve throughout the century. Very many references to the celebration of the New Year are to be found in the diaries of Evelyn, Pepys and Woodforde. Wesley, too, often mentions the festival and never more significantly than in his closing one: 'We concluded the old year with a solemn watch-night and began the New Year with thanksgiving.' In 1790 it began for him at 4.0 a.m., and no entry in any diary can be more resonant and inspiring as that with which the old Christian warrior opened his new *Journal* for 1790.

'I am now an old man, decayed from head to foot. My eyes are dim. My right hand shakes much. My mouth is hot and dry in the morning. I have a lingering fever almost every day. My motion is slow and weak. However, pleased be God, I do not slack my labour. I can preach and work still.'

VII

Naturally, too, the poor and rich depended on men of the same class for the care of their bodies and souls; indeed, the better disposed clerics of the eighteenth century not infrequently treated both. George the Third's chief medical attendant was a rector as well as a doctor, and this man certainly emerges in the latter capacity, in a more favourite light than did the monarch's professional physicians. Crabbe was not only a poet and minister but doctor; Rev. John Horne Tooke after his induction, studied medicine for the benefit of his poorer parishioners; Rev. Thomas Dawson was equally admired by the inhabitants of Hackney as both their pulpit orator and their medical attendant. To-day Wesley does not hold the high position in England as a medical adviser that he once did, even though posterity acknowledges that his medical knowledge helped him to relieve much suffering and led him to establish cheap dispensaries in many a town. His *Primitive Physic* of 1747 is nowadays more interesting than instructive, despite the author's claim that he had 'devoted twenty-six years to the study of medicine'.

He advocated toasted cheese for a cut, warm treacle on brown paper for a bruise, a plaster of brimstone for a pain in the side, whilst 'pounded garlic applied to the soles of the feet is a neverfailing remedy for hoarseness and loss of voice' and 'bruised root of crowfoot applied to the fingers is good for toothache'. Perhaps his most familiar recipe is that recommending vigorous scalp massage with a raw onion and honey for baldness; but this remedy could not claim novelty, as it had been recommended a hundred years before Wesley was prescribing. He sought diligently to discover whether the electric shock had any curative power in cases of disease. He advocated the battery for dropsy, palsy in the tongue, blindness and deafness. For hysteria he recommended that 'the patient should sit on a cake of rosin, submit to electrification for at least 30 minutes morning and night; after which sparks should be taken from him and shocks of a suitable strength administered . . . the treatment has seldom failed of the desired effect'. He appears to have been a firm believer in the efficacy of cold baths, which he recommended for ague, cancer, apoplexy and weak children. This broad conception that water had curative relations to the whole realm of disease, was certainly shared by some leading doctors of the age. Floyer, a Lichfield physician, had sensed the value of cold water in the early part of the century, whilst at its close, Currie, the famous Liverpool doctor, also advocated the benefits of cold, hot and medicinal baths. Perhaps Wesley and other medical contemporaries were responsible for the revival of sea-bathing in which mid-century people freely indulged. Another cleric of the age, Bishop Berkeley, also devoted himself to the cure of bodies and proclaimed to an astonished world that 'tar-water was the panacea for all human ills'. More specific are the two remedies for ague mentioned by Dean Swift in 1743: 'Pounded ginger, made into a paste with brandy, spread on sheeps lether and a plaister of it laid over the stomach' is the one; and 'a live spider put into a goose quill, well sealed and secured and hung low about the child's neck as low as the pit of his stomach' is the other. The Rev. Rowland Hill in the eighteenth century had an enthusiasm for inoculation, and wrote a book *Cowpock Inoculation Vindicated and Recommended from Matters of Fact*. In this book he declared that he had performed the operation on 40,000 people.

The century had its old-fashioned, homely cures inherited from superstitious ancestors. If a child had a bad cough, the parent found a dark spider in the house, held it over the child's head, repeating three times:

> Spider, as you waste away
> Whooping cough no longer stay.

The spider was then hung up in a bag over the fireplace and when the live insect had dried up, the cough would be gone. Warts were cured by making the sign of the cross on each wart with a pin or pebble; care had to be taken to make the wart bleed and to bury the pin or pebble; other eighteenth-century people cured warts by covering them with a piece of beef, which had to be stolen if a cure was to be effected. Nose bleeding was cured by wearing about the neck a skein of scarlet silk tied by a person of the opposite sex, with nine knots down the front. Epilepsy was cured by wearing a 'sacramental shilling', i.e. one out of the alms collected at Holy Communion, and then made into a ring.

L

Toothache was prevented by dressing and undressing the left leg and foot before the right one. The period had its well-known quack-doctors in Taylor, and in Ward, famous for his 'headache essence' in James, known for his 'fever powder', as well as in some notorious women like 'Crazy Sally', the Amazonian quack-doctor, who gained fame and fortune as a fashionable bone-setter.

The professional physicians of the period went in for nostrums quite as weird as any of those recommended by quacks or clerical practitioners, and professional dispensing enacted certain processes of barbaric complexion like those practised by the peasantry. Smallpox, which then attacked a third of the people, was treated with 'Mice fried alive'. Another preventive was to 'Take 30 or 40 live toads, burn them in a new pot to black cinders or ashes and make them into a fine powder. Add live earthworms, hog-lice, frog's-liver and the like. Dose to be given three times a day. ... Some physicians also recommended this mixture as a wonderful Cure of Dropsie.' And with unconscious humour or prophetic certainty, the mess is later on recommended 'as a certain help for those that are ready to die'. A professional cough cure of 1760 prescribed: 'Boil 3 or 4 snails in barley-water or tea-water; the mixture will be of good service', and the addition of chalk in tea-water was advocated 'as it is a great sweetener of the Blood'.

Some of their medicines were more agreeable to eighteenth-century palates than the foregoing and the 'Balm of Gilead', with its brandy foundation, was then a highly popular physic, whilst wood-strawberries were credited with remarkable medicinal virtues. Held in the mouth these wild berries were warranted 'to comfort the gums and heal ulcers'. Dr. Culpeper praised them highly as 'excellent to cure the liver, the blood, the spleen, or a hot choleric stomach, to freshen and comfort fainting spirits'. Hoffmann, the royal physician, with a remarkable medical ancestry and one who enjoyed a European reputation for eighteenth-century medical skill, asserted that they cured tuberculosis, whilst Linnaeus, the great eighteenth-century biologist, botanist and naturalist, recommended them to assuage the pangs of gout.

As for the prescriptions and treatments of the more ordinary medical men who flourished in that century, those of the mid-decades are freely described by Smollett, who would perforce be familiar with the recipes, manners and characters of such practitioners. Then it was customary for the apothecary to visit sick people; afterwards he went to a coffee-house where he would find the doctor he was accustomed to consult, describe the symptoms, and receive a prescription and directions for further treatment. Except for the well-to-do, the doctor rarely saw the patient.

Items of medical charges sometimes appear in eighteenth-century vestry accounts. Indicative of such are the following:

'Allow'd for phisicke & Chirurgerie for severall pore Peeple'	00–16–06
'Pd for geting ye widdy Hammund bled and uther chairges for her and y^m y^t help'd and look'd to herr'	00–02–06
'To dockter tubbie for Administring fissake to jno Bolton in siknes'	00–01–06
'Pd doccter Yull for Cureing yung Tiler of the eyche'	00–02–00
'Payd for plaisters and salve for yeere'	03–00–00
'Pd for john hines his wife when in Travaile of childberth'	00–05–00

'Helein old jim brown his legge' cost 10/–; a 'bleding' cost 6d., whilst 'heeling a boyes arme' was 4/–.

A preserved bill rendered by a mid-century doctor to a patient runs as follows:

'Robt Cearison his bill aug^t y^e 7, 1752.

Item: a purg.	00–01–00
„ y^e 8 a cordle	00–03–00
„ y^e 10 a purg.	00–01–00
„ y^e 11 d^o	00–01–00
„ y^e 13 d^o	) 00–01–00

octobber 26, Recd the Contents of y_s bill p' me.'

whilst a later receipt is almost as illiterate:

'Aprell y^e aiteen. Resav'd of jhon dixe sen^r the som of 3 pund fore the Ceure of betlye, and godye boise arme and godye whipe, vich is in fooll. By me ——.'

Perhaps the patients did not take their medical attendants too seriously. In the seventeenth century, the Rev. Robert Herrick—who has much charming poetry to his credit—wrote a *Litany to the Holy Spirit* which has tender and beautiful lines, but which also contains verses that would be ill-adapted for modern hymn-singing.

> When I lie within my bed,
> Sick in heart and sick in head,
> And with doubts discomforted,
> Sweet Spirit, comfort me.

When the artless doctor sees
No one hope but of his fees,
And his skill runs on the lees,
    Sweet Spirit, comfort me.

When his potion and his pill,
Is of none or little skill,
Meet for nothing but to kill,
    Sweet Spirit, comfort me.

A hundred years later in 1763 a very popular couplet expressed much the same opinion of current medical skill:

The cannon-shot and doctor's pill,
With equal aim are sure to kill.

The early nineteenth century saw Immermann displaying vivid fancy and quaintly original humour in *Münchausen* concerning current medical prowess. After describing how he kept the entire College of Physicians suspended in mid-air for three months, he goes on with:

'Though this was meant as an innocent frolic, it was productive of much mischief to several respectable characters amongst the clergy, undertakers, sextons and grave-diggers; they were, it must, be acknow-ledged, sufferers; for it is a well-known fact that during the three months the college was suspended in the air, and therefore incapable of attending their patients, no deaths occurred, except a few who fell before the scythe of Father Time and some melancholy objects, who, perhaps to avoid some trifling inconvenience here, laid the hands of violence upon themselves and plunged into misery infinitely greater than that which they hoped by such a rash step to avoid, without a moment's consideration. If the apothecaries had not been very active during the above time, half the undertakers in all probability would have been bankrupts.'

In those days many illnesses were attributed to ill-wishers or to the supernatural, and therefore called for curative means not to be found in the surgery. Lunacy, epilepsy, deaf-and-dumbness were all due to evil spirits. (The word 'influenza' is but an abbreviation of *influenza della stella* and implies that the stars had been baleful.) In such illnesses, witches and warlocks and weird recipes were called upon to effect a cure. According to Grose, 'A Halter wherewith anyone has been Hung, if tyed about the Hed will cure the Hedack. . . . A ded mon's Hond is supposed to have the Quality of dispelling Tumours.' . . . It seems as if the hand of a person dying a violent death was deemed particularly efficacious, so it very often happened that 'nusses and mothers bring children to be stroked with the Honds of Executed Criminals, even whilst they are Hanging on the Gallows'. A piece of murderer's skin or hairs from his head, particular bones of a dog or a monkey and the like had curative properties in the minds of the eighteenth-century ignorant masses.

Kingship *per se* could cure scrofula, if the monarch but laid his hand on the victim, and faith in such touching continued well into the third George's reign, although this royal cure had failed lamentably in the case of Johnson who was treated by Queen Anne in 1712 and by Prince Charlie in 1745. Lesser folk were sometimes credited with such miraculous powers, and even a scientist of Boyle's distinction, attested to the cures of diseased bodies he had seen wrought with a hand or magnet. On the borderland of superstitious quackery and imposture, were the cures effected by qualified doctors like Mesmer and his eighteenth-century disciples. These men had consulting-rooms which were profoundly silent, dimly lighted, specially scented, whilst the patients sat around a simmering vat. Like the slightly later phrenology, the science of mesmerism attained a great degree of popularity not only with the credulous and ignorant; among patients were some of the most eminent and learned people of the eighteenth century.

The century knew a fair amount about drugs, especially the general effects of such drugs as alcohol, opium, belladonna, and of certain purgatives and emetics. But the chemists and doctors were without any accurate conception of the why and wherefore of these effects. History suggests that they tried out their medicines on dogs, prisoners and sometimes on themselves. Still, drugs were fairly freely used during the century, and even a stolid country-man like Walpole was addicted to opium. And yet the century's roll of chemists included such men as Black, Cavendish, Lavoisier, Priestley and Stahl, who gave an impetus to chemical research and led the abler doctors to see the medicinal and surgical value of certain drugs and gases.

Dentistry was probably never a skilled profession during the whole century, even though artificial teeth of bone and ivory were being made round about 1750. As late as 1876 the *Lancet* declares that there were only fifty dentists in the United Kingdom who possessed in reality any medical or surgical diploma. In such circumstances, extraction was the only treatment of caries, &c.

Probably every doctor and apothecary then extracted teeth, but dentistry was also practised by village blacksmiths, barbers and watchmakers. History says that Dr. Monsey, physician to Walpole, was in the habit of extracting his own and other teeth sentenced to be drawn, by fastening them securely with a piece of catgut to which was attached a bullet. With this bullet and a full measure of powder, a pistol was charged and so teeth were removed by this original method. Grimaldi, the famous clown of the century, eked out his living by dentistry and advertised that 'he could draw teeth or stumps without giving the slightest uneasiness in the operation', and offered to wait upon people needing such attention. Evidently his claim was not baseless, for in 1760 he was appointed dentist to Queen Charlotte.

Spectacles with both concave and convex lenses were known in this century; fixed glasses did not, however, gain immediate popularity, and the well-to-do preferred to use 'perspective' glasses or lorgnons. The happy idea of printing in paper letters recognizable by touch was also developed in 1784, and by 1800 there were at least four special institutions for the blind to be found in England.

They seem to have been much kinder to their blind than they were to those afflicted with mental disorders, for generally the treatment of the insane provoked much brutality, and even George III was roughly handled during his periods of insanity. Usually lunatics were chained by the neck to the wall and flogged at intervals. By the last decade of the century, some doctors seem to have realized that such usage was not calculated to restore alienated intellect to its proper tone, and in 1791 Tuke established the first humane asylum at York. Perhaps it was the influence of such humanitarians that led to the closing of Bedlam on holidays and Sundays in about 1770. Up to then, quite respectable citizens found mutilation and deformity merely amusing, and had escorted their families to madhouses to see the demented at their antics.

Nevertheless, the century had seen a general advance in all forms of medical treatment. In 1745 it saw barbers and surgeons separated into two separate gilds or corporations. It saw 'plague' become a thing of the past; its close saw 'jail-fever' largely overcome by better ventilation and personal cleanliness; it saw smallpox mastered by Jenner. Scurvy was reduced considerably among sailors by Captain Cook's advocacy of free soap for sailors, and the compulsory carrying of lime-juice on ships. It saw midwifery improved under Dr. Smellie in 1740 and by the founding of special hospitals. It saw Coram push forward the building of the Foundling Hospital in 1740 and Hanway advocate the Magdalene Hospital in 1760. Not only were there special places for lying-in, small-pox, fever, male and female lock institutions, &c., but many of the old infirmaries were revived and fifty new ones established up and down the country. During that century Guy's, Westminster, St. George's, London and Middlesex hospitals were all founded.

Perhaps many of the hospitals were regarded less as curative places than as establishments where the apprentice-doctors might experiment; for by the end of the century it had become increasingly customary for these apprentices to spend some time at medical schools, and to undertake supervised medical and anatomical study. Less and less were surgeons classed with barbers; more often did doctors visit patients and not rely on the apothecary's diagnosis and treatment. By 1800 Jenner, Cheyne, Cullen, Brown, Fothergill had considerably furthered the study of medicine, whilst thanks to Chiselden, Sharp, the two Hunters, Cruikshank, Haller, Albinus and Camper there was real knowledge of the minute structures of animal tissues and of the modifications in form and structure exhibited by various groups of animals. Surgeons by then were no longer mere advocates of bleeding, and their operations were no longer based on rule-of-thumb methods. By then, too, Gall had given a new orientation and new inspiration to the anatomy of the central nervous system.

Perhaps this emphasis on anatomical study led to the grim trade of body-snatching, mention of which comes in the famous Edinburgh murder trial, *Tale of Two Cities* and in Stevenson's inferior *Body Snatcher*. Certainly the dreadful business flourished in the closing years of the eighteenth century and in the first decades of the nineteenth. As early as 1768 Laurence Sterne was hauled out of his tomb by such miscreants, and as late as 1826, one reads of three cases addressed to Edinburgh, and marked 'bitter salts' being seized at Liverpool docks, and found to contain eleven bodies. This nameless material for medical observation had come from a cellar under a clergyman's school where nineteen more bodies were found; they had been taken from the workhouse cemetery and were being sold in Scotland at from £6 to £10 each for anatomical purposes.

Nor was all well with the hospitals. Many of them proved to be hot-beds of disease, whilst in-going and out-going patients were faced with many charges, not unlike those to be found in eighteenth-century prisons. On entry patients had to find 19/6 for 'berial fees' which were returnable if the patient recovered; but beadles, porters, &c., were allowed to demand many odd shillings for things like 'papers', 'attention', &c.

CHAPTER VII

GOVERNMENT, LAW AND ORDER

I

IN the days of Queen Anne, politics were governed by petty causes; great talents were turned to paltry purposes; politics were a mere game in which success meant office, power, dignity and wealth, a game in which the viler forms of opportunism were freely shown. Treason was a thing of common occasion, and many names among the highest were tarnished by acts of grossest treachery. Corruption and bribery sustained Walpole in office for twenty years; the Duke of Newcastle for still more years controlled ministries, since he was able to command the votes of a third of the members of the House of Commons through his ownership or management of so many pocket, close and rotten boroughs. Nor were the Whigs more corrupt than the Tories; both parties ruled by corruption throughout the century and used it unblushingly. As late as 1800, and in order to effect the Union with Ireland, the Irish Parliament was packed; in their House of Commons were seventy-two place-holders and pensioners of English nominees; fifty-four peerages bought consciences and a million and a quarter pounds were given to borough-holders to console them for the loss in the sale of seats. The Government even bribed the Press, and thus the Union was passed by the most corrupt Parliament ever created by the ingenuity of man.

The spirit of political honesty and freedom, as the term is now understood, had not by 1720 begun even to glimmer upon the counsels of statesmen. As a contributor to *Johnson's England* puts it:

'From 1688 England settled down to aristocratic government with a limited constitutional monarch as titular head. The contemporary liberal theories of Locke made but little headway in the country though they found more fruitful soil in France, and when amended or orientated by Rousseau and Montesquieu were later to furnish an abundant crop of political ideas.'

Early eighteenth-century England was to read the admirable political pamphlets of Addison, Defoe, Steele and Swift; but these, like Locke's treatises, were fruitless, for 'the vast majority of the people were then quite indifferent about the forms of English

government; they knew that political authority was securely
settled in the hands of the aristocracy and that mere argument
about its nature and theory was not worth while'. Perhaps, in
Essay on Man, Pope suggests the current political tone and temper
of the times with his dual assertion that 'whatever is, is best' and
that

> For forms of government let fools contest;
> Whate'er is best administered, is best.

Johnson had much the same opinion:

'I would not give half a guinea to live under one form of government rather than another; it is of no moment to the happiness of the
individual.'

Rousseau, Montesquieu, Paine and Godwin gradually introduced the idea of a positive democracy and made it a doctrine in
the world of politics. But such a notion was challenged by Burke
'who bluntly denied reason as being a possible right basis for
politics, who could not conceive any English government except
that by territorial aristocracy in the interests of the nation at large
and especially in the interests of commerce, and who asserted that
the accumulated experience of an hereditary governing class was
something real and valuable'.

Inquiry into the economic conditions was almost stagnant under
the Whig regime, if one ignores the slight manifestations of Hume
and Tucker. About 1775 Thomas Spence drew attention to social
questions and a year later came Adam Smith's *Wealth of Nations*,
which recognized the subjection of all social phenomena to natural
laws. The century's closing years saw the writings of Malthus and
Saint-Simon, who still further crystallized the social question as it
is termed to-day. These two writers and the later social thinkers,
Owen and Fourier, proclaimed the principle of individual freedom
as distinct from privileged restriction, as a positive axiom of
economics and government.

Despite the activities of these men, parliamentary franchise
rights advanced but little during the century, and in 1796 *The
Times* is reporting two elections as follows:

'Launceston Election results:

Hon. Mr. Rawdon and Mr. Brogden	12 votes
Dalkeith and Garthshore	11 ,,

The contest was a hard fought duel between the Duke of Northumberland and the Duke of Buccleuch. Both Parties have spent a great
deal of money; but the former has carried the day.'

'Shrewsbury Election. The State of the Poll on Monday was Sir W. Pulteney 1607; John Hill Esquire 834, Hon. W. Hill 832. The Election will cost Sir Richard Hill £100,000 at least; the Expence to each Party is about £1,000 per day.'

In some constituencies the right to vote was a negative one, namely that the voter should not be a Dissenter or a Roman Catholic and had not been on the poor-rate. In some, a particular pigeon-loft or a certain pig-sty conferred the vote on its State-Church owner, whilst in many a borough permission to vote could be bought and sold, so long as the buyer was not hampered with religious scruples. Thanks to careful purchase, &c., by the end of the century the parliamentary franchise was almost entirely in the hands of patrons and corporations, and in this way the aristocracy secured supreme command of the Commons. By 1800 it was estimated that only one person in fifty had a vote, but when individual cases are considered the facts sound worse. As late as 1832, Glasgow with a population of 200,000 and Edinburgh with 150,000 had only thirty-three voters apiece; Yorkshire then was a parliamentary undivided county with four members, all of whom were elected by a negligible number of electors controlled by three wealthy families. On the other hand, Stamford, Grantham, Cirencester, Newton-le-Willows, Ilchester, Helston and Haslemere had each two members of Parliament. Old Sarum also returned two members, even though the place had not a single voter. Dr. Borlase, the historian of Cornwall in the eighteenth century, said 'the county has a greater number of boroughs than any other in Great Britain and sends as many members almost as the kingdom of Scotland'. Seventy-five members were returned by thirty-five electorates which did not among them number sixty voters; 300 members were returned by 160 separate persons. One of these persons, a peer of the realm, returned no fewer than eleven, whilst another returned as many as nine. Such gross disproportion continued right up to 1832, when the First Reform Bill disenfranchised fifty-six of these decayed boroughs, and liberated from them 143 members who were assigned to places hitherto unrepresented at Westminster.

Naturally most of the land magnates sent their sons and relatives as members for these pocket-boroughs, and paid no consideration as to the experience of the members for the task assigned to them. In one eighteenth-century Parliament there were forty miners, several of whom had not reached the age of seventeen.

Lord Torrington, afterwards Duke of Albemarle, was only fourteen when he not only sat but spoke in the House, and then with a deplorable flippancy. Taunted by a senior with 'presuming to legislate before he had sowed his wild oats', this very youthful member retorted that 'he could not imagine a better place than the Commons wherein to sow them, as there were so many geese there to pick them up'. It was of such members that Burke said, 'they were swaddled and rocked and dandled into legislation'. Pitt and Fox were both minors when elected to membership; the latter, however, had reached the age of nineteen before election. But he was in office before he reached manhood, and the one was Prime Minister and the other Leader of the Opposition by the time they were twenty-three.

As members of Parliament eighteenth-century politicians treated themselves and their friends very well. Parliament paid the 'incorruptible' Pitt's very large private debts and gave him a pension of £3,000; Perceval's smaller services to the country were rewarded by a grant of £60,000 and an annuity for his widow and son; Walpole got a pension of £4,000 a year for himself and sinecures for his family. Eighteenth-century Parliaments inherited or set up a large number of sinecures in the 'Tenths Office', 'Outlawries Office' and 'Exchequer Office'. Some posts had picturesque titles such as 'Felacers', 'Exigenters', 'Uncorkers of Ocean Bottles'. 'Tellerships of the Exchequer' got £500 or more annually and their holders had no duties to perform.

A Prime Minister's son got £800 a year as 'Auditor of the American Revenues', another office without duties. Pulteney, the Leader of the Opposition, held the insignificant but lucrative post of 'cofferer to the Household'. Steele was 'Governour of the Royal Stables', Locke, Prior and Addison were 'Excise Commissioners', Congreve was 'Commissioner for Licensing Hackney Carriages'— all lucrative sinecures that freed the holders from the corrosion of care. Even as late as 1800—twenty years after Rockingham's purge of such useless posts—it was estimated that more than a million and a half pounds were paid out annually in sinecures. Gibbon, who held high office at the Board of Trade, where he got a thousand a year, says of his duties: 'I enjoyed many days and weeks of repose without being called from my library to the office.' Lord Grenville, as Foreign Secretary, obtained the 'Auditorship of the Exchequer' at £4,000 per annum and held the post forty years without once entering the Exchequer. More

sought after than such exchequer auditorships was the post of
Paymaster-General; in the eighteenth century it was a quick road
to fortune through its perquisites. But even ordinary members
expected to be well paid for the votes they gave. No wonder the
indignant Burke denounced members, and described departments
in Whitehall 'as a sort of gently ripening hothouses where
Members of Parliament receive salaries of a thousand a year for
a certain time, in order to mature at proper season a claim on
two thousand'.

The constituencies themselves seem to have been singularly slow
in appreciating the value of parliamentary representation, and up
to the end of the century few, if any of them, thought of keeping
any control over those who nominally spoke for them in Parliament. Nor, indeed, did the members think it necessary to maintain close contact with their voters; many a member had never
even seen his constituency, and far more had never spoken to any
of their electors. The days of election addresses and mass meetings
were still far distant, whilst canvassing by personal visits was
never resorted to before the eighties. One of the first instances of
such canvassing is that in the Westminster election round about
1784, when the Duchess of Devonshire is reported to have supported the candidature of Fox, and to have been remarkably free
and easy with the voters.

On the other hand, eighteenth-century elections were most
robust affairs. Then the voter had to say publicly whom he was
supporting, and, accompanied by a band of friends armed with
sticks, he had to fight his way on to the platform; for candidates
hired ruffians to prevent opponents from recording their votes. In
the first quarter of the century Defoe speaks of the elections as
'being so scandalously mercenary'. In the middle of the century
Fielding's election scenes in *Don Quixote* and *Historical Register*
gave ludicrous representation of the corrupt arts of politicians
and the venality of corporations. In the last quarter Churchill
writes:

> And they will best succeed, who best can pay:
> Those who would gain the votes of British tribes,
> Must add to force of mind the force of bribes.

A caricature of that period shows 'Punch, candidate for Guzzle-
down', with a wheelbarrow full of gold, which the candidate is
distributing to the electors with a ladle. Below it runs:

See from the Treasury flows the gold,
To show that those who are bought are sold!
Come, Perjury, meet it on the road—
'Tis all your own—a waggon load.
Ye party fools, ye courtier tribe,
Who gain no vote without a bribe,
Lavishly kind, yet insincere,
Behold in Punch, your selves appear!
And you, ye fools, who poll for pay,
Ye little great men of a day,
For whom your Favourite will not care
Observe how much bewitch'd you are.

Horace Walpole declares that the royal household dabbled in this political corruption, and in a letter of 1747 he writes: 'they say the Prince has taken up £200,000 to carry the elections—which he wont carry; he had much better have saved it to buy the parliament after it is chosen.'

In his memoirs the same writer gives very vivid pictures of the drinking and guzzling at election times. Smollett and Fielding also describe the coarse society, rivers of ale and mountains of beef which disgraced election feasts. Pictures of such scenes still survive on Hogarth's canvas. *Polling Day* shows the paralytic, maimed, deaf, and dying carried up the election steps to record publicly their vote. 'A drunken voter is dropping lighted pipe ashes on the candidate's wig; a hideous old hag is picking his pockets; a boy is brewing oceans of punch in a mash-tub; a man is blowing bag-pipes in his ear; a fat parson close by is gorging the remains of a haunch of venison; a butcher is pouring gin on his neighbour's damaged head; an alderman—a very mountain of roast beef—is sinking back in a fit whilst a barber is trying to bleed him; brick-bats are flying in at the windows; the room reeks with the stale smell of heavy viands and the fresh vapour of gin and punch, whilst the very air is laden with discordant howls, thick oaths and ribald songs.' At all contests it was an 'Eatanswill' time, and the following is one agent's disbursements made on behalf of his candidate for parliamentary honours at the close of the century:

'To eating 16 freeholders above staires for sir John at 3/3 a head. To eating 11 more below staires and two clergymen after supper £1-5-0. To six beds in one room and four in another at two guineas; every bed with three or four electors in a bed every night. To ale, porter, punch, rum for the first night and day as near as I can say £29-13-7. To shaving, dressing and cropping the heads of 42 freeholders for sir John £2-5-6.'

In the matter of liquor this Sir John seems to have escaped lightly, for another election return of the same year shows an expenditure of over £300 on this item alone. (Incidentally the foregoing bill is interesting as regards the apparent promiscuity of bed-companions in the eighteenth-century. It indicates that by 1799 beds were being charged for in hotels; although many inns even then did not debit guests for beds or accommodation if one judges from preserved accounts. Usually beds were free; so no wonder that eighteenth-century travellers always carried their own sheets and rugs.)

Accounts of a general election in Preston in 1768 give other details. The voting was spread over the period between March 21 and April 2, and was 'preceded, accompanied and followed by much tumult, rioting, demolition of houses and injury to life and limb . . . lawless bands of colliers from Chorley contributed their quota to the use of physical force. . . .' There was 'not a whole window in the town at polling time' and such was the disrespect shown to persons 'that the very mayor himself was once seized in Fishergate and put under the pump'. This employment of paid physical force, corruption and bribery lasted throughout the century and there are instances on record where over £20,000 was spent on the candidature of one man alone. Indeed, it lasted till well into the nineteenth century, and Lord John Russell, writing to Queen Victoria in the heat of the Reform Bill controversy, said: 'that the whisper of a faction should prevail against the voice of a nation is unthinkable . . . that he is sorry to add that bribery, intimidation & drunkenness have been most prevalent at the last elections, and that in many cases the disposition to riot has only been checked by the appearance of the military.' With such methods of election it is no wonder that an historian, thinking of a typical parliament in the closing years of the century, writes: 'The vast majority of the members are hard-drinking, hard-living, gambling, raking ruffians who batten on the King's Bounty and who vote black is white, good is bad, with uncompromising pertinacity and unappeasable relish'; or that Dr. Johnson in 1779—when the idea of abolishing a separate Parliament for Ireland and of uniting it with that of England was mooted—said: 'Do not make an union with us, Sir; we shall unite with you only to rob you.' And, of course, both critics knew or knew of eighteenth-century statesmen who had made high office ridiculous, such as Newcastle, Lovat, Bute, Dashwood, Grafton, Bedford, Wharton,

Sandwich, Clare, and had seen a Lord North slumber and blunder along doing a vast amount of injury to his country.

II

These 513 members for England and forty-five for Scotland conducted their parliaments differently from modern ones. In 1715 they abandoned the former triennial system of parliamentary returns for the septennial one, but without consulting the country on the change. They discussed most questions with closed doors; they forbade reports on debates until the Press challenged the embargo and won a victory; they allowed only a memorandum to be made of their deliberations to be preserved, and they appointed Hansard alone to make the official report of the proceedings in the House. And, of course, there were no printed lists of the divisions. On the other hand, they knew full well that their patrons and the King would be told how they had voted.

As a body they never seem to have seen anything wrong in the electoral system nor in the flogging that went on in prisons, workhouses, Army and Navy, nor in the press-gang method of recruitment which persisted till 1835. Even the famous Navy revolt of 1797 did not cause them undue alarm, and they were unmoved about their penal code and their magistrates. They were unperturbed about their corrupt Church, civil service and judiciary; the welfare and education of children was no concern of theirs. They saw nothing wrong in refusing a Dissenter or a Roman Catholic the right to serve voluntarily in Army or Navy, to sit in Parliament, vote at an election, attend a public school or university, become a barrister or solicitor or teacher, to sit on the bench, to own land or to obtain legal security for a loan right up to the American War of Independence. They were apparently unconcerned that a full third of the revenue was lost through smuggling.

As a body the wealthy abhorred taxes on land and property and they did not like those imposed on possessions peculiar to the rich. In 1776 the House of Lords told the Commissioners of H.M. Excise to make sure that all persons were paying their taxes on plate. Wesley was favoured with such a request and he replied: 'I have two silver tea-spoons in London and two in Bristol. That is all the plate which I have at present, and I shall not buy any more while so many round me want bread.' But it was not only on plate that the parliamentary financiers imposed taxes; they put them on watches, clocks, guns, hair-powder, horses, wheeled vehicles, bricks and cotton; even sugar, salt, tea, malt, soap, candles, newspapers, chimneys and windows did not escape them; for they preferred the elastic and fertile revenues derivable from the use of the commonest things.

Excise duty on soap ranged from a penny to threepence a pound, and often equalled 100 per cent of the total manufacturing costs. Salt was another highly taxed commodity; often the duty represented an amount totalling forty times the net cost of production. Newspapers in some years had to pay fourpence a copy; ordinary paper yielded in taxation threepence per pound, whilst the tax on candles ranged from a halfpenny to $3\frac{1}{2}d.$ per pound. Pitt's famous budget presented soon after Wesley's death went still farther; it imposed 'an annual tax of 5/– on every clock within a house, 10/– on gold watches, 7/6 on silver ones, 10/– on every horse and 3/– on every dog. Bricks had to pay 5/– per thousand and small paving tiles 2/6 per hundred. Hats when new had to pay from 3d. to 2/– according to quality, whilst every four-wheeled vehicle had to pay £8 per annum and every two-wheeled one four guineas.' Perhaps the only tax the industrious could evade was that of a guinea for hair-powder; yet this tax would hit hard all those who claimed respectability in society, for hair-powder was still very common as late as 1795. That upon dogs, levied for the first time, excited considerable discontent and ridicule. It was such taxes that led the lampoonists to write *Billy's Budget*, which gives a tolerably comprehensive view of the various items of which it consisted:

> Should foreigners staring at English taxation,
> Ask why we still reckon ourselves a free nation,
> We'll tell 'em, we pay for the light of the sun,
> For a horse with a saddle—to trot or to run;
> For writing our names;—for the flash of a gun;
> For the flame of a candle to cheer the dark night;
> For the hole in the house, if it lets in the light;
> For births, weddings and deaths; for our selling and buying;
> Tho' some think 'tis hard to pay threepence for dying;
> And some poor folks cry out 'These are Pharaoh like tricks;
> To take such unmerciful tale of our bricks';
> How great in financing our statesmen have been,
> For our ribbons, our shoes, and our hats may be seen;
> On this side and that, in the air, on the ground,
> By act upon act now so firmly we're bound,

One would think there's not room one new impost to put,
From the crown of the head to the sole of the foot.
Like Job, this John Bull his condition deplores
Very patient indeed, and all cover'd with sores.

However amusing to modern eyes such a recital of eighteenth-century taxation may be, the imposts were no joke to the eighteenth-century poor, for they probably raised the cost of living fivefold between 1750 and 1800.

In those days the poor simply did not count in the eyes of the aristocracy and wealthy manufacturers. Members of Parliament never seem to have thought it their business to understand and control the forces of the hour, and so they let the industrial revolution proceed unchecked on its ugly course. Right up to the days of Lord Shaftesbury, governmental interference in social and economic concerns was not opposed, simply because such interference was undreamed of. In the middle of the century there were many complaints in Parliament of workmen's combinations, and the multitude of petitions and cross-petitions revealed the existence of strong associations of workers. But Parliament never dreamed of investigating the validity of the petitions or cross-petitions; it simply replied with Acts 'to prevent the organization of labour', and as late as 1799 it was enacted 'that all persons combining with others to advance their wages or decrease the quantity of their work . . . might be committed to the common gaol or to the house of correction'. If a strike resulted, then Parliament allowed masters 'to deduct 10 per cent. a week from the workers' wages until the employers' losses in profits had been made up' after work was resumed. In Parliament's eyes, poverty was solely due to worklessness, and to be out of work was solely due to laziness; that in its turn could be cured effectively by thrashings, and so 'wardsmen' in every parish were supplied with whips, and according to credible accounts, they not infrequently thrashed a fellow till his clothes were in ribbons. Even when late eighteenth-century Parliaments realized that worklessness and poverty might be due to other causes than laziness, they could only concoct such remedies as 'the greater employment of more and younger children' and the wholesale pauperization to which they resorted in 1795, when more than a quarter of the country were 'on the rates'. During the second half of the century Parliaments were very busy passing the thousands of Enclosures Acts, Acts for Preserving Game, 'Combination' Acts against workers and devising new

taxes on commodities, &c., all of which tended to make the poor
desperate and the wild reckless. The capital punishment for
felonies was increased from 160 to 253, public executions were held
every six weeks and dozens at a time were hanged; even the
hanging of young boys and girls shocked no Parliament.

Perhaps it is unjust to lay the lapses and deficiencies of a century
at the door of its Parliaments, for these same eighteenth-century
ones contained their full share of eminent, capable and humane
legislators. Carteret was a man of immense ability; Somers,
Cowper, Hervey, Wyndham, Townshend, Grenville, Rockingham
were men of austere character; Pulteney, Fox and Pitt were some
of its debaters, whilst Chatham's stately presence, magnificent
voice and superb declamation have never been rivalled in Parliament and few ministers have ever fired a nation to greater passion.
Walpole displayed predictive and financial genius; of him Coxe
said, 'He found our tariff the worst in the world and he left it the
best'. To Burke political questions were vivid, real and intense,
and even to the semi-sane Lord George Gordon, moral intensity
was essential, and his inflammatory harangues against the perils
of popery and severities of the penal laws, showed that even an
eighteenth-century political firebrand might have a capacity for
righteous indignation. The Rockingham Ministry of 1766 was
composed of upright men with good sense. They reaffirmed the
personal liberty of the subject, took a strong stand against 'general'
and promiscuous arrest warrants and the seizure of private papers,
and in thirteen months did more good for the individual, than any
other eighteenth-century Parliament was to do during twenty
years.

Besides numbering eminent individuals the eighteenth-century
Parliaments developed greatly the machinery of political government. The century saw the growth of Cabinet responsibility.
Walpole's first Cabinet only numbered five: First Lord of the
Treasury, Lord Chancellor, Lord President of the Council and
two Secretaries of State. The office of First Lord of the Admiralty
was constituted in 1752, the Lord Privy Seal in 1755 and those for
Home and Foreign Affairs in 1782, whilst that of Colonial Secretary only just fell outside the century in 1801. It saw the institution of the formal opposition as an integral part of parliamentary
debate and saw the Commons gradually secure the power of the
purse and become more dominant than its sister House. By the
end of the century it began to 'challenge royal wisdom and

prerogative, and in December 1785 the Commons passed by two
to one the following revolutionary proposal:

'That it is now necessary to declare that to report any opinion or pretended opinion, of His Majesty upon any bill or other proceeding,
depending in either House of Parliament, with a view to influence the
votes of the Members, is a high crime and misdemeanour, derogatory
to the Honour of the Crown, a breach of the fundamental privileges of
Parliament and subversive of the Country.'

Such a resolution led the way for Peel realizing that no English
Minister could rule with the support of the monarch only, and
that he needed the approval of the majority of the electors. Yet
almost throughout the century, the king and heir apparent were not
only essential parts of the constitution, they were also an integral
part of politics. The monarch presided at special cabinet meetings
till in the eighties; the cabinets resembled privy councils rather
than an assemblage of ministers, for present at them were a large
number of people like the clerical hierarchy, law-lords, territorial
magnates, &c. The Prime Minister was not allowed to choose all
his cabinet ministers; so few ministries of this century were uniform
in policy, however well they may have combined for administrative purposes. Even Pitt's administrations did not imply a prime
minister at the head of a really homogeneous ministry. But owing
to his personal dominance over George III, together with the
immense increase in the volume of public business produced by
industry and the French wars, the monarch was gradually pushed
from power, and cabinet membership became increasingly connected with the administration of the departments of Government.
Similarly there was no party discipline; but the regimentation of
the monarchs or of forceful ministers, gradually gave a veneer of
integration. With the accession of George III the Civil List came
in for revision. Up to then the sources of revenue appropriated
to the service of the Civil List had been settled on the Crown. This
list played an important part in the history of the struggle on the
part of that king to establish a royal ascendancy. With it the
monarch had been able to create places and pensions for his supporters in Parliament and under the colour of royal bounty,
bribery was practised on a large scale. All previous attempts to
investigate this list had been resisted by the kings, and Lord
Chatham declared that the funds were spent in the corruptions of
M.P.s. In 1782 the second short-lived Rockingham Ministry
abolished a large number of useless offices and secured some super-

vision of the royal expenditure. Still it was not till well into the nineteenth century that such civil expenses as the salaries of the judges, ambassadors, officers of State and pensions granted for public services, were detached from the grant to the royal household.

III

Wesley seems to have been singularly unmoved by the misdeeds of eighteenth-century Parliaments, and little affected by the democratic movement that was spreading through the country in his closing years. He was, of course, a nominal Tory, a believer in the divine right of kings, and perhaps the most remarkable examples of his political blindness were his belief in the American policy of Lord North's administration and his stand against Catholic Relief Bills. His natural bias was to respect things as they were, and in his eyes institutions, customs, systems, so long as they had not become actively mischievous, were good simply because they could boast pride of antiquity. And after all the relations of might and right are governed by a sliding scale, and it is very difficult to say anything conclusive about them at the time. Right supersedes might as reason dissolves and re-creates necessity; indeed, rights are a series of ever more subtly domineering mights, and the higher they rise the less they need to defend or inflict themselves. A man of Wesley's calibre would probably try to blend liberty with authority under the rule of reason. The difficulty of thinking right was stupendous in the eighteenth century; and even that difficulty paled before the difficulty of living right, which Wesley unquestionably accomplished.

A cursory examination of his sermons and *Journal* would suggest that he was well aware of the manifold political hypocrisies of his age, and that he had advanced views on tariffs, unemployment, intemperance, gambling, the land question, luxury trades and on the wrongs of the people. Certainly his *Thoughts Upon Slavery* in 1774 is a vivid appeal showing grace, grit and gumption. Unquestionably too, he was the first religious teacher in England who charged religion with social offices. Whilst still at Oxford, he and his Holy Club began to put into practice their firm belief in the saving power of education. They visited the prisoners in the jail once a week, admonished them of their vices and instructed their children. They set up a school, and taught boys and girls to read and write, inspected their knitting and sewing and tested their catechism. At the neighbouring workhouses they did similar work. In other words they anticipated the activities of the now highly-applauded University Settlements. 'His human sagacity later showed itself politically-minded when he established dispensaries, semi-public libraries, orphanages for the destitute and schools for children. He showed also that he sensed the need for pensions and medical benefits, and he certainly denounced usury, pawnbroking, speculation.' The distribution of wealth was often in his messages and he preached the most rigid doctrines concerning the accumulation of riches, asserting 'that I call upon God to record upon my soul, that I advise no more than I practise'. Instances of such practice are unending. At Oxford he lived on £28 per annum and gave the rest (£92) of his fellowship to the poor. As a writer and publisher it is affirmed that he gave away over £30,000 to charitable purposes. And when he was eighty-two years old he writes:

'On this and the following four days, I walked through the town and begged £200 in order to cloathe them that needed it most. But it was hard work, as most of the streets were filled with melting snow which often lay ankle-deep; so that my feet were steeped in snow-water from morning till evening.'

Such examples prove that at heart he was practically benevolent and that whatever may be said about the absence of pungent, direct political economy in his messages, his actual life was based upon such Utopian political principles as 'love rather than selfishness', on 'self-denial and not on personal desire'.

He also made indirect contributions to the political problems of his days. The Evangelical Revival both of Chapel and Church was almost entirely due to Wesley. This revival saturated the masses with a passion for a better life—personal, moral, mental and social—whilst the quickened spiritual vitality among the wealthy produced many a philanthropic spirit. From such spirits came the zeal for education, a movement for social purity, the advocacy of temperance, prison reform, factory legislation and the emancipation of slaves. Wilberforce, Hannah More, Sadler and Oastler were all products of the Revival, whilst Robert Raikes and John Howard were both personal friends of Wesley.

It is not suggested that Wesley's primary concern was with the social conditions of the eighteenth century. It was not. Like Paley and many another eighteenth-century divine, Wesley displayed relatively little spirituality in political feeling; then religion and politics were things apart. But Wesley's apparent political detachment did not preclude him from powerfully affecting the social conscience of eighteenth-century England which, in its turn, was to affect the politics of England. As a result of Wesley's life-work, the social conscience of England was probably never more alive than between about 1785 to 1840. And in that period this conscience worked on two postulates which had become inherent in the beliefs of Methodists and Evangelicals, and which in Wesley's eyes were axiomatic. They were (1) that the soul was infinitely more important than the body and (2) that help from the State was much inferior to self-help, worse in moral immediacy and, in cumulative effect, a *reductio ad absurdum*, seeing that such assistance weakened the fibre. Perhaps these hypotheses were not understood or believed in by professional politicians; at any rate Methodist political detachment often caused slighting comments from politico-economic historians, and motive is certainly a matter in which one age or generation is apt to misjudge another. Unquestionably Cobbett expressed a jaundiced view of these hypotheses, which consciously or unconsciously animated these late eighteenth-century Methodists and Evangelicals, when in 1834 or so he declared: 'the bitterest foes of freedom in England have been and are the Methodists'; called them 'ruffians and sectaries' and regretted 'that hooligans are no longer allowed to break up their field-meetings'. Probably the clear-brained, single-minded Wesley's detached attitude towards politics was that so long as man, 'the highest product of creation is rotten, the whole structure must be proportionally infirm; but make him sound and the surrounding elements will partake of the perfection embodied in their loftiest manifestation'. In that case he would not think the follies of society, corruption of Parliaments, harsh crime and poor laws, &c., worth unmasking while there was this higher game to fly at. 'His one aim was to found a *civitas Dei*; to make saints not citizens.' On the achievement of this object one sees directed the resolute and austere concentration of his mind and energies. It was for this he husbanded himself with economy. Leslie Stephen best sums up this aspect of Wesley's life when he decides that Wesley's aim was 'to stamp out vice, suppress drinking and debauchery, to show men the plain path to heaven'. And to do these three things was indeed a full-time job for any man in the eighteenth century.

Eighteenth-century Methodism made an indirect contribution

towards future political administration. The method of government adopted in the new Methodist chapels taught the adherents to share responsibilites, to develop pride in their successes, to be jealous of their reputation; in a word to learn the give and take necessary in the control of all enterprises shared by many. Such a training disciplined its members and such chapels formed admirable nurseries for future electors, members of Parliament and statesmen.

IV

Local government, as we understand the term, fell into the hands of the corrupt during the seventeenth and eighteenth centuries; a very big downward step from what had obtained in the fifteenth century.

There was no elective local government, no county councils, not even parish councils throughout Wesley's lifetime. There was an immense variety of municipal constitutions in the country; but probably none had a genuine method of election. Often these corporations were the descendants of the medieval guilds of the town, and consequently were more concerned with their own trade than with the proper government of the town. The history of some of these eighteenth-century corporations also shows that they were more concerned about making their individual fortune at the town's expense, than of arranging what was best for the townspeople. Membership of these privileged bodies was often a property right, and the provision of civic feasts was more important than the provision of sanitation, paving, street-lighting, &c. Even by 1800 reformers never seriously turned their attention to municipal reform, and grants and endowments which ought to have been spent on town improvement were sometimes deflected into the pockets of mayors and councillors. And like eighteenth-century Parliaments, towns then had useless posts that enabled the holders to make fortunes at the town's expense, and corporations often sold such occupations as 'ale-taster', 'coal-metre', 'corn-metre' to the town. In 1768 London sold the two last-named posts for £6,510 and £3,300 respectively, whilst at the end of the century, Manchester's richest banker held that of 'Muzzler of Mastiff Dogs and Bitches'.

The parish was held responsible for its poor, sick, children, old people, vagrants and idlers; but from 1601 to 1834 the adminis-

tration of relief was in the hands of magistrates, vestries and overseers. At Wesley's birth England had had a century's experience
of poor-law administration; by then it had a presumably complete
and systematic oversight of the poor in the parishes to which they
belonged, and certainly it had overseers of the poor, test work,
workhouses and compulsory poor-rate assessments. But there was
no uniformity in the administration; each locality was left to raise
its rates and distribute its funds at discretion. Parliament had, in
1723, encouraged adjacent parishes to found and support a
'Union Workhouse', fostered such unions in 1782 and in 1795
blessed the 'Speenhamland' experiment by which wages were
supplemented with parish relief. Much about this time it had
recommended the appointment of 'Guardians of the Poor'.

Rates for the most part were collected in a haphazard way in
the eighteenth century, for till well towards the end of the century,
few streets had a name or houses a number.

Nevertheless they had the germ of assessment in their collections.
As far back as 1547 it was enjoined 'that the curate of every parish
shall, according to such talent as God has given him, exhort his
parishioners to remember the poor according to their means and
the need there be for such help'. Where the exhortations of the
collectors, clergy, churchwardens and bishops had failed, the
bishop was allowed to send the 'obstinate' householder who
refused to contribute to the parochial fund, to appear before the
justices, and these justices might 'cesse, tax, and limit upon every
such obstinate person so refusing, according to their good discretion what sum the obstinate person shall pay'. And if he 'should
prove still obdurate, he could be committed to prison'. At the
end of the seventeenth century, Aubrey confirms the idea of such
assessment.

'There were no rates in those days, but the Church Ale did the Business. In every Parish the Wardens arranged a Feast with Plenty of
Good Ale, followed by a Collection to which every Householder present
was expected, perhaps compelled, to contribute in Accordance with his
Status, for the Relief of the Poor and the Conduct of the Parish Affairs
during the ensuing year.'

In the early eighteenth century, Whitsuntide was the occasion
chosen for the 'collection', and merry-making was combined with
the transaction of parochial business. The actual administration
of poor relief was less pleasing than was the collection of the
funds.

Often there was no incitement to industry or perseverence and much favouritism was shown in the distribution, and cases are quoted where 'shiftless poverty was bequeathed from pauper sire to indolent son', a heritage leading to the old cry 'once on the rates always on the rates'. These idle incapables did not mind if they, their wives and children had to wear a badge on their right sleeve adorned with a big capital 'P' indicating that they were in receipt of poor relief, nor did they object to being forbidden to move about from parish to parish.

At all the workhouses 'test-work' was authorized, and overseers were expected to raise weekly 'a convenient stock of flax, hemp, wool, thread, iron and other necessary ware and stuff to set the poor to work'. Often the workhouses were farmed out to a contractor who undertook to feed and clothe the inmates for a fixed sum, and he made what profit he could out of their labour. Such an arrangement led Crabbe to write:

> Alternate Masters now their Slave command,
> Urge the weak efforts of his feeble hand,
> And when his age attempts its task in vain,
> With ruthless taunts of 'lazy poor', complain.

The younger inmates of the workhouses were often hired out to farmers and factory-owners, and contractors with gangs of children and juveniles would tour the countryside at special times or hire them to the mills.

As buildings, workhouses were often mere pens, and Crabbe in *The Village* pictures them and their occupants in the following:

> Theirs is yon House that Holds the Parish Poor,
> Whose walls of mud scarce bear the broken door;
> There, where the putrid vapours, flagging, play,
> And the dull wheel hums dolefully through the day;
> There Children dwell who know no Parent's care;
> Parents who know no Children's Love dwell there.
> Heart-broken Matrons on their joyless bed,
> Forsaken Wives, and Mothers never wed;
> Dejected Widows with unheeded Tears,
> And crippled Age with more than Childhood fears;
> The Lame, the Blind, and, far the happiest they,
> The Moping Idiot, and the Madman Gay.

Crabbe's picture is most doleful, but perhaps it is not fully comprehensive; for eighteenth-century workhouses were not only the scene of hard, unwearying toil, but there was no regular provision concerning diet, and discipline was probably most cruel. A decade after Wesley's death, James Neild describes how he saw a boy aged twelve in Norwich Workhouse, who was fatherless and whose mother had run away: 'He had round his neck an iron collar called a yoke, with four projecting prongs, secured by a large clumsy iron padlock. Upon one leg was a strong iron ring, fastened near the ankle like a handcuff, to which was attached a massy chain about four feet long; at the end of this chain was a log of wood two feet in circumference. With these encumbrances he slept every night. . . . Every Sunday he was locked up by himself all day and night with his irons on.'

In addition to this parish poor there was the vagrant train for the overseers to deal with. This numerous body, legally described as 'sturdy beggars, incorrigible rogues, idle vagabonds', depended for a subsistence on begging and stealing. Parish officers provided for them 'places of work', 'houses of correction', and at both them and workhouses, there was a 'fasting' room. Fasting and whipping were thought to be the best remedies for all such troublesome persons in the eighteenth century. What actually transpired in fasting and whipping rooms can only be imagined, for it was not till 1790 that the law allowed 'guardians of the poor' and Justices of the Peace to visit such rooms. Nor was it till 1816 that the law enacted that 'it was not lawful for any governour, guardian or master of any house, industry or workhouse to chain and manacle any poor person of sane mind'. A provision significant of what had passed within the walls during the whole of the eighteenth century.

v

On wrong-doers, especially vagrants and poachers, the landed J.P.s administered a drastic code of punishment. These magistrates were allowed to decide questions of law and fact, could please themselves what evidence they would hear and could sentence prisoners without a jury and without publicity. They had another privilege that was extremely important; whenever Parliament wished to 'learn local facts and feelings' they simply consulted such magistrates. They were paid no salaries for their work and time, but these 'trading justices', as they were called, were allowed to take their income out of the fines they imposed. Nor was it till 1792 that they were abolished even in London.

Fielding, himself a magistrate, said, 'Eighteenth-century magistrates are never indifferent in a cause, but then they get nothing from either side'. And he, Richardson and Smollett often refer to their far-reaching powers, proceedings and pronouncements. Methodists often suffered at their hands, for they were confused with vagrants, &c., and the early years of Methodism record the ignorance and misconduct of these minor justices. Above them were the High Sheriff and the Lord Lieutenant of the county; but neither concerned himself much with what the J.P.s did.

The spectacle of those who administered justice in the important courts or those who performed the duties of civil servants is equally depressing. Up to 1855 appointments to the civil service and the judiciary were purely by nomination, and both civil servants and judges were rare creatures, and where salaried, were paid out of the King's purse. Thus offices, whether administrative or judicial, were not given to ability and experience, but to favourites or to the highest bidder. One Lord Chancellor sold masterships in Chancery outright; another, Scott of Eldon, appointed his son to four separate offices in the Chancery Court, a third appointed a duke as registrar to the Chancery Court at the early age of thirteen. It was the same story with the administrative offices. Most government employees held what were called 'offices of profit', and by reason of that position, enjoyed the right or were able to effect a claim, to receive payments and dues which would recompense them for their labours. Pepys has preserved for us the principles and practices of one of the most upright officials of his day; nowadays he would be ignominiously dismissed for gross corruption. Like other government offices, the law then had its sinecures such as 'Prothonotary of Durham', 'Chief Justice in Eyre (North of Trent)' at £2,250 per annum; financial rewards for doing no judicial work at all. The public trials of such well-known criminals as Eugene Aram, Dr. Dodds, Jonathan Wild give an idea of the corruptness prevailing even in the High Courts of Justice. Others give an idea of the unfairness, the cursing, swearing, savagery, &c., of other judges. Yet the century had its striking exceptions. There was the humane Earl of Mansfield. Mr. Justice Pratt, who presided over the Wilkes's trial in 1763, conferred a permanent benefit on the English judicial system and vindicated the fairness of English justice. Lord Kilwarden always interposed the shield of the law between tenants and landlords in Ireland.

VI

The criminal law that these magistrates and judges were told to administer was as brutal and ferocious as the class it sought to terrify into decency. During the first half of the century, there were some 160 felonies punishable by death and the loss of all property; the second half saw the number increased to 253. In this half, Parliaments seem to have spent a good deal of their time in keeping down the poor, in devising new sources of taxation calculated to press heavily on the wretched, in passing new Enclosure Acts and in framing fresh Acts for Preserving Game. Then the death-sentence had to be passed for any theft of articles valued at 5/- or more, and it was no uncommon thing for boys and girls aged ten to be hanged without mercy, and as late as 1791 two lads in their early teens were gibbeted for such thefts. The death-sentence was given for pickpocketing over 1/-, for cutting down a river-bank. Such executions were conducted on a wholesale scale, and every town of any size had its 'hanging day' every few weeks; in 1776, 223 persons were hanged in London alone; in 1785 twenty were hanged outside Newgate Jail on February 2 and on April 28 another nineteen. Such butchery led Horace Walpole to write in the nineties, 'It is shocking to think what a shambles this country is grown', and Wesley says that in 1785 he 'preached to 47 criminals all under sentence of death at Newgate'; at which service 'there was something awful in the clink of their chains'.

Few people were as squeamish as Wesley. Utter callousness of the criminals pervaded all ranks of society. Usually the prison chaplain preached a 'condemned' sermon on the Sunday preceding the executions 'during which the coffins lay on the table and around which had to stand the condemned prisoners'. On 'hanging days', as the death-carts rattled along to Tyburn or the town-gallows, pavements and windows would be crowded with spectators. Ringside seats to view the execution at close quarters could be bought at from 6d. to 2/-. Even the principals were expected to regard the affair as a joke; and not infrequently they badinaged with onlookers, bawled out a dying confession which had been prepared for them, or complained that the leg-irons and handcuffs were too tight, and that 'the pain distracted their thoughts from those spiritual reflections which were now so peremptory'. Case-hardened criminals were, of course, stupefied

with drink, and dressed in their best clothes, they tried to gain
the popular verdict of 'he died like a gentleman'. Such great
eighteenth-century spectacular rogues as 'Dick Turpin, Tom King,
"Blue-skin" Blake, Jack Sheppard all seem to have been good performers on the scaffold, and Jerry Abershaw, terror of the Kingston
district, went to the gallows with a flower between his lips'. Fielding
has delineated the unseemly methods of execution, the Tyburn
gallows with its permanent erection of three posts, wooden
galleries and crowds of paying spectators. He does not, however,
suggest that the method of execution necessarily resulted in instant
death. Johnson complained, 'Men are to be hanged in a new way;
Tyburn itself is not safe from the fury of innovation'. This was
true. At Tyburn, the condemned person standing in a cart had
his neck encircled with a taut rope, whereupon the cart was
driven away leaving him suspended. At Newgate, &c., the
prisoner stood on the ground and jailers jerked him up into mid-
air by means of a rope slung over a beam. Neither method of
execution would necessarily mean instantaneous death, but
rather in that from asphyxia. Hogarth's pictures show the prison
chaplain lolling in his carriage, ready to read the funeral service
at the gallows, quite unmoved by the ordeal. They also show a
tall, lean figure with lank hair who sits in the cart with the condemned criminal, exhorting him to repentance. He is Silas Told,
who occupied himself for many years with attending malefactors
and visiting workhouses. This Methodist died in 1778, and
Wesley writes:

'I buried what was mortal of honest Silas Told. For many years he
attended the malefactors in Newgate, without fee or reward; and I suppose no man for this hundred years has been so successful in that
melancholy office. God had given him peculiar talents for it; and he
had amazing success therein. The greatest part of those whom he
attended, died in peace and many of them in the triumph of faith.'

Boswell says that the discontinuance of these hideous public
executions was discussed one evening in 1773 at the Literary Club,
and Johnson thus delivered himself:

'No Sir, it would not be an improvement. They object that the old
method draws together a number of spectators. If they did not draw
the spectators they would not answer their purpose. The old method
is most satisfactory to all parties; the public is gratified with a procession; the criminal is supported by it. Why should all this be swept
away?'

Nevertheless the Tyburn procession was swept away ten years after Johnson's pronouncement. After 1783 executions had to be arranged at the different prisons themselves; but public opinion was so vehement, that hangings had to be carried on outside the jail's walls.

Eighteenth-century justice was not always satisfied even with execution. The ferocious punishment of being hanged, drawn and quartered was still awarded to the traitor; for the law was still in force that 'he should be half-hanged, disembowelled and then struck into four quarters'. Perhaps still more savage was the code which condemned a woman, guilty of murdering her husband, to being burnt alive. The main roads approaching the gallows in all the principal towns were bordered with avenues of 'gallows-trees', each garnished with its ghastly fruit. Sometimes bodies were exposed on public bridges for days before burial, and the heads of the rebels of the 'Forty Five' rotted on Temple Bar till late in the century. Highwaymen were often left dangling in chains from boughs as a warning; pirates were tied to a stake till 'at least three tides had passed over them'.

This love of entertainment afforded by public punishments was also catered for with the pillory, ducking-stool and scold's bridle. The more permanent of these correctives were usually to be found in the town centre, whilst the stocks and whipping-post—a stout column of oak firmly wedged in the ground—were hard by the parish church. Thus the public could enjoy the spectacle of punishment meted out to courtesans, common scolds, brawlers and like delinquents. It is barely a hundred years since Parliament abolished the pillory; it was supposed to be for the punishment of cheats and minor criminals, but in the eighteenth century it was the usual way of degrading political and religious offenders. One of its most famous victims then was Defoe, sentenced to stand in the pillory for three days for his satirical attack on the Church's prosecution of Dissenters. Instead of pelting him with garbage after the usual fashion, the crowd laid garlands about him, and stood round him cheering him and drinking his health.

Another source of punitive amusement was the barrel lined with nails, into which convicted women were thrust and then trundled down the hillsides amidst general hilarity. A popular sight for Londoners was to visit the Bridewells on whipping days, when women, stripped to the waist, were flogged in public as long as the visiting alderman desired, for minor offences or prostitution.

Branding was imposed up to 1717 on runaway slaves, malefactors, gipsies, vagabonds, and the letter 'W' was stamped on thumb or breast with a red-hot iron, whilst persons convicted of petty theft were branded on hand or ear with the letter 'M'. And this branding was done in open court. Gradually judges were empowered to sentence felons for transportation instead of branding them, and in 1779 they were allowed to impose fines or whippings instead of open-court branding for minor crime.

Naturally these degrading public punishments simply stimulated and fostered all the worst instincts of the mob, and gave great opportunities for ribaldry by facetious prisoners, who provided cheap entertainment for simple, callous onlookers. A century when respectable citizens found the antics of the insane simply comic and deformity merely funny, would naturally find its rougher elements highly diverted by the public punishment of supposed or actual crime.

Then there were the physical punishments applied in camera to suspected wrong-doers. Thumbscrews, spiked necklets, contracting handcuffs were some of the 'strong and sore tortures' applied to extract confessions from prisoners up to 1772, when the *peine forte et dure* method of extracting evidence was abandoned.

VII

Persons charged with serious crime had frequently to undergo the mental torture arising from a long wait before trial. The assizes or 'jail-deliveries' were held in some places once a year, in others every three years, and in some only once in seven years. Yet guilty and innocent alike had to languish in jail awaiting trial.

Persons convicted on one of the many capital charges were sometimes transported to convict settlements instead of being hanged. Such transportation continued till half-way through the nineteenth century, when the Colonies objected to receiving any more of such unwanted immigrants. In 1718, owing to the shortage of white labour in America, the Government adopted the device of handing over convicts to contractors at about £20 a head. For years there was great demand for such felon labour, and when the supply ran short, the English suppliers do not seem to have stopped short at adopting the press-gang methods to supplement it. Such legitimate and illegitimate traffic continued up to the American War of Independence, whereupon England had to find other fields for her unwanted, erring sons and daughters. In the last quarter of the century, Australia and Van Diemen's Land furnished the home country with fresh outlets for her many convicts. At the colonial places the felons were locked up from sunset to sunrise, all wore heavy leg-irons, all were heavily flogged on the slighest excuse by the official 'scourger'. They were housed in hulks, stockades, barracks or caravans, and men, whose sole offence had been that of poaching a rabbit, quickly degen-erated and became brutalized. Another eighteenth-century way of reducing the number of home prisoners was to swell Army and Navy with 'pardoned' felons, 'released' debtors, whilst the popula-tion of workhouses was now and then decimated, by impressing into the services lusty, superfluous vagrants and paupers.

As for the English prisons themselves, such pictures as Hogarth's *Harlot's Progress*, or *Cryes of London*, or *Humours of the Fleet*, together with Defoe's *Moll Flanders*, &c., give some idea of the horrors that happened within their walls. These were the days when prison governors were men who had paid large sums for their positions, and who looked to the prisoners for their income and the means to replace the capital they had sunk. In 1724, the Warden of the Fleet paid Lord Clarendon £5,000 for the office; he went but seldom to the prison and he sold subordinate positions to bidders at exorbitant prices. No proper books regarding the reception and discharge of felons were kept and so many of them got 'lost'; the wealthy ones quickly reappearing at large. 'No brigands were more successful in wringing ransom out of their victims, than the keepers of prisons in the eighteenth century out of the unfortunates who came within their power', says one historian; even prisoners who were pronounced innocent, were detained for months until exorbitant and illegal dues had been extracted. Mere debtors were subjected to similar duress, and Neild gives many examples of these eighteenth-century illegal dues of which the following is typical:

'Original debt'	1–0
'Expenses to recover debt'	8–11
'Fees exacted by gaoler'	15–8

And the debtor would have to pay this extra 24s. 7d. or be imprisoned with felons for at least another three months.

Like most eighteenth-century details, the prisons had their in-congruities and not all the prisoners fared badly. A 'darling of the

N

people' like Wilkes, whilst in prison, had rare and costly delicacies presented to him by his admirers. But with the vast majority, matters were far otherwise. Howard, who spent his life in ameliorating the lot of the distressed prisoners and in so doing spent £30,000 of his own money between 1773 and 1790, makes it quite clear that everywhere in England the prisons were a disgrace to humanity. The poor wretches were flung into subterranean dungeons, into wet and noisome caverns, into hideous holes. The old 'Habeas Corpus' Act was sound theory, but inconvenient for the strong arms of the eighteenth century; jails were useful for despotic leaders, for bigoted Churchmen, for rapacious money-lenders. Incidental examples of this rapacity are shown in the preserved papers of Thomas Guy, founder of the famous hospital. These entries show that he often redeemed debt prisoners in Wesley's youth. He 'paid £1–16–8 for Wm. Smith a poor weaver who had been in prison for a long time for debt'; '£1–4–8 for Jane Middleton Widow and Children, very poore and a prisonnier 20 weeks'. . . . He also released Eliz. Tomkins 'very poor, almost naked, a prisonnier for 10 months' and 'Bartholomew Nevill, a poor industrious man, one arme, sells oringis in a barrow about our streets, a prisonier for 12 munse'. No wonder eighteenth-century prisons were always densely overcrowded. Official food was rank, nauseous, scanty and, moreover, was subject to the jailer's caprice; so in effect, prisoners really depended for nourishment on outside friends, or the charity of the benevolent. Even water was doled out in cupfuls, whilst bedding was putrid straw, reeking with accumulated filth. All prisoners were heavily ironed; drunkenness was universal and unchecked; gambling was common; vice and obscenity were everywhere. Vicious intercourse, sickness, starvation, cruelty, chains, awful oppression and culpable neglect faced men whose only crime was that of owing a very few shillings. Johnson said that 'he computed the number of prisoners in one day in 1759 for small debts was upwards of 20,000 and that he calculated one in every four died from the irons, thumbscrew and bad feeding, whilst jail-fever wiped out quite as many'.

VIII

It is to the credit of a few magistrates, judges, juries, writers and philanthropists that these laws and punishments were being attacked even in this century. Goldsmith expressed himself thus:

'Nor can I avoid even questioning the validity of that right which social combinations have assumed of capitally punishing offences of a slight nature . . . when by indiscriminate penal laws, the nation beholds the same punishment affixed to dissimilar degrees of guilt, the people are led to lose all sense of distinction in the crime, and this distinction is the bulwark of all morality.'

This opinion was strongly supported by Romilly and Howard, and in the nineteenth century resulted in considerable mitigation of the severity of the law. For even in the eighteenth the law left some loopholes.

Up to 1725 any one fleeing from the law, could claim 'sanctuary' in a consecrated building and it is still possible to see some of these ancient 'sanctuary-knockers'. 'Benefit of Clergy' was another and often successful appeal against sentence. By this loophole, those who were in what were called 'minor orders', could still demand to be tried by ecclesiastical authorities and not by the judicial ones. To obtain such eligibility, the applicant had to prove capacity to read a verse from the Bible. So everybody who could read, might easily obtain exemption from punishment for his crime, as by this century, Church authorities practically exacted no punishment on their wrong-doers. Contrariwise, most Church authorities were in sympathy with the penal code and it was an easy matter to 'fail' the candidate who applied for 'benefit of Clergy'; thus by the mid-decades of the century, the literate man who stole a sheep or a hare was really treated as though he were illiterate. Lay judges and juries also often evaded the death-sentence by such subterfuges as declaring the property stolen was not worth 5/–, by such singular technicalities as acquitting a prisoner because the accused had two Christian names, whereas only one was given in the indictment, or because some name had been incorrectly spelled. It was not till the early nineteenth century that Bentham supplemented Goldsmith's previous argument, by pointing out that certainty of punishment was more effective than severity, that severe punishments induced juries to acquit criminals and thus the certainty of punishment was diminished.

On the question of Punishment this eminent jurist later was to make such revolutionary declarations as 'all punishment is mischief; all punishment in itself is evil'. Almost as revolutionary to the general attitude towards crime were the appeals of Howard and Mrs. Fry for satisfactory buildings to be used as prisons, and who became more or less directly responsible for such prisons as Millbank, Wormwood Scrubs and Dartmoor.

IX

In spite of the prodigious number of people who managed to get hanged or transported, the eighteenth century was by no means a bad time for the many wrong-doers. It was the golden age for pilferers and such specialized thieves known as 'mudlarks', 'light-horsemen', 'heavy-horsemen', 'highwaymen'. Brawlers, bruisers, bullies, tramps infested every town and village. Smuggling was conducted on a wholesale scale and public feeling was with the offenders; at any rate it seems to have required a regimental officer and twenty men to act as escort for a single notorious smuggler. In 1733 it was estimated that the loss to the revenue by smuggling on tobacco alone amounted to a third of the whole duty; that less than a third of the tea imported passed through the Customs; that quite half the brandy and much of the silk imported, contrived to evade duty. On moonless nights long lines of mounted smugglers, each with his horse laden with tubs, filed silently along; they showed their familiarity with squire and parson so far as to use the church itself as depot for contraband goods. In 1773 Wesley mournfully writes that 'Rye would do many things gladly, but will not part with the accursed thing of smuggling'. Not only Rye went in for 'free-trade' in tea, sugar, snuff, silks, gin, brandy, &c., but the Cornish smugglers, led by 'King Nick' in the mid-century, acquired national renown. This Nicholas Buzza owned a fleet of armed smugglers, cheated the revenue out of thousands a year, fooled the riding-officers times out of number, beat off the militia and fought big privateers. And this romantic idol of the West Country, the hero of song and story, was said to have been 'a powerful local preacher'. What Wesley could not persuade his followers to abandon, Pitt's measures of 1788 accomplished, for they withered the trade. The century saw a decline in piracy as well as in smuggling. Exquemeling is the great authority on the exploits of the early eighteenth-century buccaneers, and Charles Johnson writes extensively on the English pirates of the period. From them one hears of the famous Captain Avery who was dubbed the 'Arch-Pyrat', and whom his admirers called 'the flower and pattern of all bowld mariners'; he was the hero of Defoe's *Captain Singleton*, and of a play *The Successful Pyrat*. Another was Edward Teach, nicknamed 'Blackbeard', and who was probably the character on whom Stevenson based his Long John Silver. A third was Captain Misson who founded a socialist

republic in Madagascar; his biographers say he was kindness itself
and only slaughtered a victim when unavoidably driven to do so,
and even then with the greatest reluctance. In the words of
Byron:

> He was the mildest manner'd man
> That ever scutt'd ship or cut a throat.

Another was Bartholomew Roberts who was said to have
accounted for 400 ships during his brief and brilliant career. He,
like the smuggler Nicholas Buzza, was a strict teetotaller and a
strict Sabbatarian. Indeed, many of these eighteenth-century
pirates were declared to be evangelical; certainly many of them
had a clergyman aboard, although the clergyman's duties included those of brewing rum-punch for his shipmates, and of
having sole charge of the corkscrew.

                                X

   In this century England qualified herself for the bad pre-
eminence of being the most drunken nation of the civilized world.
In an evil hour of the first quarter of the century, the Government
decided to improve the revenue by encouraging distilleries in
England. From 1724, gin-drinking became the rage; in a dozen
years every sixth house in London was a grog-shop; a population
of under six millions was consuming nearly twice as many gallons
of the liquid annually. Even easy-going Parliaments were shocked
at such growing consumption, and in 1736 they imposed a tax of
20/– per gallon on gin and called for an expensive licence to retail
it. The tax was largely inoperative, since it merely increased
smuggling and led to such accepted devices as selling gin under
names like 'Old Tom', 'Red Biddy'. It evoked too, such a spate of
ballads, lampoons and satires on the parliamentarians themselves,
that they allowed the Act to become a dead letter. Eighteenth-
century doctors raised their voices against these spirits, and half-
way through the century, they asserted that there were many
thousand incurable cases of disease directly attributable to gin.
Hogarth attacked the bane and in his *Gin Lane*, created an awe-
inspiring picture of its ravages. It was so cheap and powerful that
retailers in London were accustomed to hang out painted signs
announcing that customers could be made drunk for a penny,
dead-drunk for twopence, with the additional incentive of 'Straw
to lie on Free'.

Still gin had its ancient competitor to contend with, and one of the most popular songs of 1757 was the *Beer Drinking Briton*, which vaunted the wholesome effects of beer, and pressed its claims over gin, wine and other spirituous liquors. The chorus ran:

> Let us sing our own treasures, Old England's good cheer,
> The profits and pleasures of stout Bri'ish beer;
> Your wine-tippling, dram-sipping fellows retreat,
> But your beer-drinking Britons can never be beat.

In 1760, the brewers of London alone were said to have turned out over 35 million gallons of beer. These figures sound almost astronomical. Perhaps other towns were not brewing to the same proportional extent; at any rate an East-Anglian publican found it necessary to encourage consumption, and he propounded and practised a unique method for the recovery of old drinking debts:

'Notice is hereby given, that all Persons indebted for Strong Beer to Mr. William Gray at the Sign of the Fountain in St. Benedict's Parish, Norwich, that if they will come to His House and spend Sixpence in Jorams of Beer Reddy Munni, for every sixpence they so spend, sixpence more shall be set off everyone of their Respective Debt. Provided the Persons so Indebted do in that Manner drink themselves out of Such Debts within the Space of Six Months from the Date hereof; but Uppon Failure thereof, they shall be prosecuted According to Lawe.'

Details of eighteenth-century towns and villages show that there were hundreds of disorderly public houses, 'taps', 'mug-houses', 'beer-shops', 'taverns', &c., even in small places. At the end of the century, one of these towns with a population of 40,000 or so, had 400 public houses habitually open till midnight, many of which opened on Sundays too at 4.0 a.m. A high percentage of them were supported entirely by the worst characters, and in the main centre which 'was a positive circus of crime . . . there were upwards of 30 saloons and other places of public resort appropriated to thieves and prostitutes' and that independently of these '. . . there were hundreds of dens of vice within three minutes' walk of the square'. Of 'evil-houses' there were upwards of 300 in this town and at every one of them wine, rum, gin, &c., could be procured; in one street alone twenty-two of these establishments could be counted. The harpies living in them were said to number upwards of 1,200 with double that number lodging elsewhere. Most of these women were at the same time professional thieves,

and as the report says 'they could rob without fear of legal consequences'. Male thieves practising regularly in this town were
calculated to number 1,000; fitful exponents were assessed at 500,
dock specialists 600, with a reservoir of 1,500 beginners under the
age of fourteen. This 'mass of vice' was said to cost the town under
review, upwards of £700,000 per annum. No wonder that John
Wesley, no teetotaller himself, reckoned, 'drunkenness is one of
the great evils of my day', and adds, 'gin drinking affects all
ranks of society, desolates town and country, and subjugates the
English people'.

When drunkenness was so rampant and when standards of
personal and public morality were so low, it is no wonder that
mob law and mob manners ruled in most of the big towns. Newspapers of the first half of the century contain countless chronicles
of acts of robbery with violence, in broad daylight. Riots broke
out on the slightest provocation. Lecky's pages abound in almost
incredible stories of vice and crime, open and rampant in the
streets of the biggest towns. Ladies attending Court functions had
to be guarded by servants armed with blunderbusses 'to shoot at
the rogues'. Respectable women could not venture in the streets
after nightfall without the risk of being grossly outraged, whilst
defenceless men were subjected to abominable tortures. Children
and adults were held to ransom. Pedestrians were insulted by the
hordes of chair-men and linkboys, whilst a very popular amusement of servants in private houses and waiters in taverns was to
hurl pailfuls of foul water on to the passer-by. The aristocratic
'Mohawks' added to the street terrors, whilst in the country 'and
on the fringe of every town, gipsies added their share to both confusion and danger'. Fielding gives pictures of the 'lawless arrogance of the rabble on the river' as well as in the streets, 'of the
brutal language that was followed by brutal action'. Smollett
declared that 'thieves and robbers were now become more desperate and savage than had ever appeared since mankind was
civilized'. In 1782 Horace Walpole writes: 'Owing to the profu-
sion of housebreakers, highwaymen and footpads—and especially
because of the savage barbarities of the two latter who commit the
most wanton cruelties—if one goes abroad to dinner, you would
think one was going to the relief of Gibraltar'.

The filthy narrow streets seem to have been always crowded in
this century with coaches, phaetons, chairs, wheelbarrows; with
fops, chimney-sweeps, porters bearing heavy burdens; with

(according to MacCarthy) 'bullies, bailiffs, cutpurses; with funerals, christenings, weddings, street-fights; all mixed up in inextricable confusion. . . . Nobody placed any restriction on hawkers and there was a very babel of street-cries of orange-girls, chair-menders, broom-sellers, ballad-singers and those bawl-ing for the poor distressed prisoners'. Hogarth's *Enraged Musician* adds other noises to this street row: iron-shod wheels on cobbles, clatters of hoofs, bells on reins, newspaper-boys, barrel-organs, fiddlers, apple-women, whilst even the coaches and 'penny-post' had to announce their presence with horns, rattles, whistles, &c. Other writers add their testimony to the noises and dangers of the streets in the metropolis. Sir Roger de Coverley seems to have been terrified by the London brawlers; Gay in *Trivia* recounts more deafening cries and adds to the perils to person and pocket undergone by foot-passengers, whilst Johnson says of the Strand itself:

> Prepare for death if here at night you roam,
> And sign your will before you sup from home.

The old men who acted as 'watch' during three quarters of the century, who made their rounds to see that nothing was unusual, announce the hour and state the weather conditions, were utterly incapable of dealing with such chaos and mob-rule. They were veritably of the Dogberry and Verges type; each parish was sup-posed to have its own men and all were jealous of any intrusion into their preserve by another officer. As late as 1788 the *Morning Post* was describing them as 'decrepid old Dotards'.

The history of Bow Street runners and careers like that of Jonathan Wild, 'principal thief-taker in Great Britain', give an idea of another unscrupulous company of men who were supposed to protect the public. Equally illuminating are the stories of the 'watches' in provincial towns who were unsuccessful in dealing with a population just emerging from a long spell of turbulent demoralization. Often these 'watches' were the boon companions of brawlers and wrong-doers; indeed, they were recruited from the very class against whom they were supposed to protect. Suspen-sion and dismissals for drunkenness, brutal conduct, sleeping on duty, &c., were daily occurrences; many of them were convicted as receivers of stolen property, keepers of 'dens of infamy', friends of 'mug-house' proprietors. A uniform comprising a beaver 'topper', blue frock-coat, broad belt, silver buckles and buttons and white pantaloons, would be far more appealing to these be-whiskered officers than any quixotic fastidiousness about doing their duty. As a body they were totally unfitted to deal with the Augean stables of vice to be found in most eighteenth-century towns, and it is little wonder that dragoons, militia and naval men often had to do duties now associated with the police.

CHAPTER VIII

EIGHTEENTH-CENTURY LANGUAGE

I

In this chapter a deliberate attempt has been made to select examples of phrases, words, spellings, meanings and pronunciations which probably characterized many of the writers and most of the speakers of the eighteenth century. Whilst selected from a variety of available sources, the examples have been chosen so as to illustrate the present speech practices of dialect speakers who have characteristic differences. Thus these examples of archaisms may accordingly strike the reader as erring in deficiency or redundancy, and further, that the excess of iteration is accompanied by an absence of phonetic notation. But to those ordinary readers, who know and appreciate some of England's dialects, perhaps these shortcomings will be excusable, and it is hoped that the examples chosen will show that the vocabulary, grammar, spelling and pronunciation of many so-called illiterates, are not the irrational outcome of sheer ignorance and rusticity. Some of them may even prove that the speech and writing habits of many a peasant, have haunting associations with those of the eighteenth-century *élite*. Unquestionably they are also the ever-diminishing survivals of a number of standards, current in different regions as late as the eighteenth century.

'For despite the efforts of the B.B.C., the powerful activities of the motor-car, the force of ever-changing population, the benign influence of schools and the printing press, many of these outlaws of the rules of modern orthography and of grammar and of vocal utterance continue to flourish in many a corner of the land.'

II

The vagaries of eighteenth-century English grammar are all the stranger when it is borne in mind, that long before its dawn, grammarians had dealt exhaustively with this aspect of language. In 1624 *A Perfect Survey of the English Tongue* had been written by a man named Hewes. Sixteen years later there was another production with an even more flamboyant title:

'Orthoepia Anglicana: or the first principall part of the English Grammer, Teaching the Art of Righte Speaking and Pronouncing English with certaine exact rules of Orthography and Rules of Spelling of Combining Syllables and Directions for Keeping Stops or Points between Sentences and Sentences. A Work in Itself and never Known to be accomplished by Any Before. No lesse Profitable than Necessary for all Sorts as well Native as Foreigners that Desire to attaine the Perfection of our English Tongue. Methodically composed by the Industrie of Simon Daines, Scholemaster of Hintlesham in Suffs in 1640.'

Ben Jonson perhaps never knew of this 'industry', or perhaps he disputed its accuracy, for he too wrote another seventeenth-century English grammar with less sonorous claims. In 1711 Brightland produced another text-book on English grammar; Wesley one in 1748 and Bishop Lowth a third in 1762, whilst Lindley Murray brought out the most lasting one in 1795. In 1818 even Lindley Murray had to yield in popularity to the self-taught William Cobbett, whose grammatical axioms were unquestioned for generations by the English-speaking people.

These grammars are still interesting because they indicate the perpetual, uncontrolled changes in English language and reveal the eighteenth-century attitude towards inflexions, accidence and syntax. Most of the grammarians assumed a pontifical attitude towards the subject, and the majority of them tried to graft the elaborate syntactical forms of Latin grammar on to the old English stock. Especially during the first three quarters of the century, most writers fell in with that fashion and so their work, from a grammatical standpoint, is very mannered, pedantic and full of pleonasms and appositions. Periphrasis also affected their grammatical constructions. Such mannerisms led them to phrase sentences which, nowadays, could be considered defective when regarded from a grammatical angle. Writers of national fame were responsible for such solecisms as: 'Their strength or speed, or vigilance were given in aid of our defects.' 'Who should I meet, but my old friend. . . .' 'Every person's happiness depends in part upon the respect they meet with in the world.' 'Both minister and magistrate is compelled to choose between his duty and his reputation.' 'Let me awake the King of Morven, he that smiles in danger, he that is like the sun.' 'The greatest masters of critical learning differ among one another.' 'No book has been published, since your departure of which much notice is taken.' And even a Gray could write:

And many a holy text around she strews,
That teach the rustic moralist to die.

Grammar, as understood to-day, did not advance greatly during the century. Defoe never got so far in it as to realize the logical defectiveness of a form like 'between you and I', a solecism that was also used by Foote. The Verney papers are full of phrases like, 'how things goes there', 'he has never gave me a moment's alarm', 'he has gotten', 'he and me was a-going', and of using 'I' when, according to modern rules, it should have been 'me'. Other papers indicate that they said 'As I were going', 'you have gotten'. Newspapers printed 'The canals were froze over', 'I catched it up for a moment'. Chesterfield wrote, 'English is but little spoke in France', and Wesley, 'the moment I awaked', 'her husband has forbid her to speak to me'. Richardson wrote, 'he don't know you'; Boswell senior objected to Johnson because 'he keeped a school', and later, Byron was to write 'there let him lay'. Frances Burney says that Court circles and the 'Blue-Stocking Club' regularly used phrases like 'she done her part', 'he hasted back', 'she sung', 'you writ to me', 'he oped the door', 'the place stunk', 'all sweared it was dead', and that the use of 'telled, selled, catched, gived, comed, seeked, getten, tooked, never seed it', &c., was well established.

Throughout the century there was but a very thin veneer of classical education. This, together with the increase in the means of communication and the marked urge for authorship in more and more ranks of people, gradually made written English more flexible and less tolerant of the grammatical niceties tabulated by the eighteenth-century grammarians. As the century waxed and waned, the infinitive 'to' was increasingly omitted whilst comparative adjectives and adverbs were increasingly confused: 'nothing is finelier fancied', 'the dispute grew high, while Deborah, instead of reasoning stronger, talked louder', 'horrid troublesome', 'extreme delightful'. Old adjectival terminations were gradually dropped, and 'glassen, oaken, oaten, silvern, tinnen, hornen, artistical, sympathetical, academical, fantastical, aristocratical, dogmatical', &c., became less pronounced. Less and less concern was shown to distinguish 'although' from though, 'amongst' from among, &c. Single and double negatives were used with some freedom; double negatives were freely employed to make the negation more vehement: 'I have no pears, no apples, no . . . no nothing at all.' The adverbs 'ever' and 'never' grew to be interchangeable; some abandon was shown in the employment of the adjective 'no' for the adverb 'not'. Pronouns were used haphazardly. Often personal ones were obtruded: 'The mistress she wrote and said . . .' 'For coming to see jno hines his wife.' The demonstrative 'them' was commonly used for 'those': 'Them are the men I saw.' 'I saw them boys.' 'There' was often added to make the statement more demonstrative: 'Them there are the men I saw.' 'Give me them there books.' Distinctions between the nominative and accusative were often ignored: 'Me and my wife is going.' 'Shall us go?' Many a district still preserved the A.S. 'héo' for 'she', which they pronounced 'hoo', whilst in others they used a pronoun like 'his-self'. 'Mine' and other possessive pronouns were employed without the complementary noun, and elliptical sentences like 'Come to mine' (my house) and 'I will go to yours' (your home) were common. Prepositions were increasingly relied on to mark with greater precision the relationships vaguely indicated by case in previous days. Not infrequently they terminated a sentence, nor had they their modern rigid combinations with particular nouns, verbs, &c. Eighteenth-century people said 'I can insult over him', 'she would not hear to that at all', 'recorded his vote spite of anyone', 'had servants tending upon him', 'serve for vinegar to the servants', 'she looks goose-eggs', 'delivered a book to have a dozen of hats for same', 'I have a good portion which they cannot hinder me of', 'I desire of you to get', 'out in health', 'told him on it', 'he took care to do it by his lifetime'. The well-known English custom of using nouns for verbs and vice versa was then widespread, but there were differences in usage from modern practice: 'Where do you inn to-night?', 'I will go and sheet the bed', 'he was put prentice to', 'she never made a revoke'. The auxiliary 'do' gradually lost its former periphratic use, but throughout the century it was used more extensively, both grammatically and idiomatically than it is to-day in rural England, with its many 'he do say', 'I know what they do be', 'he has done his do'. Towards the end of the century it became confined only to emphatic assertion. Still it had not gone entirely, and in the last decade writers are still saying 'the cocks do crow and the bells do toll', 'every evening did she light a candle'. On the other hand 'got' needlessly started to oust the principal verb 'have' and relegated it to the auxiliary position, and late eighteenth-century people were in the habit of saying, 'he has got three apples', 'have you got the paper?' The antiquated form 'be' for the present indicative was freely used, and 'here he be' was heard almost everywhere.

All these changes in the volatile grammar of the eighteenth century are perhaps best realized when it is seen that, at the end, the class which remained educationally exclusive, was using largely such grammatical forms as 'a-footing, a-walking, you was, was you, you has, that's him, its me, I don't know as y'll like it, they dont seem to drink like they youst to, it looks as if it were going to rain, he dont understand, for to go, he has getten that much, will us go?, you and me was a-going, &c.' They were also displaying considerable uncertainty about the past tenses of such verbs as swim, run, go, ride, drink, write, take, keep, ring, &c., and could still use meaningless phrases as conversational links. Their 'I say', 'says I', 'says he', 'well', 'you know', were simply original parataxis or co-ordination of language. 'Look you', 'Listen', 'Say', &c., used quasi-interrogatively, were mere devices to draw attention to what was about to follow, a contrivance that appears in the line of the hymn:

> 'Say, shall we yield Him, in costly devotion?'

They also employed such anachronistic turns of phrase as 'The sublime Longinus, in somewhat a later period . . .', 'grew up to be a fine girl and a handsome', 'he was a proficient in music', 'she ought not speak whilst supper is making reddy', 'and what for should I mind my own affairs?' 'It is not, quoth he, so easy', 'Far I said, from simple', 'But how was he astonished at finding . . .', 'Oh, said I, not that twould be ravishing', 'they not can help', 'her first place it was', 'in service to the squire', 'had a present made him of a Delft cup', 'half after three'.

As far as mere grammar is concerned, probably the biggest contribution made by this century was the firm establishment of the uninflected form 'its' for the Old English neuter 'his'. Milton and Shakespeare had only used it tentatively, and Dryden is the first great literary authority who seems familiar with its modern usage. Another contribution of almost equal merit was the eighteenth-century revival of 'that' as an indeclinable relative pronoun, despite the opposition offered by Addison in his *Humble Petition of Who and Which*. Bishop Lowth, another of this century's grammarians, also protested against its resuscitation and wrote: 'this abuse has long been growing upon us and is continually making further encroachments.' Later, another eighteenth-century divine, the

Rev. Horne Tooke—who was a pioneer of English philology— demonstrated that it was not an eighteenth-century innovation, and rightly declared that it had a fine literary ancestry and was in accord with the idiom of the English tongue.

Wesley's text-book attempted to deal with some of the eighteenth-century grammatical uncertainties, particularly with the past tenses of verbs. He insisted on the use of the preterite for the passive participle; thus he required the forms 'hath rose', 'had strove', &c., arguing that both were the imperfect and the passive participle for rise and strive. He gave 'writ' or 'wrote' as the imperfect, but 'written' as the participle for write and he preferred 'rent' instead of 'rend'. Although John's grammar gave 'rend' as the present tense and 'rent' as the imperfect, Charles Wesley consistently gave 'rent' for the present tense. Both these forms seem to have been used indifferently by Shakespeare and other writers, till well into the eighteenth century, though probably the practice of using the preterite instead of the participle was commoner in the first half of this century than ever before. Perhaps, too, the growing band of writers were endeavouring to reach a consistent usage, either by making the preterite serve regularly instead of the participle (as recommended by Wesley), or by distinguishing between the two forms (the fashion that ultimately prevailed). In 1758 Byrom wrote a sarcastic poem on Wesley's grammatical axiom, called the *Passive Participle's Petition* and which runs:

> Till just of late, good English has thought fit
>   To call me written, or to call me writ;
> But what is writ or written, by the vote
>   Of writers, now hereafter, must be wrote;
> And what is spoken, too, hereafter spoke,
>   And measures never to be broken, broke.
>
> I never could be driven, but in spite
>   Of Grammar, they have drove me from my right.
> None could have risen, to become my foes;
>   But what a world of enemies have rose.
> Who have not gone, but they have went about,
>   And torn as I have been, have tore me out.

The Lancashire poet was certainly wrong in thinking many of the proposed new usages to be due to Wesley's decrees, and therefore invented by him; they occur more or less in all writers before him, and they continued till well towards the middle of the century.

Byrom did sense, however, that grammarians would have to yield to the speech-practices of democracy; so he closed the 'Petition' with:

> Let all the learned take some better heed,
>   And leave the Vulgar to confound the due
> Of preter sense and participle too.

Johnson, forgetting or ignoring the many English grammars that had already appeared, and thinking of the chaotic condition of the eighteenth-century English grammar, remarks: 'In a language subjected so little and so lately to grammar, such anomalies, even in good writers must frequently occur.'

Those eighteenth-century writers and speakers who had not been hampered with a classical education were naturally impatient with much of the prevailing grammatical minutiae which the pedants were anxious to impose on English; thus language became increasingly simpler and 'rules' of grammar more and more ignored. Their native sense seems to have told them that endeavours to graft the elaborate syntactical forms of Latin or Greek grammar on to the old English stock were absurd. And if they lost their way in the eighteenth-century grammatical jungle, they hacked a way out by freely fabricating terms by tacking together, off-hand, two or more words, no matter what part of speech, into one compound adjective, by means of the terminal syllable 'ly'. An excellent example of this method is to be seen in Crabbe's *Parish Register*. A profligate fellow had run away, and left several illegitimate children to be maintained by the parish, and on him a widow vents her just wrath, by calling him 'a toss-potly, stuff-gutly, smoke-baccoly, whore-mongerly, starve-bastardly vagabond'. And it would not be easy to condense more compression of vituperation into the same number of words. Moreover, in *Robinson Crusoe*, Defoe had shown that a clear and distinct style could be achieved by using ordinary words in their ordinary spoken way; Swift in *Tale of a Tub* and Steele in his *Spectator* essays had performed similar service. Swift, Hume and Hazlitt all pleaded for a homelier style of writing and fewer grammatical shackles, and in these particular essays their style of writing was masculine and their phrasings a succession of hard-hitting sentences—elements that greatly appealed to the new reading public. Wesley's *Rules of a Helper*, too, are masterpieces of swift, terse, abrupt English and exemplify Hazlitt's specific advice.

III

Eighteenth-century penmanship calls for as much attention as does its grammar, for it helped to affect the ordinary spelling.

Preserved MSS. show great variety in such graphic dominants as size of letters, slant, shape, alinement and continuity. Speaking broadly, the early skilled scribes of the century seem to have liked flourishes and long tails to their letters; yet a number of them preferred very narrow curves for the letters 'm', 'n', 'u', and their 'c' often resembles a dotless 'i'. Their capitals had many forms depending on individual taste, and many not infrequently recall the gothic designs, whilst their a, d, e, g, h, k, p, r, t, v, w, x and y were not unlike modern German forms. As the century progressed, the modern 's' form became firmly established, though it did not oust the old type, with the result that practically every scribe used both shapes for the small 's', selecting the one chosen largely according to place-position. During the century, probably every school made a fetish of hand-writing, and as there was a host of writing-masters of the eminence of Opie, Baskerville, Snell and Seddon, who conducted classes for adults, by 1800 most English scribes were employing the French style or Italian hand, and there was a growing preference for a plain round-hand style of writing.

But, as is to be expected, the handwriting of the century shows great variety in personal form and perfection. That of Queen Anne, George II and Prince Charlie was somewhat crooked and club-footed, whilst that of the Regent and Clarence was much neater and smaller and more complicated and decorative than was their forebears. The MSS. of Addison, Gray, Voltaire, Hume, Campbell, Keats, Coleridge and Gibbon show that their writing was very neat and precise; and that of Locke, Dryden, Pope, Goldsmith, Blake, Burns and Scott is also very easy to follow. Rather less easy to read is the penmanship of Swift, Steele, Sterne, Johnson, Sheridan, Crabbe, Southey and Byron, whilst that of Fielding, Thomson and Burke is somewhat blurred, clubbed and disorderly. The eighteenth-century writers who liked decorative penmanship and meandering loops included Pepys, Defoe, Smollett, Richardson, Bentham, Horace Walpole, the Edgeworths, Franklin, Leibnitz, Goethe and Schiller.

Wesley's calligraphy was rather crowded, although the spacing between the words, phrases and lines was remarkably even. Not

o

infrequently he joined consecutive words, and he freely used abbreviations like s^l (shall), y^s (this), &c. As his eyesight weakened, this crowding effect and his reliance on contractions became less pronounced; otherwise his penmanship remained almost unchanged during his sixty years of correspondence, and in his late seventies, as in his twenties, it is always clear, vigorous and harmonious, and his punctuation invariably punctilious. He always used a firm if small round hand with a marked slope; he preferred capitals that were slightly decorative, and like many contemporaries, he made no difference between the capitals 'I' and 'J'. He went in for a biggish ampersand, looped d's, tailed k's, slightly looped initial strokes in 'm', 'n', &c., returned half-loops in 'g' and 'y', uncrossed t's, rounded r's and the Greek form of 'e'. Of the prevailing forms for the letter 's', he made increasing use of the roman model.

Probably some of these eighteenth-century writers were familiar with the typewriter. As far back as 1714 a Henry Mill took out a patent for an instrument which he described as

'an artificial machine or method for the impressing or transcribing of letters, singly or progressively one after another as in writing, whereby all writings whatsoever may be engrossed in paper or parchment, so neat and exact as to not be distinguished from print'.

His machine is said to have been clumsy and useless; it certainly led to no practical results for any widespread use of typewriting.

Throughout the century's course the capital 'I' did not win universal recognition, and it is quite common to find the first person pronoun written with a small 'i'. To keep this inconspicuous letter distinct, various scribal expedients were employed, such as tailing it or placing it between inverted commas. The letters 'j' and 'y' were somewhat suspect; not infrequently they were used as variants for the small 'i'. The more learned of the day began, however, to differentiate between the pair, and so they used 'i' for the vowel sound and 'j' for the consonant sound. Sometimes 'y' was used to indicate the open 'i' sound; a ruling that led many to write 'Ytalian, coincydence, doctryne, favouryte, py (pie), and per contra to write waie, busie, almightie, ordinarie'. Similarly, this class of writer began to regard 'u' as a vowel and 'v' as a consonant. But the great majority of the then writers were inclined to regard u, w, v, or i, j, y and other combinations as mere variants, without distinction in value and perhaps possessing a mere position rank, just as had the long and short forms of the small 's'. In any case, spellings like vpp (up), vnder (under), euery (every) were very common. Other orthographical variants which again implied little more than personal preferences were ph for f, s for c, ks for x, &c., and the form selected by the scribe was really a mere accident; the choice often producing forms like prophanation, sox, exite, exelent, Dickson. For the greater part of the century 'z' and 'y' sounds were sometimes represented by the same symbol. The learned gradually began to use 'z' to replace an obsolete letter that denoted a soft palatal sound something like 'y', and especially so in such names as Menzies, Mackenzie. The confusion arising from this interchange has led to the persistent English mis-pronunciation of names like the foregoing, and of Dalziel and of the word capercailzie.

Many eighteenth-century scribes did not observe such refinements of calligraphy as dotting the 'i' or crossing the 't'; there were limits to the capacities of quill pens and rusty inks. On the other hand, most of them appended long loops to many of their letters, liked the fancifully-looped symbol for 's', used strokes unnecessarily and, whenever possible, employed red ink for the opening letter of their deeply indented paragraphs. They favoured a multiplicity of capital letters and without any discernible principle of action. Yet at the same time they wrote the courtesy titles of Rev., Mr., Dr., Sir or Lord with a small letter. Not infrequently Christian and surnames started off with small letters or were indicated by doubled small letters, and such names as 'ffrench, ffoulkes, ffebruary' appeared. Places, days and months were often spelt with small letters, but the prevailing fashion was to indicate dates with numerals. Inverted commas were used profusely and not merely to indicate direct speech. Their other principles of punctuation also seem to have been largely a matter of personal taste and so are often bewildering to a reader. The apostrophe 's' was used haphazardly; writers known to have had a university education wrote 'Gods help, mans hat, his' book, your's truly, it's clothes' as frequently as the modern accepted forms. Perhaps the punctuation devices of professional writers like Swift and Sterne are even more amazing than those of less-known scribes. On the other hand, many of Chatterton's MSS. show long passages with hardly a single stop or comma.

In this century penmanship was not regarded as a pre-eminent accomplishment by exalted persons, and the hand-writing of Prince Charlie and George II was consistently slovenly and illegible. Towards the end of the century, there was a distinct attempt to acquire the copper-plate style of writing, and many of the MSS. of parish and religious officials showed that they could write quite as well as their educated contemporaries, whilst their spelling and punctuation were little more original than those of Marlborough, Swift or Smollett. In those days many of the writers tried to keep secret their messages, and employed such devices as writing the first line in the ordinary way, the second from right to left, the third upside down or with combinations of such devices. Now and then quaint drawings besprinkled their MSS. or replaced words and phrases. To further baffle the curiosity of strangers, many public men of that era had forms of shorthand which were almost personal. Timothy Bright had invented a system as far back as the days of Queen Elizabeth, which he called 'Characterie: An Arte of Shorte, Swifte and Secrete Writing by Character'. This system, like that of the later Bales, depended mainly on arbitrary marks for certain words. The seventeenth century saw Willis and Rich invent symbols for letters as well as new arbitraries for words. Most of the many shorthand authors also kept to special symbols for letters; but these symbols varied with each of such individual inventors as Mason, Tiffin, Lyle, Angell, Mavor, and so the forms were most conflicting. Another inventor with a highly individualized system of symbolical signs was Wesley, and for years his arbitraries eluded all attempts made to read his *Journal*. Of this eighteenth-century group of 200 or so shorthand inventors, perhaps Byrom gained most fame; his method of 'stenography', 'polygraphy' or 'brachygraphie'—as it was variously called—gained him election to the Royal Society, whilst his pupils included Horace Walpole, Chesterfield, the Duke of Devonshire, Bishop Hoadly and Charles Wesley.

Probably all such men sought after secrecy rather than speed in the matter of shorthand. Some writers who sought for speed rather than secrecy went in occasionally for other forms of word-condensation. Many of them tried to revive the lost Old English thorn, and so wrote a corrupt y^e, y^t, y^m for the, that, them; sometimes their abbreviations took such forms as w^ch (which), gr't (great), fi'ld (filled), w^{th} (with), l^{ps} (lordships), y^r ob'd^t ser^{nt} (your obedient servant). Yet at the same time, these same writers would not hesitate to split many a word that is now compounded: my self, no where, how ever, some how, &c. Additional evidence of this protracted conservatism in penmanship, was also revealed by their arithmetical calculations; even at the end of the century, arabic numerals had not entirely deposed the roman figures, and many a keeper of accounts did his additions and subtractions through such cumbrous agency.

IV

The free and easy choice in grammar and writing which characterized the fashionable English in the eighteenth century, also showed itself in their spelling. And this was not due to any absence of dictionaries. The seventeenth saw quite a number of such manuals, whilst the eighteenth had still more. In 1753 Wesley produced one with the high-sounding title of

'The Compleat English Dictionary, Explaining most of the Hard Words which are found in the Best English Writers. By a Lover of Good English and Common Sense. N.B. The Authour assures you he thinks this is the Best English Dictionary in the World'.

Despite Wesley's sonorous claims for this small manual, his dictionary was outclassed two years later by that of Johnson.

These seventeenth- and eighteenth-century dictionaries differed greatly in their spelling forms for words, for etymology was scarcely born. Many early eighteenth-century scholars still assumed that Hebrew was the original language of the world; still more attempted to link their mother-tongue with the classical languages. Leibnitz had somewhat undermined such ideas, by teaching philologists to adopt sounder reasoning principles than they had hitherto employed. But it was not till 1784 that Sir William Jones—one of the most accomplished linguists England has produced—suggested the Aryan ancestry of Sanscrit, Greek, Latin, Gothic, Keltic and Persian, and in so doing focused the first feeble rays of light on philology. Such light was intensified in the early nineteenth century by Schlegel, Grimm and Bopp, who made scientific analyses of language, traced their phonetic laws and investigated the origin of grammatical rules. Such scholars were the first to penetrate the minute details of linguistic phenomena, and appreciate the words and phrases of cognate dialects; nobody in the eighteenth century really condemned the existing lawless etymological combinations, and the baseless fancies of many lexicographers.

When considering the spelling peculiarities of the eighteenth century, it must be remembered, too, that many playwrights, novelists and poets left questions of spelling and punctuation to the printers. So in order to obtain a real view of eighteenth-century orthography, one should turn to original MSS., actual letters, diaries and so forth. These throw a vivid light on the orthographical antics of the day. Official secretaries to religious and charitable societies spelled much as they pleased. In one of these records, there are eight different ways of spelling 'shoes' and seven for 'diet' in as many pages. But such inaccuracies were not the product only of simple souls or professional scribes.

Queen Anne could write and spell little more than her name and that not always in the same way; Marlborough, the Young Pretender and George II never succeeded in overcoming the anomalies of English spelling. Simple things like names of places and people had varied forms with different writing hands. The spelling of many a surname was then a pure accident and eighteenth-century records give many orthographic variants for the same name. The Smiths and Smythes were of the same stock. Every one knows how Ben Jonson spelled his name; yet his father and grandfather and brothers were 'Johnstones of Annandale'. A testator's name often appeared in three or more different forms in his will; brothers would spell the family name differently. Sometimes a man would spell his names differently as he grew older; as a young man the Duke of Wellington spelled his name 'Wesley', later he changed it to Wellesley; Nelson as a youth spelt his Christian name Horace; Bubb Doddington used a single medial 'd' as often as not. Probably the educated Wesley family remained constant to the well-known form; but the 'in-laws' of that family varied it. John Wesley appears as 'Westley', 'Westlay', 'Wesseley', 'Wezley', 'Wesly', 'Westlye', &c., in different parts of the country and even in the same circuit records. To a less degree the name Whitefield was changed, whilst the contractions permitted in Christian names, produced: 'Tho., Jno., Jonn, Jo., Joram. (Jeroboam), Mikel (Michael), X.ofer (Christopher), X.tians, X.mass, Rafe (Ralph), &c. As for ordinary words, the wealthy and educated went in for similar spelling vagaries. Johnson, who found the ways of spelling and writing unsettled and fortuitous, reduced the vocabulary of the educated to some degree of uniformity as regards spelling. But up to the mid-century, if not to a much later period, spelling was greatly affected by two dominating forces: (a) By the use of commutable pairs of letters such as 'i' and 'y', 'u' and 'v', 'c' and 'k', 'qu' and 'c', which permitted such spellings as 'lyon, mie, thie, haue, vse, euen, neuer, ancle, anker, scul (head)', &c., and which made 'quoddle and coddle', 'quackle and cackle', mean exactly the same thing. Terminals with 'er' or 're', 'el' or 'le', &c., were interchangeable, and 'ed' or 't' were employed for past participles, methods that allowed writers to put 'theater, meter, dropt, dreamt, ceast, kilt (killed), &c.' Another termination 'full' was allowed one or two final 'l's.' (b) In the same period, most writers spelled by ear, and so there were other epistolary eccentricities. 'S' and 'z' were commutable, and some individuals preferred harsh consonantal terminations, whilst others tried to secure sweetness or liquid fluency—a variation that led to many differing spellings of the termination 'tion', &c. These ear-spellers were a numerous company, and they reflected differing euphonic niceties: 'wash' ranged from 'waisch' to 'wesh'; 'soon' from 'sune' to 'sooin'; 'either' from 'aythur' to 'oahther'; 'boil' from 'bile' to 'boyil' and so on. 'Cheen' (chain), 'tred' (thread), 'quod' (quoth), 'sermont' (sermon), 'spettacel', 'intossicate', 'pund', &c., simply indicate pronunciations which the writer preferred. Even when spelling was not affected by these two forces, many a scribe managed to be individual. In his dictionary, Johnson held on to forms like 'skeptick, politiks, horrour, parsnep'; Webster's spelling book of 1783 gave such forms as 'center, meter, favor, honor, traveler', &c. Letters and diaries of the writing men and women of the century reveal forms like 'authour, compleat, reseve, tryd, haveing, giveing, musick, onyons, doggs, chiney, steddy, sparrergras (asparagus), coffy, diner, choclit, cabbidge, biskit, frute, gozebury's, nuttmegg's, expences, woolen, cloathes, childe, famalys, frends, yow, yew, yu, neerer, enuf, seldum, uppon, uther, thett, sittisen, tradgedy, nekst, aks (ask), akd (ached), seasd, carryd, therefor, a-clock, interleck, truely, hav, deth, thru, chappell, spaw, spaa, spo, quire (choir), antient, cattel, sillibub, cillibub, syllabub'. Some of these forms are undoubtedly simpler than the ones selected by the eighteenth-century lexicographers, and have, moreover, a sounder etymological background.

v

When the vocabulary of the highly educated people of that century is reviewed, it is found that they had a boundless command of language. Milton, Clarendon, Butler, Baxter, Bunyan, to say nothing of the more remote Herbert, Waller, Walton, Jonson, Shakespeare, Bacon, Sidney, Hooker, Lyly and Spenser, had made the arsenal of words, extensive and powerful before the century dawned. Their own writers added considerably to the store. It was, moreover, a century when oratory in Parliament and the leading pulpits ranked high, and the prevailing eloquence was most vehement.

Naturally, too, this century's vocabulary was enriched with new words from commercial, social, artistic and literary sources. Among many now common were then new: 'operation, speculation, balcony, battalion, record, preliminary, communication, gentlemanly, scientist, juvenile,' &c., many of which were suspect for years and heartily disliked by some of the writers of the age. Other new words then of questionable propriety were 'brainy, constraint, embarrassment, sentimental, interesting, bore, funny, genius and home-sick', whilst Franklin opposed 'improved, noticed, progressed, opposed', &c. Some of the objections were based on philological grounds, but the greater number of these words were suspect 'because they indicated the vulgar form of grandiloquence, conspicuous in journalistic style'.

Despite classical objectors new trades, new ideas, new conquests swelled the word reservoir. Mechanical inventions for farm and workshop brought a host of new words or words with a new significance: 'cop, mule, snarl, slivers, roving, throstle, goose-neck, punch-bowl' were among them. English victories and trading in India made people acquainted with numerous East India words like 'bangle, bungalow, jute, shampoo, calico, chintz, loot, jungle, rice, muslin, toddy'.

Especially in the first and last quarters of the century, France added many words and phrases to the English tongue: 'corps, depot, canteen, soup, coupon, chaise, police, machine, cushion, chandelier', and especially those connected with dress and fashions. French cooking terms entered elegant English homes and they grew used to 'foie-gras' and 'things bisque, soufflé, braisé au gratin', &c. Gallic terms like 'au naturel, sacré bleu, touché, bon Dieu, bien, congé, vraiment, ma fille, milieu, sortie, écarté, route, fête, valet, souffrant, goût, n'est-ce pas, parvenu, par exemple, joie de vivre, ennui, allons, penchant, à-propos, tête-à-tête' and a hundred others besprinkled the daily conversation of the English jeunesse dorée. French idioms invaded the literary tongue and made the English acquainted with unusual placings of adjectives in 'heir apparent, notary public, letters patent, bishop elect, sum total'. There was also the stilted use of the third person as means of expressing respectful courtesy.

Even the poor made cheerful attempts at anglicizing French words and phrases and they freely used kickshaws (quelquechose), frumenty (froment), armery (armoire), fash (se fâcher), jaloose (jalouser), megrims (migraine), in disabils (en déshabillé), saveloy (cervelas), pompoms (pompons), trucking (troc pour troc), pansy (pensée), causeway (chaussée), dullor (douleur), &c. Some of these French words attained only a regional popularity and the Scots used words unknown to the English, that were directly drawn from France. The north preserved ashet (assiette), motty (mot), moised (O.F. moison) and gormandized (gourmandise). Men of the Fens wore their pawts (pattes); East-Anglicans talked about their hoogo (haût gout); those in Essex had their beever or bevor (O.F. beivre), and south-east men talked about lanners or lanyers (lanières), whilst many a southerner indelicately called his slice of fruit cake a 'gashy' (gâchis). Devonshire used 'more blue' with the significance of 'morbleu'; west countrymen talked of tantrums (trantran) and of 'pingling food' (épingle). Lead miners in the Mendips referred to jawms or jambs (jambes). Worcestershire people declared watery fruit was 'lashy' (lâché) and talked about 'goose-gogs' (gogues), whilst a favourite apple was the 'belliborion' (belle et bonne). In more than one area they talked about a 'tass of tea or rum' (tasse), called bijoux 'bighes', a corpse a 'mort', and a boarded floor a 'plancher'. Their power of digesting foreign words and phrases was less transparently successful when they converted 'Caton fidèle' into 'cat and fiddle', 'bocage' into 'birdcage walk' and 'joie' into their 'jo'; whilst their 'Jews trump' was a mere corruption of French words. The French 'pour' invaded the speaking tongue and people said: 'they let in their swine for to trample their corn-seed', 'come for to see', 'for bring us to Lea', 'what's best for rid us of'. Never was intercourse between France and England closer than in the closing years of this century, nor were opportunities of acquiring French with a good accent, ever more favourable. Such a condition affected greatly eighteenth-century English vocabulary, phrasing and even utterance.

Latinisms, &c., too were very pronounced in this century, particularly during the first quarter. 'Inertia, propaganda, ultimatum, bonus, maximum, insomnia, extra, prospectus, deficit,

platitude, emigrant, vaccinate, detect, dentist, tandem, perspective, alias, impetus', &c., came into daily use. Greek translations
made the people familiar with 'basis, crisis, panorama, geology,
criterion', whilst the turnpike trusts made them well accustomed
to the Greek word for a tax, 'toll'. These new Greek words also
comprised literary terms like epic, lyric, elegy, comedy, idyll,
theatre, pantomime, scene, dactyl, rhythm; rhetorical terms like
theme, topic, paragraph, phonetics, analysis, dialect, syntax,
phonetics, synonym, climax, emphasis, phrase, period, comma; and
scientific terms like technology, botany, calyx, petal, parasite,
anaemia, antiseptic, diagnosis, &c. Johnson revived the classic
euphemisms of Lyly, Greene and Nash; he inculcated a love for
polysyllabic words, for stiff, balanced phrasings and pompous
language. A good farmer became 'a skilled agriculturist', an
apothecary 'a pharmaceutical chemist', a teacher 'a pedagogue',
the gospel 'the evangel'. The beginning of the century heard the
people using in connexion with their churches, words like
perirrhanterium (porch) and superliminare (threshold); the end
found them fond of naming their amusement places, &c., 'pantheon, eidouraneon, phantasmagoria', and one hears then of a
new comb widely advertised as Blackwell's Rostrakizion. Not infrequently, educated people wrote and even spoke to one another
in Latin; John and Charles Wesley often did so and the former
conducted most of his correspondence with Count Zinzendorf in
that tongue. Walpole had to use Latin to speak to King George
as the one knew no German and the other no English. Up to 1731,
Latin was always used in courts of law in all the presentments,
indictments, pleadings and in all legal documents.

During this century Italy gave England many words for music,
poetry, paintings, &c., such as 'concert, sonata, pianoforte, duet,
soprano, contralto'; or 'canto, stanza', or 'model, vista, minia-
ture, pastel', as well as 'casino, bronze, faience, arcade, terra-
cotta'. Much about the same century, Spain added to English
dictionaries 'alpaca, carmine, flotilla, cigar, quadrille', whilst
from contemporary Greek and American sources came 'tapioca,
camera, bathos'. Our Hanoverian sovereigns brought in their
train such words as 'waltz, marshal, bear-garden, plunder, carouse,
poodle, caboose, seltzer, gin, mangle, landau, mangel-wurzel and
swindler'. They also led us to use 'kibble', 'fob-off' and 'pretty
fellow' where pretty has the un-English significance of prompt and
alert coming from the German 'prachtig'.

On all these immigrants, our forebears exercised the well-known English power of absorption, digestion and metabolism, and the new words gradually lost their foreign appearance or pronunciation, and in some cases their original meaning. Synchronously, the increasing means of communication were breaking down the old linguistic barriers of dialect, and every newly opened district was adding its quota of old English words that had been preserved almost intact by its dialect speakers and returning them into speech currency. About that time Scotland gave to England such words as 'gruesome, uncanny, glamour, murk, feck, cosy, scree, ran-dan (spree)'. Alongside the assimilative power thus shown towards new words, word creation became more and more intuitive and scores of good compounds of English elements were coined to replace the fashionable Latinized words. Saxon prefixes and affixes became much commoner and 'coldish, latish, dampish, youngster, oldster', &c., were freely heard, whilst writers like Gray, Goldsmith, Scott and Wesley revived the ancient fascination of 'unblamable, unaired, unparticular, unquiet, unstill, unget, unthrift, unidead, unfriend, disgustful, disremember, inequal, inobedient, sprightful, strengthy, duteous, powerable, misdoubt'.

Sports, mannerisms, particular men and literary characters together with some places also added to the storehouse of common words and phrases. The century saw come into general use 'high feather, show fight, high flown, crestfallen, cocksure, coxcomb, play the deuce, a clean pair of heels, outdistance, scoot, pit against, above board, within an ace, force one's hand, stalemate, cock and bull tale, top dog, hard-bitten, well plucked'. Those moving in refined social circles were fond of compounding words with alternating sounds, and this century freely used, if it did not actually coin, 'clink-clank, fiddle-faddle, tittle-tattle, clap-trap, jim-jam, pell-mell, wishy-washy, shilly-shally, wabble-wobble', whilst their 'hob-nob' came from their convivial drinking habit of 'give and take'. Empty minds naturally expressed themselves in empty phrases and impoverished speech, and the childish habit spread to the peasantry who then used 'rags and jags, rap and scrap, titter-totter, crawli-mawli, freeli-fraili, roly-poly, tip-top, hokey-pokey, hugger-mugger, clook-cleek, coxy-roxy, mee-maw, wew-wow', &c. It even invaded literary circles, and Pope and his contemporaries used 'namby-pamby, hurly-burly, hoity-toity, snick-snack, riff-raff, topsy-turvy', &c., 'Galvanic, volt, buhl,

dahlia, fuchsia, mesmerism, Wesleyanism,' &c., came from some
of the century's eminent men, whilst 'fribble, fop, hoyden, prude,
puff, languish, plagiary, lilliputian', &c., recall principal characters in eighteenth-century stories and plays. Even a Wesley
could follow the practice when he wrote: 'He is then a kind of
jack-catch; an executioner-general.' From places were then
coined such words as 'cambric, calico, gauze, port, lumber,
cashmere, poplin, landau, swede, worsted', &c.

Whether it was from mannerism or word-consciousness,
eighteenth-century people sought after alliteration. From the
countryside came such telling eighteenth-century phrases as 'live
and let live, a fine fleece and a fat carcase, muck's the mother of
money, spic and span, butch a bullock'. The new turnpike roads
were not regarded as an unmixed blessing, and farmers then
expressed themselves with "Tisn't the hunting nor the hurdles,
that makes the holes in the horse's hoofs; 'tis the hammer, hammer,
hammer on the hard high road', whilst the half-starved mill-
operatives said of the farmers, 'farmers fatten most when famine
reigns'. Although none of the writers of this century ever
approached the lovely alliterative lines of Milton or Shakespeare
or the later Tennyson, it was one of them, Churchill, who coined
the well-known quotation of 'apt alliteration's artful aid', whilst
Sterne, Swift, Johnson, Congreve, Paine and E. Young produced
respectively the well-known alliterative phrases of 'the shadows
lengthen as the sun declines', 'chew the cud of politics', 'clear
your mind of cant', 'put your best foot foremost', 'these are
the times that try men's tempers' and 'a fool at forty is a fool
indeed'.

It could not have been a highly developed sense of word-
consciousness which led the young exquisites of the eighteenth
century to struggle for predominance in such verbal fatuities and
puling expletives as 'zounds, lud, la, sdeath, odso, sirrah, marry,
snails, byrlakin, O Lard, O Gord, prithee, rat me, burn me,
rabbit me, drat it, gads life, stap my vitals, split my windpipe,
oons, godsoons, ecod, egad' and many other vapouring symbols of
affection. Cowper counted these senseless oaths among 'the pests
of conversation', and he called their users 'half-swearers, who split
and mince and fritter their oaths'. Probably it was the craze for
slickness that then produced corruptions like 'pon Rep' (on my
reputation), 'pon hon', 'thats poss', 'slife', 'sdeath', 'Gosh',
's'welp me', 'Fore Gord', 'spossible', 'cab' (cabriolet), 'nob'

(nobleman), 'mob' (mobile); that manufactured such words as 'tip' (to insure promptness), 'tot' (to add together), and called their I O Us their 'vowels'. They contracted 'Brighthelmstone' into Brighton, 'Bethlehem' into Bedlam, 'on the ticket' into on tick, 'fibble-fabble' into fib, 'nipperkin' into nip and 'humdudgeon' into dudgeon. The practice affected their grammar and the literature of the period shows that those moving in exalted circles said, 'I aint heard him say', 'The professions beant all of a mind', 'It wornt fit to be seen', 'Ise think so', 'We's let him go'. Perhaps they had found Johnsonian English pedantic, circumlocutory, and laboured; but even that could not have been so boring as these weaklings' clipped, bald, dull phrasings, the utterances of people too languid or emasculated to speak language with any vigour at all.

This artificial society was also fond of hounding to death for a brief time some inoffensive word, utterly regardless of the word's derivative or accidental meaning. Amongst the afflicted were 'vastly, grim, pretty, nauseous, filthy, plaguey, mortifying'. Such mis-use of words allowed women to be described as a 'nonsensical miss', 'terribly bonnie', 'cruel kind', 'prodigious amiable' and men as 'monstrous gallant', 'pretty fellows', 'sweet sirs'. Both could look 'mighty well' and be 'mortal proud' of a special garment. Examples of the union of such contrary epithets and stark unsuitabilities could be multiplied; they were very common indeed among the set of fashionables who used 'toad' and 'bun' as terms of endearment, who expected their dears to be delighted when described as 'a tulip among women' and who were 'proud to be foxed' that is, drunk.

In addition to this silly mis-use of words, their intellectuality further showed itself in a spate of slang: 'Strike me ugly, strike me dumb, strike me blind, mug-up, pop off, in a hole, gave me the griffin, tommy (food), tom-noddy, thingummybob, slavver, crony, funk, fudge, chum, champion (fine), corker, snorty, fly (artful), cram, scrag, gammon, flam, dibs (cash), pop-shop, bung, gob,' &c., were some of their coinages. The adjectives 'queer' and 'rum' together with the nouns 'rhino', 'ticker', 'hick', 'potwalloper' were also frequently in their mouths; but these they had probably copied from the thieves of their days. Fashionable affectation led to the adoption of slang words and phrasings in the smart language of the times; and although the practice received severe castigation from Swift and Hazlitt, this slang grew to enormous dimensions and spread to all ranks, and in 1795 a big *Classical Dictionary of the Vulgar Tongue* was issued which gives some idea of the incredible amount then used. A review of Grose's book indicates too, that many of the words and expressions were mere barbarisms. The review also shows that the vast majority of them failed to outlive the probationary period every language imposes upon durable words. Quite ninety per cent. of those recorded then have now passed completely out of use among English-speaking people. A peasant naturally shows little alert feeling for the shades of meaning of language in actual use, or any sensitiveness of the associated meanings that attach themselves to certain words. Nor is youth the age of fastidious criticism. So one is not surprised to find the forms of slang used by these groups, already far advanced in decay, or at least beginning to show taint. Nevertheless, their employment of slang phrases like 'come off it', 'fire him', 'not in it', &c., could have been defended, since they had been used by some of the greatest writers of the past, whilst their 'skin of the teeth' could be found in the Bible of 1611.

Although the foregoing examples of eighteenth-century slang had crept into the literature, perhaps they never belonged to the dignified vocabulary of the period. Some of the eighteenth-century phrases which were very popular hovered on the border-land of what was allowed by the guardians of pure English. Among these were the older ones of 'What the dickens', 'play a good knife and fork', 'odds-fish', 'a dab at so and so,' 'half-seas over', &c. The *Gentleman's Magazine* in 1755 discussed the validity of 'spic and span', in 1767 'at sixes and sevens', and later 'put the man's eye out' (for the immoderate dilution of spirits), and 'an't please the Pigs'. 'According to Cocker' was used throughout the century as a clinching argument even by the learned. Apparently this seventeenth-century writing engraver was credited with many accomplishments: the authorship and execution of fourteen sets of writing copies, of an arithmetic that ran into sixty editions and of an English dictionary. 'Like billy-o' also had a big vogue in the eighteenth century and was said to owe its origin to a Rev. Joseph Billio, a dissenting minister of extraordinary energy and enthusiasm who flourished about 1700. 'Right as a trivet' arose from the eighteenth-century pronunciation of Truefit, the 'supreme Bond-street peruke maker, whose wigs are perfect'.

VI

One feature of the eighteenth-century vocabulary common to all classes, was the marked use of very coarse language. Oaths, adjectives bristling with objectionable virility, and nouns now considered as obscene were then heard on every hand. From the youngest to the oldest they could twang off obscenities; there was 'nothing about heaven or earth, or the human body and its functions, but even a lady would whip out the name fair and square by way of conversational adornment. Mothers addressed their children in the language of a drunken bully, and gentlemen were in the habit of rapping out a dozen of interjectural oaths' every time they spoke. In 1775, Sheridan makes Bob Acres say: 'Damns have had their day'; only to be replaced, however, with much worse verbal opulence. Throughout the first half of the century Court circles revelled in low conversation and titled ladies indulged in and encouraged coarse talk. History says that Prime Minister Walpole regularly used words of indefensible indecency when discussing the domestic problems of George II and his consort. Professor Adam Smith is reported to have used the most disgusting language when talking to Dr. Johnson. Governor Nicholson, head of one of the colleges, approached by a student, 'did fly into such a rage and did curse and swear so loudly, that a sea-captain, who lay asleep, sprang from his bed and neglecting to affix his wooden leg, came hopping through the halls in his shirt, thinking the building to be a-fire'. Judges swore on the Bench; chaplains cursed inattentive soldiers and sailors at divine service. A servant, speaking of a visitor, says, 'she swore so dreadfully, I knew she must be a lady of quality'. Plays by D'Urfey, Behn and Sedley had a grossness of expression that defies exaggeration; Congreve makes his heroines anything but pure in their conversation. Angelica (*Love for Love*) is evidently meant to be all that a charming young Englishwoman ought to be: fresh, fascinating and dainty; but she is made to speak in a manner that would be strong for a barrack-room. Eighteenth-century words, connected with normal bodily functions, sound harsh and uncouth to modern ears; but these were the days when very shy and timid ladies freely and loudly expressed their condition of excessive perspiration as a 'muck-sweat', and described companions who were at once loquacious and foul-mouthed, by the expressive term 'muck-spouts', and when Hazlitt had to write, 'The English, it must be owned, are a foul-mouthed nation'.

Modern refinement has euphonized or discarded such eighteenth-century words and phrases and they are no longer heard in polite ears. It has also abandoned many old-English words with which that century was very familiar. Current among the educated and well-to-do then were: 'swig (drink), rip, dude, spark, moppet, hisself, futtocks, trollop, burthen, kerchief, news-sheet, albeit, haply, parlous, any when, dish of tea, bespoke, beauteous, troke (business), flyte (shrill abuse), anent, nab (catch), budging (going), abide (endure), moil (toil), totty (drunk), dry (thirsty), chuck (throw), blab (gossip), mort (heap), ruinate (lay waste), fuff (puff), sackless and fushionless (lacking energy), ken, mair, thrang, scuff (neck), tosspot, tit (minx), job (piece of work), whopper (a great lie), cop (capture), pal, a-gate (on the way), lap (enwrap), fleyed (frightened), mucky, slutch (mud), cap (to pass comprehension), fratch (to bicker), shive (piece of bread), spetch (mend), fettle (condition), clam (starve), receit (recipe),' and thousands of others which had been preserved by the dialect-speakers of that century. Modern writers have abandoned the use of 'that' for so or of 'right' for very and do not make their educated characters talk of things being 'that big', 'proper vexed', or 'right worried'. In those days the writers often used 'but' instead of than and 'an' instead of if. Addison has 'we were no sooner sat down, but she said . . .' Fielding: 'No sooner did they acquaint my brother but he immediately wanted . . .' Others had: 'An I knew less of the world . . .' 'An thou dalliest, then I am thy foe.' 'He is bigger nor it,' &c.

VII

As with other centuries, the eighteenth had its full share in the change of meaning in words themselves, and many everyday words became elevated or degraded in significance and narrowed or widened in meaning through the course of these hundred years. Examples of the first pair are evidenced in 'terrace, marshal, amiable, traveller, conjurer, brave, ancient, eminent, liberal, valiant, gazette, spinster, delicate', and in 'brat, gossip, demure, harlot, rascal, consummate, farrago, unctuous, perspicuous, wench, slut, puny, insolent, bully, trollop, imp, egregious'. Of the second pair, examples are to be found in, 'wife, passenger, audi-

ence, manure, punctual' and in 'help, witch', &c. Many a word
then had a significance it no longer possesses. 'Daft' simply meant
gentle, 'rash' swift, 'forward' alert, 'stupid' amazed, 'dapper'
brave and sprightly, 'stout' foolish, 'witty' pert. 'Sullen' was a
mere variant for solemn; 'strange' implied mild disapproval;
'honest' had a depreciatory meaning and was generally applied to
one's inferiors. 'Pure' had little elevation of meaning, and Swift
declared that an 'almond pudding is pure good'. 'Enthusiasm'
had an objectionable meaning, implying something akin to mad-
ness; and a tombstone in York Minster praises an eighteenth-
century clergyman 'for having preached for thirty years in this
church without enthusiasm'. 'Conversation', 'extravagant', 'mansion' then implied little more than intercourse, wandering and
dwelling do to-day. 'Crafty' and 'knave' for the majority of
eighteenth-century speakers meant skilful and lad; whilst 'angel',
'fond' and 'kind' had not their modern elevation of idea, but conveyed rather the notion of messenger, foolish and related. 'Silly'
to the majority of town-dwellers had then acquired its conception
of foolish; yet to many of the English it still had its ancient significance of simple, lowly, unpretentious, and thousands of them
probably still talked about their 'silly homes' as some in the rural
parts of Cumberland do to this day. To thousands of the
eighteenth-century country folk the word 'soft' meant half-witted,
and 'rare' meant splendid; whilst 'fog' implied rank grass, and
'dub' was a deep dark pool and could mean an ocean. Many of
the memoir-writers by 'incontinent' meant immediately, by
'neatness' purity and by 'complexion' disposition. Even by 1800
the word 'editor' had not its modern implication; then people
addressed their communications to the 'Conductor of *The Times*',
whilst clergymen meant simply 'impartial' by indifferent when
they prayed: 'And grant unto his whole council, and to all that
are put in authority under him, that they may truly and indifferently minister justice.'

'Saucy, bobbish, naughty, rag-a-bash, mudlark, rapscallion',
&c., then had no light-hearted significance, but were often the
gravest complaints made against a prisoner on trial for his life.
'Balmy' was then still a word of poetic import; and appearing in
dignified vocabularies were 'guts, phizz, blubber (weep), diddle,
mizzle, bamboozle (mystify), booze, soss, fuddle, jobation, clap,
(fasten), twaddle, tickle (insecure, delicate, changeable), rig-
marole, frump, clink (lock-up), traipse, pip (in a depressed state),

P

slippy, spry, sniffy, sock (hit hard), jiffy, toddle, stingy, suck in (cheat), chap (fellow), rumpus, rant, potter about', &c. 'Sup' was then a dignified noun and verb and Wesley often advised his patients 'to sup it in the morning fasting'. 'Pate' and 'skip off' were serious enough to appear in eighteenth-century Bibles; the one in Psalm vii. 16, and the other in Acts xiv. 14. 'Old codger' perhaps still retains its eighteenth-century familiarity, but 'wise-acre' is now somewhat disrespectful compared with its usage then, whilst 'old fogy' is thoroughly respectable compared with its implication as used by the eighteenth-century soldiery.

Wesley's hymns, letters and diaries also exemplify this perpetual change in word meanings. He used 'vulgar', 'resent', 'prevent', 'propriety', 'tenant', &c., in the Latin or primary sense of these words, which is far other than the modern daily signification. His brother's use of 'unitarian' implied little more than does 'Moham-medan' to-day. Certainly he could not have been thinking of the beliefs of such men as Milton, Newton, Locke, Lardner, Watts, Price, Priestley, Franklin or Wedgwood when he penned:

> The Unitarian Fiend expel
> And drive his doctrines back to hell.

Like Gibbon, when the historian refers to the rise of Islam, and when he talks of 'unitarian banners', 'unitarian armies', the hymnologist must have had 'The Prophet' in mind. Perhaps the following verse of Charles Wesley is the most forceful example of the damaging effects of time on English vocabulary:

> Satan his thousand arts essays,
>   His agents all their powers employ,
> To blast the blooming work of grace,
>   The heavenly offspring to destroy.

Clearly the primary sense of words tends to get blurred in the derived meanings and associations.

VIII

Not all the preceding examples of eighteenth-century methods of writing, spelling, punctuation and word-stores are drawn from the work of the literary giants of that era. Some are from the material connected with eighteenth-century chapels, churches and other public bodies. It may be argued, therefore, that some of the examples are simply indicative of the linguistic habits of dialect-speaking persons. And yet, however brief a consideration of the language and speech of the eighteenth century may be, none would be adequate without some reference to the dialects used throughout the country; for dialects, as independent of literary English, were then spoken by the vast majority of the people. These dialects, whether of locality, class or occupation, differed greatly from one another, and many people would very imperfectly comprehend the speech of another district. To appreciate adequately even the best marked dialects then prevailing would require a phonetic alphabet on each of their distinctive linguistic habits. Research into the comparative syntax and phonology of dialects is both difficult and elusive, and it is doubtful if the secrets of their speech melody can be revealed. In a book of this range such descriptions are impossible; consequently a mere sketch must suffice.

A scholar like Wesley, in his travels, would detect the old northern dialect when in places north of a line drawn from Morecambe Bay to the Humber; when in Dorset, Wiltshire, Somerset he would hear remains of the old south-western one; when in the heart of the country he would note traces of the old midland pronouns and verbal inflexions and would meet hundreds of people speaking an English that Shakespeare would have known; whilst Kent would provide him with still more marked differences. Of all these major dialects, the one that would be most musical to Wesley's ear would be the east-midland, then spoken from Lincoln to London. It was the one he heard in childhood; it eventually became the cradle of modern standard English speech, and so is the one that shows least variation from it. But in Wesley's days it was not a question of three or four dialects, but of hundreds. Owing to the isolation of place and absence of education, the differing accents, intonations and even vocabulary would have a very narrow range, and villages ten miles apart would have quite a different form of speech; an Oldham man would have been recognized as a stranger by his speech when in Rochdale; and though the dialect of Dorset might have been understood in Somerset or Wiltshire, it was nevertheless perfectly distinguishable from either of them. So, in the course of his travels, Wesley would hear speech in a drone or shrill whine, sing-song speech, staccato speech, speech with a drag or a drawl, odd, splay-mouthed utterance, speech in ascending chromatics and speech with pronounced nasalized vowels, &c., any of which characteristics would indicate to him his probable whereabouts. The north-east would be told in the strong and strident consonants; much of Yorkshire by abrupt and angular terminations; south Lancashire by flat vowels. The rough vibration of the soft palate would reveal itself in the burr of Northumberland, and common everywhere in the north would be the old gutteral h, k and g. The narrowness and tenuity prevailing in East Anglia would be the precise reverse of the sonorous, mouth-filling tones of northern England. Sussex would then show itself in the broadened vowels as 'faace', 'larder' (ladder), when 'a' was shortened into 'e' as 'fleg', 'reg', 'thet' or in the broad 'ai' when day was pronounced as 'dy' or in the softened 'th' sound when think was pronounced 'fink' and with as 'wiv'. The varying flectional differences of the present participle and the indicative present would also tell him at once whether he was in the north, midlands or south.

A student of language, such as Wesley was, would grasp the facts that dialects are highly individualized and localized, that, with a population remaining unmixed in the same habitat, the ideas they would need to express would be of a concrete character, and so the vocabulary would never be extensive. Their word-system had not to provide for the innumerable accessories of civilization, with its innumerable shades of thought, ideas and abstractions; their language would be related to a simple world of primarily natural things. He would realize also that dialect-speakers always prefer clearness to grammatical correctness, and brevity to both clearness and correctness, and further, that the ear always finds that agreeable which the organs of utterance find facile. Thus to him the omission of the final consonants, elision of initial vowels and slurrings, would be the result of the natural tendency of the speakers to reduce expenditure of muscular exertion and of breath in speaking to a minimum. Similarly, the clashing syntaxes, the varying vowel-lengths, the differing consonants, sluggish lip-action, decay of palatalization, gliding juxta-positions, vowel mutations, avoidance of the glottal-stop, &c., called not merely for better education on the speaker's part, but the imperative need for plain, vigorous talk from the preacher. And, of course, he was too much of a gentleman to find in his followers' apparently faulty forms of diction, a source of superior contempt, as did most of the few educated of his day, who seem to have regarded the retention of dialect-speaking as mere bovine callousness.

Writers on Wesley's preaching oratory stress the fact that his sermons were full of intensity and couched in homespun English. Yet what could be more natural? His aim in life was intensely practical, his interests were in men rather than in ideas, his sympathies were evoked rather by the experience of individuals than by great movements. His hearers were for the most ignorant of English as he knew it; so he had the common sense to rely on fervid and mobile feelings and on language that was simple and terse. To get this necessary simplicity and directness, legend has it that Wesley in his early evangelizing days, read over his sermons to an old maidservant and crossed out every phrase that she did not grasp immediately. There are other explanations. Wesley the preacher would know the homely tones of Izaak Walton, Bunyan, the Prayer Book and the Bible of Wyclif, Tyndale, Coverdale and especially those of the Authorized Version. From such sources he would learn to prefer the concrete word to the abstract, the direct to the circumlocution, to take the short word before a long one, to use transitive verbs and active voice in preference to the weaker passive, and the preterite for the passive participle; in other words to adopt the style and grammar most likely to appeal to dialect-speaking hearers. Again as a preacher, he would know the sermons of Usher, Donne, Fuller, Andrewes, Baxter, Jeremy Taylor, who preached in the golden age of the English pulpit. Thus many of his sermons have the plain, but energetic style of attack on the consciences and hearts of hearers as have those of Bishop Hall, a century before him, and of Archbishop Tillotson, who died before Wesley was born.

Such an attitude towards dialects also led Wesley to write with sterling simplicity; his prose has the muscular form and incomparable vigour with which the bulk of English people then spoke. It shows that he perfectly understood the value of Saxon words and single syllables and he never allowed latinity to overload a sentence, whilst his emphatic repetition of arguments gave an exemplary value to the use of written English during the middle quarters of this century. Thinking about 'style', Wesley is reported to have said: 'I dare no more write in a fine style than wear a fine coat.' But with all his plainness of speech, he was too sensible to follow eighteenth-century Quakers with their superstitious rejection of the growing commoner forms of speech.

An English scholar of Wesley's calibre and travelling experience would also perceive that a great number of words, phrases and sounds common to most of these differing dialects, had their source in Chaucer, Malory, Spenser and Shakespeare. There was the old English distinction in the use of 'thou' to familiars and of 'ye' to superiors; there were such pronouns as 'hisn, ourn, theirn, un (him), a (he) and ee (you); such plurals as childer, een (eyes), housen, shoon'; such verbal forms as 'mum (must), moent (must not), mid (might), wol (will), dun (did), knowed, telled, selled, etten (eaten), skriked (shrieked); a-doing, a-dying, a-skirting' and the equally common adverbial forms 'a-bed, a-nights, a-Sundays'; such adjectival comparisons as 'more tender, ancienter, worser, famousest, tuneablest'. Their very words were often pure old English: 'tackle (undertake), ax (ask), pike, skift, shift, at after, lick (beat), wick, rheum, neck-cloth, widow-man, nightrail, musiker, flummoxed, quiddity, anunst, afore, atween, agone, addle (earn), mackly (similar), surelye, happen so, jannock, ligge (lie), twisel (to fork).' These, together with such pronunciations as 'mooest, gooen, cauf, &c.,' still happily persist in many a northern dale. Others of equal ancestral pride are now heard only in the extreme west, such as 'suent, bowerly, wisht, question-less, unkid, niffed, minch, forwarder, quilkin (frog), airey-mouse (bat), pin-bone (thigh)'; such grammatical forms as 'iddn, teddn, youm a vool, I be sure, that do interest they, listen to I, thik fancy tale wont do for I, tell we who tis, any one of they things, 'tis she's story I be telling, the sensiblest she, bestest', and such pronunciations as 'woon' (one), 'wold' (old), 'puddn', 'larnin', &c.

Others boasting all the glamour that antiquity can confer and heard in the eighteenth-century country districts, have now almost ceased to be current coin anywhere. Among these were: 'gorbellied, belly-slave, bloody bones, rot-gut ale, bung-nipper, swallocky, ellenge, abbey-lubbers, thole (endure), utch, stuggy, podgy, towser, num-scull, mump-head, slack-twisted, vizards, roughneck, fooster, slobber-chops, splay-mouthed, sauce-box, rakehelly, knotty-pated, clay-brained, chuckle-headed, jobber-nowell (stupid fellow).' Other wonderfully comprehensive old English words like 'bray' and 'bramish' are now obsolete, and so are full-throated ones like 'bully-mung' and 'bumbaste'. Food that is hard of digestion is no longer described as 'belly-vengeance victuals'. Perhaps many of these old English words, then rich with the fruitful tone of time, can be spared, but there is big loss from decay in the use of 'mistress, sun-down, home-along, up-along, back-along, come-along-of it (outcome), downscrambled, down-daunted, wife-high, wife-old, dimpsy-light, sun-way, bed-lier, lonesome, nuncheon, generality, teen, sweal or swale, fain (rejoice)', &c. Most of the preceding examples of the eighteenth-century current speech are rich in picturesque appeal, or are vibrant with mellowed associations. But not all those used in those days can be attributed to previous great English writers; some of them are undoubtedly of dubious ancestry, whilst the birth of many others will remain a dark mystery, until the mists presently surrounding them are penetrated. Meanwhile, they should be regarded kindly—as benighted illiterates of the past—just as we regard the rich and racy elements in English character itself.

Towards the end of Wesley's life, the most salient characteristics of these eighteenth-century multiple dialects would be less marked in the growing towns because of the improving roads, the effect of the Sunday schools and the gradual transfer of the population consequent on the industrial revolution; for naturally the people could not spread and mix without dialectic disunity. Traces of this disunity are perceptible in 'Tim Bobbin's' dialect writings and there are critics who localize to a pin-point his eighteenth-century south Lancashire use of 'aw' (all), 'doff' (do off for me), 'beawt' (without), 'bawn' (going), 'to oss' (to essay), 'nobbut' (nothing but), 'welly' (wellnigh), 'olez' (always), 'oader' (order), and 'rid' (rode). From our standpoint, more important than this philological precision, is the fact that Byrom slightly, Collier conspicuously, employed the broad and racy and expressive Lancashire dialect as a literary vehicle, and have thereby preserved the oddities and peculiarities of eighteenth-century Lancashire rusticity and phonology. Perhaps the friend of eighteenth-century intellectual *élite* and aristocracy would have been indignant at being linked with a Rochdale schoolmaster, but Byrom's occasional use of the vernacular, necessarily brought into the limelight other and greater work in the same speech, and led writers like Smollett, Sterne, Richardson and Fielding—when painting the manners of actual rustic life—to use actual rustic dialect. Further, Byrom's and 'Tim Bobbin's' rusticity and that of the much greater Burns, is singularly allied to a literary sense and to a high technical finish and all three gave a warm-hearted record of rustic love, gaiety, superstition and piety in the appropriate vernacular. By so doing they kept the current of English vocabulary fed with fresh streams of idiomatic speech, and prevented standard literature from becoming anaemic through mere refinement. Moreover, the spirit of the times was rebelling against the very speech of the superior class; ordinary folk refused to deal with 'the reality of life in joyless and pallid words'. Thus racy and vigorous words of the eighteenth-century dialect-speakers, words of unimpeachable lineage, were kept alive and at the same time, the full-blooded, able-bodied recruits from the vernacular, reinvigorated the vapid and attenuated conventions of eighteenth-century English vocabulary and literature. So, however apparently ungrammatical, inelegant and awkward, the vernacular literature of this century may appear in some eyes, it can never be regarded as being devoid of merit.

IX

Speculation on the intonation of the eighteenth-century superior social people is hazardous if not impossible; conjecture on their actual word-pronunciation is also difficult as the dictionaries are somewhat contradictory, and deductions from the poets and phonetic letter-writers are often surprisingly elusive. Nor are the puzzles resolved as the century wanes to its close; throughout, one feels that there are more doubts than certainties in many of the deductions. In those days, spelling and pronunciation depended on local or class dialects, time of adoption, successive fashions in pronunciation, and most of all, on the taste and fancy of the person. Further, the great bulk of the people would be totally unconcerned about euphonic niceties.

Even to-day, when spelling is practically fixed, much of the pronunciation is still a matter of private judgement, and in simple everyday words like 'amen, again, ate, often, wont', &c., there is no consistency. The value of vowel sounds in words like 'direct, apparent, premier, finance, envelope, economic, envelop, leisure, isolate, patriot' leads to more individuality than uniformity. Few public speakers agree on their sound-divisions of words like 'official, effective, offences, oppression'. Questions of accent cause difference of opinion regarding delivery of words like 'decorum, decadent, chastisement, interesting', &c. In words like 'invalid' and 'contrary', a change of pronunciation may imply a change of sense. In the eighteenth century, the uttered speech of private life was far more fluctuating, and varied according to the age, class, education and habits of the speaker. With all that century's limitations of intercourse, there could be little language snobbishness or exclusiveness, and so it could not be taken then, as it is to-day, a very sure criterion of a man's social status and education.

Spelling in letters, memoirs, diaries, &c., suggests that it is highly probable that they said shuite (suit), coo (cow), hoose (house), enew (enough), crissmiss or kirs miss (Christmas), crisscross (Christ's Cross), allus (always), venter (venture), Inglish (English), respeck (respect), grund (ground), grosser (grocer), sate (sat), sitch (such), nevvy (nephew), idee (idea), eether and ayther and ohther (other), varmint (vermin), hunderd (hundred), sez (says), yerb (herb), yerth (earth), yill (ale), picters (pictures), torter (torture), sud (should), offen (often), cubberd (cupboard), valy (value), bankit (banquet), likid (liquid), passell (parcel), passon (parson), beckingd (beckoned), weel (well), vawse (vase), miraciluss (miraculous), nowt (nothing), carrit (carrot), misell (myself), hissell (himself), tha (thou), fower (four), prodistant (protestant), wutt (hot), histry, desprit, natshral, sperrit, boiy, watter for history, desperate, natural, spirit, boy, water. The spellings suggest a multitude of sounds for even simple vowels and consonants. 'Sup' appears as suppe, soop, sowp, zoop, zup, according to locality; 'cut' was spelled kot, cot, kuytte, kut, kytte, kitte, cytte, kyt, kette, kit; 'master' had the forms maistre, mayster, mastur, maystre, meister, mastre, misster, muster; 'half' ranged from haff to oaf by way of hayve; 'put' from pit to poot; 'soon' from sune to sooin; 'chain' from cheen to chayine and 'pound' from pund to pahiend. Their spellings of dream, dead, foal, cheap, &c., would suggest that many still preserved the old English pronunciation of these digraphs.

Eighteenth-century poets suggest other pronunciations: Swift made rhymes of doom and perfume, speak and mistake, dream and name, least with taste and wheat with wait; Goldsmith made fault and ought, fate and deceit rhyme; Pope has rhymes of cheat and great, fellow and seller, sex and neglects, shire and year, witches and breeches, gate and ate, God and awed, farthings and gardens and

> O woman, woman! when to ill thy mind
> Is bent, all hell contains no fouler fiend.

Watts made rhymes between door and her, Wesley between cease and confess, he and Doddridge between God and abroad, loud, evil and devil, up and hope, here and care. Other hymnologists made here rhyme with are, home with tomb, sweat with feet, come with doom, rude with brood, poor with store, there with fear, and join with thine. Other examples indicate that 'we and way', 'our and are', 'mulled and mould', 'solid and sullied', 'cool and coal', 'peer and pear', 'boast and boost', 'mossy and muzzy' were to many people pairs of homophones. In the days of Wesley it seems reasonable to assert that 'July' had the vowel sounds one now hears in 'newly', and that 'china' was pronounced 'chayney'. 'Tea' for the major part of the century evidently rhymed with 'bay'; but 'sea' went both as 'see' and 'say' according to the speaker's personal predilection. There were other words besides sea at the wavering stage of pronunciation such as bass, bouquet, terrace, lieutenant, colonel, trait, cambric, cretonne, &c., and posterity has compromised, by accepting the two eighteenth-century distinct sounds for most of them.

The eighteenth-century dictionaries confirm some of the differing pronunciations used in those days. Jones's *Practical Phonographer*, publisher in 1701, suggests that they said 'sommut, forad, backerd, nater, jester (gesture)'. Baker's *Rules for True Spelling, Writing and Speaking English* of 1742 gives: 'stummick, cooshin, spannel (spaniel), Izic (Isaac), ankerchay (handkerchief), medsun (medicine), fur (fire)'. Elphinstone's *Principles of the English Language and of English Grammar* of 1765 gives: 'futer, sence (since), ef (if)', and John Walker, who enjoyed a great reputation because of his *Rhyming Dictionary and Rhetorical Grammar* issued in 1785 gives, ejucate, injean (engine), ojeus (odious), higgus (hideous), baa (bar), yer (you), mi (my) uv (of), vur (for), ooman (woman), lanskip (landscape), cheer (chair), lunnon (London), obleege (oblige), sarvint (servant)'. And all these four authorities claim to reproduce the 'words as pronounced in Court and University Circles'. All four, moreover, would be able to consult the *Art of Pronunciation*, by Robert Robinson, published in 1617, a manual showing a remarkable grasp of the principles of phonetics.

English is a volatile language and one would have difficulty in dogmatizing as to how exactly words sounded in the eighteenth century even with the help of the phonetic spellers in their letters, poets' rhymes and the dictionaries. Leigh Hunt however, offers some slight help. In the earlier years of the nineteenth century he is said to have analysed the speech-sounds of actors like Kean, Kemble and Mrs. Siddons, and he asserted that they said: 'vartoo, conshince, sentimint, rint, innocint, sartin, fardyng, marcy, youst (used), oringis, fust (first), nuss (nurse), mistriss, prybit, bullitts.'

Late eighteenth-century statesmen are said to have produced, 'witch (which), nothink, maks (makes), sodaine (sudden)'. Frances Burney says that people moving in refined circles were saying at the end of the century: 'purtest (protest), saftly, thenk (thank), lardship, satisfectery, fice, plice, sot (sat), desart (desert) and respitt (respite).'

Turning to the dictionaries for information about the minutiae of eighteenth-century pronunciation, it would appear that early in the century the initial aspirate was fully sounded, and Ben Jonson said that 'which, what, wheel, whether' were sounded in his day as 'hou-ich, hou-at, hou-eel, hou-ether'. Apparently the aspirate lost its old universal sanction among the educated during the eighteenth. They habitually wrote, 'an home, an humble servitor, an harmless thing, an hottle (hotel).' In 1787 Elphinstone notes that 'many Ladies and Gentlemen and Others have totally discarded the initial h, where it ought to be stressed' and suggests that 'this omission was common to all regional dialects, except those of the very North'. It was probably this growing decline in, and mis-use of, the aspirate which led to the witty *Petition of the Letter H to its Decided Enemies* appearing a little later:

> Whereas by you I have been driven
> From Home, from House, from Hope and Heaven,
>   And plac'd by your Most Learned Society
>   In Evil, Anguish, Anxiety;
> And used without the least Pretence
> With Arrogance and Insolence,
>   I hereby ask Full Restitution
>   And Beg you'll change your Elocution.

The 'petition' only seems to have provoked the retort:

> Whereas we've rescued you, Ingrate,
> From Hell, from Horrour, from Hate;
>   From Horseponds—Hanging in a Halter,
>   And consecrated you in—Altar,
> We think you need no Restitution
> And shall not change our Elocution.

The dictionaries show that final consonants were often omitted, and certainly scribes wrote: 'thousan, scaffel (scaffold), thinkin, goin, ole (old), houns (hounds), ros-beef, cummin.' Elphinstone says the final 't' must not be sounded in 'sect, corrupt, respect, greatest, direct, reflect'. All the eighteenth-century lexicographers agree with the dicta of Gill, Butler, Wallis and Cooper—the seventeenth-century dictionary authors—'that the final "b" of lamb, thumb, climb, dumb, &c., must be silent'.

The dictionaries indicate that many medial letters were unsounded as the 'l' in 'folk, walk, milk', whilst many a phonetic scribe wrote 'on'y, haff, tawk (talk), cauf (calf), saumon (salmon), fawse (false), fawte (fault)'. The medial 't' was apparently ignored in 'glisten, often, listen, thistle, ghostly, costly, waistcoat'; the medial 'r' in first, and many wrote cuss, puss, nuss for curse, purse, nurse; whilst son-y-lawe, souljer, ylond, grummle, thusty, li'l, le'er, passley, passon, represented son-in-law, soldier, island, grumble, thirsty, little, letter, parsley, parson.

Before the eye was accustomed to print, there was a good deal of confusion and actual ignorance of the respective functions of the letters 'w' and 'v'. Evidently many said 'wocalist, wessel, convivial, wisit, wittles, wixen'. In the closing years of the eighteenth century, Walker mentions this speech-habit and regards 'vich, werry, walence, woyce', &c., as 'a blemish of the first magnitude that occurs among Londoners and not always those of the Low Order'.

The ingrained desire for ease of utterance, suggested by the foregoing speech-habits, showed itself in other ways. Letters and syllables were telescoped, so to speak, and 'cleric' became clerk, 'chiminey' chimney, 'foundery' foundry, 'furrowlong' furlong. 'Mistress' was corrupted into missis and 'madam' into mum. Such syncope spread still farther and initial vowels or syllables got lost through want of an accent. 'Esquire' dropped to squire, 'easterling' to sterling, 'especial' became special, 'amend' mend, 'affray' fray, 'despite' spite, 'escheat' cheat, 'hydropsy' dropsy. 'Cute' was the mere aphetic form of acute. Such sound elision spread among all classes, and plays of the period suggest that they were saying 'prentice' (apprentice), 'tice' (entice), 'maze' (amaze), 'fra' (from), 't-other', 't-event', 'th-element', 'i-faith', 'better-n' (better than), 'more-n', 'wi-em', 'ha' (have), 'an-if' (and if), 'ud' (would), 'for-t' (for it), 'do-t', 'pay-t', wunt (will not), shunt (should not), hant (has not), giz (give us), don (do on), &c.

Sometimes sounds were inserted to facilitate pronunciation, and in not a few cases posterity has adhered to these eighteenth-century adventitious aids to vocalization, as in num(b)er, passe(n)ger, wet(t)est, hand(i)craft, chronic(l)e, gen(d)er, em(p)ty, thun(d)er, though it has abandoned those then used in Hen(e)ry, chemist(e)ry, &c. Sometimes finals were added to ease utterance as in peasan(t), ancien(t), gizzar(d), parishion(er), practĭtion(er), which are still preserved although posterity no longer has lemon(d), gardin(g), gown(d), scholar(d), muslin(g), bin(g), lawn(d), height(h).

Whilst eighteenth-century speakers did not sound the 'w' found in sword, swollen, sworn, &c., they seem to have been punctilious about retaining the difficult enunciation caused through the sounding of the initial 'w', 'k' and 'p' in such words as 'knock, knob, kick-knack, knee, wrap, wrist, wretch, pneumonia, psalm, pseudo'. The dictionaries suggest that they stressed the harsh initial sound in card, kind, &c., and that they preserved the difficult 'u' sound when they said union, universal, university, which they invariably prefaced with 'an'. In more than one district, the educated preserved the difficult sound of 'l' in would and should and even in could; an appreciable number sounded the guttural 'gh' in night, fight, &c.; a bigger number would still roll their r's, and more still would pronounce the termination 'tion' as two-syllabled, and without a trace of the modern 'sh' or 'zh' sound. On the other hand when 'th' was followed by 'r', the aspirate was often silent as in throat, thread, through, &c., and many wrote and therefore said wiv, tred (thread), smore (smother), tudder (the other), sevent, fift, fourt, clodding (clothing), quod (quoth), moe (more), bahd (bird), chech foaks (Church folks), lenf, strenf (strength), and even dafter (daughter). In contrast many used the old 'murther' style, and Wesley always preferred the form 'burthen'.

Vowel sounds and lengths probably changed greatly during the course of the century, and the almost imperceptible shades of sound between a short 'i' and a short 'e', or between a fully-voiced 'g' and a voiceless 'k', were increasingly ignored. Playwrights put into the mouths of their characters such sounds as 'pritty and pratty; nat and net (not); mun and mon (man); stane and stooan (stone); muster, mister, mayster; mericle (miracle); aut (out); canduct, jay (joy)'. 'Sleek' was often narrowed into slick, 'peel' into pill, whilst 'pert' was sometimes and in some areas broadened into peart.

The 'ou' sound was then, as now, a problem, and one of their tongue-twisting couplets suggests the varieties of utterance the combined vowels could yield:

Though the tough cough and hiccough plough me through,
O'er Life's dark Lough, my journey I pursue.

The phonetic scribes indicate that they used other letters than 'ou' to represent the sounds they made for many of these words, whilst their employment of 'oo' instead of 'ou' in words like court, courant, course, about, &c., suggests they pronounced them with the French 'ou' sound.

The digraphs 'ea' and 'oa' provided other sources of confusion. Probably many of the speakers retained the Tudor sound, which is still preserved in 'great' and 'broad'; but there is written evidence that some of them separated the two vowels and pronounced each distinctly, as dialect-speakers still do in words like 'tea, sea, dear, moat, road, boat, loaf', &c.

Scansion of eighteenth-century poetry clearly indicates that they sounded the 'murmur vowel' after most emphatic consonants and that they said 'cup(pe), had(de), length(e), gold(de)', &c.; and certainly many wrote in their prose 'bishoppe, sinne, naile', &c. Scansion and balance suggest that they gave the 'i' in doctrine and favourite with a long sound, just as they did the first 'i' of italian and the second 'i' of coincidence. Scansion also indicates that their accents did not always fall on the same syllables as they do to-day. Very probably they pronounced ,'lunatic, mischievous, revenue, algebra, contumely, character, theatre, contrary, acumen, library, blasphemous, remonstrate, compensate' and many other three-syllable words with the accent on the medial syllable. In such nouns as 'converse, record, doctrine, instinct, interest, comrade, grimace, aspect, details, product, insult, uproar, barrier, surface, product, chapel' the accent often fell on the last syllable, on the third in 'military', 'coincidence', 'temporary', 'lamentable', 'superfluous', 'nomenclature', on the fourth in 'abominable' and on the first in 'political' and 'corollary' as uttered by the majority of speakers. The earlier hymns of the Wesleys also suggest accenting of words other than that of to-day. In these cases, scansion calls for the accent on the first syllable in 'acceptable', 'cemented', 'successor'; on the second in 'obdurate', 'primarily' and on the third in 'executor'.

Although many a turn and tang of rural English recalls the speech of the eighteenth-century *élite*, it is also evident that, by Wesley's death, the great majority of English speakers had begun to challenge the foppish elegance and deliberate artificiality of the wealthy's Frenchified utterance, had realized that it was effete, debased, affected and probably inaudible, and had found in it a source of innocent amusement. By then they had started to question their social superiors' many privileges, to doubt their intellectual standards and to challenge old-established institutions. So they would not be inclined to regard the patricians' grammar, vocabulary, speech habits as the outcome of enlightenment, but rather as mere fastidiousness and the result of vanity. Privilege, pedantry, and even purism had to yield before the tide of the prevailing usage of the majority. There is also another aspect of the problem. Despite the many grammars, dictionaries, and books on style, which had appeared during the seventeenth and eighteenth centuries, one hears famous writers deploring the absence of all 'rules'. Dryden wrote: 'How barbarously we yet write and speak! And I am sufficiently sensible in my own English; for I am often put to a stand in considering whether what I write is the idiom of the tongue, or false grammar and nonsense couched upon the specious name of Anglicism'. Some decades later, Warburton prefaced his edition of Shakespeare with: 'The English tongue is yet destitute of a test or standard to apply to in cases of doubt or difficulty. We have neither Grammar nor Dictionary, neither Chart nor Compass to guide us through the wide sea of words.' He wrote that three years before *Johnson's Dictionary* appeared. But even after all the dictionaries by Johnson and his copiers, De Quincey felt it necessary to observe: 'We have no sufficient dictionary and we have no work at all, sufficient or insufficient, on the phrases and idiomatic usages of our Language ... there is not a celebrated authour of this day (except Mr. Wordsworth), who has written two pages consecutively without some flagrant impropriety in the Grammar, or some Violations more or less of the vernacular Idiom.'

CHAPTER IX

LITERATURE

I

As periods of literature do not necessarily change with the exact beginning or end of any particular century, perhaps the simplest way of refreshing the memory is to list the names of the more celebrated writers of the eighteenth. Such a list will prevent the obvious danger of falling into too hasty generalizations from an imperfect statement of facts, consequent on narrowness of space.

GROUP A. Dryden, Evelyn, Farquhar, Locke, Pepys and Wycherley are some of the writers who died in the early years of the eighteenth.

GROUP B. Addison, Bentley, Berkeley, Byrom, Chesterfield, Cibber, Congreve, Defoe, Gay, Lady Mary Wortley Montagu, Pope, Prior, Ramsay, Richardson, Savage, Steele, Swift, Vanbrugh, Watts and Edward Young represent a number born in the seventeenth century but who wrote extensively in the first quarter and half of the eighteenth.

GROUP C comprises some of those who lived their lives in the eighteenth: Akenside, Burke, Burns, Chatterton, Churchill, Collins, Cowper, Fielding, Foote, Franklin, Gibbon, Goldsmith, Gray, Hume, Johnson, Macpherson, Percy, Shenstone, Adam Smith, Smollett, Sterne, Thomson and Walpole.

GROUP D is a list of writers who were in their writing prime in the latter part of the eighteenth century: Beattie, Bentham, Blake, Burney, Crabbe, Dibdin, the Edgeworths, Gifford, Hannah More, Paine, Sheridan, Horne Tooke and Arthur Young.

GROUP E contains some of the brilliant men who had proved their future worth before the eighteenth closed: Campbell, Cobbett, Coleridge, Landor, Malthus, Rogers, Scott, Sydney Smith, Southey and Wordsworth.

GROUP F includes some born in the eighteenth but who did no lasting literary work till the nineteenth: Austen, Barham, Byron, Brougham, Carlyle, de Quincey, Elliott, Grote, Hallam, Hazlitt, Heber, Hood, Hook, Hunt, Irving, Keats, Lamb, Milman, Moore, Napier, Peacock and Shelley.

The preceding names are only indicative of the groups. Among the omissions are some poet laureates who made a considerable noise in their day, but whom posterity has treated as so many charlatans. Even if groups A and F are excluded from consideration, the names remaining show that there was a bewildering variety of literary styles in the eighteenth century and that such a jostling crowd of writers, dealing with swarms of ideas, cannot be pushed into a pigeon-hole and dismissed with a label. Among them are writers, who, though close together in time, are nevertheless most diverse in theme, impulse, mastery and technique; with their individual clamorous assertion of self-independence and their mutual dislike for one another's peculiarities of thought and literary expression, they would form an uneasy company if lumped together. Further, the diminishing insularity of England in this century makes it necessary to list some foreign writers who affected, or were affected by our own writers.

Beaumarchais, Buffon, Chénier, Diderot Mme de Staël, Fénelon, Fontenelle, Marivaux, Montesquieu, Prévost, Rousseau, St. Pierre, St. Simon and Voltaire are a few of the French contemporaries, whilst among the contemporary Germans were Bürger, Fichte, Goethe, Gottsched, Herder, Humboldt, Kant, Klopstock, Lessing, Münchausen, Novalis, Richter, Schiller and Wieland.

II

The lists show at once that in eighteenth-century literature there are all the elements of marked contrasts. Many of its novels and poems may nowadays seem the recital of a series of erotic pleasures. Defoe wrote a story with an improper title giving fair warning of its questionable contents; Swift, a poem whose very memory is shocking; an anonymous writer penned the *Essay on Woman*, which is odious; Frederick, Prince of Wales, wrote some verses on his wife, which may be full of rapture but which are also enriched with the most outspoken description of her various charms of person. And yet it is doubtful if, in the novels at any rate, the authors displayed that sexual-obsession of the modern psychoanalyst, and certainly no period of English literature has ever seen so many moral tales specially written to make people good. Eighteenth-century authors wrote pages on superficialities, on routs and masques, ribbons and laces, yet in the same period were produced the long-drawn-out death-bed agonies of *Clarissa*, the melancholy perfection of the *Elegy*, the brooding despair of *Ossian*, the dreary lamentations of *Night Thoughts*. Amateurs of the horrible will find their taste catered for in eighteenth-century nightmare tales of wreckers and their accomplices, of

Q

privateers, ghosts, vampires and ghouls; yet the century saw the
rustic graces, and the description of simple homely things by
Burns, Crabbe, Cowper, Goldsmith. Political verse of classic precision and perfection and charged with power can be found, and,
at the same time lampoons of impulsive immaturity, full of
fantastic slang and slap-dash doggerel. The eighteenth century
had some of the greatest parliamentarians ever known to English
history: men of tingling vitality and colossal self-assurance; yet,
compared with the seventeenth or the later centuries, it is strik-
ingly weak in political autobiographies. A little of its poetry has
genuine vigour and passion; some of it has grace and melody; more
has polish and perspicuity; but much of it is intolerable priggish-
ness, false emotionalism and stagey impersonations. In this century, literary judgements, based on sound foundations, were being
gradually formed and ruthlessly delivered; yet these competent
critics poured out base and servile adulation over the poor productions of the wealthy. Whatever branch of eighteenth-century
literature is viewed, it seems impossible to guarantee a brief,
balanced estimate of these widely differing writers with their
paradoxical powers.

Perhaps the reason for this extraordinary variety of work,
thought, and expression, traceable even in the strongly-individu-
alized writers of this century, lay in the conditions under which
they lived. Although none lived with the avenging sword of the
State suspended over his head as did Milton and Spenser, still they
had to express themselves warily. Walpole, who had endured
many a bitter attack from writers, retaliated with his 'Licensing
Act' of 1737 by which he hoped to curtail not merely adverse
attacks on the stage, but also those initiated by essayists and
lampoonists. The Act led the essayists to use a cloak of anonymity
and to adopt a precision of style which veiled their trenchant
severity; novelists, whilst giving their readers glimpses of the
eighteenth-century lordly houses, only ventured on the ironical
expression of their clear-sighted view of the lives led by the
inhabitants; diarists and letter-writers who refused anodynes and
blinkers to their troubled souls, had to express themselves in a
form of shorthand lest they should be assailed by the ruling
powers. Only reckless writers with no reputation to lose, or those
who were highly placed and wealthy, or those who were protected
by the mighty ones of the period, dared for fifty years to express
themselves forcibly. Yet nearly a century before, Milton had

championed liberty for writers, and had tried to sweep away any controlling 'brutish hand'. His *Areopagitica* had declared 'it cannot but be a dishonour and derogation to the author, to the book, and to the privilege and dignity of learning' when work was censored, and had asserted, 'I endure not an instructor that comes to me under the wardship of an overseeing fist'. This noble and eloquent attack on Press censorship was forthright in its protest, and thundered and echoed down the eighteenth century. So eventually, its influence, together with the courage shown by Cave and Johnson, won freedom for the Press and kept it. Then there was the question of payment of their work. Up to the middle of the century, writers of eminent merit were sure to be munificently rewarded by the Government with a pension or a sinecure post, when they expressed thoughts that pleased the rulers. Those of less ability might get a lump sum or a post as tutor or librarian, &c., in a ducal home, if they lavishly complimented their patrons. But by Johnson's heyday, literature had ceased to flourish under the patronage of the great, and had not yet begun to flourish under the patronage of the public. Probably it was Wesley's small tracts that revealed the discovery that when literature really becomes democratic and takes root among the masses, a writer's fortune is assured. For the greatest part of this century, unless writers were subsidized one way or another they were very badly off; their work was ill-paid and copyrights were flagrantly ignored; knavish printers merely pirated anything they wanted. This piracy was so bad that some dramatists would not print their plays, and a strict watch was maintained in the theatre itself to stop listeners from transcribing comedies and dramas. History has it that Holcroft, the eighteenth-century cobbler-pedlar-stableboy-dramatist-novelist was sent to Paris in 1784 to pirate Beaumarchais's *Marriage of Figaro*, that he heard the comedy ten times, memorized it completely and translated it for English audiences. Nevertheless, the century had its well-known and reputable publishers. Throughout its course it knew of the Cambridge University Press, and it saw the establishment of Rivingtons, Longmans, Green & Co., Eyre & Spottiswoode, John Murray, Sampson Low, Marston & Co., and it was in that century that Baslett flourished, who gained a peculiar niche in the publishing world, with his 'Vinegar' Bible.

III

The assertion that it is impossible to find a single phrase or even chapter which would adequately describe the variety of literary work in the eighteenth century, becomes more evident when attention is given to the different forms of literature. At the beginning of the century, Addison, Swift and Steele made essays periodical and popular with the educated. In these essays political intrigues, piratical adventures, feminine coteries, State embassies, fashionable parties, parliamentary ambitions, country life, &c., are treated in a tone that is ever changing from grave to gay; facetious banter gives place to biting ridicule and both alternate with philosophical reflection according as one reads the mocking satire of Swift, the quiet raillery of Steele, the dignity of Addison and the later grave morality of Johnson. With the decline or death of these great four, the charm of the essay evaporated. Their feebler successors relied on abstruse themes and elaborately allusive styles which wearied the changing reading public; the common people began to prefer the 'dog-snap and cat-claw, curse and counterblast' of the political squibs and lampoons. So for fifty years the essay languished and was not revived till Lamb showed that it could be employed in a lighter manner and on lighter subjects and still remain grave and decorous.

In Drama the first decades of the eighteenth saw the airy fancies of Farquhar, the broad humour and strong comic vein of Vanbrugh and the fine masterpieces of Congreve, which were, however, completely overshadowed in popularity with the bare-faced brutalities of Etheredge, Shadwell and Wycherley. The middle part saw the light comedy of Gay and Cibber, and the criticism of public affairs by Fielding and Foote. The latter part saw the *Good-natured Man* and *She Stoops to Conquer* by Goldsmith and saw Sheridan raise drama to supreme levels. In dramatic technique Sheridan and especially Goldsmith, avoided all previous melodrama and produced excellent dialogue and well-delineated characters. Excellent as these were, popular taste probably preferred Colman's *Broad Grins* and Mrs. Inchbald's *Farces*, or her melodramas *Married Man, Wedding Day, Midnight Hour, Maids as They Are*, &c., most of which were tainted by a morbid and exaggerated sentiment. As for other details connected with the theatre, the century saw new plays produced and many new theatres built in Bath, Nottingham, Manchester. London's old 'Dorset Gardens', which, according to Dryden, was 'like Nero's palace, shining all with gold', was outclassed by Haymarket, Covent Garden, Sadler's Wells, Drury Lane. It saw the censorship of plays set up by Walpole in 1737—a censorship that he would have liked to extend to novels and to the Press. In that year Fielding's *Historical Register* so attacked the Government that Walpole determined to muzzle playwrights. By means of a bogus play, he frightened Parliament into establishing the play censorship with its restrictive influence, and from that time onwards all plays had to be submitted to the Lord Chamberlain for approval.

IV

In literary diction itself there is again this characteristic bewildering variety and contradiction, which adds to the precariousness of isolating a particular period in literature, and to the difficulty of putting a label on it. The poets of the century practised most rhythms and rimes, freely exploited the laws of prosody and developed such special metres as the anapaestic measures, the heroic couplet, the triplet, the quatrain, whilst Thomson's *Season's*, Young's *Night Thoughts* and Cowper's *Task* still offer some of the best examples of blank verse after Milton. In didactic verse Pope and Cowper rose to supreme heights, whilst the eighteenth-century lyrics, pastorals, odes, elegies, ballads and satires are still considered first-rate productions. Yet despite these individual excellencies it was left to Scott, for a poet to take possession of the general public, to produce verse that could be read and memorized easily, and which, moreover, had the perfect ring of sincerity and strength. Perhaps the hymnologists had played no insignificant part in this introduction of poetry to the general public. They seem to have preferred the 'square' forms of poetry in their C.M., L.M. and S.M. metres, but Charles Wesley composed hymns in metres that had never been used before in divine worship. He introduced valuable poetic novelties into hymnology, fresh metrical schemes, and made free use of jolly anapaests of 66.9.D, &c. And whilst his hymns are usually full, splendid and stately, more of them are animated and easy-flowing. Such hymns as these played no inconsiderable part in leading ordinary people to like rhymes with sharp, quick rhythms and to love heartiness and melody in their secular songs and songs of praise. Perhaps some of his metrical structures, nowadays labelled 'irregular', may have been a factor in causing Wordsworth in his *Intimations of Immortality*, and especially Coleridge in *Kubla Khan*, to break away from the restraints of couplet and stanza and to make rhymes and pauses fall, just where and when emotion demands them.

In Wesley's lifetime there was an almost complete transformation of poetic matter. In his youth the old French classical school of thought and expression remained supreme, and culminated in Pope. The age of Queen Anne asked that poetry should be smooth and trim, with points neatly contrasted; it disapproved of enthusiasm, sincerity in opinion, forcefulness of language. Decorum and restraint were the watchdogs on all poetry, so its poems were deficient in feeling. Pope even managed to make the Odyssey agreeable to that age, by clothing it in the habit of the day. Tales in verse declined in power and appeal, despite the admirable exceptions shown in *Tam o' Shanter* and *Battle of Hastings*. Prior with *Henry and Emma*, Gay with *Shepherd's Week*, Pope with *Rape of the Lock*, had all tried to resuscitate this grand old English form of verse, but without success. Even the *Deserted Village* and the *Elegy* fail as tales in verse; for they have only the germs of a tale, germs that get lost in meditation and moralizing. This fear of being considered 'enthusiastic', this hesitation to convey genuine feeling in convincing language, gradually made poetry decline into senility by 1750. Charles Wesley then wrote his *Wrestling Jacob*, which not only fired latent religious fervour, but marked the wide breach between the work of professional poets and what is genuine poetry. It exemplified a return to Milton's dictum that poetry should be 'simple, vivid, passionate'. It showed that manly poetry, couched in everyday speech, was more pleasing to the general public than the current delicate flowers of classical culture. Moreover, this new poetry was not dominated by any class-consciousness. It also re-introduced into verse the former personal note, and therefore it had fire and fervour. These new poets were writing from actual spiritual experience, and they tried to make as radiant and vivid an echo of that experience as they could. Indeed, so intense was this new personal note and so moving was the experience, that it is even now practically impossible to *read* some of these eighteenth-century hymns, without a thrill as from another world. Professor Moore puts it thus: 'This magnificent literary result does not arise from any excellent skill in phrase or form, but rather because

phrase and form were coined so as to transmit something of that
reality, taught in the experience of the man who wrote them.
Symbols are sometimes employed to extravagance; yet their final
impression is the apprehension of the close and glorious reality
that transcends all imagery.'

Sometimes this eighteenth-century literary imagery is offensive,
but line after line of *Wrestling Jacob*, and similar hymns by Wesley,
Watts, Toplady or Doddridge, are noble, masculine and clear.
The language is distinctive of the period, but a spirit of real devotion breathes through them all, and so makes the dry bones live.
Such hymns restored to public favour the forgotten religious
poems of Wedderburn, Dickson, Wither, Milton, Taylor, Ken and
Addison which were notable for melody of rhythm, structural
skill, and especially for the warmth and reality of their religious
feeling. Even Chatterton felt this sense of fervour and reality, and
could write stanzas indicative of the new poetic spirit:

> O God, whose thunder shakes the sky,
>   Whose eye this atom globe surveys,
> To Thee, my only Rock I fly.
>   Thy Mercy, in Thy Justice praise.

> If in this bosom aught but Thee
>   Incroaching, sought a boundless sway,
> Omniscience could the danger see,
>   And Mercy, look the cause away.

> The gloomy mantle of the night,
>   Which on my sinking spirit steals,
> Will vanish at the morning light,
>   Which God, my East, my Sun, reveals.

These verses show an intensity not only rare in the boy poet, but
rare in the professional poetry of his days.

With their lyrical sincerity, spontaneity and enthusiasm, these
Methodist hymnologists anticipated Burns, Wordsworth, Scott,
&c. The hymns drove away for ever the existing eighteenth-
century limited poetical appeal; they led directly to the *Lyrical
Ballads* of 1798, which finally extinguished the century's craze for
satiric-didactic poetry in heroic couplets. From the time of
Wrestling Jacob, genuine poets studiously avoided every feature of
the century's earliest work; thus the lucid, polished, fastidiously
exact poetic style of the first decades, was made to adjust itself,
through the agency of Methodist verse, and without jolt or jar, to
new poetic work of all kinds: description, dialogue, reflection,

characterization. Thanks to these hymns, enthusiasm was no longer avoided, and genuine feeling rather than mannered expression became the poet's goal. In literary circles, enthusiasm was no longer regarded as something irregular, abnormal, common; as mere exaggerated feeling and uncurbed eccentricity. Although Shaftesbury was to define it as 'a kind of natural inebriation', he was also to admit that 'it is the only expedient against this evil of uniformity'. Byrom was to ask and answer his own question:

> What is enthusiasm? What can it be
> But Thought, enkindl'd to a high degree.

And this enthusiasm, which gradually penetrated Wesley and permeated the Methodist spirit in the religious sphere, was to produce a revival of belief in inspiration even in the literary world. Such a revolution was to lead to poetic work in marked contrast with that done in an age of reason, common sense, class-distinction, decorum and scholarly restraint.

This revolution in literary diction was not so evident in the field of prose. As a body eighteenth-century novelists were inclined to exploit figures of speech; metaphors were sustained too long and elaborated with too much detail; occasionally, as in *Clarissa*, they escaped the writer's control. The sustained metaphors had also been accompanied by an immoderate liking for sonorous syllables and for distended sentences. In the mid-decades sentence-structure grew more and more complex; Richardson, Fielding, Smollett, Hume and their successors went in for lengthy descriptions and lengthy approaches; they wrote convolute sentences, strung precariously from one dependent clause to another; they and especially Gibbon, exploited the genitive which involved a great enlargement of the sentence, and later de Quincey was to revel in elaborate involutions, untiring amplitude of description and richness of verbal ornament. Yet Paine, Cobbett and Wesley avoided these massive, balanced structures and preferred direct, pithy, masculine sentences, descriptions that are terse, language that is vigorous, portraits that are lifelike, details that are striking and sympathy that is obviously sincere.

v

Of the certain things that one could affirm of this century's literature, one would be that it had no poets who were the equals of Milton and Shakespeare on the one hand or of Shelley and

Byron on the other; and that it saw no great creative work of many-sidedness or a conjunction of grand conceptions with the emotional sublime. Speaking in broad terms it would seem that the great majority of its poets are simply poets of culture rather than poets by nature; that trite phrasing, meretricious gilding, predominance of words over thought, and of style over substance, was the hall-mark of the great majority. Even Goldsmith, Thomson and Cowper are more distinguished for taste than for depth of feeling. Sallies of wit are found instead of sublimity of description; elegance of language replaces bold strokes of invention; refined expression is substituted for genuine pathos. And yet the century saw peculiar literary genius. It saw the deliberate emphasis on the pictorial side of poetry; in scores of poems by Thomson, Cowper, Campbell, Southey, Scott, Burns there is natural scenery in all varieties: of lake, mountain, dell, forest, ocean, bold headland and gushing fountain or sweeping river. To many a modern reader, this particularizing style may seem too assertive; certainly it led to very close attention to every detail and almost anticipated the pictorial artistry and verbal opulence which, later, were to be more fully developed by the Pre-Raphaelite Brotherhood and Tennyson.

Eighteenth-century poems and novels for the first time thought the manners, amusements, follies, absurdities, virtues, conventions, &c., of ordinary people worth recording. Defoe dealt with waifs and strays, pickpockets, wretched women, soldiers, apprentices, merchants; Fielding sketched the lives of court ladies, country gentlemen, broken captains, also those of bullies, valets, adventurers, and delineated coffee-houses, gaming tables and taverns; Goldsmith dealt not with ambitions and great passions, but with the life of a simple family, and Crabbe thought the village poor worthy of portraiture. It saw great historians like Hume and Gibbon give accounts of the conditions of the people, in addition to treating constitutional changes and political incidents.

This century's Goldsmith stands in a class by himself as the author of a novel every one reads, of verse from which excerpts appear in every anthology and of a play which still fills a theatre with a laughing crowd. It also saw Blake, Chatterton and Macpherson, who have their own unique niches in English literature. It saw in Sheridan the most famous dramatist since Shakespeare's day, the most brilliant orator of an age which regarded oratory as one of the greatest arts, and the almost unrivalled

humorist of the world. It saw the rise of such women writers as
Maria Edgeworth, Hannah More and Frances Burney, who
opened up the way for Jane Austen and the Brontës. It saw produced such lasting things as the homely poems of Burns and
Crabbe, the satires of Dryden, the moral epistles of Pope, the
lovely lyrics of Collins, the rustic graces of Goldsmith and Cowper.
It saw laid the foundation of modern English hymnody. Its stories
and essays will always be read and its outstanding comedies
always played. It was an age of song-writing and not least of
convivial song-writing.

Some of its individual masterpieces have already been mentioned. Among others were *Robinson Crusoe*, *Pamela*, *Joseph
Andrews*, *Tom Jones*, *Roderick Random*, *Peregrine Pickle*, *Humphry
Clinker*, *Tristram Shandy*, *Evelina*, &c. 'How Sleep the Brave', 'Ode
to Evening', 'St. Cecilia's Day', 'Cottar's Saturday Night',
'Windsor Forest', 'The Task', 'Deserted Village', &c., are still
regarded as some of the best and purest of English poetry. This
artificial century saw born such fine war poems as 'Scots wha hae',
'Rule Britannia', and the 'Marseillaise', as well as such national
songs as 'Auld Lang Syne', 'Yankee Doodle', 'Sally in our Alley',
'God Save the King', 'Gentlemen of England', 'Tom Bowling',
'Jolly Miller', 'Hearts of Oak', 'Farewell Manchester', 'Flowers o'
the Forest', 'A hunting we will go', 'Vicar of Bray', 'Ye Banks and
Braes', 'Home Sweet Home'.

Its literature also gave to posterity such characters as Beau
Tibbs, Dr. Primrose, Gentleman in Black, Vicar of Wakefield,
Squire Booby, Squire Western, Sir Roger de Coverley, Parson
Adams, Parson Trulliber, Tristram Shandy, Rev. Yorick, Dr.
Slop, Uncle Toby, Corporal Trim, John Gilpin, Tony Lumpkin,
Sir Gregory Gazette, Jerry Sneak, Partridge, Timothy, Mrs.
Grundy, Mrs. Malaprop, Lady Teazle, Anthony Absolute, Bob
Acres, Lord Foppington—a multitude of characters drawn with
brilliant skill, perfectly natural, and types of men and women
found everywhere in eighteenth-century England.

Its popular plays produced phrases that were not only then in
every one's mouth, but are still heard on every hand: 'Not worth
a rush', 'That accounts for it', 'Keep on moving', 'That's your
forte.' The century's thinkers and writers also provided their
quota of lasting phrases, which, having lost their first brilliance,
have now passed into everyday coin: 'distance lends enchantment
to the view', 'love and murder will out', 'the eternal fitness of

things', 'God helps them that help themselves', 'God tempers the wind to the shorn lamb', 'that man has an axe to grind', 'honesty's the best policy', 'the amiable weaknesses of human nature', 'handsome is as handsome does', 'he who fights and runs away, may live to fight another day', 'where ignorance is bliss, 'tis folly to be wise', 'rich beyond the dreams of avarice', 'a little learning is a dangerous thing', 'poetic justice with her lifted scale', 'masterly inactivity', 'disciplined inaction', 'instinctive genius', 'the end must justify the means', 'some folks are wise, some are otherwise', 'hope springs eternal in the human breast', 'agree to disagree', 'to be prepared for war is one of the most effective means of preserving peace', and 'Monday is the parson's holiday', are only a few of them.

VI

Leaving the minutiae of literary criticism, one turns to three aspects of a sort of literary work which may be said to have characterized the eighteenth century.

1. The letters and diaries of the eighteenth have a thrilling and historical appeal when read in MS., quite apart from their intrinsic value as literature. There are scores of famous collections of journals, letters and diaries; perhaps those of Swift, Steele, Gray, Cowper, Horace Walpole, Wesley, Mary Heber, Lady Mary Wortley Montagu are some of the most pre-eminent.

In many of the letters the old, stilted and stiff superscriptions and subscriptions of earlier days were preserved, when the writer was a junior member of the family or a mere female. One of these juniors writing to his ducal brother begins:

'Right Worshipful, My Singular Good Brother, as my duty is, with entire re-graces. I commend me unto you whose honour, joy and prosperity, I beseech the Blessed Trinity to increase daily, as I would have my simple person.'

The family tutor or librarian, writing to his employer, starts off:

'Right Reverend and Worshipful Master, I commend me unto your Good Mastership, ever more desiring to hear of your Good Welfare, the Which I beseech Jesu long to Continue unto your Hearts Desire.'

An earl ends his letter with

"I have the Honour, my dear Cousin, to be Y^r Most Devoted, Humble and Ob^{dt} Servant.'

The apparently unnatural obsequiousness and appeal for heavenly grace which characterized many of the eighteenth-century family letters, also invaded eighteenth-century business communications, and canvassers always declared

> We have the Honour to Be,
> With the Utmost & Profoundest Respect, Sir,
> Your Most Humble Ser^{nt}.

It even entered prosaic shipping accounts, and two bills of lading dated 1796 and 1800 begin with: 'shipped by the Grace of God' and conclude with

> 'God send the Good Ships to their Desir'd Ports in Safety. Amen.'

Many eighteenth-century home-letters seem strangely precise and unnatural as regards their beginnings and endings. Yet the domestic letters of Marlborough, Sydney Smith, Garrick, Johnson, de Quincey, Nelson, Collingwood, Cobbett show that they could occasionally be pretty, playful, tender and admiring, and some of their love-letters are masterpieces of ardour, good sense and earnestness. Those of Sheridan to his wife equal those of any age for phrasing, whilst his salutations are most fanciful—strangely unlike the orthodoxy of his generation; not infrequently they anticipate later hyperboles, periphrases and circumlocutions.

In the leisurely eighteenth century, they seem to have had un-limited time for strange-sounding salutations, flowery phrases of benediction, apparent unnaturalness, quaint spellings, neat but flourishing penmanship. Even Samuel, John and Charles Wesley, when distinguished graduates, always prefaced letters to their father with 'Hon^d Sir' and declared themselves to be 'Your dutiful Son'. To their mother, sisters and friends the two younger sons used much more natural phrasings, and in his letters to his col-leagues, John Wesley dropped many of the prevailing flourishes and superficialities; these letters, whilst remaining invariably courteous and formal, were direct, pithy, forcible and expressive, and now and then humorous. His more important letters like those to the bishops are a marvel of logic and literary condensa-tion; he compressed into a few words what would have taken most eighteenth-century people pages of paragraphs. In the one called *Calm Address* and in *Thoughts on Slavery* he showed good wording, apt quotation and an almost unrivalled faculty for suggesting a multitude of thoughts to readers, and of inducing the readers to think for themselves.

Eighteenth-century diaries are somewhat easier in their phrasings than were the letters penned by the same people. Usually the entries are short and business-like, whilst every now and then the spiritual and the pleasantly mundane elements seem to be harmoniously blended. Keeping a diary was a general practice in this century, and hundreds of them can still be examined. Thanks to the privacy of their recording system, these diarists were in a unique position for shedding strong light upon the lives of the people, and many of the diarists seem to have observed the habits, dress, manners and speech of their fellow men with close fidelity of detail and in a way that gives a lingering glamour of romance. Wesley's *Journal* especially reveals an accumulated and remarkable store of intimate knowledge of different people and places. Of these diaries Birrell said: 'there lies in them the most amazing record of human exertion ever penned or endured.' Perhaps they have not the quaintness and humour of Evelyn, Pepys, and Woodforde, but the author of *Omar Khayyám* declares them 'to be written in pure, unaffected, undying English'.

2. The second general striking feature of eighteenth-century literature was its satire, irony, brutality. Writers and caricaturists knew their public—men of strong stomachs and dull brains —whose passions could only be inflamed, and their comprehensions reached by means of the crudest lines and the most unblushing exaggeration in colour, line or words. Hogarth, Sayer, Gillray, and Richardson flayed prevailing customs and practices, hit off the ludicrous, attacked social follies and satirized habits and pretensions, often in gross forms and exaggerated caricatures. Dryden had a special faculty for satire; Pope's *Dunciad* has malignity and petulance, whilst his *Frenzy of John Dennis* is coarse beyond words: Johnson's political contributions to the *Gentleman's Magazine* were ridicule laced with brutality, and he could dismiss the death of the greatest soldier of his days, and one of England's best essayists in a line apiece:

> From Marlborough's eyes the streams of dotage flow,
> And Swift expires, a driv'ler and a show.

Swift's *Tale of a Tub* was mainly reckless satire, whilst his *Drapier's Letters*, and those of the unknown Junius, set the country ablaze with shocking personalities most thinly veiled, and with the sarcasm that withers and scorches. Chesterfield's bitter, sarcastic tongue and pen spared neither sex, rank, relation, power, profession, friend or foe from his glittering, pointed verbal weapons. Illness, death-bed, deformity did not save eighteenth-century victims from metrical abuse; even excellence was not spared. Swift ridiculed the music of Handel, Pope the scholarship of Bentley, Gray the abilities of Shaftesbury and the eloquence of Rousseau. Byrom's lines on Handel were considered witty; yet they merely run:

> Some say, compared to Bononcini,
> That Mynheer Handel's but a ninny;
> Others aver, that he to Handel
> Is scarcely fit to hold a candel;
> Strange all this differ, there should be,
> 'Twixt Tweedle-dum and Tweedle-dee.

Gifford, a man of letters and publicist, thought he was displaying Corinthian polish and brilliant touches of satire, when he dubbed opponents 'monsters of turpitude' and 'reptiles gorged with bile'. Pope called Lord Hervey 'mere white curd of asses milk'; Burke described Lord Chatham 'the grand artificer of fraud' and his supporters 'a parcel of low toad eaters', whilst Swift said of one of his opponents 'he is the most universal villain ever known'. Lesser lights like the literary bravos Churchill and Savage, wrote the *Rosciad*, *Epistle to Hogarth*, &c., things that bristle with scurrilous personalities. Newspapers like the *Craftsman* attacked by articles, verses, epigrams every thing or person that could possibly be connected with Walpole. A Tory paper, *The Post Boy*, in March 1714, seriously observes:

'That to desire the Whigs to forebear lying, we are sensible would be a most unreasonable request, because it is their nature, and their faction could not subsist without it.'

A misfortune to a Dissenter could not be referred to without a sneer. *The Weekly Packet* in 1715 has the following:

'On Monday last, the Presbyterian minister at Epsom broke his leg which was so miserably shatter'd, that it was cut off next day. This is great token that those pretenders to sanctity do not walk so circumspectly as they give out.'

This intemperance of thought that is clothed with gratuitous censure, entered into the disputes between eighteenth-century religious factions. Just as some of the people were malicious in drink, some were brawling and virulent under the influence of religious feeling. Broadly speaking, savage animosity among

Christians was normal in those days; and vomited venom had characterized the seventeenth-century religious disputes. Then the Quakers were the object of the vilest abuse from those calling themselves Christians, and their religion was held in derision by Anglicans and Dissenters alike. Bunyan had denounced them as 'the greatest enemies to the Christ of any men under Heaven . . . the notablest liars and corrupters of the sayings of the people of God, yea, and of the Scriptures also, that ever I came near in all the days of my life'. And later the Quakers gave as good as they got. Similar unredeemed vulgarities marked the wordy clashes between the Church and the Deists in the first half of the century. A preacher then said: 'the scarlet whore of Babylon is not more corrupt either in principle or practice than the Church of England'; a clergyman declared Archbishop Tillotson to be 'a traitor who had sold his Lord for a better price than Judas had done'.

The Methodist-Calvinistic controversy about 1772 was another occasion for unprofitable controversy and for distressing hubbub, marked with bitter, personal abuse and violent, frothy vituperation. One would have to go far to find more detestable literary assault and battery than that with which Toplady and his co-religionists assailed Wesley. They described him as 'the most rancorous hater of the Gospel system that ever appeared in this land . . . a low and puny tadpole in Divinity . . . governed by satanic shamelessness and satanic guilt'. A few years later, Rowland Hill, a graduate of Cambridge and a minister of the Gospel, described the founder of Methodism 'a venal profligate . . . an apostate miscreant . . . a wicked slanderer', whilst he termed Methodists 'a ragged legion of preaching barbers, cobblers, tinkers, scavengers, draymen and chimney-sweepers'. And into the mouth of Wesley the author of 'Rock of Ages' puts the following satiric doggerel concerning the author of 'The God of Abraham praise':

> I've Thomas Olivers, the cobbler;
> No stall in England holds a nobler;
>   A wight of talents universal
>   Whereof I'll give you a brief rehearsal:
> He wields beyond most other men,
> His awl, his razor and his pen;
>   My beard he shaves, repairs my shoe,
>   And writes my panegyric too;
> He, with one brandish of his quill
> Can knock down Toplady and Hill;

> With equal ease, whene'er there's need,
> Can darn my stockings and my creed;
> Can drive a nail or ply the needle,
> Hem handkerchiefs and scrape the fiddle;
> Chop logic as an ass chews thistle,
> More skilfully than you can whistle;
> And then when he philosophises
> No son of Crispin half so wise is;
> Of all my ragged regiment,
> This cobbler gives me most content;
> My forgeries and faith's defender,
> My barber, champion and shoe-mender.

Bad as this is, it is fairly mild compared with another attack by another Calvinist in the *Gospel Magazine* in 1780, when the slanderous abuse took the form of a dialogue between 'Old John and Old Nick'.

Sometimes much better writers joined in the religious verbal battles. *Humphry Clinker* is largely a caricature of Methodist preachers; Burns's *Holy Fair* is a savage attack on the ignorant ranters of his day; Foote had a farce called *The Methodist* which, independent of its personalities, was a violent satire upon Methodists, and through them upon the more religious part of the community; it contained a considerable quantity of coarse language and some rather exceptionable morality. When Charles Wesley questioned the propriety of elevating Coke to the dignity of a bishop prior to going out to America, he turned his brother's decision into metrical ridicule with:

> How easy now are bishops made
> At man or woman's whim;
> Wesley, his hands on Coke hath laid,
> But who laid hands on him?

When excellent people like Whitefield, Toplady, Rowland Hill, Charles Wesley could pen and voice brutal language like the foregoing, it is no wonder that another religious iconoclast could write a hymn beginning:

> We are the sweet selected few,
> The rest of you be damned;
> There's room enough in hell for you,
> We wont have Heaven crammed:

or that a devout Quaker, protesting against the arguments of another sectarian, could thus deliver himself:

'Thou fiery fighter, thou bastard that tumbled out of the mouth of the Babylonish bawd, thou mole, thou tinker, thou lizard, thou bell of no metal but the tone of a kettle, thou wheelbarrow, thou whirlpool, thou whirligig. O thou firebrand, thou adder and scorpion, thou louse, thou cow-dung, thou ragged tatterdemalion, thou Judas; thou livest in philosophy and logic which are of the Devil.'

Clearly the religious criticism of conflicting sects did not go in for precise expression, but preferred a riotous welter of abusive phrases and mixed metaphors to sound reasoning. Such strong language was however, germane to the times, and then, as now, it was used to cover weak thought. Besides, these were the days when the veneer of education was extremely thin even among preachers, so their understanding would be quickly intoxicated and their imaginations allowed to run wild; no wonder such men tried to cloak their mental inertia and deceive their hearers' minds with mere pretentiousness. Wesley, too, had his excesses of language which stir consternation among his admirers of to-day. But these excesses appear thin and pale, so far as scurrility gives tone and colour, when compared with the outpourings of many of his reverend contemporaries: Still he sometimes attacked local magnates, and gave them a piece of his mind about their conduct and life, and turned them to public contempt with rough and rasping ridicule. Happily there were honourable exceptions to this vulgar abuse between religious men. Law, Doddridge, Clarke, Price, Priestley, Clayton, Tindal conducted their religious differences in spirit of remarkable delicacy and caution for eighteenth-century protagonists.

Caricaturing of public people was another form of satire, irony and brutality that started in the days of George I. Such satire was often very broad, and a man like Wolcot had a keen eye for the ridiculous, and was endowed with a wondrous facility both of diction and brush. Scurrilous ballads were then very popular, and were full of the coarsest and grossest abuse against the monarchs, their favourites and courtiers; they were sung, bawled, shouted all day and night in the public streets, for the subjects of the royal Georges made no secret of their dislike. In his *Reminiscences*, Horace Walpole says nothing could be grosser than the ribaldry that was vomited out in lampoons, libels, squibs, broadsheets, window-pictures and every channel of abuse against the Sovereign and the Court. All the scandals attached to the Hanoverian family, and preserved in the early Jacobite songs,

R

were plentifully raked up. Once when George II was absent in Hanover, the following large notice was affixed to St. James's Palace:

'Lost or strayed out of this House, a man who has left his Wife and Five Children to the Parish. Whoever will give Tidings of him to the Churchwardens of St. James's Parish so that he may be got Again, shall receive Four Shillings and sixpence reward. N.B. This Reward will not be Increased as Nobody judges him to be worth a Crown.'

When Frederick Prince of Wales died, the sorrow of the people took this form:

> Here lies Fred,
> Who was alive and is dead.
> Had it been his father
> I had very much rather;
> Had it been his brother
> Still better than t'other;
> Had it been his sister
> No one would have missed her;
> Had it been the whole generation
> Still better for the nation;
> But since 'tis only Fred
> Who was alive and is dead,
> There's no more to be said.

When the sense of their inability to make changes for the better was too poignant for abusive expression, writers sometimes sought relief in forced humour. Byrom summed up the imperturbability of the ordinary man of the eighteenth century regarding the rival claims of Stuarts and Hanoverians for the English throne with:

> God bless the King. I mean our Faith's Defender,
> God bless—no harm in blessing—the Pretender;
> But who Pretender is or who is King,
> God bless us all; that's quite another thing.

Johnson, too, could be pathetically comic, and there is solemn burlesque in his lines:

> Hermit hoar, in solemn cell,
>   Wearing out Life's evening gray,
> Strike thy bosom, Sage, and tell
>   What is bliss and which the way.
>
> Thus I spoke and speaking, sighed,
>   Scarce represst the starting tear.
> When the hoary Sage replied:
>   Come, my Lad, and drink some beer.

Eventually even the illiterate found burlesque and humour in their sufferings. The iniquitous 'tommy-shops' provided them with such verbal humour as is to be found in 'tommy-rot', 'good tommy-spot'. Even the gallows afforded them sources of humour; their friends were 'gallows-birds' and had 'gallows-faces'; the braces that suspended their trousers were nicknamed their 'gallowses', and country people regularly called hemp 'neck-weed'. Their cynical humour led them to describe a favourite flower as the 'sweet-william' so as to recall the activities of the Bloody Duke of Cumberland, and an ugly old woman was styled a beldam (belle dame). Their broad and brutal humour led them to apply coarsely cheerful nicknames on acquaintances with physical defects or distinctive habits. The man with a short leg would be called 'stumpy Dick', the woman with a villainous squint, 'squinting Sally', and because of inertia, many an eighteenth-century man was known as 'old Dosey'. Distinguished members of learned club-societies got labelled 'old codgers' or 'lunatics', whilst Lord Townshend who conferred inestimable benefits on English farming communities by introducing the swede, was simply known to his peasantry as 'turnip Townshend'. Every village seemed to have its 'Gentleman Tom' and 'Pious Joe', and sacrilege often entered this form of rural humour and many a first Methodist was dubbed 'Jimmy Jesus', 'Sammy Christ', 'John Lord', whilst those of the Pharisee breed were quickly labelled 'creeping Judas', &c.

These few examples out of the wealth of eighteenth-century satiric brutality and humour show that to the people, incongruities were at first intolerable but finally amusing; they also show that the eighteenth-century English had a genius for keeping a solemn face over the follies which they rather relished than endured. Vitriolic satire is usually found in the early crusading days of any political or religious movement, when one is grimly in earnest and positive in the belief that things can and must be altered; then is the time for violent attack and impassioned protest rather than for laughter. Later, when it is realized that for good or ill, the world goes jogging on its way much as before, we begin to laugh at things we are powerless to amend. Eighteenth-century memoirs typify this changing attitude and abound in examples of the wit, punning, and repartee of Parr, Porson, Horace Walpole, the 'Blue-Stocking Club', Johnson, Horne Tooke, Dr. Burney and Sydney Smith. These people often donned the mask of levity, rather than

that of tragedy. The eighteenth-century Horace Walpole perhaps
best summed up this situation when he declared: 'Life is a comedy
to the man who thinks; a tragedy to the man who feels.'

3. Although newspapers were known in England in the seventeenth century, they had only a very small circulation. One called
the *Weekly News* appeared in 1622; another, *Kingdom's Intelligence*, in
1662, whilst the *Gentleman's Journal* was the first magazine in 1692.
In 1709 appeared the first morning paper, the *Daily Courant*.

The idea of a leading article as a factor in the shaping of public
opinion began with such leader writers as Swift, Defoe, Steele,
Bolingbroke, Pulteney in the *Review, Examiner, Craftsman*, by which
was waged the keen political struggle of the first half of the
eighteenth century. In the second half Smollett and Murphy
were engaged to champion the cause of Bute in the *Briton* and
Auditor. But when John Wilkes and Churchill established the
North Briton, they quickly surpassed the Government papers in
ability and virulence. Many of these earlier dailies were remarkable for the eminent force and versatile genius employed upon
them; the leading articles were pungent, direct, forceful and often
libellous, and there is no wonder that Walpole tried to muzzle not
merely the stage, but the Press, for he was often a writhing victim
of these onslaughts. To defend his administration, Walpole
engaged a special writer, William Arnall, and paid him £3,000
a year out of the Treasury funds.

Most of the papers mentioned have now disappeared or lost
their identity; but others like *The Times, Glasgow Herald, Lloyd's
List, Belfast Newsletter, Gloucester Journal, Yorkshire Post, Norwich
Mercury, Observer, Northampton Mercury, Tatler, Spectator*, which still
flourish, were also born in this century.

As to-day, advertisements were a feature of the eighteenth-
century newspapers, although their form and nature have undergone considerable changes. Then there were advertisements concerning marriage for money, advertisements 'for companions'
from gentlemen who candidly announce that 'matrimony is not
intended', and from ladies who 'were seeking a protector'. Very
frequent are the advertisements for runaway servants. Forgotten
tea-gardens, coffee-taverns, theatres, music-halls and clubs appear
in these eighteenth-century columns. Wigs, powders, patches,
lotteries, street cries, ballads, lampoons and especially quack-
medicines and their vendors appear in eighteenth-century advertisements. Judged by modern standards these advertisements were

somewhat paltry as regards space and lay-out but they made a still more blatant use of the modern superlative.

Chimney-sweeps and rat-catchers advertised with remarkable candour and self-assertion: 'W. Hunt of Woodrising, taylor and Rat-catcher in aprelle last, att the hous of Mr. Robt. Adley in woodton, catched in one fortnite, no lesse than 1418 RATS, the Truth of Which will be attested by the Neighbourhood. The eminent Rat-catcher is now bespoke with at Woodton hall.'

'The greatly celebrated CORDIAL Balm of Gilead is happily calculated for the Weak, the Sickly, the Infirm. In all inward Decays, Debility, Lowness of Spirits, Weakness in either Sex, it affords the Most Wonderful Relief.

Prepared by Dr. SOLOMON,

Author of The Guide to Health and other valuable works at his House, Solomons Place, Liverpool.

Price half a Guinea a bottle.

Is there no Balm in Gilead? Is there no Physician there? Why then is not the Health of the Daughter of My People recovered? Jer. viii. 22. The Lord hath caused medicines to grow out of the earth, and he that is wise will not abhor them; for with such doth he heal men and take away their pains. Ecclus. xxxviii. 3, 4.

'The Balm of Gilead is a most noble medicine, compos'd of some of the choicest natural balsams and strengtheners in the whole Materia Medica. The process is long and laborious and requires the most nice and minute attention. Not a single drop can be produc'd under six weeks digestion; and the elements from which it is compos'd are obtain'd with still greater labour and difficulty. The Discovery of it has cost the Proprietor Amazing Sums, great Loss of Time, repeated Experiments and Close Application to Practical Chemistery; and it Affords him no Small Gratification to avow, that in offering it to the Public, he invades No Man's Property, nor imitates any Medicine Known in Public or Private Practice. The Experiment he has made with it upon a Variety of Diseases would almost Exceed Belief.'

The prescription for this northern cure-all has been lost, but it is thought that it contained rich spices, herbs and what not, generously laced with strong old brandy. It became famous in every inhabited part of the globe; scarcely a ship left an English port without cargoes of it, and it secured a fortune for its inventor. The 1782 advertisements of Dr. Graham for his 'Temple of Health' were just as bombastic, whilst those vaunting Dr. Brodum's 'Guide to Old Age' and his 'Botanical Syrup', appearing in The Times as late as 1798, equalled any previous ones in flamboyance.

Doctors advertised themselves with much verbal opulence and listed the forty or more coffee-houses at which they would call daily in a given order and at which 'they were ready to serve any lady or gentlemen'. Butchers advertised in lyrical terms their 'welch moutton which they engage to be seven years old, at which age moutton is at its Highest Perfection'. Coffee-taverns proclaimed their 'water-gruel of which 'tis not yet thoroughly known, but there comes such a company as drinks usually four or five gallon apiece in a morning'. Puff in Sheridan's *Critic* says concerning advertising language: "Twas I first taught them to crowd their advertisements with panegyrical superlatives, each epithet rising above the other, like the bidders in their own shops. From me they learn'd to inlay their phraseology with variegated chips of exotic metaphor.' And judging from the late eighteenth-century advertisements of professional men and tradesmen, they learned their lesson well.

Sometimes, however, the advertisements were straightforward affairs:

'A Gentleman has enquired of me for a Reputable Gentlewoman about 30 years Old, of Good Breeding, Comeliness, Prudence and 5 or 600£ in Munni, Land or Joynture. Such an One his Friend would match with, tho' on the Square, he Deserves far more Fortune which he Minds less than his Good Likeing.'

In the year Wesley died another would-be husband listed not only the positive qualities he expected to find in a bride, but he also detailed her possible disqualifications.

'Wanted immediately, a woman who would be pleas'd with a husband; she must be sound of mind and limb, of a moderate fortune, tolerably handsome and not subject to drunkenness. She must not scold but once a month, must comb her hair at least once a week, and, above all, she must neither chew tobacco nor take snuff, as it always gives me heartburn to have my diet peppered. A woman of this description may find a place by applying to J.R. of H——, who possesses every requisite to qualify him for a husband.'

'A negro maid went away from her Master's House; a negro maid aged about 16 years, much pitted with the Small Pox, speaks English well, haveing a piece of her Left ear bit off by My Dog, and hath on a strip'd stuff wascote and petticoat.'

Norwich Gazette in 1722 advertised that 'Mr. Rob[t] Robinson in Norwich, near Bedlam, has Great Choice of Good Second Hand Coffins to Sell for Ready Money'. There is no mention how the advertiser came into possession of his gloomy chattels, which were designed to serve two or more occupants in succession. But one cannot read the advertisement without being haunted with grim visions of a midnight trade then widely practised.

Advertisements for 'places under the Government' were often seen in *The Times* at the end of the century and 'gentlemen with 500£ or 1,000£ would be treated with'. One in 1796 runs: 'To be sold a permanent place under Government, the Salary being 76£ per annum nett; attendance not required more than twenty times in the year, and for about two hours each time . . . the duty is agreeable and in the Line of a Gentleman and can at all times at small expence be executed by a deputy. What Offers?'

As for general news, these papers were mainly filled with wearisome tales of gallantry, brutal abductions, silly bets, murders, executions, privateerings, the unsavoury records of matrimonial agents, the little chapels in May Fair, the shameless business of Fleet marriages, masks, masquerades, balls, sudden deaths from excessive drinking and so forth. 'Sales of wives' are frequently mentioned. Throughout the century, working-men seem to have thought that such transactions were legal, if they sold their partners in open market, and had taken the precaution of putting a halter round the woman's neck. Quite at the end of the century even *The Times* reports such transactions. Prices seem to have ranged from sixpence to three and a half guineas, and evidently many were withdrawn from auction because they had not reached the reserve price.

The newspapers chronicled the exploits of jockeys, watermen and pugilists, and the sayings and doings of Johnny Moore, Tom Spring and company were fully recorded especially in *The Boxiana*. Fashionable duels were reported *in extenso* and in most jaunty fashion, whilst the detailing of blows, wounds, &c., was nauseating.

Most of the reporting was done in so-called sprightly English, but which was really nothing but patches of indecent ribaldry. Dullness gave way to pertness, and such pertness marred the first issues of the *Morning Post, Morning Herald, Morning Chronicle*, which as late as the eighties, courted popularity by detailing the most indelicate scandal, that ought to have been offensive to public morality and taste. Even in the mid-nineties *The Times* was almost as arch and facetious as its competitors. It was of such journalists that Pulteney, a great pamphleteer and politician of the century, had said 'they are a herd of wretches whom neither information can enlighten nor affluence elevate; low drudges of scurrility, whose scandal is harmless for want of wit and whose opposition is only troublesome from the pertinaciousness of stupidity'.

Their sense of proportion and their conception of style are perhaps best revealed by samples:

'Old Bailey Sept. 24th 1790. The following Prisoners received Sentence of Death: John Griffiths for Sheep Stealing, Wil. Pearson for a Robbery in an open Field near the King's Highway, Eliz. Hill for stealing Goods to the value of 15/– privately in a Shop, Sara Dauncer for the same Offence, John Spenser for horse Stealing, Erick Falk for Forgery, John Lewis for assembling with 20 persons and more, to the Disturbance of the Public Peace and Beginning to Demolish and to pull down a house.'

Chester 1753:

'Last Thursday was married at St. Bridget's Church in this City, Mr. Robert Allen an eminent Pawnbroker aged 75 to Miss Catherine Powell of about 17, youngest Daughter to Mr. Powell, formerly Peruke-Maker but since left Business, all of said city, a young lady of such sedate, womanly Carriage, as Becomes One of these Times her Age, nothing of the giddy Young Damsel, appearing either in her Dress, or Behaviour, which certainly was one of those Captivating Charms, as well as her Beauty (which is extensive) that enamour'd her Antient Lover with a Desire of Joining Hymen's Knot, that he might pass the Remainder of his Hoary Life, with one so Agreeable as She is, having surprising Wit, with Abundance of Eloquence and in Her is centr'd Virtue, Meekness, Humanity and Other Qualifications, which will render the State very happy and an handsome Portion.'

Sometimes eighteenth-century newspapers purported to review books and works of art. In this they succeeded in being as silly and flippant as they were with their ordinary reporting. The *Westminster Magazine* criticized two large quarto volumes with three words, 'learned, critical and ingenious', dismissed a volume on science with 'crude, obscure, bombastic', one on regal antiquities with 'curious, useful and pleasing'. Another newspaper, towards the end of the century, pronounced the authors of a learned and illustrated manual on painting 'a hellish bad painter and a damned bad writer'. Even Cowper could review the Rev. Henry Venn's collected sermons as 'a repository of self-righteousness and pharisaical lumber'. Broadly speaking, throughout the century newspapers were not conducted with much taste, independence, responsibility or sense of power.

And yet some of that century's writers should have made excellent journalists. Defoe, with his power of word-spinning, his education in the school of life, his capacity for popular reassurance, and the confidence trick of his imagination, should have attained the highest degree of proficiency in that field of literature. Swift could have contributed columns of vigorous and provocative comments, and would have done solid work in combating the illusions, prejudices, conventions and meannesses that clog and petrify life. Johnson could have written dignified, thoughtful 'leaders', and would never have hesitated to extract the sharp whine from minor politicians, or the retailers of cheap shoddy. Horace Walpole would have been admirable as 'Our London Correspondent', 'Man about Town' or 'Club Members'; for he was always a professor of tradition in art, literature, politics, and could pose as a person attached to the fashionable or dominant party, animated to that end by instinct rather than by acumen or conviction. He moved in most circles of any social importance; he knew how to praise just that mellow and polite England of which country houses, swagger clubs, orthodox church are the comfortable symbols.

The early eighteenth century saw the first attempts at reporting to the public what took place in Parliament. At first these reports appeared monthly and contained mere indications of the speeches. Then the *Gentleman's Magazine* began to publish reports of the debates. From 1728 to 1771 these reports were constantly challenged, for the Commons considered it 'an indignity to and a breach of the privilege of this House for any Person to presume to give in written or printed Newspapers, any account of the Debates or Proceedings'. They were quite satisfied with Hansard, their official recorder. But Cave, by his parodies in the *Gentleman's Magazine*, and especially John Wilkes, led the public to victory in this contest between the House of Commons and the Press. Letters from correspondents do not seem to have been published till the *Public Ledger* and *Public Advertiser* accepted them during the sixties; and it was in the latter newspaper that first appeared the celebrated letters from 'Junius' in 1769.

Sunday newspapers were a feature of eighteenth-century journalism; perhaps they were not good ones, and probably Wesley regarded them much as did Crabbe, who wrote:

> No changing Season makes their Number less,
> Nor Sunday shines a Sabbath on the Press!
> Then lo! the Sainted Monitor is born,
> Whose Pious Face some sacred texts adorn;

As Artful Sinners cloak the Secret Sin,
To veil with Seeming Grace the Guile within;
So Moral Essays on his Front appear,
But all is Carnal Business in the rear;
The fresh coin'd Lie, the Secret whisper'd last,
And all the Gleanings of the Six Days Past.

The first religious newspapers were published round about 1770, and eight years later Wesley started the *Arminian Magazine*, so as to defend and maintain those doctrines which were then being reviled with abominable scurrility by the Calvinists in their monthly papers, *Spiritual* and *Gospel*. Despite such excellent titles Wesley had occasion to write of them:

'they have no regard to good nature, decency or good manners; nor to truth or reason; all these are set utterly at defiance . . . their arguments are worthy of Bedlam and their language worthy of Billingsgate.'

The paper used for magazine and newspapers was rather poor material; type was small and somewhat irregular, whilst the aline-ment was imperfect. Printing presses did not improve greatly from the days of Caxton till 1800, when the Earl of Stanhope invented a press allowing for larger sheets and which permitted 300 impres-sions an hour to be worked off the machine. The newspapers were quite wet when sold, and they had to be dried before a fire to make them acceptable by particular readers.

The early newspapers of the century, like the *Daily Courant*, had pages 14 in. by 8 in. with a printed area of 11 in. by 6 in. The news was printed in two columns per page and on one side of the paper only, whilst the entire newspaper was a single sheet and therefore contained only two pages. A hundred years later, many newspapers had pages nearly 18 in. by 12 in.; the news was printed in four columns and on both sides of the paper, whilst the entire newspaper might have four such pages.

Eighteenth-century statesmen saw in newspapers an easy way of increasing the national revenue, and they quickly instituted the 'newspaper stamp', a red mark indicating that the tax had been paid. This tax was at first a halfpenny per half-sheet; but it was raised again and again so that by 1797 practically every organ of the Press was paying at least $2\frac{1}{2}d$. per issue. By then, however, the newspaper habit was firmly established. In 1753 the number of newspapers paying tax averaged over seven millions a year; by 1770 the number paying the 'stamp' averaged a million a month.

Round about Wesley's death, *The Times* was boasting that it had a circulation of between 4,000 and 5,000, and with such a circulation, clearly it was coming into new importance. With this multiplication of people who could read, the number of competing separate newspapers greatly increased, and one hears Dr. Johnson grumbling that 'journals are daily multiplied without increase of knowledge'. For in addition to regular newspapers and journals, the public could buy things called 'broadsheets', which simply reported one or two exciting bits of news; these broadsheets were 'somewhat secret in machination, unchecked by criticism, very brutal in language and violent in ideas'.

In addition to the newspaper stamp, the papers had also to pay the State an 'advertisement tax' on every advertisement they printed. At first this tax was a shilling and imposed regardless of space or position occupied. Later the tax was differentiated according to size and position of the advertisement, and might be anything up to 5*s*. 6*d*. per issue. It was a profitable tax, and in 1800 newspapers were paying from £500 to £1,000 per annum on this impost alone. The advertisers themselves do not seem to have been heavily charged for their advertisements by the newspaper proprietors, and there are records showing that leading papers charged about 2/– for a $2\frac{1}{2}$ in. space in prominent places.

Most newspapers could be seen at the private circulating and lending libraries, which by the end of the century were very popular. At these places, it was customary not only to borrow and read newspapers and books, but also to use them as gambling dens.

CHAPTER X

EDUCATION

I

EIGHTEENTH-CENTURY poor parents were quite untroubled about their children's education; they looked upon their offspring as possible wage-earners from the age of four. Wealthier parents then looked upon infancy and adolescence as a kind of mental, moral and physical disease rendering the victims unfit occupants of a civilized home. So, to free themselves of the children's presence, they either employed menially-treated, badly-paid tutors or sent them early to boarding-schools.

Stories by eighteenth-century writers and school anecdotes of eighteenth-century famous men, indicate that at all the better-known schools bullying was rife, even to the torturing of small boys by big ones with spurs, and that fighting was encouraged. School buildings were usually old, deficient in light and air, with barred windows, massive doors, enormous bolts, and in every way giving the gloomy aspect of a prison; everything about them was cold and repelling. Tone was bad. At Winchester the boys regularly drank flip, had brandy parties, smoked twist; at both Eton and Rugby the boys on occasion grew so obstreperous that the militia had to be called in to quell riots. Wesley says the younger boys at Charterhouse were tyrannized over, and that the older ones were allowed to exercise the physical privilege of stealing food from the younger ones' plates. Cowper's life at Westminster—then the most eminent of public schools—was one of sheer torture and horror; the memory of his school was so persistent that, when he was fifty-three, he wrote *Tirocinium*, which is a bitter attack on public schools and their products. Fielding asserted that 'public schools are the nurseries of all vice and immorality'.

Many of the masters at them have had talents and even good dispositions, but a large number seem to have been disgraced by licentiousness, and to have been dependent upon a whole arsenal of punishments in order to maintain any sort of discipline. Johnson declares that no schoolmaster of his day ever tried to distinguish between ignorance and negligence, and would unmercifully beat a boy, equally for not knowing a thing as for neglecting to know it. Gibbon writes: 'By the common methods of discipline, at the expense of many tears and some blood, I purchased a knowledge of Latin syntax. . . .' Of Oxford he writes: '. . . to the university I acknowledge no obligation . . . the months I spent at Magdalen proved the most idle and unprofitable of my whole life.' Johnson felt much the same about the same place where 'he treated the authorities with the grossest disrespect', whilst Gray, the donnish recluse, viewing the situation from the opposite angle, 'shunned the crew of dissonant college-dwellers at Cambridge'. Wesley, looking at Oxford without its 'Holy Club', wrote:

'I loved the very sight of Oxford; I loved the manner of life and esteemed many of its institutions. But my prejudice in its favor is considerably abated.'

Later he affirmed:

'The moment a young man sets foot in either Oxford or Cambridge he is surrounded with company of all kinds, except that which would do him good; with loungers and triflers of every sort; with men who no more concern themselves with learning than religion.'

And judging from the acid comments of writers who pursued their studies in the early decades of the nineteenth century, these schools and universities do not seem to have improved. Southey, who made a poor show at Westminster and Balliol, refers to them as 'places where I got little or nothing'; at Cambridge, Wordsworth was 'stiff, moody, violent'; Shelley was expelled from Oxford 'for contumacy', and Byron declared that Cambridge Trinity 'added little to his knowledge of academical learning, but there he qualified himself to graduate in boxing, drinking, gaming'. Hazlitt, who only knew teaching institutions by their products, is most contemptuous: 'Any one who has passed through the regular gradations of a classical education and is not made a fool by it, may consider himself as having had a very narrow escape . . . the least respectable character among modern politicians was the cleverest boy at Eton . . . you will hear more good things on the outside of a stage-coach from London to Oxford than if you were to spend twelve months with the heads of the colleges.' Lord Holland, a late eighteenth-century aristocrat, described education at Oxford as 'pedantry without training, insolence without learning, intolerance without firmness'. So the evidence of widely differing men like Swift, Defoe, Gray, Johnson,

Eldon, Chesterfield all agree on this point, that both universities were neglectful and inefficient in the performance of their duties. Thackeray infers that the other places which should have been centres of light and training grounds, were just as bad. At Charterhouse the senior boys seemed to have assumed all the privileges of men before they quitted the seminary; they smoked cigars, chewed twist, practised inebriation, fought duels, bet on cock-fighting, loved bull-baiting, diced for big sums. In this era, wealthy boys who had reached a certain age, were allowed their own private servants at school and university. Many of them kept horses, phaetons, coaches, &c., and as pupils, were allowed to entertain in lavish manner. At the end of the century and early in the nineteenth, John Mytton was said to have lived at the rate of £800 a year when a boy at Westminster school, and to have been allowed to keep his own pack of hounds when he was ten years old. Perhaps it is no wonder that eighteenth-century schoolboys and undergraduates tippled, diced, duelled with a zest that could hardly have been bestowed upon better causes.

II

Despite this weighty evidence on eighteenth-century educational particular failures and shortcomings, history proves that there was genuine progress in education, especially in that for girls and the poor.

Theory of education, too, received much attention. In 1697 Locke wrote his *Thoughts on Education*, and the better professional people were influenced by his ideas. In this book Locke bewailed 'the poor quality of some schoolmasters', grieved over 'the mixed herd of unruly boys, the lax morals and the rowdy ways', and deplored 'the tyranny of Latin grammar, themes and versions'. He stressed the importance of good company, of making learning attractive, of banishing drudgery and overmuch memory work. He affirmed his belief in the almost unlimited power bestowed by education, and ascribed very little importance to natural endowment. Nowadays few teachers would agree with Locke's observations on the unimportance of original endowment, just as modern psychologists would discredit his theories on perception. But every one would consider as sound his plea for the establishment of a school in every parish, and that all children between the ages of three and fourteen should be obliged to attend one. This idea of compulsory education for all was never adopted by any eighteenth-century Parliament, although Adam Smith revived a lower ideal in 1776, when he advocated the establishment of district schools which should be partially maintained at the public expense. But Smith thought that the pupils should pay to attend such proposed institutions, should not be compelled to attend them, and that freedom should be obtained at any time by passing an easy qualifying test. Other writers followed Locke in the field of educational philosophy. In 1741 Isaac Watts wrote his *Improvement of the Mind*, in which treatise he recommended the very close study of logic and astronomy from an early age. Apparently he was not troubled about his puny frame and constant ill health, or did not attribute them to his own school training; at any rate he recommended a course of study calculated to endanger a boy's physique. Dr. Priestley wrote his *Course of Liberal Education* in 1765, Mrs. Chapone her *Letters on Mind Improvement* in 1774, V. Knox his *Liberal Education* in 1781 and Godwin his *Enquirer* in 1797. The last-named sounded a very modern note when he defined his teaching method as 'an incessant recurrence to experiment and actual observation'. Most of these philosophers or religious writers stressed the moral application of all lessons, and anticipated the famous verbal memory business which, later, masqueraded as education under a Gradgrind.

Better known people sometimes wrote in a direct manner on education, notably Mary Wollstonecraft and Hannah More, whilst Johnson and Goldsmith suggested rather casually the new theory that parenthood in itself gave a right to an opinion on education. The two ladies even tried to put their theories into practice in girls' seminaries and charity schools, whilst Goldsmith and Johnson went farther, and made short-lived attempts at actual teaching. The former failed lamentably, and the latter's private school must have resembled an ogre's den. Sometimes too, the wealthy and clever men of the eighteenth century formulated doctrines for the education of their own sons. The brilliant fourth Earl of Chesterfield coached his heir in the famous *Letters to my Son*. These letters are full of elegant wisdom, keen wit, admirable portrait painting, exquisite observation and deduction; but in them there is instruction for the boy on how to seduce women. In fairness, it must be remembered that these objectionable letters merely reflect the morality of the age, and that the author only reduced to writing the principles of conduct by which, deliberately or unconsciously, the worst and best of his wealthy contemporaries were governed. That these particular letters did not shock the moralists of the age is proved by the subsequent work of a Dr. Gregory. For towards the end of the century, when this old-fashioned moralist had made the discovery 'that women might be considered as our companions and equals', he wrote *Father's Legacy to His Daughters*, which was a mild feminine edition of Chesterfield's more famous work. This duly execrated attitude towards sexual laxity, makes the modern moralist forget that the eighteenth-century nobleman urged far more powerfully other things on his son. He was 'to be scrupulously jealous of the purity of his moral character and keep it immaculate, unblemished, unsullied'. Equally seldom is it recalled that in these letters there is unflagging incitement to strenuous living, and that the external graceful accomplishments Chesterfield desires for his son 'must come from grace within . . . that a vital sense of decorum operates not merely in manners, but in studies, in morals, in religion'.

Two other eighteenth-century noblemen, Lord Holland and the Earl of Chatham, may be said to have shaped their sons' education. Both Charles James Fox and William Pitt were intended for ministerial office from the cradle, and although the two peers employed contrasting training methods, both achieved their objective. This notion of specialized training for future occupation was also greatly encouraged by Pestalozzi, the late eighteenth-century educator of international importance. Even at the age of five, the training selected for each individual was to bias in favour of ultimate profession. Thus different systems of discipline and education were advocated for the potential clergyman, naval or military officer or physician. For the last, Pestalozzi recommended the serious study of anatomy at the age of five, and suggested the desirability of allowing the infant to carve the family duck or turkey, whilst the embryo soldiers 'should from infancy be accustomed to the loss of a meal, having one at irregular hours and despatching it quickly'. Just before 1800, another wealthy man who had put his ideas on infant and junior training into practice with his numerous offspring, expressed rather more orthodox opinions. In 1798 Edgeworth published his *Practical Education*, and if one can overlook the heavy morality inculcated, and make some allowance for the sex-prejudice he shows, one will see that he had sound ideas on the question of educative toys for children and that he anticipated Froebel in many details. He urged, for example, that the temperament and abilities of the individual children should be given special attention, and made the then astounding declarations that 'sluggishness must be distinguished from slowness' and of 'nothing upon compulsion', that 'lessons on any particular point should be very short' and that 'there must be variety of stimulus'.

But none of these English amateurs and writers made an impression on eighteenth-century education like that produced by Rousseau in 1762 with his *Emile*. He electrified the superior social section of the world by urging that even the noblest mothers should nurse their offspring, and that all boys, even the wealthiest, should be taught a trade. He amazed his friends by stressing the dignity of parenthood; he astonished tutors by declaring that education should be approached from the pupil's end and not from the teacher's. An altogether new doctrine of 'hardening off' young people was propounded, and many an heir to a dukedom was brought up on the spartan-red-indian training principle. Whatever absurdities the author and first disciples may have committed in the flush of enthusiasm, the idea did call for respect of the child's individuality. Importance was attached to sense-training and to realistic studies generally; an active part was assigned the child in his own education, and the law of consequences was made to work from the start. All this was so much to the good, but the beneficence of Rousseau's theories was largely restricted to sensible tutors and dissenting academies; for the famous schools either ignored the new doctrine completely, or made a farce of its implications. Still, owing to the sensationalism of the principles, and the personal influence of Voltaire and Rousseau, French ideas on education gradually permeated England's wealthier class during the second half of the century to a marked degree. Not all the English accepted this foreign contribution; Wesley, for example, had very little patience with Rousseau or his doctrines. 'Surely a more consummate coxcomb never saw the sun', he writes in one place. Likewise he saw no sense in Rousseau's affirmation that 'nature intends children to be children before they are men', nor in the plea that 'adults should love childhood, encourage its sports, its pleasures, its lovable instincts'. The two men were poles apart; the one based his educational system on what he thought the child-mind was like, whilst Wesley based his practice on what the child-mind ought to be like.

s

III

As for the actual studies pursued in the well-known public schools of the eighteenth century, there is every sign that the lads had to work very hard; every day they were at lessons from six in the morning till six at night. The classical tradition dominated the teachers' minds; Greek and Latin were obligatory and the boys had to talk Latin when in the playgrounds, and most of the lessons were given in that tongue. Such heavy stress made many an eighteenth-century man readier to talk and write Latin than English. The subsequent influence of this emphasis showed itself in literature and politics. Great writers like Johnson, &c., expected their readers to be reasonably good latinists, and to possess a sound knowledge of classical mythology; certainly they never troubled to explain their allusions, or to translate their quotations. Ministers of the Crown freely quoted Homer and Euripides in the House of Commons, and declaimed solemn hexameters of Lucretius and Virgil. Inspired by the shooting beam of the rising sun through the windows of the Senate-house, Pitt interspersed his great speech on the Slave Trade with:

> Nos . . . primus equis Oriens afflavit anhelis,
> Illic sera rubens accendit lumina Vesper;

a beautiful and apt impromptu that would delight and grip his auditors. The mother-tongue was somewhat despised, and certainly held a very minor position in the curriculum. Mental science, metaphysics, epistemology, ethics, aesthetics, logic— classed together as 'philosophy'—were very important in the schools; the teachers were supposed to analyse the clashing chimes of such seventeenth- and eighteenth-century philsophers as Hobbes, Descartes, Spinoza, Leibnitz, Locke, Toland and Berkeley, Hume, Priestley, Kant. On the other hand, mathematics was considered an inferior subject and was therefore neglected in these schools, despite the fact that Brahe, Napier, Galileo, Kepler, Newton, Pascal, as well as Eüler, Mayer, Legendre and Laplace had each added considerably to eighteenth-century mathematical knowledge, and that Gunter had made many useful mathematical inventions with his chain, line, quadrant and scale. Other forms of science, too, could also boast such honoured names as Bradley, Maskelyne, Herschel and Lagrange for astronomy, and such as Stahl, Glauber, Snell, Huygens, Boyle,

Galvani, Coulomb, Volta, Nollet, Franklin, Priestley, Cavendish, Black, Lavoisier, Buffon, Linnaeus, &c., for new facts concerning the physical characteristics of matter, plants and animals. The century saw the invention of the Leyden Phial, and the realization that lightning is nothing more than a gigantic spark. Yet, despite such facts and rolls of honour, astronomy, electricity, chemistry, physics and botany were almost ignored in these schools. Handicraft was never attempted in them, whilst organized games were practically unknown. The boys played a sort of cricket, guerrilla football, fives and tennis, but even lusty youths were equally enthusiastic over hoop-bowling, see-saw, marbles, top-spinning, puss-in-the-corner, kite-flying and battledores. They enjoyed leaping with poles, and one of the chief delights at Eton was to slide down the stairs from cloisters to kitchen. On the other hand, 'Shrove Tuesday' cock-fighting, &c., were encouraged at most of them during the whole century and were still allowed at Manchester Grammar School as late as 1815.

Particularly in the mid-century, these youthful aristocrats were encouraged to acquire foppish manners and affectations, and other forms of what was considered elegant behaviour. Men were then admired for their strut and pose, their tailoring, because they 'could sweep a magnificent leg' . . . or 'interlard their conversation with French phrases'.

Neither Oxford nor Cambridge was a great centre of learning and research during the century, nor were university chairs always given to outstanding ability. Cowper spoke of professors as 'representing ignorance in stilts'; Porson wrote the following epitaph on a Fellow of his own college:

> Here lies a Doctor of Divinity,
> Who was a Fellow, too, of Trinity;
> He knew as much about divinity
> As other fellows do of trinity.

Amherst, editor of the *Craftsman*, said: 'there were debauchees acting as professors of Moral Philosophy and astronomy teachers who had never in their lives looked soberly upon the stars.' History records the appointment of Bishop Watson to the Cambridge professorship of chemistry about 1764, although at the time 'he knew nothing at all of chemistry; had never read a syllable on the subject nor seen a single experiment in it'. In 1776 Adam Smith wrote: 'In the University of Oxford, the greater part of the public professors have for these many years given up altogether even the pretence of teaching'; for at both universities many of the professors were absentees and paid a miserable pittance to deputies. It was of such men that Gibbon said: 'they well remembered that they had a salary to receive and only forgot that they had duties to perform.'

But even in this detail, the eighteenth century shows its customary conflicting characteristics; for it was the era of university dons of the eminence of Porson, Jebb, Sherlock, Bentley, Blackstone, of men of learning like Hearne, Tyrwhitt, Lowth, Warton, Twining and Jones. It saw the foundation of a dozen or so more university 'chairs', and the start of the mathematical tripos. Yet, in spite of the ability of these great eighteenth-century English scholars, the rallying points for educated opinion during this century, lay not in the English universities, but rather in the academies of art, science, medicine, letters and music which then flourished in France, Germany and Russia.

Perhaps the two universities themselves realized that their work was of little good. Undergraduates entered at the age of fifteen; the wealthy ones were called 'Gentleman-Commoners' or 'Fellow-Commoners', whilst at the other end of the social scale, were the Servitors or Sizars who were paid to render menial service for the wealthier ones, and were permitted to follow the lectures. The 'finals' again favoured the wealthy; for the scions of nobility were admitted to a degree without even the formality of an examination. In *Roderick Random*, Smollett gives a vague idea of the oral examination for the M.B. degree, and Lord Eldon one of that for law. Until Blackstone's time students of law seem to have been dependent on two law books written two centuries before for any legal theory they could acquire. What was very necessary, in order to qualify, was a denunciation of the Pope, the forswearing of transubstantiation and the production of a certificate that they had received the Sacrament according to the rites of the Church of England. Perhaps the energy demanded from students by the universities in the eighteenth century is summed up in the couplet:

> Granta, Sweet Granta, where, studious of ease,
> Seven years did I sleep, then got my degrees.

After such a university course, the young heir usually made the grand tour of which contemporary novels, diaries and letters give copious details. Dean Tucker and Adam Smith also furnish details

of this education by travel, and of it they speak most contemptuously. Generally the young man brought back with him a few
new recipes for strange dishes, and some newer notions of vice
than he had set out with. The best of them also returned with
pictures, books, statuary, musical instruments, bulbs and trees for
the family mansion.

IV

Owing to the faith of their fathers, the sons of wealthy Dissenters
could not attend existing public schools or either university, and
so they were educated at Dissenting academies. And although
Dissenters were lumped together in an amorphous mass by their
Anglican rivals, they were by no means a uniform group; so their
hampering religious prejudices led to the establishment of Presby-
terian-Dissenting academies, Independent-Dissenting academies,
Quaker-Dissenting academies, &c. Some of the best-known of
these in the eighteenth century were those founded in London,
Bridgwater, Taunton, Warrington, Bridgnorth, &c., which in
time gradually provided the best education possible for boys in
England. In them a very modern note was sounded, for education
was closely linked to life. Writing of Morton's Academy at
Newington, Samuel Wesley said: 'This Academy was indeed most
considerable, having annext a fine garden and a fishpond, and
within, a laboratory and some not inconsiderable rarities with air-
pump and the thermometre and all sorts of mathematical instruments.' This attention to Nature study, physics and chemistry
was, of course, sneered at in the public schools, whilst the rise of
mathematics in academic esteem, provoked in the last quarter of
the century the skit:

> See Euclid proudly spurns the Mantuan muse,
> While gentle Horace wipes Maclaurin's shoes;
> There Homer learns the theory of light,
> And tortur'd Ovid learns to sum and write.

Nevertheless some eighteenth-century Churchmen realized that
the education given in Dissenting academies was superior to that
of the public schools, and in time they were able to claim among
old pupils, Anglican stalwarts of the eminence of the Earl of
Oxford, Archbishop Secker and Bishop Butler. Samuel Wesley
saw in them too, not only rivals to Winchester, &c., but also

sources of proselytism. He thus proceeds to say: 'at these schools severall people of quality, knights and baronets sons are to be found, who are there to avoid the debaucheries of the universities . . . these sucking academies proselytize sons of the wealthy, and jeopardize the future of Oxford and Cambridge.' On leaving such schools, Dissenters who wished could proceed to one of the Scottish or continental universities.

Only a word need be said about the 'grammar' schools of this century. Most of them rose out of the ashes of the old monasteries and were then sorely pressed; their buildings were in disrepair and their scholars few in numbers. During the first quarter of the century some of them were fairly efficient, then eighteenth-century cupidity supervened, and the endowments were shamelessly abused. Late in the century some attempt was made to regularize the situation, but in 1795 the Lord Chief Justice after a public trial into their administration, declared, 'that schools with very large endowments to them are empty and have not a single scholar; everything is neglected by the so-called schoolmasters but the receipt of salaries and endowments'. Nevertheless, some of these eighteenth-century 'grammar' schools gradually expanded into such public schools as Christ's Hospital, Dulwich, Sedbergh, Bedford, Bradford and Birmingham.

In that century some of the flourishing merchant companies and individual philanthropic business men founded a number of schools which have since risen to eminence in different towns. The 'Friends' then established two which still flourish at Saffron Walden and Ackworth.

Naturally John Wesley was greatly influenced by the different Dissenting academies when he founded Kingswood in 1748. Perhaps he was specially influenced by those of the Moravians at Herrnhut, and by that of Dr. Doddridge at Harborough, where the head had stressed the value of English as the teaching medium and had demanded the serious study of the mother-tongue. At Kingswood life was more strenuous than in any existing public school; the children rose at 4.0 a.m. and went to bed at 8.0 p.m., tea and coffee were rarely supplied, food was very simple, and the spartan founder insisted on two meatless days every week, whilst Friday had to be a day of abstinence, when the children fasted till 3.0 p.m.

The curriculum was equally formidable; there were the three R's, English, French, Latin, Greek, Hebrew, natural philosophy,

metaphysics, logic, ethics, history and geography. The text-books
are described *in extenso* in Volume XIV of *Wesley's Works*. This
educational dictator wrote most of the grammars to be used, and
revised or abridged all the other books for his scholars' use, prefacing
them with detailed instructions to the teachers on how they were
to be employed. He believed so firmly in his teaching principles
and in his 'corrected' text-books that, after sketching out a four-
year academic course to be followed between the ages of twelve
and sixteen, he concluded with the remark: 'if those of tolerable
capacity do not advance more here in three years than the generality of students in Oxford or Cambridge do in seven, I will bear
the blame forever.'

His disciplinary system was equally forbidding. 'Tender
parents, so-called, who are indeed offering up their sons and
daughters unto devils, have no business here; for the rules will not
be broke in favour of any person whatsoever.' Play for its own
'was unworthy of a Christian child' so it was forbidden entirely at
Kingswood. 'Chopping wood, digging in the garden, drawing
water were healthy occupations and far more profitable exercises
... he who plays as a child will play when he is a man'; whilst 'the
prejudice they might acquire at home against the strict rules of
the school' was a convincing and conclusive argument against all
holidays. 'I will kill or cure; I will have a Christian school or
none at all.'

In defence of this monastic doctrine on discipline, play and
holidays, the times must be considered. In the eighteenth century,
flagellation was quite common in homes and schools, and neither
sex escaped. Rank only was the barrier between the birch and
victim, and even the youthful, erring sprigs of nobility took their
punishment vicariously through their 'whipping' boys, who had
to accept the punishment meted out to the noble offender. Pages
could be written on the domestic birch, birch in the boudoir,
school punishments, and discipline in charity schools. Perhaps
corporal punishment declined in severity and frequency some
thirty years after Kingswood was founded; at any rate in 1775,
Johnson affirms: 'There is now less flogging in our great public
schools but then there is less learned; so what the boys get at the
one end, they lose at the other'; and Gibbon writes: 'the domestic
discipline of our ancestors has been relaxed by the philosophy and
softness of the age.'

As for Wesley's strictures on play, it must be urged that in the century, 'school play' was little more than coarse violation and demoralization. Similarly his views on 'holidays' were probably very popular with eighteenth-century parents. Half a century after his pronouncements on this point, a very popular school which advertised that it was an institution 'where youth are genteely boarded and expeditiously qualified for Commerce and Profession' further attracted parents by the satement: 'As long experience has convinced the Schoolmaster that the usual Vacations tend to Impede the Progress of Education, his Pupils do not visit home but at the particular Request of their Father.'

<h2 style="text-align:center">v</h2>

The seminaries for eighteenth-century girls seem to have been more docile establishments than were the boys' schools; indeed, many of them seem to have been polite prisons where anxious parents might send their daughters out of harm's way. At the beginning of the century, Swift says that common opinion restricted women's reading to books of devotion or household management: 'anything else might turn their brains.' Defoe describes those of his day as 'places in which their youth is spent to teach them to stitch and sew and make baubles; they are taught to read aloud, and perhaps write their names or so; that is the height of woman's education'. The ardent feminist, Lady Mary Wortley Montagu, writes in 1752, 'we are educated in the grossest ignorance and no art omitted to stifle our natural reason'. In 1778 Johnson remarks 'all our Ladies read now, which is a great extension'. Later still, Shelburne, the first Marquis of Lansdowne, and a statesman with enlightened political views, 'thought a little spinning and some moral training of course' was all the education needed by the women of his class; for 'women are domestic animals and should never be taught to go from home'.

A review of the curriculum in Mrs. Teachum's 'Little Female Academy'—probably a typical boarding-school of the period—shows that these girls' schools carefully avoided the appearance of any thoroughness outside the domestic arts and deportment. Even late-century Miss Pinkertons advertised that

'Young Ladies are Compleately Finish'd in Ev'ry Polite as well as Usefull Branch of Education viz. French, Musick, Dauncing, Deportment, Writeing, Fine Work, Plain Work, Childe-bed Linnen.'

Probably the teachers confined their attention to singing, the harpsichord, guitar, reading aloud, fanciful penmanship, 'casting of accompts' and the 'use of globes' (geography). Embroidery was greatly stressed and the beautiful conventional 'samplers' they worked can still be seen. French was taught at most of them, and probably well taught, by one of the many visiting teachers every girls' school then had; for by the middle of the century French had gradually superseded Latin as the general medium of international thought. But the greatest importance was laid on 'deportment'. A nineteenth-century mother is speaking of the 'Pinkerton' type of school existing in 1790 when she says:

'Decorum was the imperative law of a lady's inner life as well as her outward habit. Nothing in the academy that was not decorous, was for a moment admitted. Every movement of the body in entering or quitting a room . . . in taking a seat or rising from it was duly criticized. . . . There was kept in the back premises a carriage for the purpose of ascending and descending with calmness and grace, and without any unnecessary display of ankles.'

Physical shape, too, was sought after in these institutions, and secured by means of 'backboards', 'stocks', 'iron collars', &c., worn during lessons. These pieces of machinery were intended to have not only a corrective effect on poise and deportment, but were meant at the same time 'to curb excessive volatility of temperament'. Feminine fortitude and self-control were regarded as elements of decorum, and were specifically inculcated by means of witch-stories, by testing the pupils with 'ghosts', &c., whilst blanket-tossing was considered an admirable method of 'hardening a young lady's nerves'.

Maria Edgeworth seems to have been satisfied with this female education; round about the close of the century she writes: 'Stop at any good inn on the London roads and you will find the landlady's daughter can shew you her framed drawings, play a tune on the spinnet and support a dialogue in French of a reasonable length.' But Mary Wollstonecraft, a more vigorous supporter of women's rights, had in 1792 called for 'a thorough education and not for ladies alone, but for the middle-class girls as well', whom, she believes, 'to be in a more hopeful state' than are the former. Other writers, too, felt that this schooling was neither satisfactory nor thorough. *The Times* in 1795 has: 'When a Tradesman's Daughter is taught to jump a dance, to play a tune and spit French, she is fit for anything—but a wife', and the lampoonist writes in 1798:

Whilst Miss dispises all domestic Rules,
But lisps the French of Hackney boarding-schools,
And ev'ry Lane around Whitechapel bars
Resounds with screaming Notes and harsh Guitars.

Hannah More's description of the girls in Farmer Bragwell's
Somerset home, also suggests that this improvement in female
scholarship was not invariably well received nor yet put to good
use. Many a contemporary diary suggested also that 'learning
may be a great danger for the female mind and our Mary has now
reached a pitch of education that soars high above the Fifth
Commandment'. Contempt for the speech and manners of their
parents, for the task of nursing them in sickness, ability to spend
but not to keep accounts, accomplishments of cutting paper,
strumming the harpsichord, concocting toilet-washes, &c., were
not calculated to raise the countryside's opinion of higher education for women.

Wesley saw something other than 'decorum' and 'deportment'
in these schools and their devices; he charged them with being,
'places of pride, vanity, affectation . . . If parents wished to send
their daughters headlong to hell', he says, 'let them send them to
a fashionable boarding-school'. Nor was he alone in this judgement. Another staunch advocate of sensible education for
women, Mrs. Montagu, describes the process of schooling in
vogue at the end of the century 'as a dedication to the pomps and
vanities of the Devil, in complete defiance of baptismal vows'.

Nevertheless, higher education for women was spreading among
the wealthy, and the last-named critic had the honour of institu-
ting the well-known eighteenth-century 'Blue-Stocking Club',
which was designed to encourage sound education among fashionable women and at the same time to counteract their avid passion
for gambling. In spite of a good deal of pompous nonsense, pretentious patronage and foolish absurdity at these assemblies, there
was a warm welcome for every follower of science, for every rising
genius, for doctors, lawyers, bishops, actors and critics, and
certainly neither the women nor the men who forgathered were
there to vie with each other in costly attire. They failed to rival
the famous French feminine *salons*, but they attracted to their
gatherings men like Johnson, Stillingfleet, Goldsmith and Burke.
The last named was so impressed with the meetings, that he
thought the emancipation and capacity of the women were the
most important contribution made by the eighteenth century to

national progress. Naturally the meetings were lampooned, and
the satire of one writer beginning with:

> Hannah More's pathetic pen
> Painting high th' impassion'd scene,
> Carter's piety and learning;
> Little Burney's quick discerning;

had more truth in it than he suspected or intended.

VI

The recreative reading done by these well-to-do eighteenth-
century children and adolescents is amazing to modern eyes.
During the last quarter of the century they were introduced to
*Peregrine Pickle, Tom Jones, Pamela, Moll Flanders, Roderick Random,
Humphrey Clinker*—'abridged for the amusement of youth'; abridged
it is true, but not at all in the direction one would have expected
for young people. Their more personal library also included
Juvenal, Virgil and Homer, Newton's works, Locke's *Human
Understanding*, Temple's *Essays*, Bacon's *Advancement of Learning*,
Steele's *Christian Hero*, Taylor's *Holy Living and Holy Dying*,
Fielding's *Trial of Wild*. In their desks would be found, too, a
spelling book, a dictionary, a book of compliments, instructions on
dancing, advice to a son (or daughter) and the Prayer Book. Included among those recommended as suitable for young ladies
were *Domestic Medicine, The English Housewife*, containing the
'inward and outward vertues which ought to be in the Compleat
Woman', and Culpeper's *Midwifery*.

For the direct teaching of manners and morals teachers relied
on books of manners, courtesy books, hell-fire books, in which
morals and manners were inculcated by the recital of horrible
stories of martyrdom and punishment; stodgy volumes sicklied
over with pale didacticism and full of gloating piety. Foxe's *Book
of Martyrs*, Baxter's *Call to the Unconverted*, Janeway's *Tokens for
Children or the Conversion, Lives and Joyfull Deths of Severall Children*
are some examples. The publisher Newbery must have considered
them as unsuitable, and in 1750 he commissioned Mrs. Barbauld,
Mrs. Trimmer, Mrs. Chapone, Mrs. Bonnington and company to
write special stories for children. They responded with such titles
as *Juvenile Errors Corrected, Looking Glass for the Mind, Legacy for
Young Ladies, Useful Lessons for Little Misses and Masters, Mother's
Advice to her Absent Daughter*. Contemporary French tales by

Berquin and de Genlis specially written for the young are just as boring. *Proper Use of Time, Interested Kindness, Obligingness and Complaisance, The Little Gamblers, The Three Cakes* are titles sufficiently revealing the subject-matter of the stories. Day's *Sandford and Merton* of 1783 was far more popular than any of the foregoing and was a sort of anglicized *Emile*. Popular though the book was with several generations of eighteenth- and nineteenth-century children, it undoubtedly owed its vogue to the abundance of incident in it, rather than to the didactic strain running through it. As late as 1795 Maria Edgeworth wrote her stilted *Letters for Literary Ladies*, whilst another produced *First Principles of Religion and the Existence of the Deity Explained in Conversations Adapted to the Capacity of Infant Minds*. The great bulk of children's books of that century, as well as those of the early nineteenth century are terrifying documents. Accidents, tragedies, punishment and death stalk through the pages in ghastly shape—a foil for the comforts which religion alone can supply. They were far worse material for juveniles than were *Babees Book* or *Boke of Curteisie*, which used to be given to fifteenth-century children and adolescents. And if one judges from the comments towards general reading provoked by such material, and made by the smug young heroine in Hannah More's *Cœlebs*, it is no wonder that the method was a complete failure. This small girl, asked why she is wearing a crown of woodbine, replies:

'O sir, it is because this is my birthday. I am eight to-day. I gave up all my gilt books with pictures this day twelvemonth and to-day I give up all my story books, and am now going to read only such books as men and women read.'

Eighteenth-century parents and teachers never seem to have grasped the idea that some books are meant to provide a pleasant relaxation, or to develop comprehension and appreciation of the writer's thoughts and feelings.

Even Dr. Johnson hazarded the opinion that such books as were presented to eighteenth-century infants and juveniles were unsuitable, and that children required their imaginations raised by tales of giants and fairies, castles and enchantments, and Charles Lamb said of them 'they only starved their hearts and stuffed their little heads'. Lord Chesterfield, looking on these authors as uncouth pedants, said of them: 'Let blockheads read what blockheads wrote . . . stick to the best written books in any language.' The one purpose of these 'edifying tales from real life' was to turn the young from their carelessness; to put old heads on young shoulders; to induce, as Arnold of Rugby later expressed it: 'a thoughtfulness which would hasten their progress from the follies of childhood to the more stable behaviour of the grown-ups.' Even at the end of the century the two Edgeworths would draw a moral lesson on every available occasion and from every subject taught, and Hannah More wrote her *Cheap Repository Tracts* with the same motive. Although written with the express purpose of 'making poor people good and contented with their lot', blessed by a bishop as highly praiseworthy and printed by the million, it is amusing but not surprising to think that most of them were eventually shipped off to distant islands; they are revoltingly inept and tedious. Perhaps nothing better could have been meant, but certainly nothing could have been more ineffective.

This heap of didactic, indigestible reading matter offered to the eighteenth-century young is all the more astonishing when it is remembered that by then Aesop, La Fontaine and Perrault had all been well translated into English, and that *Robinson Crusoe*, *Arabian Nights*, *Goody Two-Shoes*, &c., had all seen the light of day. No wonder as the century closed, money-making publishers poured out other matter for the increasing number of general readers, and flooded the countryside with 'chap' books, or cheap paper-backed books like the *Fortune-Teller*, *Accounts of the Ghost of Mrs. Veal*, *Dreams*, *Nun and Cavalier*, *Cupid's Whirligig*, *Mother Bunch's Closet Newly Broke Open*, *Fifteen Comforts of Matrimony*, *Accounts of the Lives*, *Behaviour*, *Dying Words of the Most Remarkable Convicts*, *The Newgate Calendar or the Malefactor's Bloody Register*, *Cry of the Oppress'd* or *True Tragical Account of the Unparallel'd Sufferings of Multitudes of Poor Imprison'd Debtors*, &c. These dreadful out-pourings roused the ire of John Wesley, who thereupon became a pioneer for the provision of 'penny tracts' of his sermons, contro-versial pamphlets and hymns which were printed in very much better type and on much better paper. In later years he extended the ambit of his publications, by reproducing 50 volumes in a series called *The Christian Library*; this series included abridgement of books by the great Anglican divines, English Nonconformists and translations of Pascal, Bengel as well as reproductions of the works of Milton, Herbert and Bunyan. As the series had a phenomenal sale, the success testifies to the native sanity of this new reading public.

VII

The Church of England's charity schools established under the auspices of the S.P.C.K. in 1699 aimed at teaching the children of the poor between the ages of seven and twelve simple reading, writing, arithmetic and the catechism. The Independents, too, were interested in this movement and early in the eighteenth century they also had many charity schools under their control, and in 1740 Griffiths Jones is said to have got together some hundred schools and 10,000 scholars in Wales 'who were taught to read in a single year'.

The charity-school movement spread rapidly all over England, and it is calculated that the Anglican Church by 1702 had 350 such schools with some 8,000 scholars, and that twenty years later both totals had been quadrupled. It was during this progressive period that Addison declared these schools 'were the glory of the Age we live in and the most proper means that can be made use of to revive it out of its present Degeneracy and Depravation of Manners . . . they seem to promise us an Honest and Virtuous Posterity'.

Church interest in them waned about 1727 and their welfare was left in the hands of individual clergymen and village squires, and from that date they varied greatly according to the prevailing whim of the lady of the manor. Often they were conducted in the church porch, and the instruction was as miserably inadequate as the material provision; sometimes the master was blind or crippled, and as late as 1837 a teacher at one of them is reputed to have said, ''tisn't much they pay us and 'tisn't much we teach um'. These masters had to eke out their livelihood in various ways; one was liable to interruption in his academic labours as 'his wife kept the village mangle which he is obliged to turn for her'. Goldsmith has given a picture of one of them, in which he is described with sweet, pure humour. 'Tim Bobbin' gives more precise details and we learn from him that the curate who was the head master, got £10 per annum and that as assistant 'Bobbin' got as much, that when he was promoted to the headship he got the entire staffing salary of £20 a year, that he had to teach twelve boys and girls for nothing, and that the fee payers only came occasionally when the spirit moved them, or when their parents had weekly pence for the schooling. Despite the superhuman difficulties, some charity schools had their brilliant successes; one notable product was

Warren Hastings, who spent a few years in the charity school at
Daylesford, a second was Hutton, the great mathematician, who
was a scholar at the Jesmond charity school, whilst Dyer the great
eighteenth-century historian-antiquarian, was a third. Both
Hogarth and Reynolds had fathers who taught in such institutions. These charity-school children wore a distinctive dress:
'leather breeches, coloured stockings, coats of a quaint cut in
green, grey or black; flat caps and two pieces of fine linnen fluttering under their chins and called "bands". Girls had frocks and
coats of wonderful cut and colour, white aprons and special
mob-caps.'

Villages that could not afford a master relied on some respectable old dame, who, for a pittance and an extra petticoat or so
from the lady-patron, was content to teach the alphabet and pot-
hooks, plain sewing, the dropping of curtsies and such portions
of the Church catechism as she had not forgotten. Shenstone has
pictured one of these institutions:

> In every village marked with little spire,
> Embower'd in trees, and hardly known to fame,
> There dwells, in lowly shed and mean attire
> A matron old, whom we schoolmistress name;
> Who boasts unruly brats with birch to tame;
> They grieven sore, in piteous durance pent,
> Awed by the power of the relentless dame;
> And oft times on vagaries idly bent,
> For unkempt hair, or task unconned, are duly shent.

Such schools flourished through the century and in 1806 a House
of Commons Committee reported that some 50,000 children were
still attending similar institutions.

Every worthy lady of the manor cared for the village women,
children and sick; she was at home in every cottage, would visit,
give help and advice and often acted as village doctor or nurse.
Usually she maintained a 'charity' or 'dames' school and with the
spread of the idea of 'practical' education, many a lady of the
manor changed the very objective of such institutions. These
'special' schools became more and more numerous from the mid-
decades of the eighteenth century. At them girls were taught
straw-plaiting and lace-making or specially trained for domestic
service. The girls started to attend such schools from the age of
seven or nine and stayed there till they were fourteen or sixteen.
As a distinctive mark the patrons usually insisted on cropped hair,

and large round cloaks with tight-fitting hoods. Food was plain and hours were long; early rising, punctuality, extreme neatness of dress and servile humility in behaviour were compulsory; cookery, laundry-work, needlework, cleaning, &c., formed the main curriculum; reading and writing were not always included in the instruction. This absence of emphasis on the rudiments of knowledge would not concern the patrons of the schools. Even after Parliament had made grants to the schools conducted by the National Society and British Foreign School Society, the Charity School Commissioners found in 1837 that in Oxfordshire 'only 24 of these schools teach the three R's, in eight the curriculum is not stated, three teach reading only and seven reading and one other subject'.

These eighteenth-century 'special' schools should not be confused with the 'lace' schools run by employers of labour. The Rev. Thomas Mozley says of his Northamptonshire parish school:

'This school was but half fill'd. It had a rival too strong for it. The village of misery and dirt was the scene of a beautiful and delicate manufacture. As many as an hundred maidens and girls made pillow-lace. Near 30 small children were pack'd in a very small room (called the lace-school), and kept at their pillows from six in the morning till six at night.'

Returning again to his 'charity school' Mozley goes on: 'the village school draws children from holes and corners worse than caves and from out-of-the-way places worse than deserts.' This somewhat casual conclusion to his remarks on the schools, suggests that the teachers had other obstacles militating against steady education, and impeding the securing of a high standard of instruction and attainment, besides those arising from a constant stream of admissions and withdrawals and capricious attendance, and in addition to the obstructions arising from the limitations of accommodation and equipment.

Besides these varying types of schools, the eighteenth century had self-appointed educators. The *Morning Post* in 1788 makes mention of a man living near to Reading, who announced that he 'is a Barber, Peri-wig Maker, Surgeon, Parish-Clerk, Scool-Mayster and Man Mid-Wife' . . . he promised 'shaves for a penne, cuts hare for toopense . . . yung Ladys genteely edicated, Lamps lited by the year or querter, yung Gentlemen also taut there grammer Langwage in the neetest manner; grate ceare takin of theyre morels and Spelin'. Existing then in very great numbers were residential schools, staffed by men almost as ignorant as this southern coach. Hundreds of private schools of the calibre of 'Dotheboys' Hall' then throve particularly in Yorkshire and Lancashire. All had fine-sounding manorial names; all advertised a pretentious, silly, muddled curriculum; all stressed their 'great care of the morals and deportment'; all emphasized 'practical' education and 'excellent eatage'. Actually the education was beneath contempt, the lads were probably employed as servants on farm and land, the discipline was ferocious and dietary as scanty as that doled out to workhouse children. Perhaps foolish parents were tempted to send children there, because of the baits that the fees were only a few pounds per annum, and because these institutions did without holidays the whole year round.

VIII

The most virile signs of increasing vitality in the eighteenth-century educational organism were shown by the foundation of Sunday schools. Robert Raikes, the Anglican banker, started the best known one in 1780 in Soot Alley, a part of Gloucester that did not belie its name, and whither a number of ragged urchins were lured with buns and hot potatoes, there to be taught 'by four decent women'. He was not, however, the first pioneer in the movement. Wesley had anticipated the idea in Georgia in 1737; the Rev. Theophilus Lindsey had started one in his Catterick parish in 1763, whilst Hannah Ball was, by 1780, running one in High Wycombe.

It was lucky for the movement that Raikes took a non-sectarian attitude from the outset, otherwise support would have been meagre and the founder's efforts foredoomed to failure. As it was he got support from both Wesley and the Bishop of Gloucester, and the movement spread rapidly in both Church and Dissenting areas. Hours of attendance now seem excessive; from 10 to 12 in the mornings and from 1 to 5.30 in the afternoons, including attendance at the neighbouring church or chapel. But as these were the days when small children worked fourteen hours a day in mines, mills, &c., perhaps they did not regard the Sunday sessions intolerably long.

The first teachers were paid 1s. 6d. a Sunday and were expected to teach the alphabet and simple reading. Raikes stressed this need for reading power, and he seems to have realized that there

T

was a greater wealth and satisfaction to be got from genuine books, rather than from mere moral tales. In his earlier days he had lent all his volumes to prisoners, and although in 1780 he had only a very limited supply, he strongly encouraged his Sunday pupils to borrow them. He saw too the value of personal cleanliness, and though his teaching can hardly be called hygiene, he insisted upon clean hands and combed hair from his scholars. The success attending the Sunday schools was immediate and astounding. Soon after their inception, it was affirmed that 20,000 children were receiving Sunday schooling; in August 1785 the London Society for Sunday Schools was founded and in ten years that society claimed that 'there were 65,000 scholars in their 1,000 schools and that nearly 100,000 spelling-books, over 24,000 Testaments and 5,000 Bibles had been distributed'. Contemporary activities by the Rev. Thomas Charles of Bala were almost as richly rewarded in Wales, if one judges from his statistics.

Figures like the foregoing almost suggest that thanks to Sunday schools, all England was becoming literate by the end of the century. That achievement was still far away; as late as 1834 it was asserted 'that only one in fifty persons could read or write', But this cold fact should not dim the fair renown of Raikes. In his day it was a great triumph in itself to see the simple teaching of the New Testament in a clear light, unencumbered with controversial and sectarian interpretations; it was also a great thing to keep clear of the sort of party politics which then inhibited the actions of many pious and well-meaning people. The greatness of his influence in the sphere of secular education is not easily estimated. He was not alone in calling attention to the dangers of ignorance and squalor; but his experiences in endeavouring to convey to quite untaught children and adults, the simplest ideas in religious or moral teaching, were most useful in helping him to frame his demands for education on other days than Sundays. He must, therefore, be considered a pioneer of ordinary day-school education in influence if not in fact, and remembered when the work of Owen, Bell and Lancaster is considered.

IX

The earliest systematic attempts to educate the English poor stand to the credit of the Quaker, Joseph Lancaster, who in 1797 and at the age of nineteen, opened a school for poor children in

Borough Road, Southwark. The movement was successful, and soon Lancaster travelled up and down the country, an apostle of education for the poor, and an advocate of a new teaching method. Unfortunately the movement excited the suspicion and antagonism of the clerics, who thought they alone were capable of imparting even secular instruction. Violent attacks were made on Lancaster and his training system by the ecclesiastics and their supporters, and the 'National School Society' came into existence in 1811 'to check the success of the schismatics'. Lancaster's system of monitorial instruction in schools was invented by Dr. Andrew Bell, the eighteenth-century clergyman who had tried out the method in Madras. In 1797, after his return to England, he wrote a pamphlet on this system of mutual tuition, as he was convinced of its universal applicability. His plan was but coldly received, until Lancaster's Southwark school had met with such success, and until the Church feared that the patronage of day schools might rest entirely with Dissenters. Thereupon Anglicans resolved to set up similar institutions in which Church principles should be inculcated, and in 1807 Bell was called upon to organize a system of schools in accordance with such views. As far as teaching methods are concerned the two sets of schools were identical, for Lancaster conducted his schools in strict accordance with Bell's principles, even in such a detail as using sand-trays for the teaching of writing. Both pioneers seem to have been subject to irritable vanity, and violent quarrels broke out between them, quarrels that were conducted with characteristic eighteenth-century freedom of language. If the methods of the two men have not continued to live in the schools, they were certainly instrumental in calling into existence two societies which laid the foundation of English elementary education.

As for the statesmen of England, although nearly every European Government interested itself in public education during the eighteenth century, they remained quite unmoved. Its importance had been preached to them by Blackstone, Adam Smith, Bentham and Malthus, but no parliament of the century ever showed a trace of the imagination or zeal for education that was being manifested by the Fredericks of Prussia, Maria Theresa in her Empire, Turgot, Condorcet or Napoleon in France. Every English statesman seemed content to leave education for the poor entirely to voluntary organizations, to charity schools or Sunday schools.

A few details on eighteenth-century ideas concerning infant teaching methods, discipline and general school equipment may interest some readers.

Mrs. Wesley describes how she taught her children to read:

'At five they were taught the alphabet which most of them learnt in one day; next day they were put to spell and read one line and then a verse of the first chapter of Genesis.'

As she was a remarkable woman and as her children were highly gifted, there is perhaps no need to marvel at the success of a method far and away harder than the old horn-book of the Tudors. Mrs. Barbauld, who posed as a pioneer of infant readers and reading methods at the end of the century, seems severer than was Mrs. Wesley; her *Early Lessons* is a document according to which infants are expected to start reading at the age of two. Less austere teachers were by then teaching the alphabet by means of big pieces of cardboard 18 in. by 12 in., each having a giant letter on them and ornamented with pictures of the nobility and emblems of royalty. However much these pictures may have appealed to the learning infants, such teaching of the alphabet would not be so delightful as that described by Prior eighty years before:

> To Master John the English maid,
> A hornbook gives of gingerbread;
> And that the child may learn the better,
> As he can name, he eats the letter;
> Proceeding thus with vast delight,
> He spells and gnaws from left to right.

At the end of the century the 'battledore' appeared. This was a three-leaved oblong card which contained, besides the alphabet and numerals, a fable or didactic story in verse or prose, the morality of which was often more excellent than the style.

Although educative toys had been advocated by the Edgeworths, playing with dolls was discountenanced; nor were nursery rhymes recommended. 'Why should we suffer them to indulge in playing with dolls?' . . . 'Why should the infant-mind be filled with fantastic visions instead of useful knowledge?' &c., were rhetorical questions admitting of no answer to the eighteenth-century teacher. Instead of 'Mother Goose' rhymes—certainly available for teachers from the middle of the century—they were given informative verse from such collections as *Poetry Explained for the Use of Young People*, *Good Resolutions*, *Paul Pennylove's Poetical Paraphrase of the Pence Table*, *Hymns for Infant Minds*, &c. And these rhymes, like their prose, were always in a moral, minor, miserable key. Tales from the *Parents' Assistant, Moral Tales* and other dreary clouds of moralizings, were preferred by these infant educators to the fables and tales by Aesop, La Fontaine or Perrault.

By then Blake had sung of infant innocence and charm, but eighteenth-century teachers and parents for the most part remained convinced that what is good for the young must be unpleasant, and that the ideal child was the one who showed marked signs of premature manhood. The old sour doctrine of 'breaking their wills early', of 'a child should be governed by fear' rather than by love were followed. Even a sensible, affectionate mother like Mrs. Wesley could give such advice as: 'Let a child from one year old be taught to fear the rod and to cry softly; from that age make him do as he is bid if you whip him ten times running to effect it.' Undoubtedly eighteenth-century parents of piety, learning and discernment would have condemned as mere sentimentality much of the modern experimental teaching of infants, and would have regarded as mischievous nonsense, the present careful avoidance of overt discipline. In those days every school, from the 'dames' to the famous public ones, had as part of their essential equipment the birch, the stool of penitence and the big false face with the crowning word of Dunce in big capitals.

The buildings or teaching rooms were mainly ramshackle affairs; dull sunless apartments with primitive ventilation and heating systems, and furnished with antiquated tables and chairs. The conditions under which charity schools, &c., were conducted would be infinitely worse. In 1820 one reads that John Pounds, the founder of 'Ragged' Schools, instructed in his Portsmouth cobbler's shop forty children in a room 18 ft. by 6 ft., and that the girls and boys sat on old boxes. They were taught to read from old hand-bills, writing on slates, some easy addition and subtraction, to cook plain food and mend their own shoes. All other accounts suggest that these teaching rooms were very dingy and depressing and overcrowded, whilst the lavatories, &c., indicated an utter disregard for the simple proprieties of life.

The paper on which the children were taught to write even in the well-known schools was very poor; it would be expensive, too, as then it was hand-made. The ink used was usually thick, sludgy stuff made from special soot; quills were used as the writing implements, for though a steel pen had been made in Birmingham for Dr.

Priestley in the last decade, the invention was neither immediately popular nor successful. Lead pencils of poor quality were being used in the last quarter of the century, but it is very doubtful if they appeared in schools. Blotting-paper of a coarse, grey character was sometimes used, but most writers as late as 1775 used pumice or sand scattered on the written word to dry the ink, and right up to the end of the century pupils in schools would be expected to possess a little 'pounce'-pot containing sand.

On the master's desk in these eighteenth-century schools would be 'brass candlesticks, snuffers, snuff-dishes, penknives [for the quill pens], recording ink and pounce-pots'.

CHAPTER XI

CHURCH AND CHAPEL

I

Two of the eighteenth-century memoir-writers, Horace Walpole and Lord Hervey, are extremely bitter about the corruption, pluralism, pride of prelacy, &c., then existing in the National Church. Both had unrivalled opportunities of getting their information, as one was son of a Prime Minister and the other the confidential friend and adviser of the chief dispenser of Church patronage. Contemporary historians like Lord Chesterfield and Phillimore also refer to the insatiable greed and sycophancy of the higher clergy. Cobbett is equally severe in his strictures, whilst the author of the *Extraordinary Black Book* of 1831 is detailed in his recital of abuses of the revenues of the National Church. These authorities show that the revenues were used as a sort of outdoor relief for the aristocracy, and that by their hold over family livings, the wealthy managed to make the State Church infamous. They assert that one nobleman had forty livings at his disposal; another twenty-five, and that hundreds of them had from a dozen to a score apiece, and declare that towards the close of the century the Church of England was costing seven times as much as that of France for far fewer adherents.

Among their many particular instances of this corruption they quote the following. A close relative of Lord North, the Prime Minister, was a bishop at thirty and later secured the Winchester see, the most lucrative in the country; altogether this cleric got over £1,500,000 from the Church's funds, and later quartered on to the State Church his sons and sons-in-law to the tune of thirty livings. Of these, one was a priest-in-charge at a tender age, and another had eight livings and drained away upwards of £300,000. The Right Reverend pluralist, Lord Hugh Percy, Bishop of Carlisle, got over a quarter of a million from the State Church, to say nothing of the canonries, prebends and rectories of his son and numerous sons-in-law. The Beresfords did well from family livings in this century; one got over £350,000, another just under £300,000, a third netted a quarter of a million and the fourth, who had only four livings at one and the same time, got £58,000.

Altogether this family of landed proprietors got from the Irish Church, through their eight clerics, a million and a half pounds. The Earl of Cork also took care of his relatives; one brother had two bishoprics, a son-in-law was Bishop of Tuam and a nephew Bishop of Waterford. The Reverend Lord John Thynne, who was a landed proprietor with an income of £13,500 a year, had himself made Canon of Westminster for fifty years at £2,500 per annum and at the same time rector of a village in Somerset. Lord Normanton was not only a peer of the realm, but a prelate of the Irish Church for nearly forty years. The Manners at the close of the century held eight English and twelve Irish sees; one of them, who held the Canterbury see, had also many pluralities, and it is calculated that the reverend gentleman drew some £650,000 from the Church; at the same time he looked well after his sons and daughters, and took care that it should provide for his family. Similar examples of the aristocratic plunder of the Church revenues are shown in the eighteenth-century story of the Edens, Hobarts, Stewart-Murrays, Vernons and Wodehouses, &c. From none of these lay-rectors or reverend-aristocratic holders of sees and livings did the State Church receive any distinguished service. No wonder that the learned Franciscan Father Piette declares:

"Every roué or questionable character, every piece of human wreckage felt he had a call to the empty livings. A great number were pushed forward by the nobility who had the right of nomination.'

Perhaps Milton's stinging gibe of 'hireling wolves whose gospel is their maw' aptly describes the majority of such nominees. The ecclesiastical prizes were consistently withheld from hard-working clerics who had nothing to recommend them but devotion, piety and years of faithful service.

The binding chains of an oppressive hierarchy, due to the gross abuse of traffic in family livings, were further strengthened by the trade in pluralities, and pluralism is often mentioned in the newspapers of the century's last decade. In his *Legacy to Parsons*, Cobbett declared that '332 parsons shared 1496 parishes and that another 500 clergymen held 1524 more livings'. History records one clergyman as holding two livings together worth £1,200 a year, and how he got the work done at both by a couple of curates at a total cost of £84. Watson, the Bishop of Llandaff, lived practically all his life at Windermere; at the same time he held a university chair at Cambridge and fourteen livings in Hunts.,

Shropshire and Leicestershire. Nor was he the only bishop who rarely saw his see. One of the best bishops of the period, Dr. Porteous, thought it no wrong to hold a country living as well as the Chester see. As late as 1785 Paley thought the evil of pluralities was insuperable, and suggested that the non-resident incumbent 'should at least distribute the tracts of the Society for Promoting Christian Knowledge' as a substitute for his ministrations; a third excellent bishop in 1796 thought that 'considerations make non-residence a thing to be connived at', whilst Archbishop Secker attributed the 'development of a new sect, pretending to the strictest piety' simply due to clerical absenteeism. Nor was it till 1838 that State and Church combined to do away with pluralities and absenteeism.

Not only was the Church cursed by traffic in livings and by absenteeism, but the rapacity, avarice, pride and luxury of some of its leaders were notorious. Perhaps because of their ancestry, most of the wealthier clergy assumed an arrogance of demeanour that was singularly out of keeping with their apparent calling; indeed, their very mode of life was so closely allied to that of the aristocracy as to be indistinguishable from it. Archbishop Hurd always travelled with the pomp and circumstance afforded by the attendance of twelve servants about the episcopal coach. Of Dr. Blackbourne, Horace Walpole wrote: 'This jolly old Archbishop of York had the manners of a man of quality, and though he had been a buccaneer and was a clergyman, he retained nothing of his first profession except his seraglio.' A favourite story in circulation was that Archbishop Blackbourne had as butler, Dick Turpin, and it was not long before people began to notice that on every night that the bishop and butler left Bishopthorpe, the North Mail was held up and robbed. Cornwallis, the eighty-seventh holder of the Canterbury see, is perhaps kindly described when he is termed 'a merry old soul'; another, having the same exalted position, so trained his grandson that he became a leading light of the infamous Medmenham Brotherhood. And, of course, such episcopal worldly pride affected some of the younger clergy. 'Some of the most distinguished coxcombs, drunkards, debauchees, gamesters who figured at places of public resort, were young men of the sacerdotal orders', declared Dr. Stoughton.

In striking contrast with this tepid zeal for diocesan work, these same bishops were most punctilious in attendance at Court and in the House of Lords, where they gave unwearying support to the hundreds of repressive Game, Crime and Enclosure Acts. And it is Macaulay who calls attention 'to the unquestionable and instructive Fact' that, when the political power of the Anglican hierarchy was at its zenith, national virtue was at its lowest. With such clerics figuring among the Church's leaders, there was naturally lowered religious vitality in the State Church. Such a condition meant in its turn that Society became so frankly irreligious or atheistic that even a Voltaire was slightly shocked, and said: 'there is only just enough religion left in England to distinguish Tories who had a little from Whigs who had none'; whilst a Montesquieu sums up his remarks on English life with the conclusion 'that there was no religion in England. Every one laughs if one talks of it. . . . In France I pass for having too little religion; in England for having too much'. It was the existence of such clergymen and bishops that led Swift to make many harsh and terrible statements about the deans and bishops that he knew; that caused Leighton to speak of 'the eighteenth-century Church as one of the most corrupt in its administration', made a statesman describe the Church 'as the biggest den of thieves in the whole world', and led many a one to despair of its continuance. In 1750 Burnet is said to have refused the Canterbury see 'because it was too late to try and support a falling Church', and much later, when matters were better, Arnold of Rugby affirmed, 'the Church, as it now stands, no human power can save'.

Bad as the National Church seems to have been in most districts and for the most part of this century, it is doubtful if it was worse than that of Germany, where the foundation of Christianity was being sapped by a coarse eudaemonism, or that of France, where it was necessary for a priest to be a count or a marquis before he was considered eligible to become a successor of the apostles.

Despite this recital of the imperfections of some of the eighteenth-century clerical hierarchy, Dean Stanley always argued that it was not the bishops who estranged the Methodists from the State Church. He maintained that some of them, like Potter, Lowth, Butler, Benson, Burnet, Wilson, treated Wesley as an equal, and with great respect and consideration. He considered that it was the ignorant multitudes, the country squires and rural clergy who made for the barbarous intolerance shown in the name of the Church to Dissenters and Methodists. Addison and Fielding seem to agree with Stanley, for they sketched country squires who prided themselves on being 'Tory fox-hunting gentlemen', who described Dissenters and Methodists as 'factious sons of whores', and who detailed with gusto how they headed the mob at the pulling down of many a Methodist meeting-house, and how they got a bear, dressed it up in a skirt, cloak and bonnet and let it loose in a prayer meeting. Undoubtedly too, the century saw thousands of 'parson Trullibers', with their pigsties, and when Wesley came to Colne in Lancashire in 1748, one reads of the enterprising curate who announced that

'if any man be mindful to enlist under the command of the Rev. George White for the defence of the Church of England, let him repair to the cross where he shall have a pint of ale and other proper encouragements'.

Perhaps this symptomatic outburst was simply an exhibition of pious jocosity or of irritated clerical vacuity. It might have arisen, however, from a sense of vengeance, for good religion has often been corrupted by the wretched and wicked prejudices which admit a difference of opinion as a cause of hatred; and so the history of many a religious sect has records of ferocious brutality wreaked by its fanatics when their creed and authority have been set at naught.

Most of these eighteenth-century clerical rank and file were indubitably ignorant, and vacillated between the grossest superstition and the profoundest scepticism, between bigotry and atheism. In their dealings with Dissenters, such protagonists piled their prejudice on suspicion and called the result 'principle'. It was a time when many a clergyman lived at the public house, adjoining and perhaps belonging to the Church; for in these days worthy folk saw nothing incongruous in their curate living like a fighting cock, in sharing there his flock's rumbustious pleasures and not dwelling in sanctified isolation. This was the type of incumbent described by Bishop Burnet with: 'our clergy had less authority and were under more contempt than those of any other Church in Europe; for they were the most remiss in their labours and the least severe in their lives'; or by an archbishop in 1768 when he said: 'Christianity is now railed at and ridiculed with very little reserve, and the teachers of it without any at all'; or by a philosopher who wrote: 'there has never been a time when ministers of religion were held in so much contempt as in the Hanoverian period ... the contempt was for the persons, manners and characters of ecclesiastics.'

There is, of course, the financial side of these clergy to be considered. To eke out their very small stipends many of the clergy
had to act as charity-schoolmaster or general factotum to the local
squire. Bishop Bentley said that in his see there were more than
600 incumbents with only £50 a year, and that many of the
stipendiary curates got less than £30, and that they lived and
died without the slightest prospect of getting more. Tim Bobbin's
father, the Rev. John Collier, was curate of Eccles; he had nine
children and was paid £30 per annum; for years the Rev. Samuel
Wesley had no bigger stipend at Epworth. Not infrequently an
acting curate got less than that amount and was compelled to
accept £20 or so from some wealthy pluralist. As one historian
puts it:

'No estimate of the piety of the English churches in the eighteenth
century would be adequate without a scrutiny of such germane facts as
(1) many of the bishoprics such as those of Bristol, Oxford, Llandaff
appear to have had incomes under £500 per annum; (2) that in the
mid-century the Bishop of York declared that half his incumbents were
non-resident and that such conditions were probably general throughout the country and throughout the century and (3) that a census early
in the century showed that out of the 5,600 known livings, more than
half carried a stipend of £50 or less and that a century later quite four-
fifths of the livings were under £150 a year.'

It is therefore no wonder that the more illiterate of the clergy
bred pigs, thought, talked, behaved and lived like mere labourers.
Often they got into debt and were hounded into prison; dozens of
them could be found in the 'Fleet' at any time, and there they
became broken-down and disreputable. For a fee such fellows
would marry a couple at any hour, without asking a question and
without taking heed of the drugged or drunken condition or even
protests of bride or bridegroom. Equally notorious were the
'Alsatian' clerics, who haunted the Seven Dials, or those who presided over the tavern marriage-shops in the King's Bench prison,
the Mint in Southwark and May Fair chapel. Right up to 1753
these ridiculous ceremonies performed by these disreputable
clergymen were legal; not till that year had weddings to be
solemnized in a consecrated building; nor were Dissenters (other
than Quakers and Jews) relieved from such restriction till 1836.

Naturally such clergymen took little heed of the Church fabrics,
&c. In his *Tour Through the Whole Island*, Defoe said of Ely
Minster: 'some of it totters so much with every gale of wind, looks

so like decay and seems so near it.' By 1750 cathedral after cathedral had fallen into a miserable state of dilapidation and decay. A little later Bishop Fleetwood declared, 'Unless the good public spirit of repairing churches should prevail a good deal more than it does at present, an hundred years will bring to the ground a huge number of our churches'. About the same period Archbishop Secker detailed 'some of the annoyances which must gradually bring our churches to decay . . . water is undermining and rotting the foundations; earth is heaped up against the outside walls; weeds and shrubs are growing in the very walls; . . . the floors are meanly paved, the inside walls are dirty and patched, the windows are ill-glazed and in parts stopped up with rags and straw . . . very many of the churches are damp, offensive, unwholesome'. Late in the century Cowper says: 'the ruinous condition of these country churches gave me great offence . . . many an one has scarce any sort of roof than the ivy that grows over it . . . the noise of the owls, bats, magpies makes even the principal part of the music in many of these ancient edifices . . . the parson's surplice is as dirty as a farmer's smock.'

For decades, the most that the authorities did was every few years to whitewash churches and even cathedrals. And of this washing device one critic said:

'I make little scruple in declaring, that this job-work—which is carried on in every part of the kingdom—is a mean makeshift to give a delusive appearance of repair and cleanliness to walls and is resorted to, to hide neglected or perpetrated fractures.'

Pepys states that it was not unusual for many a parishioner to grow sage, &c., on the family graves; Archbishop Secker had to remonstrate with many of his incumbents for using the churchyard as pasture ground for their cattle and pigs; and as late as 1775 a writer thus expresses the condition of many a churchyard:

> Here nauseous weeds each pile surround
> And things obscene bestrew the ground;
> Skulls, bones, in mould'ring fragments lie,
> All dreadful emblems of mortality.

Foolish monuments glorifying the longevity, &c., of a particular parishioner or the deeds of a parish official who had bought a font or repaired the pews and windows were admitted into churches till well into the third quarter. As late as 1764 Wesley has occasion to refer to 'the heaps of unmeaning stone and marble' he found in

Westminster Abbey. Chatterton is thinking of the monuments to
be found in Bristol Cathedral in the third quarter of the century
when he writes:

> Around the monuments I cast my eyes,
> And see absurdities and nonsense rise;
>   Here rueful-visag'd angels seem to tell
>   With weeping eyes, a soul has gone to hell;
> Here a child's head supported by duck's wings,
> With toothless mouth, a hallelujah sings.

And a monument erected in Winchester Cathedral about this
period, exemplifies the 'nonsense' of which Chatterton spoke:

> Here rests in peace a Hampshire grenadier,
> Who kill'd himself by drinking small beer;
> Soldier, be warn'd by his untimely fall,
> And when you're hot, drink strong, or not at all.

Perhaps the incumbents were equally careless about the characters and abilities of the men they engaged as parish clerks.
These uneducated, posturing fellows got trouncings from many
an observer. In 1757 Wesley describes one as 'a poor humdrum
wretch who can scarce read what he drones out with such an air
of importance' and congratulates himself that in his 'Meeting
Houses'

'it is no small advantage that the person who reads prayers is one . . .
whose life is no reproach to his profession and one who performs that
solemn part of divine service, not in a careless, hurrying, slovenly
manner, but seriously and slowly as becomes him who is transacting so
high an affair between God and man'.

Years later Hartley Coleridge remarks:

'How often in town and country do we hear our Divine Liturgy
rendered wholly ridiculous by all imaginable tones, twangs, drawls,
mouthings, wheezings, gruntings, snuffles and quidrollings; by all
diversities of dialects, cacologies, and cacophonies; by twistings, con-
tortions and consolidations of visage, squintings, blinkings, upcastings.'

II

Not all the eighteenth-century bishops and incumbents—
perhaps not the majority—were dull in conscience and apathetic
in religion, and happily time has preserved pictures of other representatives of the eighteenth-century National Church; representa-

tives who were adorned with human virtues and who were fighting
with some show of right; men who were living lives of simple piety
and plain duty. To its great credit, the National Church had
beneficent activities and some excellent clerics.

The opening of the century saw Parliament construct a dozen
or so new churches by imposing a duty on coal and thereby
realizing £350,000; it saw the Church's leaders develop societies
for the promotion of Christian knowledge, the establishment of
many charity schools and some parochial libraries, whilst its
closing years saw formed the London Missionary, the Church Missionary and the Religious Tract Societies. The century had its
'vicars of Wakefield', its 'auburn priests' and 'Sir Roger's chaplains'. It had a Gibson who exercised a vigilant oversight on the
morals of all ranks, and whose fearless denunciations of the
licentious masquerades lost him the royal good will. It had its
men of learning and ability among bishops like Lowth, Butler,
Berkeley, Paley and other divines. It had its eloquent preachers
in Kirwan and Horsley. In 1770 its Archbishop of York declared
that he had confirmed more than 41,000 persons during the past
three years, and much about the same period the Exeter bishop
had laid hands on quite as many, whilst other bishops declare
contemporaneously, that they often confirmed 1,500 a day, and
that they were 'in church from 9.0 a.m. till 7.0 p.m.'

It had its kind, large-hearted curates like John Newton, Thomas
Stackhouse, Fletcher, Romaine, Walker and Seed. Its Rev.
Stephen Hales was a great physiologist and inventor, and he probably saved thousands of lives by his advocacy of ventilating
systems for mines, jails, hospitals and ships' holds, to quote only
one of his scientific activities. The Rev. Gilbert White of Selborne
gave up ten years of his life in that century to settling some questions of ornithological details and produced one of the kindest and
most gentle of English literary masterpieces. In his *Diversions of
Purley*, Rev. Horne Tooke dissected particles till he laid bare their
component fibres. Wesley saw much good in them; and though
bitter experience had taught him that many a curate was deficient
both in learning and piety, he nevertheless affirmed, 'In the
present time, the behaviour of the clergy in general is greatly
altered for the better', and in 1780 he declared, 'I am fully convinced that our Church (of England) with all her blemishes, is
nearer the Scriptural plan than any other Church in Europe', and
'To speak freely, I myself find more life in the Church prayers

than in any formal extempore prayers of Dissenters'. Dr. Johnson, another fierce foe to all sin, remained a faithful Churchman throughout his life; Smollett, a proud, warm-hearted man who would be enraged by anything he considered unjust, asserted that 'the clergy were generally pious and exemplary', whilst the Rev. James Woodforde's diaries give pictures of an amiable, well-meaning eighteenth-century cleric.

Many of these good clergymen and bishops never quite understood Wesley and his Methodism. The theological writings and pronouncements of their leaders showed work of vigorous and scholarly minds, frankly and definitely on the side of doctrinal precision. Judged by modern standards, they tended to impose finality where no finality is, and to make static the dynamic power of the Gospel. It is also doubtful if they ever perceived that over-insistence on doctrinal precision must weaken any Church in essential force, and rob it of valuable helpers. Perhaps some of them never realized that doctrines which may be repulsive to one temperament, are to another the inspiration of boundless devotion and service to God and man. Still, some of the clerics of this school of thought, who met Wesley and understood Methodism, found mutual knowledge tended to mitigate dislike, and they grasped the fact that a code of faith, vindicated by right living, selflessness and good works, could not have anything very heinous in the way of theory.

Nevertheless, the great majority of these excellent clerics held themselves aloof from Methodism. Yet they were regular in the discharge of their sacred offices as clergymen and not unmindful, nor neglectful, of their other high and important duties. To the poor the parsonages were ever open, and not only did parishioners benefit by the preacher's precepts and example, but they were sure to find a friend in need, a comforter in their sorrows, and a benefactor and physician in the hour of illness. This class of eighteenth-century cleric loved his country, her laws, her ordinances, institutions, State religion and government. He abhorred the troubler of the State, the spurious reformer, the obstreperous, tyrannic demagogue, and the disorganizing sophist. He disliked the irregular or abnormal in anything, and hated exaggerated feelings, uncurbed eccentricity, peculiarity in thought, or mannerism in its expression. His ideal of good manners was decorum with restraint; an ideal well expressed by Nugent, a satisfying poet of the period:

Happy when Reason deigns to guide,
Secure within the Golden Mean,
Who shuns the Stoic's senseless pride,
Nor wallows with the herd obscene.

He, nor with brow severely bent,
Chides Pleasure's smiling train away,
Nor careless of Life's great Intent,
With Folly wastes each heedless day.

On the question of pain and pleasure, his religious philosophy was probably summed up in Blake's lines:

Joy and woe are woven fine,
A clothing for the Soul divine;
Under every grief and pine
Runs a joy with silken twine.
It is right it should be so:
Man was made for joy and woe;
And when this we rightly know,
Safely through the world we go.

Such an eighteenth-century clergyman of this most creditable class, whilst convinced that safety lies in keeping to the well-regulated, and whilst continuing to make 'reason the standard of all thoughts, words and actions, and firmly resolved to yield a constant and ready obedience to reason's dictates', might even have assented to Byrom's lines:

Sense to discern and reason to compare,
Are gifts that merit our improving care;
But want an inward light, when all is done,
As seeds and plants do that of outward sun:
Main help neglected, tasteless fruits arise;
And Wisdom grows insipid to the wise.

What this class of cleric really needed was the buoyant confidence and unity of those nearest to the historic facts of religion. They lacked conviction; they did not realize that the Christian Faith is not a creed to defend but a Gospel to preach, and that conviction is the sword-point that would best carry the thrust home.

Further evidence of the growth of numbers of incumbents leading quiet blameless lives, of the increasing sobriety of judgement, practical sense and developing depth of fervour, are shown by such facts as that eight clergymen of the Church of England supported Charles Wesley's pall in 1788, that during the fifty years of

U

John Wesley's evangelizing movement the initial distrust shown by many of them gave way to alliance, and that before the end of the century many of the churches had instituted monthly sacraments, whilst in some cathedrals the sacrament could be received every Sunday. Increasing care over sacred buildings and grounds was also shown. Belfries were attended to and bells that had been destroyed by the Puritans, or where 'four bells out of five had been sold by the parish parson to defray the churchwardens accounts' were replaced; one firm claiming that they alone had erected 3,000 bells by 1774. Actual belling-ringing became no longer the privilege or pastime of the wealthy who, hitherto, had rung bells when and how they pleased. Although 'change-ringing' degenerated in social repute, it became more scientific and melodious, whilst belfries were less regarded as adjuncts to the pothouses.

Public behaviour in churches also improved, and at the close of the century the naves of York, Durham and Norwich were no longer used as mere fashionable promenades, whilst the state-entry of the squire became less ceremonial. No longer preceded by footmen or negro slaves carrying food, wine, pipe and Bible did the lord of the manor enter the church and take his seat in the special pew. And as time rolled on, it became less and less customary for worshippers to be accompanied by their dogs. Hogarth's cartoon, the *Sleeping Congregation,* shows how earlier congregations used the altar-rails as hall-stand for cloaks and hats, indicates the lounging, slumbering group where all but parson and clerk are fast asleep, was indicative of early eighteenth-century church habits. Novelists of the period mention how, shut off from view of pulpit and other pews, the old-time squire used to take his ease during the service, not only by sleeping, but by eating and smoking. It seems to have been the practice during the de Coverley era for the village autocrats to have cake and wine or something more substantial during the sermon, whilst smoking during the sermon was quite common, and not unknown in Wales and Scotland as late as 1850. More objectionable than this eating, smoking and sleeping had been the early- and middle-century antics of the bright young people of the day, who, with their perspective glasses quizzed the youthful female worshippers and led an early eighteenth-century bishop to refer to them as, 'Young whelps, who in corners, make themselves merry with open railing and scoffing at the Holy Scriptures'. Probably it was the same 'whelps' who found amusement at open-air revival meetings by setting their hounds at the faithful, driving baited bulls into the crowd, blowing coach-horns, ringing the church bells, throwing mud and stones at the preachers, and who, later—when the Methodists had their own churches—found pleasure in throwing squibs and crackers among the converted.

III

As for church equipment, it may be said that family pews had become a regular part of the ordinary church furniture in the days of Queen Anne. Often these pews were built high to keep off the draughts prevailing in unheated churches. Where the church was attended by more than one well-to-do family, rivalry in pew construction supervened. Some of the great ones had canopies to their pews and had them hung round with curtains; not a few of them had a fireplace or stove with poker, tongs and shovel all complete, and nearly all were furnished with a good substantial table at which they could eat. Swift is referring to such family pews when, in *Baucis and Philemon*, he says :

> A bedstead of the antique mode,
> Compact of timber many a load,
> Such as our ancestors did use,
> Was metamorphos'd into pews;
> Which still their ancient nature keep
> By lodging folks dispos'd to sleep.

It was not till the end of the century or even till the nineteenth, that the Church authorities realized the evils and moral injustices of such pews. As late as 1798 Young, recognizing that such family pews occupied an inordinate amount of space for the few, urged that the proposed new churches should be built like theatres with 'benches and thick mats for the poor and with galleries and boxes for the higher classes'. Wesley did not like his chapels to have pews; he objected to the horse-box ones in the dark, oak-lined Octagon Chapel in Norwich on the ground that they were 'too ornate for the coarse Gospel of Christ'. He preferred that his chapels should do away with all the eighteenth-century class distinctions for worshippers; he wanted plain, backless seats for all alike, and he insisted on the separation of the sexes as were the arrangements in the Primitive Church. In 1780 he wrote: 'If I come into any new house, and see the men and women together, I will immediately go out.' He does not seem to have objected however, to the eighteenth-century use of galleries. Then, in most churches there were galleries erected in all sorts of queer places; the small ones flanking the organ or musicians' place were reserved for the charity-school children. These were necessarily very steep, and the topmost row of these unfortunates practically touched the ceiling.

Eighteenth-century pulpits were usually three-decker contrivances; the lowest box was for the parish clerk, the middle one was the reading-desk and the highest one—usually topped with a sounding-board—was the pulpit. The woodwork of the pulpit, organ case and main pew was often very fine, for in the first half of the century, Grinling Gibbons and his pupils did an enormous amount of church carving. In the pulpit there was usually the 'Hour Sand Glass' by which the worshippers could measure the length of the sermon. The Bible in some of these churches would still be chained to the desk and nearly all of them would be printed in the black letter type. Not infrequently the windows put into the churches in the second half of the century were of stained glass or were painted with scenes from the lives of Christ and the Saints. Naturally Wesley preferred simplicity in pulpits and expressed a preference for sash-windows in the growing number of his chapels; he could neither afford, nor did he desire, ecclesiastical ornamentation.

IV

The growing Methodists began to make themselves felt in the land. Their first chapel was opened in May 1739 at Bristol, and soon afterwards the movement had taken root in London, Kingswood and Newcastle; in 1771 their meeting-houses numbered 70 and by 1784 they totalled 359, whilst their further numerical progression was almost geometrical. A somewhat casual census taken fairly early in the nineteenth century suggests that in Lancashire there were 292 National churches, 85 Catholic chapels and 346 Nonconformist meeting-houses. Such figures would imply that about half of Lancashire's population were Dissenters. But neither significance nor accuracy can be attached to such calculations and deductions, for the partial census states that then one person in fifty-one was a Methodist in Lancashire and that the Yorkshire proportion was one in twenty-three. Greater evidence of the rising tide of Methodism is shown, however, through other channels. Writing to the Home Office in 1792, the Mayor of

Liverpool urged the Government to build more churches in the Merseyside villages :

'In all these places are nothing but Methodist and other Meeting houses and as all the people in the Countery are in general dispos'd to go to some place of Worship on the Sunday, they go to these places because there is none other; and thus the Youth of the Countery are training up under the Instruction of a Set of Men not only Ignorant, but whom I believe we have of late too Much Reason to imagine, are inimical to Our Happy Constitution.'

This letter is quoted *in extenso*, as it was precisely on such arguments that Parliament in 1818, was moved to spend a superfluous war-indemnity of a million pounds for the building of National churches, 'in order to remove dissent and enable the Church to counterbalance the activity of the Dissenters'.

As buildings the first Methodist chapels left very much to be desired. Wesley described the derelict arsenal, the 'Foundery' in 1740 as 'a ruinous place with an old pantile covering, a few rough deal boards put together to constitute a pulpit'. Still it had to function till 1779, when it was replaced by City Road. It was in such associations that Wesley preached twice daily at 5.0 a.m. and 7.0 p.m.

The chapels specially built for Methodism in the eighteenth century made no pretensions to architectural beauty; even those erected for other worshippers in the second half of the century were excessively plain and fitted with austere accommodation. Most eighteenth-century Methodist conventicles were small, square buildings as ugly outside as they were poor and colourless within. Their drab walls, hard, unbacked benches and bare floors typified and fitted in with the worshippers' lives. There was something almost ox-like in the very way the faithful sat; men with gnarled hands flat on knees, the women with red and coarsened hands folded together under shawl or cloak, whilst brother Such-an-one in the little pulpit read the Good Book and thundered forth his rude conception of truth. Town meeting-houses were sometimes built of stone, faced with blue-plaster, had a sanded floor, backless forms, a fireplace and a high pulpit with brass candlesticks; there was a gallery on three sides, often reached by a ladder, and the men sat on the right side of the preacher and women on the left.

Although some of these early buildings may be bare and mill-like, they often possess genuine beauty in their austere dignity of naked lines, whilst many of the wistful, unhealthy little country temples were the fruit of tremendous effort, and of a self-denial that appeals to the imagination. The Sheerness chapel of 1786 was built by direct labour freely given by the converted, whilst the one at Haslingden in 1788 was built as a speculation, cost about £800 and was let at 3 per cent per annum. Shapes varied too; there was the eight-sided chapel at Norwich, whilst that at St. Ives was 'exactly round and composed wholly of brazen slag'. Details of the hundreds erected in the eighteenth century, must lie imprisoned in many archives or greatly scattered in former or present Methodist homes. If they could be studied, they would throw further vivid light on the progress of Methodism, and afford many other details about the construction of these first meeting-houses.

v

Despite Wesley's lifelong plea that he and his co-Methodists were National Church people, and notwithstanding his assurance that he was a high-Church Tory, he and his followers were attacked by their Anglican contemporaries, who would persist in classing them with Whigs, Deists or other Dissenters. Throughout the century religious differences were confused with political differences by the vast majority of the population. The National Church was a mighty political power during these hundred years; the bench of bishops was regarded as a powerful phalanx and even the ablest statesmen had to take notice of them; the ordinary incumbent could and did influence many an election to the Commons, so that the Church had to be favoured or appeased by competing politicians. Thus parsons were accustomed to brief spells of flattery at election times.

At the beginning of the century high-Church Tories were in the ascendancy, but naturally a Lutheran like George I would not appeal to them. Thus by 1717 the National Church itself was split into two bitter camps by these political quarrels. In that year the Lower House of Canterbury displayed a turbulent spirit of revolt, and the higher clergy retaliated by suspending it for 135 years; for by then the bishops were mainly Whigs and the Lower House mainly Jacobites. The arbitrary and oppressive character of this long-enforced silence of the spirituality was very bad indeed for the well-being of the Church itself, and was probably one factor that led to its decay. Perhaps too, it was a factor in the growth of the evangelical party within the Church itself, and which led many an incumbent to welcome the appearance of the Methodists in his village.

But long before the appearance of Methodism, the war between Whigs and Tories or between 'high', 'broad' and 'low' Churchmen and between the multiple forms of dissent was raging. Not infrequently the clergy delivered seditious and libellous sermons on the shortcomings of the Whigs, and freely classed them with Deists or Dissenters; to the ordinary squire and his incumbent these simply formed an amorphous gang that had to be suppressed. Quite early in the century the very popular song of the 'Church Triumphant' started off with such a grouping of the opposition:

> Bold Whig, and Fanatics now strive to pull down
> The true Church of England, both Mitre and Crown.

Quickly the Dissenters became labelled a hypocritical set of 'schismastics', and, like Whigs, worthy only to figure on the gallows or in the pillory. A song circulating round about 1712 likens them to ill-grained dogs:

> There's atheists and deists and fawning dissenters,
> There's republican sly and long-winded canter;
>   There's schism, heresy and mild moderation,
>   That's still in the wrong for the good of the nation,
> There's Baptist, Socinian and Quakers with scruples,
> Till kind Toleration links 'em all in church-couples.
>
> Some were bred in the army, some dropt from the fleet,
> Under hulks some were litter'd, and some in the street;
>   Some are good harmless curs, without teeth or claws;
>   Some were whelp'd in a shop and some runners at large,
> Some were wretched poor curs, mongrel starvers and setters
> Till dividing the spoil, they put in with their betters.

The Whigs and Dissenters retorted with pamphlets and songs picturing in broad colours the unsanctified lives of many of the Tory stalwarts and Church clergy, and loudly proclaimed their venality and greediness. One song of the period ends with:

> They swallow all up
> Without e'en a gulp;
> There's nought chokes a priest but a halter.

Sometimes the verbal assaults were accompanied with physical battery, and in the days of Queen Anne and George I, it was no uncommon thing to destroy the houses of Dissenters, their meeting-places, and to burn effigies of their leaders.

Nor did the early Methodists escape such regrettable attentions. These attacks were most frenzied between 1745 and 1752 and in areas like the Potteries, Lancashire, Yorkshire and especially Cornwall, and largely there because the ignorant mobs, led by stupid, frightened squires and clerics, thought the Methodists were Jacobites; for many an eighteenth-century man was under the firm impression that John Wesley was a Catholic priest raising forces for the Pretender. Such physical attacks gradually died away, but the barbarous outpourings of the lampoonists seemed inexhaustible. In the year Wesley died, one of the most popular songs of the Church party started off with the first verse of the National Anthem, and then continued with:

> Old Mother Church disdains,
> The vile dissenting strains,
>   That round her ring;
> She keeps her dignity,
> And scorning faction's cry
> Sings with sincerity,
>   God Save the King.

> Sedition is their creed,
> Feign'd sheep, but wolves indeed,
>   How can we trust?
> Gunpowder Priestley would
> Deluge the throne with blood,
> And lay the Great and Good
>   Low in the Dust.

> Hist'ry, thy page unfold,
> Did not their sires of old
>   Murder their King?
> And they would overthrow
> Kings, Lords and Bishops too,
> And while they gave the blow,
>   Loyally sing.

The song concludes the insult and abuse with the comminatory verse of the National Anthem. It was answered by the satirical reply of the Whigs in their famous *Réveillé to the Church*, issued a little later, and containing the following stanzas:

> Now, now, if ever, loudly bawl
>   The Church, the Church in danger!
> Each prebend trembles for his stall,
>   And eke his rack and manger.

Peers, knights and squires in league combined,
    Protect your good Old Mother;
For should the beldame slip her wind,
    You'll never see another.

Two hundred years and more the dame
    Has tightly held together;
Her glorious motto 'Still the Same'
    In spite of wind and weather.

Her sons of Grace with tender care,
    She's fed on dainty dishes;
And none but they have had a share
    Among the loaves and fishes.

   .   .   .   .   .   .

Rouse then for shame, ye church-fed race
    With Tories true and trusty;
Turn on your foe your fighting face,
    And fit your armour rusty.

Probably neither leading Dissenters nor Churchmen wrote the fore-going politico-religious squibs. But history shows that many leading Dissenters and clergy lost their dignity and dispelled the sense of their sacred calling in such unseemly disputes. Sometimes the differences were more doctrinal than political. For years even Dissenting Churches like Congregationalists, Baptists, Calvinists, &c., regarded the Methodist movement with perplexity and doubt, if not with positive hostility. *Odium theologicum* showed itself everywhere. Temperaments that feared tolerance as the devil's lure, abounded in every sect, and unfortunate animosities were aroused. Religious iconoclasts made differing chapels and churches noisily competitive enterprises, and the more militant leaders cherished holy malice, denounced the others, and rampaged freely and wildly. They were far more intent on defeating their opponents than in arriving at the truth; most of them revelled in controversial antagonisms; few of them realized that progress in apprehension of the truths of the Gospel must chiefly come by the intercourse of minds united in friendship and fellow-ship. One can but wistfully wonder how they would fare in the land of perpetual peace, where there could be no challenging of authority, no joy of contest, no campaigns to organize and no personal abuses to reform. This sort of civil religious war broke out among the Methodists themselves, and even before Wesley's death; for the dissidents found difficulty in accommodating them-selves to Wesley's formularies of ancient mould; nor could they be

influenced to remain within the fold, by a sort of general accept-
ance, without the implication of a detailed assent. Waterland,
Warburton, Tucker, Tomline, Toplady, Hill and the leading
Quakers, as well as John Wesley, were all alike guilty of this very
bad taste. Happily there were honourable exceptions in men like
Law, Fletcher, Adam Clarke, Priestley and Horsley.

Sometimes professional writers, who boasted no sort of religious
fervour or deep political faith, engaged in this wordy warfare.
Their differing attitudes towards the dispute are perhaps fairly
illustrated by quotations from Defoe and Pope. In the one an
emotional kinship between dissent and satanism is suggested,
whilst the other implies that the religious warfare was trivial and
negligible. Defoe wrote:

> Wherever God erects a House of Prayer,
> The Devil always builds a chapel there;
> And 'twill be found on examination,
> The latter has the largest congregation.

Pope affirmed:

> For modes of faith, let graceless zealots fight;
> He can't be wrong whose life is in the right.

Fielding denounced Methodists with heedless flippancy;
Smollett treated them with contempt in novels and in his *History
of England*; Burn's *Holy Fair* was a savage satire on the ignorant
ranters of his day and his *Address to the Unco Guid* attacks the false
premises of any form of faith. Anonymous writers sometimes descended to the lowest depths, and probably many a Methodist
preacher was greeted with the popular shout of

> Here comes the Methodee parson,
> Here comes the ranter bold;
> He kissed my wife . . .

when appearing on the village greens.

VI

Probably Fielding, Smollett, Foote, Chatterton, Burns and the
anonymous lampoonists confused the early Methodist ministers
with the roaming 'hedge-preachers', just as did the general public,
many magistrates and numerous incumbents.

The bulk of these 'preachers' were mere roving adventurers
who could be 'licensed' by any magistrate to preach and beg.

Hundreds of these fellows could not even read, and fewer still could write; yet these handicaps did not prevent them from practising as preachers. One of these illiterates, asked by a licensing magistrate —who was anxious to reduce the thousands of vagrant-evangelists —how he managed to be a preacher, seeing that he could not read, replied that his friend read the Scriptures which the missioner then 'splained and spounded'. After such explanation and exposition, the charlatan usually delivered a 'Gospel' sermon. Wesley could not be but disgusted with the activities of these fellows and he often protested against 'what were vulgarly called Gospel sermons. . . . The term has become a mere cant word. . . . Let but a pert, self-sufficient animal that has neither sense nor grace, bawl something about Christ and His Blood, or justification by Faith and his silly hearers cry out: "What a fine Gospel sermon."' These self-appointed evangelists increased enormously in the last quarter of the century, and Viscount Sidmouth tried to stop their further multiplication by an Act of Parliament. Unfortunately the noble lord had made the usual muddle of confusing these tramps with Free-church ministers, and so he proposed that 'six respectable house-keepers in every parish should be authorized to certify the qualifications of a nonconformist minister'. Others besides Lord Sidmouth confused the masqueraders with Wesley's licensed preachers. In 1749 the *Monthly Review* described Methodist preachers as 'the most wild and extravagant, the most ridiculous, strolling, fanatical, delirious and mischievous of all the Saints in the Romish communion', and Chatterton, the boy-poet who would meet genuine Methodists in his home town, made the same mistake and challenged their very sincerity:

> He'd oft profess an hallow'd flame
> And everywhere preach'd Wesley's name;
>   He was a preacher and what not,
>   As long as money could be got;
> He'd oft profess with holy fire,
> The labourer's worthy of his hire.

And in a poem entitled the 'Methodist Preacher', like Defoe, the same poet seems to think there is some spiritual kinship between Dissent and satanism.

> Says Tom to Jack; 'Tis very odd
> These representatives of God,
> In colour, way of life and evil,
> Should be so very like the devil

And however much we may dispute the rightness of the title, the quatrain cannot be dismissed as mere poetic licence, when the activities of these humbugs are recalled. The lives and manners of these noisy, miserable fellows were undoubtedly execrable; in rampageous oratory, bad taste blazed out of their mouths when they dealt with their appalling doctrines of a crude hell, and their catalogues of manufactured sins.

VII

Turning from them to the more orthodox preachers, one finds that pulpit oratory in the eighteenth century naturally varied according to the varying mental, moral and spiritual gifts of the preachers. The semi-illiterates, the 'Trullibers', felt it their duty to talk to their parishioners about the general news of the day about which they were probably better informed than their flocks. As the great majority of their hearers could not read, a variety of secular matters had to be published from the pulpit, such as the publication of the poor-law assessment, days of appeal in matters of house and window-taxes, hues and cries, inquiries after lost goods, &c. Often the sermons themselves were little more than friendly talks to the assembled parish. A novelist describing such sermons in late eighteenth-century churches, makes his narrator say:

'If the curate dressed us down personally one Sunday, as like as not, he would tell us of his own failings on the next occasion. He never hesitated to mention man, woman or child by name from the pulpit and thought nothing of asking personal questions in the middle of the sermon or of telling us to open or shut a window or not to blow our noses so loudly. Then he would proceed to talk about the weather, the crops, the fishing and so gradually soar to higher things by gentle degrees.'

And however personal and pointed such sermons in country pulpits may have been, they could scarcely have outdone in frankness one preached by Wesley in Norwich, when 'I told them in plain terms that they were the most ignorant, self-conceited, self-willed, fickle, untractable, disorderly, disjointed society that I knew in the three kingdoms'. Happily fortune has preserved a mid-century 'special' sermon preached by a rural clergyman; the *British Magazine* of November 1750 has a complete account of one delivered by a 'Trulliber' of the period, and it certainly is a curiosity in theological literature. This funeral oration begins by eulogizing the ancestry of the departed, pays fulsome compliments to every principal mourner, and then proceeds to set forth 'the transcendent virtues of the deceased':

'As your memories may fail you, I shall again remind you of one or two of them. The first is, she was a good knitter as any in the county of Norfolk. When her husband and family were in bed and asleep, she would get a cushion, clap herself down by the fire and sit and knit. But, Beloved, be assured she was no prodigal woman, but a sparing woman, for, to spare candle, she would stir up the coals with her knitting pins, and by that light, she would sit and knit and make as good work as many other women by daylight. Beloved, I have a pair of stockings upon my legs that were knit in the same manner, and look at them, and know that they are the best stockings that ever I wore in my life. Secondly, she was the best maker of toast in drink that ever I eat in my life, and they were brown toasts too; for when I used to go in a morning, she would ask me to eat a toast, which I was very willing to do, because she had such an artificial way of toasting it, no ways slack, nor burning it. Besides, she had a pretty way of grating nutmeg and dipping it in the beer, and such a piece of raw cheese, that I must needs say that they were the best toasts that ever I eat in my life.

'Well, Beloved, the days are short, and many of you have a great way to your habitations, and therefore I hasten to a conclusion. I think I have sufficiently proved this man to be a good man, and his wife a good woman; but fearing your memories should fail you, I shall repeat the particulars namely . . .'

Perhaps this type of lengthy, futile requiem was not uncommon; at any rate Gay puts in his *Pastorals*:

> He said that Heaven would take her soul no doubt,
> And spoke the hour-glass in her praise quite out.

Whilst the final recapitulation makes one recall Chatterton's couplet:

> And now again we hear the doctor roar
> On subjects he's dissected thrice before.

Most sermons preached by the eighteenth-century rural divines were probably taken almost verbatim from printed collections. Many of these could be described as 'mere moral essays' and embodied in 'words of learned length and thundering sound'. Sermons without marked political bias and not specifically directed against some form of dissent, would be tame and colourless, cold and artificial, lest they should offend the squire's susceptibilities. Perhaps the Rev. Laurence Sterne's 'Yorick' sermons were never delivered from the Sutton or Stillington pulpits; if they were, they must have amazed mid-century Yorkshire congregations by their remarkable audacity, wit and graphic power. Perhaps what is more significant, is that their authorship does not seem to have injured Sterne's character as one suitable for a clergyman.

As for the recorded sermons preached by the most famous men of the eighteenth century, those by 'Orator Henley', Dean Kirwan, Bishops Horsley, Waterland, Warburton, Tucker and Lavington are remarkable for elegance of expression or forthrightness of phrasing. Those preached by Evangelicals and Dissenters are perhaps more remarkable for their variety. Rowland Hill, who might almost claim to have been both, was a very popular preacher. And yet he seems to have violated the laws of good taste in the eccentricities of his pulpit wit and humour. Probably he thought clownish antics necessary for his rural congregations, and perhaps, they in their turn, sensed that there was something deeper than clerical buffoonery in his orations. At any rate, history says: 'the intensity and purity of purpose by which he was actuated, enabled him always to retain uninjured his moral influence over his hearers.' Those delivered by many licensed preachers were probably coloured by the old Puritan doctrine of conversion and called upon the individual listener not to understand or to admire, but blindly to realize the power, mercy and love of God. As one critic puts it:

'Often these sermons were stern, rugged, ruthless as a storm; they spoke of death, hell, judgement. Most warned, few pleaded; most drove with fear of hell, few enticed with hope of Heaven.'

With their message of Fear and Repentance, these puritanical preachers must have been fierce and ruthless prophets.

Perhaps some of the first Methodist licensed preachers had such messages, and certainly Wesley had often to correct their message and preaching style. For their guidance he drew up excellent maxims on elocution and deportment, and he was specially severe in his opposition to pietism of the unctuous sort. Uninstructed pietism was suspect to him, and he always demanded the proper presentation of the Word by a clear and informed mind as well as a warm and fervent heart. To quote Dr. Bett: 'His own sermons did not over-emphasize the doctrine of retribution and he appears to have preached on hell once only, whilst out of his 500 hymns in the 1779 collection, only one of those poems has hell for its theme.' The vast majority of his preserved sermons deal with the mercy of God, the grace of God, the forgiving love of God. Naturally, too, they reflect plain common sense and are phrased in well-chosen but studiously simple English.

In mere literary qualities many of these sermons are probably excelled by the addresses of Law, Watts and Doddridge. Concerning the Rev. Dr. Watts, Johnson observes:

'He was one of the first authors that taught the Dissenters to court attention by the graces of language. Whatever they had among them before, whether of learning or acuteness, was commonly obscured and blunted by coarseness and inelegancies of style. He showed them that zeal and purity might be expressed and enforced by polished diction. ... In the pulpit, though his low stature, which very little exceeded five feet, graced him with no advantages of appearance, yet the gravity and propriety of his utterance, made his discourse very efficacious. ... In the art of pronunciation he had few superiors. ... Such was the flow of thoughts, and such his promptitude of language, that in the latter part of his life, he did not precompose his cursory sermons, but having adjusted the heads, and sketched out some particulars, trusted for success to his extemporary powers. He did not endeavour to assist his eloquence by any gesticulations; for, as no corporeal actions have any correspondence with theological truth, he did not see how they could enforce it.'

Those by Hervey, who was considered a preaching star in that century, and who 'was a sort of spiritual son of Wesley', got much greater praise from his contemporaries than posterity is likely to give them. A twentieth-century congregation would soon weary of the dreary drip of dilatory declamation he oozed. To many a modern reader his *Meditations Among the Tombs* are limp, sprawling, affected moralizings, completely invalidated by triteness and mushy emotionalism. Perhaps still more disappointing to a twentieth-century reader are the sermons by Whitefield. Possibly their astonishing success was due to the preacher's physical advantages of a good presence, attractive face and magnificent voice; to his high susceptibility, his perfect sincerity and his powerful passion. At any rate the intrinsic matter of his printed sermons seems extraordinarily weak and poor, and ill-calculated to rouse the high testimony they did evoke from able men like Horace Walpole, Chatham, Garrick, Hume, Franklin, Johnson, Bolingbroke, Chesterfield, who all knew excellence in literature, thought and oratory. These sermons even roused royal highnesses like ᵃᵃᵃᵃᵃᵃ

Frederick Prince of Wales and the Duke of Cumberland, worldly people like the Duchesses of Marlborough and Buckingham, and fops like Selwyn and Doddington.

VIII

Church music and hymn singing developed greatly during the eighteenth century. A large proportion of the wealthy were then very musical, and they probably gave an impetus towards more musical services in hundreds of churches. Even at the beginning of the century a few churches had rudimentary organs, the number of which was increased considerably during these hundred years. Usually, however, the Church dignitaries did not encourage too much music and singing, whilst 'musical services' were looked upon with actual disfavour, and Wesley could write about 'the unseasonable and unmeaning impertinence of a voluntary on the organ'. Many churches that had no organ boasted of fiddles or reed instruments; and some had small orchestras of double-bass, 'cello, violins, flute, clarinet and 'serpent' by 1800. But most churches and chapels had neither organ nor orchestra; they were dependent upon the parish clerk's pitchpipe; this instrument was made of wood plugged at the end by a movable stopper, which, pushed to certain fixed places, gave the required note as a pitch for singing.

Wesley always prided himself on the music in his chapels; his diaries made frequent reference to 'the spirit and cheerfulness of the singing . . . hymns are sung with much taste, sweetness and good feeling'. Naturally his emphasis on the religious value of music in public worship affected all his chapels and the more evangelical of the State Churches. Other Wesleys too, would be potent factors for the improvement of chapel and evangelical church music. Charles had probably a more musical ear than his elder brother, whilst his two sons and grandson attained high eminence in musical circles, and exercised great influence in religious instrumental and vocal music. But this increasing love for sacred music was not restricted to chapels and churches. Together with instrumental and vocal music, it became popular everywhere, and in the last quarter of the century, there were scores of dales which produced the *Messiah*, &c., and furnished the soloists, the instrumentalists, chorus and even conductor. Bates, a Halifax musician of the period, says:

'In these manufacturing districts the poorer classes are so to speak born musicians. They meet constantly at their own habitations or in the inns for practice. And after a hard day's toil their solace is at a glee party. So determined are these amateurs, that man, woman or child will trudge five or six miles to attend a rehearsal or to sing a roundelay with a few of their own friends.'

Other memoir-writers indicate that not only glee societies and choral clubs met for practice in the 'singing room' in the chosen inn, but that church and chapel choirs sometimes practised there. At all such gatherings it appears to have been customary to spend several minutes singing psalms and hymns before they began to practise their glees, anthems, cantatas and oratorios. It was probably this pleasant eighteenth-century singing custom that led many important choral unions always to preface their rendering of the *Messiah* with the Christmas Hymn, &c.

At these church and chapel choir practices, much attention would be given to *The New Version* by Tate and Brady, issued round about 1700. It had displaced the sixteenth-century *English Metrical Psalms* by Sternhold and Hopkins. In the last quarter of the century this displacement became more marked, for the improving choirs demanded improved melodies. By 1790 Cowper writes: 'the good old practice of psalm-singing is wonderfully improved in many churches since the days of Sternhold and Hopkins; there is scarce a parish-clerk who has so little taste as not to pick his staves out of the New Version . . . the tunes themselves have been set to jiggish measures . . . an itinerant band of vocal musicians who make it their business to go round to all the churches in their turns, and after a prelude with the pitch-pipe, astonish the audience with hymns set to the New Winchester measure and anthems of their own composing.' With Cowper, Wesley rejoiced at the disappearance 'of the miserable, scandalous doggerel of Sternhold and Hopkins'. Wesley wanted not only better tunes but improved reverence and heartiness; he told his followers 'they were to sing not lolling at their ease, or in the indecent posture of sitting, but all standing before God, praising Him lustily and with a good courage'.

During this century the paraphrase gradually gave way to the hymn, and the psalm tune to hymn tunes. To meet this new tendency, Wesley with his customary energy, overhauled the tunes he wished his followers to enjoy, and 'there was to be no repetition of words, no dwelling on disjointed syllables'. By this time Wesley

W

had made the discovery that hymns are a considerable factor in
religious worship. In one sense he had been anticipated by Luther
and the Puritans. Luther was one of the first to write metrical
verses on sacred subjects and adapt them to church melodies or to
lines of secular songs; the Puritans too, stressed the value of con-
cise and rhythmical lines and, like Luther, they did not hesitate to
introduce secular tunes into their worship. Neither the one nor
the other ever made the sanctuary walls a boundary between
musical art and religion, and both sensed that such placing of the
choral song of the church within the lips of the people, had great
religious and moral possibilities. But it was Wesley who made the
discovery that when religious words are set to appropriate music,
the effect on men's minds, thoughts and fervour is astonishing.
The preface to his hymns of 1779 still remains one of the best statements on the purpose of hymn singing. He looked upon a hymn
as 'a means of raising or quickening the spirit of devotion; of
confirming the believer's faith; of enlivening his hope; and of
kindling and increasing his love to God and man'.

The first collection of hymn tunes made by Wesley, was issued in
1742 and known as the *Foundery Collection*. It numbered some
forty-three unharmonized melodies of which posterity has abandoned the great majority. In 1761 he enlarged this anthology, and
the new edition called *Hymns with Tunes Annext* numbered some
seventy-six melodies, of which again only the theme was given.
In 1780 the previous editions were replaced with Wesley's *Sacred
Harmony*, and modern musical Methodists have considered thirty-
four of the tunes originally selected by their founder worthy of
inclusion in their latest anthology. Most of the tunes selected by
Wesley in his different collections, were of stately dignity or
possessed a dirge-like movement; most of them were written by
Arne, Boyce, Butts, Freylinghausen, Handel, Playford or Wilkins.
Characteristically, Wesley thought his editions contained the best
selection of hymn tunes in the world, insisted on the musicians
following his directions and urged their almost exclusive use in all
his meeting-houses.

There were available, however, other compilations of tunes
besides those favoured by Wesley, and by the end of the century
the more musical precentors could and did find other melodies
than those selected by Wesley. Psalms, tunes in minor keys,
chorals sung very slowly, and other relics of the old German hymn
tunes of traditional type, were gradually replaced by lilting

cadences and gracious harmonies from both sacred and profane sources. By Wesley's death tunes by Alcock, Bach, Bourgeois, Byrd, Clark, Croft, Day, Gibbons, Haydn, Lawes, Mozart, Tallis and the two sons of Charles Wesley had grown into favour. Precentors' repertoires had also been increased by a freer use of English, Welsh, Scotch, Irish, French and German traditional airs and carols, and then available for Sunday services was music that was only indirectly religious or that was frankly pagan, such as could be found in the collected musical stores of Anchor, Barton, Burney, Chalmers, Este, Green, Harrison, Howard, the two Jacksons, Moore, &c. In addition, they had at choice tune books that had only a regional popularity, such as the one called 'Leeds', that compiled for 'Lock Hospital' or the one used in Magdalen Chapel. Other sources for precentors with more catholic tastes included *Pensum sacra*, *Cantica sacra*, *Psalmodia sacra*, *Hymnodus sacer*, *Lyra Davidica*, *Piae cantiones*, as well as two with the lugubrious titles of *Seven Sobs of a Sorrowful Soul* and *Goostly Psalmes and Spiritualle Songs*. Every one of these collections has furnished melodies that are sung to-day in churches of one or other denomination. For educated eighteenth-century English precentors there was still further choice available. France then offered the *French Psalter*, the *Genevan Psalter*, Grenoble church melodies and Rouen church melodies; Germany then had available such sources as the *Gesangbuch* of Andernach, Corner, Görlitz, Horn, Klug, Spiess, Thommen, Vehe, Weisse, Wolder, and collections connected with particular places such as Bremen, Darmstadt, Mainz, Stralsund, Weimar, Wittenberg, &c. Perhaps better known than any of the foregoing German collections were Doles's *Choralbuch*, the *Geistliche Lieder*, *Heilige Seelenlust*, *Vollständige Psalmen*, *Tochter Sion Christliche Lieder*, *Katholisches Gesangbuch* and the *Kirchen-Gesänge* of the Bohemian Brethren.

Expressed in terms of tunes, by Wesley's death many a Methodist would be familiar with such well-known themes as Adeste fideles, Bremen, Coleshill, Crüger, Ein' Feste Burg, Eisenach, Farrant, Franconia, French, Gräfenburg, Hanover, Helmsley, Hotham, Invitation, Leoni, Lubeck, Luther's Hymn, Melcombe, Moscow, Nun danket, Old Hundredth, Ravenshaw, Rockingham, St. Petersburg, Wainwright, Warrington, Yorkshire, whilst scores of others, now known everywhere, would then have a local popularity.

Wesley often refers to the excellent congregational singing he heard in different chapels. Probably for such visits the adherents had previously memorized the tunes and words in honour of the visit. At less auspicious services, the singing would not always be hearty and rhythmical; for, as the bulk of the members were unable to read, it was customary for the preacher to 'give out' each line before the congregation sang the hymn or metrical psalm. Such a practice would slow down the singing to a snail's pace, must have shattered both the structure and climax of the words, would destroy the melodic stride and the vital pulsations of the theme, and have made almost a travesty of such eighteenth-century hymn melodies as Austrian Hymn, Darwall, Dresden, Easter Hymn, Jackson, Knecht, Miles Lane, Morning Hymn, Rousseau, Wareham, &c., whose glory was in their steady march. Such singing was probably done in truly reverential spirit, but it would be more impressive as an act of worship than as a performance, for it could not have been technically satisfying.

There is however, a further point of view. A man like Wesley would realize that the strength of a hymn lies not in its intellectual content, but rather in the stress which it lays upon the ideas expressed. He may have sensed that many a hymn becomes superficial because of the supremacy of the tune; for not infrequently, even nowadays, the tune may provide an unmerited popularity for a hymn. The voice tends to cling to the tune and the mind renounces the attempt to seize the meaning. In Wesley's day, hymn-singing was probably a more vital and powerful instrument of worship, than is the melodious weekly expression which it now represents. Then, hymn-singing was the spontaneous expression of a burning and living belief, the sort of faith that could not be expressed in ordinary speech. Methodist historiography compels the reflection, that distressed souls in the crisis of their religious experience, then found the verse of a hymn come nearest to an otherwise inexpressible reality. As Moore observes: 'After all, in the last resort, the Christian is cheered not by any rousing chorus or appealing melody, but by the comfortable words of his Lord and the Saints, by Faith and Trust, and without which, both hymns and tunes are vain and harmful.' It was such a belief that led many early Methodist preachers to *read* hymns to their congregations. The practice would enable the hearers to penetrate far more personally into a song of praise than does conventional singing, for it would counteract superficial acceptance of the words and ideas.

IX

An examination of the poems selected by Wesley for his hymn anthology shows that the chosen ones were mostly short, complete in themselves, terse and masculine in thought. In form they were often homely and sometimes rugged. Some of them were poetic gems, but several consisted of mere saws of prudence, moral hints, religious admonitions. Scores of them never roused religious passion nor fed the intellect; yet not infrequently they seem to have reached eighteenth-century hearts. The imagery in many a one is confused; but even these defectives exerted a wonderful power over this or that worshipper. As for the best, they have sublimity, passion, thought or divine fancy, and so unprejudiced a critic as Martineau attested that this 1779 compilation of hymns 'was after the Scriptures, the grandest instrument of popular religious culture that Christendom has ever produced'. In framing their compilation, the two brothers would be familiar with the metrical psalms and paraphrases, the medieval hymns of Bernard, Luther, Rist, Franck, Löwenstern, Rinchart, Gerhardt and Scheffler. They would also know those written by Milton, Addison, Herbert, Jeremy Taylor, Ken, Cowper, Watts, Doddridge, Byrom, Toplady, Olivers, &c., as well as those by foreign contemporaries like Gellert, Klopstock, Spangenberg and Zinzendorf. The hymns translated and composed by the Wesleys themselves are full of literary affinities. In them echo after echo from Milton, Herbert, Dryden, Cowley, Pope, Young and especially Prior strikes the ear, whilst now and then, memories of the great ancients are evoked in the phrasings.

Excluded from the collection would be many a hymn that had achieved popularity in different parts of the country, but which Wesley would consider most unsuitable for inclusion. For these were the days when the general public favoured snatches of roaring, racy, impudent ballads and coarsely cheerful songs. Moreover, religious poetry lies open to many peculiar dangers and not infrequently shows ghastly results. Wesley sensed this danger and based his selection on 'psalms and hymns which are both sense and poetry; such as would sooner provoke a critic to turn Christian than a Christian to turn critic'.

Nevertheless, many a hymn that was sung at different camp meetings, and which would be indignantly spurned by Wesley, has been preserved for the amusement of posterity. Chatterton often heard such 'hymns', and their recollection caused him to write:

> Jack, or to write more gravely, John,
> Through hills of Wesley's work has gone;
>   Could sing one hundred hymns by rote,
>   Hymns which will sanctify the throat;
> But some indeed, compos'd so oddly,
> You'd swear 'twas bawdy songs made godly.

Probably these unsavoury hymns were of lay-manufacture; but even when ministers enter the poet's region, they rarely cut a very conspicuous figure. Charles Wesley naturally could not in all his 7,000 hymns maintain the sublimity he reached in 'Jesu, Lover of My Soul', 'Hark! the Herald angels sing', 'Come, O Thou Traveller unknown,' 'Love Divine'; indeed, he could put his name to a 'hymn for children' containing this abominable verse:

> While they enjoy his Heavenly Love
>   Must I in torment dwell,
> And howl (while they sing hymns above),
> And blow the flames of Hell.

Nor could Isaac Watts preserve the pure nervous English, unaffected fervour and strong simplicity of 'There is a Land of pure Delight', 'Jesus shall reign', 'O God our Help', 'When I survey the wondrous Cross' in all his 500 hymns. Nor could Philip Doddridge retain the transparent simplicity and benevolent wisdom shown in 'O God of Bethel', 'Hark the glad Sound!' in his hundreds of religious poems. And although Cowper's 'Hark my Soul!', 'Sometimes a Light surprises' and 'God moves in a mysterious way' are among the finest in the collection, not all the Olney productions have such engaging piety. Moreover, just as in other literary fields, there are cycles among hymnologists; after the brilliant sunset of Watts, Wesley, Doddridge would come the days of the didactic hymnists, people of little freshness or individuality. But whether judged fine or maudlin by literary standards, these early hymns of the Methodists acted like a talisman in perpetuating modes of belief, and helped to fling society upon fresh and better paths.

X

Although Methodism was spreading irresistibly throughout the land by means of its hymns and its preachers and its organization, its main triumphs were among the poor and rising middle classes. The upper classes were but little affected by this religious movement, even though a religious revolution was sadly needed among them.

Nor was this due to any neglect on the part of some of the revivalists; one of these reformers who belonged to their set, freely sacrificed money, energies and even reputation to achieve that end. The Countess of Huntingdon did her utmost to recall the wealthy to better modes of life. In details such as era, length of life and force of character she somewhat resembled John Wesley. She too, had a burning call to do good; she too, desired no split with the National Church; she founded many a church and one college; she also was dictatorial and yet at the same time most self-sacrificing. She tried to absorb the mighty triumvirate, and in many eyes her particular form of dissent was considered synonymous with Methodism, so in 1749 Horace Walpole writes: 'Methodism is now more fashionable than brag; the women play very deep at both.' Both John and Charles Wesley preached in her Bath chapel or in her drawing-room, and in the fashionable congregations were many of the leaders of State, National Church, art, literature and fashionable society. John did not find the congregations congenial, and grimly remarked, 'they do me no good and I fear that I do none to them', whilst the very setting struck Charles as comical, and he wittily said, 'preaching there was like attacking Satan in his headquarters'. Not only at Bath did John Wesley preach to the wealthy without success, but also at Dublin, Liverpool, Taunton and Bridgwater, and usually he has occasion to comment after such occasions on 'fluttering things', 'butterflies', 'tittering misses', 'pious flippancy', 'gay triflers'. A man of his dignity would be disgusted with misbehaviour from so-called worshippers, whilst he could have no patience at all with people who imagined that merely to spend their unearned resources, was all the contribution they needed to make towards the welfare of the community to which they owed everything. Charles, who regularly consorted with those persons of quality who loved music and literature, also regarded the set as hopeless, and round about 1785 he wrote an epitaph on a 'Man of Fashion' which began with:

What is a modern man of fashion?

and ended with:

And lives an Ape and dies a Fool.

Cowper too, saw something amusing in these wealthy Dissenting gatherings, and in the very possibility of a nobleman being devout; and putting it into the mouth of a Dissenter, he says:

> We boast some rich ones whom the Gospel sways,
> And one who wears a coronet and prays.

Perhaps the letters and diaries of the Earl of Bath, Lord Dartmouth and Lord Teignmouth indicate that they were really swayed by the Huntingdon influence, and that they leaned towards dissent; but on the majority of the aristocracy, such influence was transitory and sporadic.

Replying to an effort to extend such influence, the Duchess of Buckingham said to Lady Huntingdon:

'I thank Your Ladyship for the information concerning the Methodist preachers; their doctrines are most repulsive and strongly tinctured with impertinence and disrespect towards their Superiors, in perpetually endeavouring to level all ranks and to do away with all distinctions. It is monstrous to be told you have a heart as sinful as the common wretches that crawl on the earth. This is highly offensive and insulting and I cannot but wonder that Your Ladyship should relish any sentiments so much at variance with Good Breeding and High Rank.'

As this duchess had royal blood in her veins she would know the true sentiments of high rank, probably too, she expressed the *élite's* general attitude towards Methodism.

However much Methodism was failing to influence the aristocracy, it was proving a great success with the rank and file of the nation. The religious services were giving the workers an escape from their visible surroundings; the music and hymns were replacing the old demoralizing theatres and fairs; the sermons were teaching them the meaning of a personal God, that human perfectibility was only attainable after redemption, and thus firing them with lofty endeavour, idealism and burning spirituality. The very organization was teaching them the elements of loyalty and community control, whilst the finance of salvation was providing them with lasting excitement and with opportunities of helping others. Such teaching and training demanded from the adherents sturdy endurance in obscurity, the facing of life without the stimulus of success or the consolation of personal triumphs; they called for rich vitality, undaunted spirit, useful lives and loyal citizenship.

Trevelyan expresses the influence of these new Methodist Fellowships with:

'Many of the more self-respecting men and women found in the Methodist chapels and Sunday Schools, the opportunity for the development of talents and the gratification of instincts that were denied expression elsewhere. The close and enthusiastic study of the Bible educated the imagination, and in chapel life, the men first learned to speak and to organize and to persuade their fellows. Much effort that later went into political, trade-union and co-operative activities were then devoted to chapel communities. . . . In a world that was made almost intolerable by avarice and oppression, here was a refuge where men and things were taken up aloft, and judged by spiritual and moral standards that forbade either revenge or despair.'

President Wilson expresses much the same idea and at the same time embodies Methodism in Wesley: 'The eighteenth century cried out for deliverance and light; and God prepared John Wesley to show the world the Might and the Blessing of His Salvation.' Birrell, thinking of the man alone, affirms: 'No single figure influenced so many minds; no single voice touched so many hearts; no other man did such a life's work for England.' Earl Baldwin said recently:

'The lives of Wesley and Whitefield were the significant factors in moulding the character of the people; and it is largely owing to the spirit which they breathed throughout England, that immense impetus was given to the reforms which took place in this country during the last century.'

Finally—and in order to return to our starting-point—Lecky's words are quoted: 'Wesley's conversion in 1738 meant more for Britain than all the victories of Pitt by land and sea.'

The celebration of the anniversary of this momentous conversion is a fitting time for Methodists to refresh their memories of the days of their illustrious Founder, and to see how and why he got the foregoing testimony from non-Methodists. Such testimony would in itself be valueless without some knowledge of the historical essentials and incidentals which form the background to the life of the Wesleys. Discussions on the Revival would be aimless and unproductive without a grasp of eighteenth-century social and cultural facts, whilst fundamental issues such as why Wesley did or said this or that, would be deliberately shirked without light on the past. Of significance, rather than of mere passing interest, are such details as the century's superstitions and politics; without them, debate as to whether or not Wesley wove his patterns of human perfectibility out of human fear and agony becomes abortive; and disputation on his apparently civil inertia is fruitless, if it is forgotten that in his day, moral aspirations condoned a lack

of clear political thinking, and that very many men of public spirit
would then have agreed with Emerson who, decades later, wrote:

'The less government we have, the better . . . the fewer laws and the
less confided power. The antidote to this abuse of formal government
is the influence of private character; the growth of the individual.'

Wesley's attitude towards the State Church and eighteenth-
century education, ideas, ideals, &c., is puzzling, if his training and
his times are unknown; whilst his personal relationships with
bishops and helpers are liable to misconception, if it is assumed
that he was unaffected by the deference then paid to birth compared with the grudging reception conceded to achievement.
Even his explosive language with its colossal assurance and stun-
ning efficiency of statement is open to misunderstanding without
an adequate conception of eighteenth-century speech habits. In
brief, it is very doubtful if one can really read his *Journal*, savour
his *Sermons*, and appreciate his lifework without this historical
enlightenment. And in securing such indispensable information
concerning their Founder, Methodists will perceive that however
great an achievement was his unwilling founding of a new
religious community, his shining fame as a maker of England's
greatness has many other bases. For he gave thousands upon
thousands of English-speaking people, directly or indirectly, a
new mind and a new spirit. Because of his influence, the adherents
of State and Dissenting Churches were revitalized, and they and
his own followers knew a higher standard of honesty as citizens,
as employers, as employees, and they learned to accept the duties
of a full life. The spread of such teaching over vast numbers fired
the philanthropists, awoke the social conscience of the country,
and stabilized the national temper, at a time when England faced
the repercussions of the French Revolution. But as every Methodist would affirm, without the momentous event of May 1738, it
is extremely unlikely that Wesley would have gained his present
standing in the religious world, nor would he have been so inspired as to secure his present niche in Valhalla. From that day
onward, his story is one of an unconquerable spirit dedicated to an
indestructible ideal. From then and from whatever angle we may
regard him, he cannot be left out of our national life. If Methodism but remembers its Wesleyan history, profits by its lessons,
and is ever ready to renew the fight for right, then Wesley's hand
will still be shaping national destinies, and he will be still at his
old work; still making history.

INDEX

Printed in Great Britain by
The Camelot Press Ltd., London and Southampton